ADDITIONAL PRAISE FOR *THE CHRISTIAN DELUSION*

"If John Loftus never wrote anything else, he will be remembered a century from now for his *Outsider Test for Faith*, which figures prominently in this book."

　　—Frank Zindler, PhD, former president of American Atheists
　　　and editor of *American Atheist Magazine*

"I'm quoted in this book as saying that treating the arguments of others fairly is simply an application of the Golden Rule. Christians regularly ask atheists to listen to their arguments and read their books. If a Christian wishes to return the favor, this volume offers atheist views on a range of subjects, presented respectfully (for the most part) yet with conviction. Christians who wish to critically examine and reflect on their beliefs will benefit from the outsider perspectives offered here. I join with its authors in encouraging you to *dare to doubt*. If you follow that courageous path, you may at times draw the wrong conclusions. If you do not, you will *certainly* be wrong at least as often."

　　—James F. McGrath, PhD, associate professor of religion at Butler University
　　　and author of *The Only True God: Early Christian Monotheism
　　　in Its Jewish Context*

"For nearly two thousand years apologists have striven mightily to show that the dogmas of Christianity are rationally defensible. For much of the Christian era critics have sought to debunk those apologetic claims. In that long tradition of criticism, there have been few works as effective as *The Christian Delusion*. The essays are incisive, rigorous, and original, shedding new light on old issues and boldly exploring new paths of argument. The selection of topics is outstanding—at once both comprehensive and innovative. For fresh insights into an old debate, *The Christian Delusion* is strongly recommended."

　　—Keith Parsons, PhD, professor of philosophy,
　　　University of Houston, Clear Lake, and
　　　author of *God and the Burden of Proof*

"John Loftus is to be congratulated for assembling such a fine collection of papers from such a diversity of fields. This book is not simply an anthology of atheist thought, but a wide-sweeping attack on the basis of Christianity. Using these various approaches, the authors subject Christianity to a rigorous critique: challenging it from the psychology of belief to the origins of morality, the historical Jesus, Christian exceptionalism, and claims of eternal truth despite the constant evolution of that religion. The end result is that Christianity is demonstrated to be just one of the many religions humans have invented for themselves."

 —James Linville, PhD, associate professor of religious studies,
 University of Lethbridge, Lethbridge Alberta, Canada

"The culture of Christianity has dominated the US, and to some extent the world, for so long that even the act of asking questions or raising doubts is scorned. But with Christian doctrine so far out of whack with scientific, moral, philosophical, and political realities, we cannot afford to leave it unanalyzed. When we do cast an objective and critical eye toward it, its ideas, arguments, and justifications unravel. The thinkers in this volume, who have the courage, the will, and the expertise to conduct that critical evaluation, have made a valuable contribution to the sea change."

 —Matt McCormick, PhD, professor of philosophy,
 California State University, Sacramento

"John Loftus cut his Christian apologetic teeth at our seminary, and I believe that he has since exchanged them for a false set. Nevertheless, in this book he has prepared a buffet with other notable atheistic chefs that 'honest Christians' dare not ignore. Many will simply refuse the menu because of its perceived poisonous entrées. But Christians need to chew on what these cooks are serving, even though much may be hard to swallow or difficult to digest. I say, 'Let the banquet begin!'"

 —Rich Knopp, PhD, professor of philosophy and apologetics
 at Lincoln Christian University, Lincoln, Illinois

"*The Christian Delusion* is an incredibly powerful book that's a must read for anyone who's ever had a doubt about God—believers and nonbelievers alike. I wish a book like this was around when I first had my doubts about Christianity. It would have saved me many years in getting to the truth."
    —William Lobdell, author of *Losing My Religion: How I Lost My Faith*
        Reporting on Religion in America—and Found Unexpected Peace

"This book systematically undermines the pillars of evangelical Christianity. It shows the arguments for the divine inspiration of the Bible, the resurrection of Jesus, a supernatural conversion experience, the necessity of the Bible for a proper system of ethics, and so on to be full of holes. It demonstrates that those who believe in the tenets of evangelical Christianity truly are deluded."
    —Ken Pulliam, PhD, who taught Greek, theology, and apologetics
        for nine years before becoming an agnostic

"*The Christian Delusion* is a comprehensive and representative presentation of contemporary skeptical thought. Anyone who wants to understand the position of contemporary freethinkers could not do much better than to read this book."
    —Matthew Flannagan, PhD, Christian philosopher
        and adjunct lecturer in philosophy for
        Laidlaw College and Bethlehem Tertiary Institute

THE CHRISTIAN DELUSION

THE CHRISTIAN DELUSION
WHY FAITH FAILS

EDITED BY JOHN W. LOFTUS

FOREWORD BY DAN BARKER

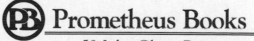

Prometheus Books

59 John Glenn Drive
Amherst, New York 14228–2119

Published 2010 by Prometheus Books

Inquiries should be addressed to
Prometheus Books
59 John Glenn Drive
Amherst, New York 14228–2119
VOICE: 716–691–0133
FAX: 716–691–0137
WWW.PROMETHEUSBOOKS.COM

14 13 12 11 10   5 4 3 2

Library of Congress Cataloging-in-Publication Data

The Christian delusion : why faith fails / [edited] by John W. Loftus.
    p. cm.
    ISBN 978–1–61614–168–4 (pbk : alk. paper)
    1. Christianity—Controversial literature. I. Loftus, John W.

BL2775.3.C47 2010
230—dc22

2009050906

Printed in the United States of America

CONTENTS

5

122160

PART 5: WHY SOCIETY DOES NOT DEPEND ON CHRISTIAN FAITH

FOREWORD

Chapter 8 of Lee Strobel's *The Case for Faith* is titled "I Still Have Doubts, So I Can't Be a Christian." Within this chapter, Strobel comforts believers who "fall prey to doubts." He assures us that doubt can actually strengthen faith.

I'm not sure why, but as an epigraph, he includes a quote from me.

> *In their most inner thoughts, even the most devout Christians know that there is something illegitimate about belief. Underneath their profession of faith is a sleeping giant of doubt. . . . In my experience, the best way to conquer doubt is to yield to it.*
> —Dan Barker, pastor-turned-atheist

Strobel doesn't comment on this, positively or negatively. I'm guessing he figures that what I said is so patently absurd that it needs no refutation. He probably knows I was mimicking Oscar Wilde's famous quip that "the only way to get rid of a temptation is to yield to it," so if doubt equals temptation, then it must be horrible.

Strobel's fluffy inspirational advice to doubters is not only erroneous (the previous chapter repeats the falsehood that Hitler was a "deliberate antitheist"), but it also stereotypes nonbelievers. He confesses that his own doubts as an atheist were motivated by the fear that "my hard-drinking, immoral, and self-obsessed lifestyle would have to change if I ever became a follower of Jesus, and I wasn't sure I wanted to let go of that." The roots of doubt, he insists, have nothing to do with the shaky truth claims of Christianity—because if we had the facts, "what we would have is knowledge, not faith." (And that is bad?) One of his interviewees assures us that "all unbelief ultimately has some other underlying reason." Many famous atheists, he claims, had a strained relationship with their father, "thus creating difficulty in them believing in a heavenly Father." Each argument of the skeptic is "just a smokescreen . . . merely a fog . . . to obscure his real hesitations about God." If we critics point out the psychological components of faith, he says, "Yes, people have a psychological need to believe—just as some people have psychological needs *not* to believe. . . . What's the reason you don't want to believe? Is it because you don't want the responsibility faith brings with it? Is it because of despair over your own incorrigibility? Or is it because you don't want to give up parties?"

How did he know!

So if Strobel is right that faith trumps knowledge, why put that faith in Christianity? Why not another religion? Strobel's expert, a minister who counsels church leaders, reports that "when it comes right down to it, the only object of faith that is solidly supported by the evidence of history and archeology and literature and experience is Jesus."

Well, which way is it? If faith is paramount, why do we need any evidence at all? Doesn't it follow that the less you know, the stronger your faith?

The most important question we can ask about any religion is this one: "Is it true?" Is the evidence for Jesus "solidly supported," as Strobel claims? When I started asking myself that question after almost two decades of preaching the Gospel, my beliefs began to unravel. The more I learned, the less respect I had for faith. Today, given the choice (regardless of my "psychological reasons"), I would rather know—or not know—than believe. *The case for faith is a case for ignorance.*

It's been said that converts make the best Catholics. Or Jews. Or fill-in-the-blanks. You have to be quite motivated to focus intently enough on the details of a new worldview to learn exactly what you are embracing. On average, converts probably have more zeal than those who got their religion simply by being born into it. Like learning a second language, it is exciting to feel you are becoming fluent, and you want to use what you have acquired to justify the effort. The very fact of changing (if not the actual facts of the religion) can give the mind an exciting feeling of newness, wonder and color of purpose that was probably lacking, or fading, in what came before. Otherwise, why change?

Perhaps it is also the other way around. If we can infer anything from the life stories of the contributors of this volume, maybe deconverts make the best critics. Or atheists or agnostics. Or fill-in-the-blanks. All but one of these skeptical authors have emerged from a religious background. Some of them, like me, were fanatical preachers—even ordained clergy—of the Christianity we now discard.

But it's a question of averages. No one in the country is more dedicated to atheism or capable of critiquing religion than my wife, Annie Laurie Gaylor, a third-generation nonbeliever. David Eller's penetrating and devastating chapters—written by a "natural born atheist"—show that what unites the authors of this volume is not revenge for having been victimized by the deceptions of religion, but a burning desire for actual facts. If we doubters do have a psychological motivation, perhaps it is the mental hunger, the intense craving to truly fill in the blanks of knowledge. As you read the following chapters, you will sense—almost palpably—the searing human drive to understand.

I was only seventeen years old in the summer of 1966 when I was "called by God" to Nogales, Mexico, to convert Catholics into Christians. I preached for a week in downtown churches and took a team of young evangelists into the streets to round up children who needed to be saved from their sins by the love of Christ. We hiked up a muddy hillside to visit some of the humble homes, and I still vividly remember my first taste of a *chile relleno*, served under a smoke-blackened *ramada* with chickens running under our feet. (When I jokingly said, "This is delicious! What's for dinner?" they pointed under the table.)

There is no way to know, but it is not impossible that one of those children who came to hear us was named Hector. I learned years later that Hector Avalos (a contributor to this book) was born in that very neighborhood. Hector, like me, became a child preacher, a true believer who happened to fall too much in love with the Bible. The language captivated him—not the *Reina Valera* or King James versions, but the original languages. Hector went on to get a PhD in Hebrew Bible and Near Eastern Studies at Harvard and is today one of the most highly respected biblical scholars in the country, the "atheist Bible professor" whose classes, I hear, are always full. He is one of those eager and helpful experts whose brain I often get to pick when preparing for debates.

Richard Carrier is another one of those deconverts who make the best critics. Or rather, a de-deconvert. Raised nominally Christian, Richard became a devout Taoist, immersing himself so thoroughly in the religion that he arrived at the place where he could see its limitations. Broadening his studies, he read the entire Bible, word for word. "When I finished the last page," he reports, "though alone in my room, I declared aloud, 'Yep, I'm an atheist.'" Today Richard is another one of those resources whose knowledge and advice on history and philosophy are invaluable, especially when it comes to the early Roman Empire.

Robert Price was a born-again, evangelical preacher with Campus Crusade and InterVarsity, starting as a teenager. He immersed himself in apologetics, but after years of convincing nonbelievers to "come to the Lord," he, too, discovered that he had learned too much, and today is one of those go-to guys, a towering expert on the (non)historicity of Jesus.

Ed Babinski is a Catholic-turned-fundamentalist-turned-agnostic, and Valerie Tarico also comes from a fundamentalist background, which might explain her fascination with psychology. Jason Long says he was "born agnostic" (weren't we all?) and returned to agnosticism after years of Christian Sunday school and Bible study failed to make sense. Paul Tobin was born and raised a Roman Catholic, dabbled a little in Pentecostalism (Assemblies of God) as a teenager, went back to the church and slowly "evolved" into an atheist.

And then there's John W. Loftus, editor of this volume, a former student of William Lane Craig, the renowned apologist, and a true-believing minister and Christian apologist who eventually "saw the light." Nobody understands better than John what it is like to believe from the inside, and no one else is in a better position to have formalized the "outsider test" for religious faith, a test that is fast becoming an indispensable part of the critical arsenal. More evidence that insiders make the best outsiders.

No one can pretend that the contributors to this volume have not given Jesus and the Bible a fair shake or that they don't know intimately what they are talking about.

Something is happening in the United States. All of the polls show that this country is becoming gradually less religious. According to the definitive American Religious Identification Survey (2009), currently the fastest growing "religion" in America is nonreligion. Between 15 percent and 20 percent of adult Americans report they are free from religion. Although only about 10 percent can be classified as thoroughly secular atheists, agnostics, and nonbelievers (about the same as this book's contributors were raised!), that is still much larger than Jews, for example, a respected minority that has shrunk to 1.2 percent. Among young people from college age to age thirty, it is 25 to 30 percent who are free from faith, the least religious generation in recent memory. I think that is exciting!

Whatever it was that happened in Europe—after centuries of deep religious history and zealous divisiveness, where today most people are totally secular and the beautiful churches stand empty—seems to be starting to happen on our own continent. What occurred in Europe was not a result of atheist missionaries diligently converting a malleable populace. It happened naturally. An evidence of a similar cultural shift on our own continent is the phenomenal organic rise of freethought clubs on college campuses. The Secular Student Alliance and the Center for Inquiry have their hands full signing up new freethought/atheist/humanist/skeptic groups, often composed of students who thought they were all alone in their efforts, only to learn that they are part of a larger movement with no followers (we are all leaders), a growing population of critical, caring young people who don't care a hoot about any "next world." They are in love with *this* world, and want to remove all obstacles to science, reason, morality, and progress.

It is obvious—and many students confirm it—that the Internet has been a real "blessing" for free inquiry. It is now impossible for religious leaders and apologists to hide the embarrassing facts of biblical scholarship. The availability of clear and documented critical information on the Secular Web (infidels.org), for example, or the Freedom From Religion Foundation (ffrf.org), or the individual Web pages of the contributors to this volume (look them up!), and many other dozens of wonderful resources, virtually guarantees that those of us who want to know—not believe—will not be starved into sectarian submission.

Another evidence of a profound change is the success of blockbuster atheist and antireligious books by Sam Harris, Richard Dawkins, Christopher Hitchens, Daniel Dennett, Victor Stenger, and others. This proves that there is a vast, growing "market" out there for skeptical ideas. (If not, who is buying all these books?) I have little doubt that this current volume will not simply be riding that wave but will be helping to propel it.

Dan Barker

Copresident of the Freedom from Religion Foundation and author of *Godless: How an Evangelical Preacher Became One of America's Leading Atheists*

INTRODUCTION

As the editor of this book I envisioned it as an extension of my previous one, *Why I Became an Atheist: A Former Preacher Rejects Christianity* (Amherst, NY: Prometheus Books, 2008), which I think of as important background reading for the chapters in this one, although you don't need to read it in order to understand and benefit from this present book. All the themes in this book expand on issues raised there. I personally think this book delivers a powerful blow to Christianity, especially when combined with its predecessor. Someone has to tell the emperor he has no clothes on. These two books help to do just that.

In part 1 David Eller, Valerie Tarico, Jason Long, and I elaborate and defend my *Outsider Test for Faith*, which calls upon believers to examine their culturally given faith from the perspective of an outsider, with the same level of skepticism they use to examine the other religious faiths they reject. Eller does so from an anthropologist's perspective, while Tarico and Long do so from the perspective of psychology. Eller argues that there is no such thing as Christianity. There are only local Christianities, since Christianity is a cultural phenomenon that is both affected by its culture and in turn affects the culture in which it thrives. Among other things Tarico argues that the sense of certainty that faith gives believers is a psychological malaise. Long shows us from several different studies that we human beings are often irrational and gullible people. Then I revisit the argument by defending it from additional criticisms. I happen to think such a test is devastating to believers who think Christianity, or any other so-called revealed religion, is true.

In part 2 are chapters related to the Bible as God's word. Edward Babinski goes into detail about the flat-earth, three-tiered cosmology we find in it. Paul Tobin then surveys what biblical scholarship tells us about the rest of the Bible. It is inconsistent with itself, not supported by archaeology, contains fairy tales, failed prophecies, and many forgeries. Then I argue that since the Bible was used by the church to justify some horrific deeds, God did a poor job of communicating his will in it. This is what I call the *Problem of Miscommunication*. The Bible cannot be God's word in any meaningful sense at all.

In part 3 are two chapters related to the problem of evil. Hector Avalos takes aim at Paul Copan's attempt to justify Yahweh's actions in the Old Testament, which utterly fail. Then I argue there is no good reason for the amount of animal suffering in the world if there is a perfectly good God. These two chapters show convincing reasons why the Judeo/Christian view of God is indefensible.

Part 4 contains chapters that question what Christians believe about Jesus. Robert Price deals with Paul Eddy and Gregory Boyd's book *The Jesus Legend* and finds their whole methodology wrong. Richard Carrier applies my *Outsider Test for Faith* to the New Testament stories about a resurrected Jesus. Then I argue that at best Jesus is to be understood as a failed apocalyptic prophet, since the prophesied new age (or *eschaton*) never occurred in his generation as predicted. Together, in one way or another, we show that what Christians believe about Jesus is not the case, to say the least.

Finally, in part 5 are chapters arguing that modern society does not depend on Christianity for morality or science. David Eller shows us how human morality arose. We don't need a god to explain morality, so consequently there is no moral lawgiver, and no argument from morality to the existence of God. If God wrote a moral code within us, he did so in invisible ink. Hector Avalos decisively answers the claim that atheism was the cause of the atrocities of Hitler. In fact, centuries of Christian anti-Semitism were more to blame for the Holocaust. Then Richard Carrier closes the book by effectively arguing that Christianity is not to be credited with the rise of science. He compiles a massive amount of material showing that Greek science was blossoming way before Christianity arose on the scene.

I want to sincerely thank each and every contributor to this volume in hopes that our combined efforts will make a difference. I think every chapter is significant and insightful, all written for the college-level reader, for the most part. Richard Carrier did a yeomen's job with peer-reviewed comments on each one of the chapters, which has made this a better book. A FAQ site to discuss this book can be found at http://sites.google.com/site/thechristiandelusion, where we will attempt to answer critical reviews of it when they appear, so look for it.

Alas, we can already predict the effect this book will have. What typically happens in every generation as Christians are forced to confront skeptical arguments against their beliefs is that instead of giving up their faith, they reinvent it. Every skeptical attack is countered by Christians in every generation in order to save their faith from refutation, and so far Christians have been successful. After all, Christianity is still around. But they do so at a high cost.

In my own lifetime I have seen Christianity reinvent itself like a chameleon changes colors. Because of the onslaught of skeptical arguments, more and more Christians are claiming that their faith is a "properly basic belief," and as such, it doesn't need any evidence to support it (à la Alvin Plantinga in *Warranted Christian Belief*). Others like William Lane Craig are arguing that the witness of the Holy Spirit "trumps all other evidence" since it's "an intrinsic defeater of any defeaters brought against it." (Question 68: "The Witness of the Holy Spirit" at http://www.reasonable faith.org). In effect, Christians have insulated their faith from contrary evidence. But this also means the external evidence does not have to support their faith, so why bother with apologetics at all? Why not just preach the Bible, as neo-orthodox theologian Karl Barth suggested?

Christians have long ago abandoned the horrible and barbaric view of an eternal fire-and-brimstone hell (thanks in no small measure to Robert G. Ingersoll in the nineteenth century) and replaced it with a metaphorical one described as "the absence of God." Now with a globally connected world of diverse, sincere religious believers, more and more Christians are embracing *annihilationism* (à la Johnathan L. Kvanvig in *The Problem of Hell*), whereby the sinner simply goes out of existence upon dying. But if this is the case, why would Jesus die for us if all he did was save us from nonexistence? And so why fear hell at all? How is it any punishment to simply cease to exist? And why bother evangelizing if this is so?

Christians are also embracing "Open Theism" in light of problems with time, relativity, and the notion of a timeless God (à la Clark Pinnock, editor of *The Openness of God*). It's now believed by more and more Christians that God doesn't have foreknowledge of future free-willed human actions. Still other professing Christians go one step further by embracing "Process Theism" or panentheism, especially in light of the fact that there is no satisfactory answer to the problem of evil for a perfectly good omnipotent God (à la David Ray Griffin in *God, Power, and Evil: A Process Theodicy*). Process theists simply deny God has omnipotence. He cares. It's just that he can't do much about it but persuade his creatures to do good. But if Christians can deny God has foreknowledge and omnipotence then why not also deny God cares for us? A few have done just that (à la John K. Roth in chapter 1 for *Encountering Evil: Live Options in Theodicy*, ed. Stephen T. Davis).

Christians are also arguing that Satan is the reason why animals have suffered for millions of years on this planet before the advent of human beings (à la Gregory Boyd in *Satan and the Problem of Evil*). In the past, apologists believed animal suffering resulted from the supposed fall of Adam and Eve in the Garden of Eden. Now in a post-Darwin world they are laying the blame on Satan's activity before a human fall, or by arguing that the fall retroactively caused natural suffering (à la William A. Dembski in *The End of Christianity: Finding a Good God in an Evil World*). Others, like R. C. Spoul and Russell Moore, have decided that in order to answer this vexing problem they must reaffirm young earth creationism.[1] And yet other professing Christians have rejected the existence of Satan and the historicity of the Garden story altogether (à la Conrad Hyers in *The Meaning of Creation: Genesis and Modern Science*). But once Christians admit there are nonhistorical myths in the Bible, the floodgates are open to consider it may *all* be mythical.

In light of the effectiveness of the scientific method of naturalism, Christians are now forced to defend their faith by arguing that "everything should be fair game" for the critical scholar—that scholars need to be open to the possibility that any claim, no matter how strange, is, technically speaking, "on the boards" (à la Paul Eddy and Gregory Boyd in *The Jesus Legend*). But once every claim, no matter how bizarre, is truly considered fair game, then what's to stop people from believing in, well, anything and everything?

Then, too, Christians are adopting Preterism (or partial Preterism), which is a view of eschatology attempting to answer the problem of Jesus' failed prophesy of the consummation of the ages after two millennia. Many Christians are now claiming these prophecies were fulfilled metaphorically in 70 CE, with the destruction of Jerusalem (à la N. T. Wright in *Jesus and the Victory of God*). But in making this case, they must claim the whole history of theology was wrong to say otherwise, and if that's true, then why should we accept anything the church has believed from the beginning?

In light of philosophical problems with regard to personal identity after death, many Christians are now claiming Jesus did not bodily rise from the grave. According to them he arose spiritually in some sense. (à la John Shelby Spong, *Resurrection: Myth or Reality?* along with others). But once this is granted, what's the difference between seeing spiritual bodies from merely seeing visions, which have no objective reality to them? Liberal Christians like these are well along the road to atheism.

Many professing Christians are even embracing the homosexual by arguing that a homosexual lifestyle is not a sin. Sixty-eight clergy in Madison, Wisconsin, in May of 1997 affirmed that "homosexuality is neither sickness nor sin" (http://www.iwgonline.org/docs/madison.html), while the US Anglican Church voted to allow gay bishops. Christians have repeatedly reinterpreted the Bible on slavery, women, democracy, science, the environment, and animal rights, as we became socially and scientifically enlightened. But then, if the Bible is this malleable, capable of being interpreted differently in every generation, how can exegetes really think they have the correct interpretation of it at all? And what's there to prevent Christians from using the Bible to support future changes if and when the world embraces socialism, homosexual marriages, assisted suicide, cloning, and family planning (like abortion)? Some already do.

The Christianity of the past was different than today's Christianity. Nearly all modern Christians would have suffered under the Office of the Inquisition with what they believe, it's so far removed. And the Christianity of the future will be just as different as the presently accepted one. Shouldn't Christians just walk away from their faith and recognize it as the delusion that it is, once it has been shown to be false? But that's not what they'll do. Instead, they will reinvent it. This happens in every generation, even if there remain pockets of Christians who embrace the views of the past. It's too bad, really. Like a chameleon, Christianity will always change its colors as the surroundings change with each subsequent generation.

So with a book like this one it'll be no different. Rather than admit the arguments contained herein have been successful, Christians will simply change what they believe in order to keep their faith. Will existentialism or fideism or mindless Pentecostalism be the wave of the future? Probably so. But for believers who are intellectually honest with themselves and the arguments, I suggest it's time to get rid of the dizziness that swirls in your head by jumping off the merry-go-round of faith.

Let me finally make a comment on the title to this book. Unlike the bestselling atheist book of all time that targets religion in general, *The God Delusion* by Richard Dawkins, this one has a more specific target: Christianity. The word "delusion," by my Microsoft Word 2002 Encarta World English Dictionary, is defined as: "1. false belief: a persistent false belief held in the face of strong contradictory evidence, especially as a symptom of a psychiatric condition; 2. mistaken notion: a false or mistaken belief or idea about something." While I personally think in most cases people are brainwashed by their culture to believe, the title is not meant to convey that believers have any psychiatric disorders because of their faith. Just keep in mind as you read through this book that *brainwashed people do not know that they have been brainwashed.*

The phrase "faith fails" in the subtitle suggests that religious faith does not stand up to rigorous scrutiny. Let me provide an example from what one Mormon said about the skeptical book *Joseph Smith and the Origins of the Book of Mormon:*

> I could probably spend a few years of my life trying to find dirt on the author of this book and likely, I would find some. The question is: why would I? Yes, it's very easy to find dirt on someone, if that's what you are looking for, because the bottom line is: *people believe what they want to believe.* If you want to KNOW something, why not ask the only one who truly knows: God? That was Joseph Smith's message. That was the message of the *Book of Mormon.* It was also the message of our Savior, who said: "Ask, and it shall be given you; seek, and ye shall find; knock, and it shall be opened unto you" (Matthew 7:7). Or you can refer to the scripture quoted by the prophet himself: "If any of you lack wisdom, let him ask of God, that giveth to all men liberally, and upbraideth not; and it shall be given him.... But let him ask in faith, nothing wavering. For he that wavereth is like a wave of the sea driven with the wind and tossed. For let not that man think that he shall receive anything of the Lord" (James 1:5–7).

I know Joseph Smith was a prophet of God. Not because some person told me, and not because some man showed me a book full of evidence (*there is much evidence for those who want to find it*). *I know, because like Joseph Smith, I got down on my knees, in faith, and asked my Heavenly Father if it was true.* You cannot know anything, but by God. What do you have to lose? *I'm not giving you my opinions.* I only invite those who wish to know the truth.... If you want to know, ask God, I promise you that He will answer if you honestly seek only the truth.[2]

This Mormon claims that people who don't believe don't want to. He's not offering his opinions either. He knows because he has the inner witness of God in his heart. And he claims there is "much evidence" for anyone seeking it. Does any of this sound familiar to other believers? That's why faith fails. Faith can lead people to justify whatever they were raised to believe—that's why. So in order to test one's faith, every believer must subject it to a brutal examination of the evidence and the arguments. There is no other way.

To honest believers who are seeking to test their own inherited religious faith, this book is for you. Our contention is that when you subject your own faith to the same level of skepticism you use to scrutinize other faiths, you will find out why faith fails.

NOTES

1. R. C. Sproul, *Truths We Confess: A Layman's Guide to the Westminster Confession of Faith* (Phillipsburg, NJ: P & R, 2006): 1:127–28. Russell Moore, "A Creationist Watches Animal Planet," *Southern Seminary Magazine* 74, no. 2 (Summer 2006): 11, http://bpnews.net/bpnews.asp?ID=21777.

2. J. C. Gregersen, "Do You Really Want to Know?" review of *Joseph Smith and the Origins of the Book of Mormon*, 2nd ed., by David Persuitte, *Amazon.com*, http://www.amazon.com/gp/cdp/member-reviews/A1U46V17JFIIII8W/ref=cm_pdp_rev_title_1?ie=UTF8&sort_by=MostRecentReview#R3O9028RW4DASK [emphasis added].

Part 1

WHY FAITH FAILS

Chapter 1

THE CULTURES OF CHRISTIANITIES

David Eller, PhD

O ne of the great mysteries is why, despite the best arguments against it, religion survives. After all, every argument in support of religion has been shown to be inconclusive or demonstrably false, yet religion persists; of course, if the case for religion in general fails, then the case for any particular form of religion, like theism or monotheism or Christian monotheism, naturally fails too. If religionists/theists/monotheists/Christians would just be rational, would just *listen* and *think*, atheists grumble, they would see their error and abandon their erroneous ways.

Ironically (or not so ironically), religionists/Christians confront the same stubborn resistance—and not only from atheists. The problem is especially acute for them when trying to "share" their beliefs with members of non-Christian religions, both other "world religions" and those "primitive" or "traditional" religions against whom Christians relentlessly send missionaries. Why don't those people accept Christianity, and why don't they accept it in the form that existing Christians practice and teach it?

I fear that discerning Christian proselytizers, who have been doing this for much longer than atheist polemicists, have discovered the answer, and it is an answer that those who want to "win" the contest and to influence society must heed—namely, *culture*. From the earliest Jesuits in the Americas to contemporary missionaries in remote villages, successful promoters of Christianity have realized—and exploited—the fact that religion is not only about, not even mostly about, "beliefs" and "arguments" but about a worldview, a way of life, and a learned and shared and *produced* and *reproduced* regimen of experience.

In this chapter, I will illustrate how the concept of culture is relevant to the understanding, practice, and success of Christianity in particular and religion in general and how some cunning Christians know this and have used it to their advantage for a very long time. I will further show how the concept of culture reduces Christianity into just another cultural phenomenon, operating by the same processes and yielding the same results as any cultural phenomenon. One of the key qualities of culture is diversity: there is no such thing as "Christian culture" but rather "Christian cultures"; indeed no such thing as Christianity but rather Christiani*ties*. This will also explain, finally, why the efforts to debunk and displace Christianity through evidence and logic—the atheist's stock in trade—have been and will continue to be largely futile. Christians are not easily argued out of their religion because, since it is culture, they are not ordinarily argued *into it* in the first place.

CHRISTIANITY AS CULTURE

Culture is the central concept in my chosen profession, anthropology. I could, therefore, present an anthropological view of the concept, which I hope that readers will seek out, perhaps in my new textbook on cultural anthropology.[1] Instead, I want to demonstrate how professional Christianity has absorbed and deployed the concept quite intentionally and remarkably effectively.

Unbeknownst to most rationalists, atheists, and academic anthropologists, Christian missiologists (those who study and teach the ideas and methods of mission work) have generated a considerable literature on the subject and actively share and perfect their craft.[2] Whole organizations, institutes, and publishing houses (like Orbis Books and Zondervan, to name but two) exist to fulfill these functions. The challenge for missionaries is that the groups upon which they descend already have their own religions and, more problematically, have their own languages and values and institutions that tend to support those religions and to make Christianity strange and incomprehensible or to defy it altogether. Smart missionaries understand that they must penetrate these barriers and invade and co-opt these languages, value systems, and institutions (which is why translation of the Christian scriptures into local languages is such an urgent goal for them), and, as quickly and completely as possible, either dominate or replace these systems and institutions with ones of their own making and in their own image.

In Winter and Hawthorne's *Perspectives on the World Christian Movement*,[3] which amounts to a guidebook for culture-aware missionaries, many of the chapters are dedicated to spreading the message of the critical importance of culture. Charles Kraft, one of the leading figures in the project, describes culture as "the label anthropologists give to the structured customs and underlying worldview assumptions [by] which people govern their lives. Culture (including worldview) is a people's way of life, their design for living, their way of coping with their biological, physical, and social environment. It consists of learned, patterned assumptions (worldview), concepts and behaviors, plus the resulting artifacts (material culture)."[4] I think that most professional anthropologists would regard this as a workable characterization of culture.

Kraft goes further, though, to enumerate several more advanced qualities of culture:

- Culture "provides a *total design for living*, dealing with every aspect of life and providing people with a *way to regulate their lives*."
- Culture "is a legacy from the past, *learned as if it were absolute and perfect*."
- Culture "*makes sense to those within it*."
- Culture "is an *adaptive system, a mechanism for coping*. It provides patterns and strategies to enable people to adapt to the physical and social conditions around them."
- Culture "tends to show *more or less tight integration* around its worldview."
- Culture "is *complex*."

Of the worldview central to any particular culture, he makes several assertions:

- It "consists of the *assumptions* (*including images*) underlying all cultural values, allegiances, and behaviors."

- It grounds and explains "*our perception of reality and responses to it.*"
- Its basic assumptions or premises "are learned from our elders, *not reasoned out, but assumed to be true without prior proof.*"
- "We organize our lives and experiences according to our worldview and *seldom question it* unless our experience challenges some of its assumptions."[5]

The immediate relevance for Christian missionization, and for our eventual purposes in this chapter, consists of three points:

1. Christianity, like any religion, is a part of culture. It is learned and shared, and it is integrated with the other systems of the culture, including its economics, its kinship, and its politics.
2. Christianity, like any religion, *is a culture.* It offers its own worldview, specific terms with which to speak and think, and specific symbolic and organizational and institutional forms. It is never *only* beliefs, but as Paul Hiebert stresses in the same volume, *Perspectives on the World Christian Movement*, it is also always feelings and values and allegiances and standards for judgment and evaluation.[6] It is a more or less complete design for living.
3. Christian missionization is a type of cross-cultural communication and cultural change. Conversion from one religion to another is, thus, *never simply a shift in belief*, as Kraft reminds us, "Significant culture change is always a matter of changes in the worldview.... [A]nything that affects a people's worldview will affect the whole culture and, of course, the people who operate in terms of that culture."[7]

From my exposure to the anthropologically informed missiology (and there are, no doubt, variations and exceptions), the Christian writers acknowledge that Christianity and its diverse Christian cultures are not one and the same thing: Christianity can take different shapes in different cultural contexts. In fact, the point of these writings is that Christianity *must* take different shapes in different contexts, so the writers urge missionaries to "recontextualize" Christianity in such a way as to fit it into the local cultures without rejecting every aspect of those local cultures but without losing the core of the religion. However, as far as they do go in recognizing the cultural nature of their religion, they do not take the final step toward seeing its own dependency and relativity, that Christianity, too,

- is one way to regulate human lives, among many other ways;
- is a legacy from its own past, evolved over time and learned from its predecessors *but held to be absolute and perfect*;
- makes sense to those inside it but no sense at all to those outside it;
- consists of its own assumptions and premises that underlie its norms, values, allegiances, and institutions;
- grounds and informs a particular view of reality and possible responses to that view;
- is not reasoned out, but assumed to be true without prior proof; and
- organizes the lives and experiences of its followers—literally provides the terms in and through which they live and experience—and is seldom questioned by them.

In other words, despite all the sensitive-sounding babble about culture and worldview, and so on, the proselytizers still think (as they would have to think in order to be motivated to proselytize) that *their* culture/worldview is the *true* culture/worldview. "As divine revelations," Hiebert explains, "biblical norms…stand in judgment of all cultures.… Truth, in the end," by which he naturally means *his* truth, *Christian* truth, "does not depend on what we think or say, but on reality itself."[8] Other cultures are cultures, you see, but Christian culture is "reality"—which betrays their actual intention and in so doing betrays the message of anthropology.

CHRISTIANITY SPREADING OUT TO CULTURE

What these missiologists are describing is the central anthropological tenet of "holism," that every aspect of culture—its religion, its economic system, its kinship practices, its politics, its language, its gender roles, and so on—is integrated and interdependent. The functioning of each part affects all of the parts, and changes to one part lead to changes in other parts. Further, dominant elements in a culture ripple through that culture, replicating themselves in various institutions and practices. Ultimately, all of the aspects of culture develop a kind of consonance, an overall consistent feel or theme.

The integration of culture is a two-way process. One of the directions is from the religion out to the rest of culture, and Christian proselytizers have understood this since what Michael Welton calls the "cunning pedagogues" among the first Jesuit missionaries. As early as the 1600s, Jesuits in the Americas invaded native societies with a "pedagogy," or teaching regimen, that was "motivated by an interest in exercising a symbolic, cultural domination over their student adversaries."[9] This carefully developed and meticulously deployed pedagogy was a concentrated and unyielding attack on the cultural foundations of native religion and culture:

> The Jesuit attack pedagogy was aimed primarily at undermining the lifeworld foundations of Indian ways of life. The lifeworld is the taken-for-granted source of meaning and action, and various spiritual-religious practices (animism) were interwoven into everyday life.... The Jesuits sought to dislodge [the shaman] from his place of lifeworld supremacy through ridicule, mockery, and one-upmanship and to insert themselves in his place. This was a brilliant, ruthless pedagogical strategy. They used their scientific knowledge of solar and lunar eclipses, tides, and the magical power of the printed word to de-authorize the shaman. They marshaled their own lifeworld resources (now increasingly penetrated by scientific forms of knowledge) to undermine the Amerindian cultural foundations and create a native fifth column in the Devil's Empire.[10]

Among the tactics used then, and ever since, was study of the local language so as to find ways to translate ideas and doctrines "from a hierarchical, patriarchal, technological, status-ridden Christian Europe into the mental universe of the Indians."[11] Armed with knowledge of the language and culture (much of which knowledge constituted the first "ethnological" materials created in non-Western settings), the Jesuits launched a multi-pronged campaign against the bases of native life and belief, especially not-specifically religious matters, like gender roles. Precontact gender relations were so critical and such an anathema to missionization because native women "had considerable power, authority, and prestige in Amerindian tribal life. Although there was a sexual division of labor, Indian cultures lacked the moral vocabulary to conceive of women as 'bad' or 'evil.'"[12] Another tool was the European-dominated fur trade, which gradually achieved the incorporation of local groups into the emergent global, colonial, economic system, teaching them disciplines and values suitable to (the lower rungs of) the new Christian/capitalist way of life.

Other explicit and finely honed pedagogical techniques used on the native peoples included ridicule and verbal attacks on traditional beliefs and practices and on native etiquette. As "educational warriors," once missionaries "sensed that the traditional lifeworld was eroding, they focused their attacks on the inadequacy of the indigenous meaning system."[13] Their weapons included the scientific skill to make natural predictions (like eclipses), literacy to argue that the written word was better and more authoritative than oral knowledge, and visual images to represent and dramatize their messages. They exploited emotion and melodrama and "studied the aesthetic preferences of their students to increase the effectiveness of their pedagogy."[14] Specifically, "the Jesuits sought to create a lavish, sensual, sacred pedagogical space to exert influence over their followers. They conducted their services and rituals with flash and pomp to provide the believers with a spiritual ambience that would awaken the senses and cast a spell over them."[15]

The anthropologists John and Jean Comaroff have discovered the same processes in a later stage of colonialism in Africa during the 1800s. Colonialism, wherever and whenever conducted, involved changes to and domination of the political and economic aspects of subject societies, together with religion and other cultural habits, such as dress, speech, marriage, gender roles, and so on. All these forms and practices, and not merely religious doctrines and rituals, carried Christian messages about what is true, good, important, and possible. Much of such cultural and even religious "knowledge" is implicit and informal, embedded in the big and little things we do all day, every day—what Jean Comaroff calls "the signs and structures of everyday life."[16] Therefore, the conversion process was designed to effect a change in these signs and structures, a "revolution in habits," that is, "a quest to refurnish the mundane: to focus human endeavor on the humble scapes of the everyday, of the 'here-and-now' in which the narrative of Protestant redemption took on its contemporary form."[17] They have also labeled this struggle "an epic of the ordinary" and "the everyday as epiphany": "it was precisely by means of the residual, naturalized quality of habit that power takes up residence in culture, insinuating itself, apparently without agency, in the texture of a lifeworld. This, we believe, is why recasting mundane, routine practices has been so vital to all manner of social reformers, colonial missionaries among them."[18]

An important nonreligious dimension of change was economics, literally farming techniques. Missionaries offered a model for "civilized cultivation" in the form of the "mission garden"; a major aspect of this new model was a reversal of traditional gender roles, in which women had done the bulk of horticultural work. The plow became a potent symbol, fences introduced conceptions of "enclosure" and property, and inequality of output—

related to intensity of labor—generated Western-style differences in wealth and status. But economic change went beyond horticulture to new institutions, such as markets and money. Modern labor and cash were part of a new "moral economy," stigmatizing idleness and "primitive production" and promoting "the kind of upright industry and lifestyle that would dissolve [tradition's] dirt."[19] Yet more mundane habits, like cleanliness, clothing, and household practices, were valued for their civilizing and Christianizing effects. Clothes not only meant covering heathen nakedness but teaching locals the proper wear and care of these articles; native clothing, it seemed to colonists, was dirty, too "natural," and lacked the necessary markers of social—especially gender—distinctions. Home became a "domestic" sphere, which became the woman's sphere, where she would literally sit, sew, and serve. But the traditional native house would not do; the house and the community had to be altered from what the Europeans perceived as "a wild array of small, featureless huts scattered across the countryside."[20] Missionary houses and buildings again acted as the model: with right angles, specialized spaces (e.g., a room for eating, a room for sleeping, etc.), doors and locks for privacy, and modern furniture, the mission structures "became a diorama" for how people should live.[21] The collection of residences that became the "town" differentiated public from private spaces, all set in a universe of square blocks and broad streets. In these and many ways, the foreigners were doing much more than bringing a new religion; they were "teaching [natives] to build a world,"[22] one in which civilization itself was expressed "in squares and straight lines."[23]

Many people, atheists and rationalists among them, still think that unless they are living in some primitive society, or unless they are being bludgeoned overtly with religious "belief," that they are safe from the influence of religion. If the presentation above has not awakened them to the multiple mundane ways in which religion pervades their lives, then they should heed the warning of Kraft, who assures his readers that religious colonization is not and cannot be a mere frontal assault on "false" religion: for the cunning cultural converter, "Christianity is to be directed at the worldview of a people so that it will influence each of [the] subsystems from the very core of the culture. Truly converted people (whether in America or overseas) need to manifest biblical Christian attitudes and behavior in all of their cultural life, not just in their religious practices."[24] Accordingly, Christianity in American and other Western societies, and other religions in other societies, actively and intentionally pursues the same course, creating a pervasive and largely taken-for-granted religious worldview that generally escapes criticism, since it escapes notice. As I have tried to warn readers in my previous work,[25] the United States and the wider Western world are heavily saturated with Christianity throughout their many large and small cultural arrangements. Whether or not they know it—and it is more insidious if they do not know it—non-Christians living in Christian-dominated societies live a life permeated with Christian assumptions and premises. Christians and non-Christians alike are literally immersed in Christian cultural waters, and like fish they usually take for granted the water they swim in.

The subsystems to which Kraft refers include essentially every aspect of culture, including language, critical life events, everyday habits, bodily habits, institutions, and even understandings of time and space.

LANGUAGE

A society's language is the first but hardly the only place to look for the subtle power of religion. Even atheists talk the language of religion, which in American society means "speaking Christian." Every religion not only infiltrates the local language but *is* a language in its own right, with its own vocabulary that has no meaning outside of that religion. For example, Christianity is rich with terminology that often has no correlate in other religions, such as "god," "heaven," "hell," "sin," "angel," "devil," "bless," "soul," "saint," "pray," "sacred," "divine," "baptism," "purgatory," "gospel," and so on. These are not neutral, universal notions but are specific to this one religion. A religion like Hinduism has its own unique lexicon, with *dharma* and *karma* and *samsara* and *moksha* and *yuga* and so on. Christians cannot "say" these things, since they do not occur in Christianity, and Hindus cannot say "Christian things" since those things do not occur in Hinduism.

But there is much more to a religion than its vocabulary; religions, like other areas of culture, include specific things to say. Some of these conventional things to say are propositional, that is, truth claims like "God exists" or "Jesus was the son of God." Many are not propositional, however. They may be utterances of power, meant to have an effect on the world, from "God bless America" to Navajo prayers for health to phrases like "abracadabra." Much of religious talk consists of scripts, routines that people perform just as surely as saying "Hello, how are you?" or "Have a nice day"; at the extreme, these scripts become liturgies, like a Catholic mass or a wedding ceremony. Religion also provides stories (which are usually intended to apply to and organize our own lives in some way) and metaphors for thinking about the world and our behavior in it. And we would be remiss if we did not acknowledge that religious language can also keep secrets, obfuscate the truth, manipulate hearers, and sometimes tell out-and-out lies. A religion like Christianity also supplies images, stories, and metaphors that pervade the culture's speech and thought. Even a short list of such ideas and illustrations highlights how Christian-soaked our speech-community is: Mark of Cain, Garden of Eden, David versus Goliath, Jacob's ladder, patience of Job, "my cross to bear," "spare the rod and spoil the child," "beat swords into plowshares," "voice crying in the wilderness," "Can the leopard change his spots?" "hide your light under a bushel," "wolf in sheep's clothing," "wars and rumors of wars," "Physician heal thyself," "lost sheep," "grapes of wrath," "cast the first stone," "through a glass darkly," and many, many more. Most atheists use most of these phrases without any thought for their source—and how the use serves the source.

CRITICAL LIFE EVENTS

Religion invades the major moments in individual and collective life. The two most obvious are birth and death. Religion does not create birth or death—although many religions like to assert that they do—but religion typically demands a role in, or even authority over, both. Many religions maintain that a person cannot be born or die "well" or "successfully" without a religious officiate and a religious ceremony on the occasion. The same is true with marriage, a social and civil bond that religion often attempts to claim as its own (one must marry "in the church"). In times of illness or misfortune, religion may barge in and insist on a role, either as reason or remedy. In times of shared alarm, such as war or natural disasters or other tragedies, religion is almost certain to show up. And religion may simply invent its own occasions and events, such as baptisms or confirmations or bar mitzvahs or the "christening" (Christ-ening) of a baby, a ship, or anything else that religion wants to lay its mitts on.

EVERYDAY HABITS

Religion is not satisfied to show up at the big occasions; promoters of religion know instinctively that it is the little things that matter most, since they occur most often and constitute the bulk of our lives. Religion thus insinuates itself into the mundane, like the food we eat: religions often carry dietary restrictions on what foods we can eat and when (in this religion no pork, in that religion no beef, in the other religion no meat on Friday or no meat at all, etc.). It also adds practices of fasting and feasting, like the Muslim fast of Ramadan or Catholic feast days. Every time you eat you may be expected to "say grace." For that matter, every time you go to sleep you may be expected to say a bedtime prayer. Religion may even show up when you sneeze ("God bless you"). And religion may shape the everyday more energetically, with regular services and ceremonies, "confessions," prayers, and so on.

One of the most overlooked ways that religion replicates itself in the everyday is in personal names. In many religions, humans are given names from the mythology of the local religion—in Judeo-Christianity: for males, *Matthew, Mark, Luke, John, Adam, Joshua, Joseph, Daniel, Michael, David*, and for females, *Mary, Ruth, Rachel, Eve*, and on and on. In Islam, *Muhammad* is probably the most common male name, followed by *Ali* and *Hussein*. Hindus often name their sons *Krishna* or *Ram/Rama*. A few Scandinavians are still named *Thor*.

BODILY HABITS

Christianity's disdain for the physical and the bodily does not mean that Christianity is content to leave the body alone. Christianity, like all other religions, sets standards for how the body should be dressed, groomed, and treated. Hair is a recurring concern for religions: many Protestant sects think hair should be plain for women and short for men, while Sikh men should never cut their hair, Hindus may wear their hair matted or tonsured, orthodox Jews may wear earlocks, and fundamentalist Mormon women wear the "high" hair piled and curled in specific ways. Facial hair excites religions too, such as the fundamentalist Muslim requirement that all men sport beards or the opposite Mormon norm that they do not.

In addition to hair styling, clothing is a prime sign of religious affiliation: the fundamentalist Mormon women recently seen in the news don similar long, specially colored dresses; Amish men adopt their suspenders and hats; Sikhs wear turbans (to contain their unshorn hair); and Muslim pilgrims to Mecca all put on the same plain, white robes. Orthodox Jews may even strap a phylactery, a small wooden box with scraps of scripture in it, on their foreheads and arms, and Muslim women may have to wear scarves or cloaks covering some or all of their face and body. Sikhs should bear a comb, a bangle, and a short sword, and both they and Mormons are expected to hitch up a customary kind of underwear.

Clearly religion dictates how one grooms and dresses oneself—not to mention religious manipulations and operations on the body, such as circumcision and "female circumcision," tattooing, scarring, piercing, and so on. Religion even extends into the personal bathing of its practitioners; many religions require various ritual washings and ablutions—more routine versions of the big Christian "baptism." Also, religions may contain specific postures and gestures, from the meditative pose of the Buddhist to the extremities of Hindu yogis, as well as kneeling, pressing together hands in prayer, making the sign of the cross over the head and chest, ad infinitum. And last but not least, religion likes to have a say in human sexual behavior, including who, when, how, and why.

INSTITUTIONS

No religion will succeed unless it can transform its assumptions into long-lasting, socially significant institutions—or, at the very least, insert itself into the existing institutions of society. The two most obvious points of entry for religion into the institutional life of a group are family and education. Religion did not invent either, but as with life events, religion likes to pretend that it did or that only its particular version of these institutions is the "right" one. Religion may attempt to dictate the terms of marriage, sexuality, child bearing, and familial roles. It may set up its own educational institutions or demand inclusion in the general "secular" institutions—with moments of silence, religious displays, or explicit prayers and religious teachings.

Another potent place for religious intervention is political or governmental institutions. In some religions, like Islam, religion is essentially law and jurisprudence, the *shari'a* law supposedly providing a guide—including a court system—for all decisions from marriage to business to war. Religious penetration of politics can take many forms, from outright theocracy as in Khomeini's Iran or Afghanistan under the Taliban (or the theocratic program of the Christian "dominionists" or "reconstructionists") to pious leadership, to hiring of clergy for the military, to religious displays on government property, to religious slogans on money, and to the phrasing of oaths and pledges. Additionally, wherever religious people go and whatever they do is likely to have the mark of religion on it, including their workplaces—where employees may erect religious shrines and employers may organize prayer groups or religious study groups.

Finally, the arts generally, from music and painting and sculpture to literature and philosophy, are shaped by religious themes: how much of the Western art of the last two thousand years has been a reiteration of Christian myths and images? Meanwhile, Greek and Roman art conveyed the religious sentiments of those cultures, as Hindu and Buddhist art has, while Jewish and Muslim art has been constrained by the principle that realistic depictions are forbidden. Even contemporary media like television and movies continue to transmit religious messages—overtly in *The Passion of the Christ* and covertly in *The Matrix* and other offerings and genres that talk about "the one" and "saviors" and such.

An important fact to remember is that if religions cannot have their place in the institutions of society, even dominate those institutions, then they will create their own. If a religion cannot control the secular schools, it will found its own sectarian or "parochial" ones or else simply "homeschool" its children. In the extreme, if a religion cannot dominate the government, it may withdraw into seclusion (like the Amish or the fundamentalist Mormons) or attempt to conquer the government (like the Taliban) or establish one of its own (like the "Christian Exodus" movement in the United States that aims to literally occupy and control its own state government and secede from the United States if necessary—visit http://www.christianexodus.com to see their plans for South Carolina).

TIME

Religions define the very notion of time for their members. This is true of large-scale time keeping, such as calendars and annual cycles. When Westerners state that it is the year 2010 or whatever, they tacitly declare Christianity's victory over time: it is the year 2010 *according to the Christian calendar*, but it is not "really" 2010 or any other year. Muslims have their own calendar system, starting from the first year of the Muslim era; Jews have theirs, Hindus have theirs (actually more than one), Chinese have theirs, Mayans had theirs, and so on. Not only do religions colonize calendrical time, but they fill the year with their events and activities, including annual "holidays" as well as shorter cycles, like seven-day weeks with a "sabbath" day inserted into each one (whether it is Friday for Muslims, Saturday for Jews, or Sunday for Christians—and for the Romans they cribbed it from). Religions even determine the macrostructure of time, whether it is "linear" with a definite end, as in Christianity, or circular with indefinite time before and after the present, as in Hinduism. At the smaller scale of time, as we have already mentioned briefly, religions shape the day, defining when the day even begins (sundown of the previous evening in Judaism, midnight for some, sunrise for others, etc.) and filling it with religious observances, such as the five daily prayers of Islam, prayer at meals and bedtime, hourly church bells, attendance at mass or church, or the like.

SPACE

Finally, religions literally colonize the physical space they inhabit. Even the most "otherworldly" religions put their sign on the material world. Every religion has its "sacred places," which may be cities where leaders or institutions are based or the religion started (as in Rome, Jerusalem, Salt Lake City, or Mecca) or locations where important religious events occurred; for many religions, specific mountains, lakes, rivers, or other features have significance and power. Religions usually need ceremonial grounds, to conduct rituals or to bury the dead ("consecrated earth"). Most religions construct sacred buildings of some sort, from cathedrals and mosques to stupas, ashrams, convents, temples, and synagogues. In addition to their own religious spaces, religions typically try to brand other public or private spaces. Many religions have an identifying design—the cross, the crescent, the star of David, the wheel of dharma, the swastika—with which they tag all the sites they can; they may also place statues, inscriptions, and other kinds of displays, permanently or occasionally (as at Christmas time). Among the most extreme examples is the "Christ the Redeemer" statue that stands over Rio de Janeiro, Brazil; the 120-foot colossus literally claims the city as its own. Religious people often carry this branding procedure into their homes and workplaces, erecting altars, shrines, icons, portraits, *mezuzahs*, or whatever the religion requires. And, like the practice of naming people after religious mythology, places are often named so as well, which literally inscribes the religion onto the map and immerses believers (and nonbelievers too) into the geographically reproduced myth-world of the religion. Think, for instance, of Christian-named places in the United States like New Canaan, Connecticut; Bethlehem, Pennsylvania; St. Paul, Minnesota; the Sangre de Cristo Mountains in Colorado, or Corpus Christi ("Christ's body"), Texas.

CULTURE SPREADING INTO CHRISTIANITY

As we said previously, cultural integration is a two-way street: culture adapts to and is suffused with religion, *but religion also adapts to and is suffused with culture.* In other words, not only does religion replicate itself through the many parts of culture, but culture replicates itself through the religion, recasting a religion like Christianity in the *culture's* own image. Loftus is insightful to stress in his introduction to this volume the adaptive capacities of Christianity or any religion. Since its inception, Christianity has accommodated itself to its cultural surroundings—and necessarily so, since a religion that is incompatible with its cultural context would be unintelligible and therefore unappealing to the people of that society. The consequence is that there is no such thing as a single, unified, global Christianity but instead many, different, local *Christianities*, which often do not recognize each other, accept each other, or even comprehend each other.

Elaine Pagels finds such religious adaptation in the very founding documents of Christianity. Each of the four gospels is a product of its particular historical moment and political perspective, written for—and against—someone; each thus was influenced by the rival or enemy of the day. Mark, generally held to have been composed first, "takes a conciliatory attitude toward the Romans" but quarrels "with the Jewish leaders—the council of elders, the Sanhedrin, along with the Jerusalem scribes and priests—who had rejected God's Messiah."[26] This Christianity is a dispute between Jewish factions. Matthew reflects the establishment of a distinct Christian identity and community, separate from "the Jews," that is, "the majority, who reject the gospel, [and therefore] have forfeited their legacy."[27] Luke, as "the only Gentile author among the gospel writers, speaks for those Gentile converts to Christianity who consider themselves the true heirs of Israel"; at the same time, he makes comparative peace with the Jewish authorities.[28] By the time of John, the historically last version, an exclusive and tight-knit Christian community has emerged, which is commanded to love each other "while regarding their Jewish opponents as offspring of Satan."[29] To say nothing of the unofficial or "noncanonical" gospels like Thomas, Mary Magdalene, and Philip, which paint yet divergent portraits of the man and his mission.

The diversity of Christianity did not end when it was adopted and institutionalized by the Roman Empire. Rather, differences of opinion—now branded heresy (from *hairesis* for "to choose")—persisted, not the least on the question of Jesus' divinity: Docetists believed that Jesus was purely divine and not human; Gnostics believed that only they possessed the "mysteries" of Jesus and could be one with him; Arianism taught that god was not three but one, that there was no biblical authority for the trinity concept (replacing it with a "unitarian" view). Books and essays were composed by Christians arguing with and condemning each other for false doctrine, such as Hippolytus's *The Refutation of All Heresies*, Irenaeus's *The Detection and Refutation of False Knowledge*, also known as *Against Heresies*, and Tertullian's "Prescription against Heretics." The only ways to settle these disputes became fiat and violence: committees like the Council of Nicaea in 325, overseen by the emperor Constantine, determined official Christian policy, while as early as 385 Bishop Priscillian of Spain and six followers had the honor of becoming the first Christians to be executed over theology.

In order to fully grasp the inescapable malleability of religions, we must consider the basic processes of culture and its subdomains including religion. However much cultures may strive for stasis and equilibrium, they are continuously subject to change and evolution. New items appear in a culture by either innovation or diffusion—innovation if inventions or discoveries are made by members of the society, diffusion if ideas or practices or objects seep into the society from another society. Simultaneously, old items are lost through abandonment or replacement. Other existing items undergo reinterpretation in the light of shifting circumstances and exposure to foreign ideas, new technologies, and changing environments. Two of the most important and recurring cultural processes are *syncretism* and *schism*, by which cultures are blended or broken. In syncretism, two or more cultural sources interact, blend, or fuse to create some new cultural mix; a fine example is the "cargo cult" phenomenon seen on Pacific Islands as a response to the invasion of Western soldiers, Western goods, and Western Christianity. In schism, a cultural element splits into two or more independent items or movements, following separate courses of development thereafter.

Christianity itself could and should be seen as an innovation or reinterpretation within Judaism; it started out as a "Jesus movement" along with multiple competing movements in Roman-occupied Jerusalem, such as the Essene and Zealot factions. As Christianity spread, local non-Christian elements diffused in while Christian elements diffused out to the local groups and religions. Christianity absorbed many influences, from the Latin language and the hierarchy of the Roman Empire to Germanic/Nordic practices like yule trees and Easter eggs. There is ample evidence to conclude that the "date" of Jesus' birth was borrowed from previous religions like Mithraism, since there is no basis whatsoever for December 25 in the Christian scriptures.

Like an avalanche, Christianity or any growing and spreading religion or culture picks up bits and pieces along the way and incorporates them into itself. But Christianity did not only fuse with local cultures, it also fissioned into separate and competing, sometimes hostile, cultures. The first great fission was the permanent split of Eastern (Orthodox) from Western (Latin/Roman) Christianity around 1054; a temporary and lesser-known schism in the late fourteenth and early fifteenth centuries left the Roman church with two and then three simultaneous and rival popes. Christianity continued to spit out schisms before and after that period, including the Albigensian/Cathar, Huguenot, and Hussite movements; one response to these developments was the establishment of an Inquisition to root out and destroy schismatics. However, Christianity underwent another irreparable rupture with Martin Luther's "Protestantism," which spawned countless imitators and competitors, such as Calvinists, Baptists, Quakers, Methodists, and so on. Christianity, if it ever was united (and it was not), was forever divided. Of course, the immediate result of these divisions was fratricidal war for more than a century.

American Christianity is thus not unique in its history of innovation, diffusion, loss, reinterpretation, syncretism, and schism, but it is noteworthy: Alexis de Tocqueville commented in 1830 that the United States was distinctive not only for its general high level of religiosity but for the diversity of its religion, the "innumerable multitude of sects" it contained.[30] Americans were great religious practitioners but also great religious innovators:

> Here and there throughout American society you meet men filled with an enthusiastic, almost fierce, spirituality such as cannot be found in Europe. From time to time strange sects arise which strive to open extraordinary roads to eternal happiness. Forms of religious madness are very common there.[31]

Indeed, the list of new and exceptional forms of Christianity born in the United States is truly impressive, while every kind of Christianity and other religion ever known to humankind can be found here as well. And those religions foreign to America, like Buddhism, were given an American stamp:

most American Buddhists practice a very different religion than, say, Thai or Vietnamese Buddhists, a distinct version of "American Buddhism."

America's religious fertility has produced a colorful pageantry. While Baptism, Quakerism, and Methodism were not invented here, they achieved their greatest success here. The period from 1720 to 1750, known as the First Great Awakening, saw the rise of a distinctive type of revivalist, evangelist, and populist style of Christianity that is still seen today. At the same time, "spiritualist" traditions like Swedenborgianism (which survives today: see http://www.swedenborg.org) mixed facets of Christianity with other features that, even at the time, were regarded as "new age." A Second Great Awakening occurred in the early/mid-1800s, much of it in upstate New York, which was actually dubbed "the burned-over district" for the plethora of religious movements that flared there. The Church of Jesus Christ of Latter-day Saints (Mormons) appeared in this era, as did the Millerites and Seventh-Day Adventists; other groups like the Shakers saw their greatest growth. Also, a movement toward "primitive" or nondenominational Christianity emerged as congregations began calling themselves simply "Christian" or "Disciples of Christ." Around 1827, William Nelson Darby gave modern Christianity one of its more enduring innovations, the notion of the "rapture," which most American Christians think, falsely, is an ancient precept of their religion. Later in the century, the Church of Christ, Scientist (Christian Science) was organized by Mary Baker Eddy, while the Watchtower Society institutionalized into the Jehovah's Witnesses.

Christianity has shown a nearly infinite capacity to multiply and morph to fit its environment; it can accommodate or integrate almost any influence. Sometimes, the result can be frightening, as with the Ku Klux Klan and the Christian Identity movement (see http://www.kingidentity.com), which blend religion with racism. Fractious and dangerous politics can mix with Christianity, as in Dominionism/Reconstructionism (see http://www .chalcedon.edu/blog/blog.php) and many "militia" organizations. Sometimes, the result can be hopeful, as with the "social gospel" of the nineteenth century and the "liberation theology" of the twentieth. Sometimes, the result is just wacky, as in the "prosperity gospel" of Oral Roberts, Joel Osteen, T. D. Jakes, and the aptly-named Creflo Dollar; the Church for Men (for a more manly Christianity: see http://www.churchformen.com/index.php and http://www.godmen.org/); the Scum of the Earth Church, for freaks and misfits (http://www.scumoftheearth.net/); not to mention Christian rap (please watch "Banging for Christ" at http://www.youtube.com/watch

?v=o5WLdvVEkpw&feature=related) or Christian rock, even a Christian version of "Guitar Hero" called "Guitar Praise." The current "megachurch" phenomenon is an adaptation to the suburban and corporate lives of many modern Christians; in the 1992 film *America's Folk Religion*, the leaders of one megachurch talk about marketing their "product" to their "target demographic." Most startlingly of all, Christianity can apparently even accommodate the nonexistence of its god, as in the "death of God theology" (an oxymoron if there ever was one) promoted in the 1960s.

All of these variations of Christianity roughly represent one possible tactic, which we will call *reforming*: the religion is reinvented for its specific time, place, and audience. A second tactic involves *retreating*, withdrawing from the cacophonous modern world into some protective religious reality. The Amish are one mild example, while contemporary "fundamentalism" is another not-always-so-mild case. In fact, some retreats are tactical retreats, preparing for a coming assault, as with the Reconstructionists or even the more mainstream Religious Right, which aims explicitly to (re)conquer American society for Christianity. As Pat Robertson himself stated:

> The mission of the Christian Coalition is simple.... [It is] to mobilize Christians—one precinct at a time, one community at a time—until once again we are the head and not the tail, and at the top rather than the bottom of our political system.... ['T']he Christian Coalition will be the most powerful political force in America by the end of this decade. We have enough votes to run this country...and when the people say, "We've had enough," we're going to take over![32]

Ironically, retreating religions almost unavoidably reform at the same time: even the most fundamentalist forms of Christianity gladly incorporate modern tools like television and the Internet, and they would have no success if they didn't.

CONCLUSION: SO MANY CHRISTIANITIES, SO LITTLE REASON

All told, by some estimates, there are as many as thirty-eight thousand sects and denominations of Christianity in the world today (we have not even had the opportunity to mention non-Western versions of Christianity or pseudo-Christian cults in this chapter). Many are not only incomprehensible but literally anathema to each other: many Christians deny that Mormons are Christians, while others condemn rap and rock as inappropriate or evil corruptions of their religion. But, by taking the notion of culture seriously, we have exposed some crucial facts about Christianity in particular and religion in general. Religions may think they are universal and eternal, but they are not. Religions may think they are special, but they are not. And, with the help of the missiologists, we have solved the mystery at the opening of this chapter: Christians are not easily reasoned out of religion since they are not usually reasoned into it. Christians, like other religionists, are not so much convinced by arguments and proofs as colonized by assumptions and premises. As a form of culture, it seems self-evident to them; they are not so much indoctrinated as enculturated. Weak analogies like "religion is a crutch" or "religion is a lens" do not convey the depth of the process. As I have written elsewhere:

> Like a pair of glasses, humans see with culture, but they do not usually see culture. Computers do not know they are running a program; they simply follow the instructions. Seeing your glasses, recognizing your program, is a rare thing, achieved by few individuals in even fewer societies. It demands a certain amount of "freedom," a certain amount of distance from oneself. It is also probably not an entirely desirable or beneficial ability: taken-for-grantedness is adaptive in a strong sense. The very opaqueness and "obviousness"...of the human world spares us from having to remake the same conclusions and judgments over and over; as some anthropologists and sociologists have emphasized, culture provides us with a set of "frames" or "scenarios" with familiar and predictable patterns and outcomes. These frames or scenarios get the average person through the average life with little uncertainty and little remainder, but only so long as the conditions in which they were forged persist.
>
> Some atheists and other critics of religion like to use the analogy of a crutch for religion—that it is something that the weak use to get them through otherwise difficult situations. The implication is that, if they were stronger (like us) they could dispense with the crutch and walk independent and free. [But] you cannot pull a crutch from underneath a cripple and expect him or her to walk. Rather, they will fall and then probably blame you for the accident. The real point is more profound but perhaps more discouraging: religion for the religious person is like culture for the cultural person—it is glasses, not crutches. And these glasses are not prophylactic—they do not help the person to see "better." *They make seeing at all possible.* Maybe an ultimate analogy for culture in general

and religion in particular is not glasses but the very eyes themselves. You could not expect to pull someone's eyes out and have them see better, any more than you could expect to take away someone's culture and have them understand and act better.[33]

Religions like Christianity—or rather, their specific local versions—are not so much "belief systems" as, like the missiologists said, worldviews and embodied realities. Each is opaque and foreign to the nonmembers, and *each is largely invisible to itself.* Hiebert explains that "so long as we live in our own culture, we are largely unaware of it. When we enter new cultures, however, we become keenly aware of the fact that other people live differently.... [W]e learn that there are profound differences in beliefs, feelings and values. Finally, we begin to realize that there are fundamental differences in worldviews. *People in different cultures do not live in the same world with different labels attached to it, but in radically different worlds.*"[34] With the information presented in this chapter, and in this book, it is impossible for Christians to remain unaware of their own religion or of the differences between religions. The hope, and the obligation, is that once people recognize the diversity, plasticity, and relativity of religion, they will see little merit in it: that which is no longer taken for granted is often not taken at all.

NOTES

1. Jack David Eller, *Cultural Anthropology: Global Forces, Local Lives* (London: Routledge, 2009).

2. For example, see Charles H. Kraft, *Anthropology for Christian Witness* (Maryknoll, NY: Orbis Books, 1997); Paul G. Hiebert, *Transforming Worldviews: An Anthropological Understanding of How People Change* (Grand Rapids, MI: Baker Academic, 2008); Sherwood G. Lingenfelter, *Transforming Culture: A Challenge for Christian Mission*, 2nd ed. (Grand Rapids, MI: Baker Academic, 1998); Paul R. Gupta, *Breaking Tradition to Accomplish Vision: Training Leaders for a Church-Planting Movement: A Case from India* (Winona Lake, IN: BMH Books, 2006); and most offensive to me and my discipline, Stephen A. Grunlan and Marvin K. Mayers, *Cultural Anthropology: A Christian Perspective*, 2nd ed. (Grand Rapids, MI: Zondervan, 1988).

3. Ralph D. Winter and Steven C. Hawthorne, eds., *Perspectives on the World Christian Movement*, 3rd ed. (Pasadena, CA: William Carey Library, 1999).

4. Charles H. Kraft, "Culture, Worldview, and Contextualization," in Winter and Hawthorne, *Perspectives*, p. 385.

5. Ibid., p. 387.

6. Paul G. Hiebert, "Cultural Differences and the Communication of the Gospel," in Winter and Hawthorne, *Perspectives*, p. 376.

7. Kraft, "Culture, Worldview, and Contextualization," p. 388.

8. Hiebert, "Cultural Differences," p. 379.

9. Michael Welton, "Cunning Pedagogics: The Encounter between the Jesuit Missionaries and the Amerindians in 17th-Century New France," *Adult Education Quarterly* 55 (2005): 102.

10. Ibid., pp. 102–103.

11. Ibid.

12. Ibid., p. 107.

13. Ibid., p. 109.

14. Ibid., p. 112.

15. Ibid., p. 113.

16. Jean Comaroff, *Body of Power, Spirit of Resistance: The Culture and History of a South Africa People* (Chicago: University of Chicago Press, 1985), p. 80.

17. John L. Comaroff and Jean Comaroff, *Of Revelation and Revolution: The Dialectics of Modernity on a South African Frontier* (Chicago: University of Chicago Press, 1991), 2:9.

18. Ibid., p. 31.

19. Ibid., p. 189.

20. Ibid., p. 282.

21. Ibid., p. 292.

22. Ibid., p. 296.

23. Ibid., p. 127.

24. Kraft, "Culture, Worldview, and Contextualization," p. 388.

25. David Eller, *Atheism Advanced: Further Thoughts of a Freethinker* (Cranford, NJ: American Atheist Press, 2007); see especially chapter 8, "Religion and the Colonization of Experience."

26. Elaine Pagels, *The Origin of Satan* (New York: Random House, 1995), p. 10.

27. Ibid., p. 87.

28. Ibid., p. 89.

29. Ibid., p. 65.

30. Alexis de Tocqueville, *Democracy in America*, ed. J. P. Mayer, trans. George Lawrence (Garden City, NJ: Anchor Books, 1969), p. 290.

31. Ibid., p. 574.

32. The Christian Resistance, "World Politics," http://www.freewebs.com/christianresistance/worldpolitics.htm.

33. David Eller, *Natural Atheism* (Cranford, NJ: American Atheist Press, 2004), pp. 124–25.

34. Hiebert, "Cultural Differences and the Communication of the Gospel," p. 377 [emphasis added].

Chapter 2

CHRISTIAN BELIEF
THROUGH THE LENS OF
COGNITIVE SCIENCE

Valerie Tarico, PhD

My father died in a climbing accident when he was fifty-nine and I was in my mid-twenties. In one of our last deep conversations before his thousand-meter misstep, he expressed his abiding hope that I would "get right with God." Dad was the son of Italian immigrants, all Catholics, who got converted by door-to-door Pentecostals some years after their arrival in Chicago. As far as I know, he never questioned his belief that the Bible was the literally perfect word of God and that Jesus died for his sins. And yet of his six children three of us, according to those beliefs, are now slated for eternal torture. To us, his religious certitude is an oddity in an otherwise rigorous engineering mind.

How should we understand it? What are the implications for our own lives?

This question could not be more important. Religious belief is one of the most powerful forces in our world. Almost half of Americans insist that humans were created in their present form sometime within the last ten thousand years, *because the Bible says so*.[1] In the Middle East, Sunnis and Shiites split over theological differences that seem trivial to the rest of us but that in their minds create tribal boundaries worthy of lethal conflict. In the United States, religion is the best predictor of political party alliance—with enormous implications for international relations, medical research, population policies, and resource management. Believers think that belief has the power to save us all. Increasingly, doubters fear the opposite may be true.

Why is Christian belief so widespread and powerful? The traditional answer is: because it's true, and people who haven't hardened their hearts recognize this when God's plan of salvation is presented to them. But cognitive science offers a new way to look at this question, not from a moral or theological vantage but from a practical vantage. What is the mental machinery that lets us form beliefs? What are the roles of reason and emotion? How well do beliefs tend to relate to external realities?

The more we learn about the hardware and operating systems of the human brain—the more we understand about human information processing—the more we glean bits of insight into the religious mind. For example:

- We humans are not rational about anything, let alone religion.
- Certainty is a feeling, not proof of knowing. It can fail to materialize even when evidence is enormous, and can manifest itself independently of any real knowledge.
- The structure of thought itself predisposes us to religious thinking. Given how our minds work, certain kinds of religious beliefs are likely and others are impossible.
- The "born again" experience is a natural phenomenon. It is triggered by specific social and emotional factors, which can occur in both religious and secular settings.

Before looking at the evidence behind these statements, it is helpful to understand why belief is so important in Christianity. For traditional Christians, belief is the heart of the Christian religion. As they conceive it, believing that Jesus Christ died as a "propitiation" for your sins matters enormously to God. It is the toggle that sends people to heaven or hell. Only if you believe correctly do virtue and service become relevant. The creedal councils, canonization of scripture, inquisitions, purges, and centuries of conversion activities can be understood only in this context.

This focus on belief is not characteristic of all religions. In the ancient Near East, the birthplace of Christianity, pagan religions placed little emphasis on belief. The existence of a supernatural world was broadly assumed because there seemed to be little other way to explain the good and bad things that happen to people and natural events like storms, earthquakes, illness, birth, and death. But the point of religion wasn't belief; it was to take care of the gods so they would take care of you and your community. The word "cult" (Latin *cultus*, literally "care") is related to the word "cultivation." We talk about cultivating ground so that it will bear fruit. These days, nonprofits talk about "cultivating donors." This kind of cultivation was what pagans thought gods cared about, and so it was the heart of their religious practice.

From the beginning, Christianity was different. Jesus worshippers cared tremendously about right belief, also known as orthodoxy. Bart Ehrman's *Lost Christianities* offers a fascinating window into the struggles that went on during the first and second centuries as groups with different beliefs about Jesus criticized and competed with each other and one of them won out.[2] Some groups (e.g., Ebionites) believed Jesus was a fully human Jewish Messiah and that Jesus worshippers must follow the Jewish law. Others (e.g., Marcionites) believed Jesus was a being from the spirit world who only took on a human likeness. Still others (e.g., Gnostics) believed that the human Jesus was inhabited by a divine "Eon" during the years of his ministry—revealing to his followers secret knowledge that would let them escape this corrupt mortal plane. Others subscribed to the Roman or "proto-orthodox" version of Jesus worship, which led to the views of Christians today. What all of these groups agreed on was that it was tremendously important to believe the right thing about who Jesus was and what Christianity should be.

This emphasis on right belief was and is unique to monotheism. For this reason, Christianity's exclusive truth claims and emphasis on right belief helped it to out-compete other religions in the Roman Empire. Polytheists can be quite agreeable to adding another god to their pantheon. Christians could persuade pagans to add the Jesus-god and then could wean them off the others. Today, in India, for example, evangelical missionaries are much more likely to target Hindus than Sikhs or Muslims who would have to immediately abandon their primary religion in order to embrace the idea of Jesus as a god.

Eastern religions do not share Christianity's concern with belief. Their emphasis is more on practice or "praxis"—spiritual living, self-renunciation, insight or enlightenment—and, among ordinary people, a sort of cult or caretaking of the gods like that practiced by Western pagans. Right belief isn't what lets you move up through cycles of reincarnation or attain Nirvana. Nor is it what gets you the favor of supernatural beings.

Just as biological organisms have many different adaptive or reproductive strategies, so religions compete for human mind–share in different ways. An emphasis on propagating belief (i.e., evangelism) and purity of belief (i.e., orthodoxy) is only one of those strategies. In the late nineteeth and early twentieth century, a movement called modernism emerged within Christianity. Modernist theologians began reexamining traditional orthodox beliefs in light of what we now know about linguistics, archaeology, psychiatry, biology, and human history. In this light, traditional Christian certainties looked less certain, and many modernist Christians have become more like members of Eastern religions in that their primary concern is with spiritual practice rather than belief. But a backlash emerged in response to modernism. People who proudly called themselves "fundamentalists" insisted that no one was a real Christian who didn't hold to the traditional dogmas. Evangelicals inherited the fundamentalist torch, and even some of the more inquiring denominations have reverted back toward emphasis on right belief.

This is the mindset that dominates Christianity in the public square. It is the mindset that sends Christian missionaries out to seek converts in impoverished and obscure corners of the planet. It is the mindset that prints Bibles to be distributed in Iraq and has organized strategically within the United States military hierarchy, seeking to create an "army of Christian soldiers." Hence, to understand Christianity it is helpful to understand the psychology of belief.

SO YOU THINK YOU'RE RATIONAL

I like to think of myself as fair-minded and reasonable. In fact, I pride myself on "following the evidence where it leads, whether I like the conclusion or not." Integrity and truth seeking are near the top of my wanted-virtues list.

The problem is—research on human cognition suggests that I am neither fair-minded nor reasonable. None of us are. And it's not just a matter of sloppy thinking. Our brains have built-in biases that stack the odds against objectivity, so much so that the success of the scientific endeavor can be attributed to one factor: it pits itself against our natural leanings, erects barriers across the openings to rabbit trails, and systematically exposes faulty thinking to public critique. In fact, the scientific method has been called "what we know about how not to fool ourselves."

In some ways, science picks up where philosophy leaves off. Philosophers, from classical times to the present, have developed sophisticated, useful lines of reasoning about knowledge (epistemology), morality (ethics), and the nature of reality (metaphysics). They have identified and learned to avoid "logical fallacies." But their approach has limitations. Without the constraints of external real-world tests, philosophers go down their own kind of rabbit trails, into a world of ideals. Philosophy assumes that if an argument can be made logic-tight, then it will be persuasive. It assumes that people can be compelled by reason. It assumes that we make moral decisions by doing some calculus that prioritizes harm avoidance or the greater good. Psychology, on the other hand, looks at how ordinary people function in everyday life and says "that ain't the way things work around here."

The way things actually do work is somewhat embarrassing. The fact is, we distort reality in a host of ways—many of which are extravagantly self-serving. We take undue credit for successes, and blame failures on external circumstances (attribution biases). We even revise history so that, in hindsight, our failures were simply to be expected because of the challenges we faced (retroactive pessimism). We retain memories of when we were kind, funny, personable, and clever, better than memories of when we were boorish and mean. On average, we expect to live ten years longer than average.[3] And virtually all of us who believe in heaven think we are going there. To put it bluntly, each of us is the protagonist in a custom-made Hollywood movie with the best possible camera angles. Our self-serving biases may have a positive function. They may play a role in fending off depression, feeding hope, and getting us to try harder. But they also help to explain why stunningly self-centered religious beliefs don't trigger any alarms.

It is easy for us to distort the evidence in our own favor, in part because we aren't so great with evidence in general. One of the strongest built-in mental distortions we have is called *confirmation bias*. Once we have a hunch about how things work, we seek information that fits what we already think. It's like our minds set up filters—with contradictory evidence stuck in gray tones on the outside and the confirmatory evidence flowing through in bright and shining color. This bias optimizes for efficiency over accuracy. It allows us to rapidly sift through the information coming at us and piece together a meaningful story line. But in situations where emotions run high or evidence is ambiguous, it also lets us go very wrong. Corporate leaders fall into group-think about the best competitive strategy. Jurors assume an accused criminal is guilty. Politicians fabricate reasons for war—certain that the real evidence must be just out of sight.

What we're always trying to do is get to a coherent plot line. Consider what it's like to read a novel: when there are too many contradictions or loose ends, or the conclusion is ambiguous, we grumble and lose interest. What we want is a story where the mysteries get solved and everything gets tied up in the end. In everyday life, we operate the same way. Our brains are constantly trying to create a smooth narrative out of fragments of information. This is true of our eyes, which make jerky movements and have actual blind spots that our brains revise to create a seamless picture of the scene in front of us. It is also true of our higher cognitive processes. The mind edits and fills in gaps.

This imaginative infill is why we experience dreams as stories. As our nighttime brain is at work on synthesizing memories, it insists on interpreting the images and ideas flashing through them in a narrative form. Alcoholics and patients with brain injuries that cause memory gaps sometimes "confabulate." When asked about missing chunks of time they make up stories about where they were and what happened. This is not intentional deception. It is the brain, faced with an impossible question, creating an answer. And once the answer is generated, the person whose subconscious created the history actually *believes* it. Our compulsion to think in "stories," to ignore threads that don't fit the plot line, and to fill in any gaps, may be at the heart of the religious impulse.

As we learn more about the human mind, even the outrages of religious belief become more understandable. How can a college-educated engineer think he just happened to be born into the one true religion? How can a doctor who looks at the evidence and dismisses homeopathy believe in the healing power of intercessory prayer? How can tourists who escaped a hurricane or plane crash believe that a god intervened to save them while letting others drown or burn? How can a minister with a high school education—or a doctorate, for that matter—be convinced after two thousand years of theological blood feuds that he knows how God meant the book of Genesis to be interpreted?

It all becomes a bit easier to understand when you realize that we humans are only partly rational. Bias is our default setting, and most of the distortions happen below the level of conscious awareness. Understanding this may let us be a little more sympathetic toward otherwise smart, decent people who hold beliefs that make us cringe. It should also make us wonder about our own blind spots. But it puts Christianity as a system in an awkward position because Christianity sanctifies belief itself. "Believe in the Lord Jesus Christ and thou shalt be saved and thy house" (Acts 16:31). Christians call themselves believers. Philosopher Daniel Dennett calls their stance "belief in belief," which shines a light on one of the core problems Christianity must face. Arriving at belief in an infallible God by way of an inerrant Bible requires an unwarranted belief in yourself.

I KNOW BECAUSE I KNOW

On a warm afternoon in June, two men have appointments with a psychiatrist. The first has been dragged to the office by his wife, much to his irritation. He is a biologist who suffers from schizophrenia, and the wife insists that his meds are not working. "No," says the biologist, "I'm actually fine. It's just that because of what I'm working on right now the CIA has been bugging my calls and reading my e-mail." Despite his wife's skepticism and his understanding of his own illness, he insists calmly that he is sure, and he lines up evidence to support his claim. The second man has come on his own because he is feeling exhausted and desperate. He shows the psychiatrist his hands, which are raw to the point of bleeding. No matter how many times he washes them (up to a hundred times in a day) or what he uses (soap, alcohol, bleach, or scouring pads) he never feels confident that they are clean.

In both of these cases, after brain biochemistry is rebalanced, the patient's sense of certainty falls back in line with the evidence. The first man becomes less sure about the CIA thing and gradually loses interest in the idea. The second man begins feeling confident that his hands are clean after a normal round of soap and water, and the cracks start healing.

How do we know what is real? How do we know what we know? We don't, entirely. Research on psychiatric disorders and brain injuries shows that humans have a *feeling* or *sense of knowing* that can get activated by reason and evidence but can get activated in other ways as well. Conversely, when certain kinds of brain malfunctions occur, it may be impossible to experience a sense of knowing no matter how much evidence piles up. V. S. Ramachandran describes a brain-injured patient who sees his mother and says, "This looks like my mother in every way, but she is an imposter." The connection between his visual cortex and his limbic system has been severed, and even though he sees his mother perfectly well, he has no emotional sense of rightness or knowing, so he offers the only explanation he can find (called the *Capgras Delusion*).[4]

From malfunctions like these we gain an understanding of normal brain function and how it shapes our day-to-day experience, including the experience of religion. Neurologist Robert Burton explains it this way: "Despite how certainty feels, it is neither a conscious choice nor even a thought process. Certainty and similar states of *knowing what we know* arise out of involuntary brain mechanisms that, like love or anger, function independently of reason."[5] This "knowing what we know" mechanism is good enough for getting around in the world, but it is not perfect. For the most part, it lets us explain, predict, and influence people or objects or events, and we use that knowledge to advantage. But as the above scenarios show, it can also get thrown off.

Burton says that the feeling of knowing (*rightness, correctness, certainty, conviction*) should be thought of as one of our primary emotions, like anger, pleasure, or fear. Like these other feelings, it can be triggered by a seizure or a drug or direct electrical stimulation of the brain. Research after the Korean War suggested that the feeling of knowing or not knowing also can be produced by what are called brainwashing techniques: repetition, sleep deprivation, and social/emotional manipulation.[6] Once triggered for any reason, the feeling that something is right or real can be incredibly powerful—so powerful that when it goes head-to-head with logic or evidence, the feeling wins. Our brains make up reasons to justify our feeling of knowing, rather than following logic to its logical conclusion.

For many reasons, religious beliefs are usually undergirded by a strong feeling of knowing. Set aside for the moment the question of whether those beliefs tap some underlying realities. Conversion experiences can be intense, hypnotic, and transformative. Worship practices, music and religious architecture have been optimized over time to evoke right-brain sensations of transcendence and euphoria. Social insularity protects a community consensus. Repetition of ideas reinforces a sense of conviction or certainty. Forms of Christianity that emphasize right belief have built-in safeguards against contrary evidence, doubt, and the assertions of other religions. Many a freethinker has sparred a smart, educated fundamentalist into a corner only to have the believer utter some form of "I just know."

Given what I've said about knowing, how can anybody claim to know anything? We can't, with certainty. Those of us who are not religious could do with a little more humility on this point. We all see "through a glass darkly," and there is a realm in which all any of us can do is to make our own best guesses about what is real and important. This doesn't imply, though, that all ideas are created equal or that our traditional understanding of "knowledge" is useless. As I said before, our sense of knowing allows us to navigate this world pretty well—to detect regularities, anticipate events, and make things happen. In the concrete domain of everyday life it works pretty well for us. Nonetheless, it is a *healthy mistrust for our sense of knowing* that has allowed scientists to reach beyond everyday life to detect, predict, and produce desired outcomes with ever greater precision.

When we overstate our ability to know, we play into the fundamentalist fallacy that certainty is possible. Burton, author of *On Being Certain*, calls this "the all-knowing rational mind myth." As scientists learn more about how our brains work, certitude is coming to be seen as a vice rather than a virtue. Certainty is a confession of ignorance about our ability to be passionately mistaken. Humans will always argue passionately about things that we do not know and cannot know, but with a little more self-knowledge and humility we may get to the point where those arguments are less often lethal.

WHY GOD HAS A HUMAN MIND

As the story goes, Jesus was a human, fathered by a god and born to a virgin. He died for three days and was resurrected. His death was a sacrifice, an offering or propitiation. It brings favor for humans. He lives now in a realm where other supernatural beings interact with each other and sometimes intervene in human affairs.

Gradually the mainstream of the American public is becoming aware that none of these elements is unique to Christianity. Symbologists, or scholars who specialize in understanding ancient symbols, tell us that the orthodox Jesus story, as it appears in our gospels, follows a specific sacred or mythic template that existed in the ancient Near East long before Christianity or even Judaism. In part this is due to the flow of history. Religions emerge out of ancestor religions. Though the characters and details merge and morph, elements get carried through that allow us to track the lineage. The Gilgamesh and Noah flood-hero stories are similar because the Hebrew story descended from the Sumerian story. The same can be said of the

Sumerian "Descent of Inana" and the Christian resurrection story.[7] Even religions that exist side by side borrow elements from each other, in a process scholars call *syncretism*, something Eller has shown us in the first chapter.

But another reason for similarities among religious stories is that all of them are carried by similar human minds. To quote cognitive scientist Pascal Boyer, "Evolution by natural selection gave us a particular kind of mind so that only particular kinds of religious notions can be acquired.... All human beings can easily acquire a certain *range* of religious notions and communicate them to others."[8] Our supernatural notions are shaped by the built-in structures that let us acquire, sort, and access information efficiently, especially information about other people.

You may have heard the old adage "If dogs had a god, God would be a dog; if horses had a god, God would be a horse...." Humans are more inventive than dogs and horses, and not all human gods or magical beings have human bodies. They do, however, have human psyches—minds with quirks and limitations that are peculiar to our species. Philosopher John Locke believed that the human mind was a *tabula rasa*, a blank slate. We now know this is not the case. Because we need to learn so much so fast, certain assumptions are actually built-in. This allows us to generalize from a few bits of data to a big fund of knowledge. It lets us know more than we have actually experienced or been told.

Let me illustrate. If I tell you that my "guarg," Annie, just made a baby by laying an egg and sitting on it, your brain says: *Guargs* (not just Valerie's guarg) *are nonhuman animals that reproduce by laying eggs.* You have different categories in your brain for animal reproductive systems, and putting one guarg in the egg-laying category puts them all there. To oversimplify, we have a built-in filing system. Most of the labels actually start out blank, but some of them don't. The preprinted labels appear to include human, non-human animal, plant, human-made object, natural object.

A large percentage of our mental architecture consists of specialized "domain-specific" structures for processing information about other humans. We *Homo sapiens sapiens* are social information specialists; that is our specialized niche in this world. Our survival and well-being depend mostly on smarts rather than teeth, claws, stealth, or an innate sense of direction, and most of the information we need comes from other humans. Our greatest threats also come from our own species—people who seek to out-compete, exploit, or kill us. For this reason, our brains are optimized to process information from and about other humans.

HOW DOES ALL OF THIS AFFECT RELIGION?

Here is a concrete example. Our brains have a specialized facial-recognition module. Much of what is known about the inborn structures of our minds comes from studies of infants and brain injuries, and we know about the facial recognition module from both. Shortly after birth, babies are uniquely attracted to two circles with a slash beneath them, which is representative of a face. Later on, brain injury or developmental anomalies can produce a disorder in which people cannot recognize faces (including their own!)—even though other kinds of visual processing are perfectly intact. This is called *prosopagnosia*. Most of the time, though, our facial-recognition module overfunctions rather than underfunctions. In ambiguous situations—looking at clouds, rocks, lumps of clay, or ink blots—we have a tendency to see faces. Our brains automatically activate the facial recognition machinery even though it doesn't really apply. Through history people have seen gods, demons, ghosts, or the man in the moon looking at them. Christians, whose interpretation of hazy shapes is further shaped by belief in specific supernatural persons, see Jesus, the Virgin Mary, an angel, a demon, or even Satan.

This illustrates a broader point that cannot be overemphasized in understanding the psychology of religion: when faced with unknowns and ambiguities, our brains activate inborn information modules even when they don't really apply. We take unfamiliar situations and even random data and perceive "simulacra," meaning patterns that are inherent, not in the external world, but in our own minds. Furthermore, our pattern-recognition systems err on the side of being overactive rather than underactive. This tendency is called *apophenia*. It is alarming to look at a face and not see it immediately as a face; it is quite common to see a face in an array of leaves or shadows.

When we look at the world around us, we instinctively see more than faces. We also "see" kindred conscious beings. Humans (and some intelligent animals) have developed a capacity called "theory of mind." We not only have minds, we imagine that others have them, and we think about what they might be thinking. To guess what someone else might do, or to influence what they might do, it is tremendously helpful to know what they want and what they intend. Theory of mind is so important in navigating our way through society that we can think about it several steps removed:

I can imagine what Brian is thinking about how Grace intends to respond to Janet's preferences. Furthermore, because our brains process information about minds differently than information about bodies, we can imagine human minds inside of all kinds of bodies (think stuffed animals, pet rocks, or cartoon characters) or without any body at all (think evil spirits, poltergeists, or God).

Because our theory of mind is so rich, we tend to overattribute events to conscious beings. Scientists call this *hyperactive agency detection*. What does that mean? It means that when good things happen somebody gets credit and when bad things happen we look for someone to blame. We expect important events to be done by, for, and to persons, and we are averse to the idea that stuff just happens. We also tend to overassume conscious intent, that if something consequential happened, someone did it on purpose.

This set of default assumptions explains why the ancients thought that volcanoes and plagues *must* be the actions of gods. Even in modern times, we are not immune from this kind of attribution: for some Christians, Hurricane Katrina happened because God was angry about abortions and gays; the Asian tsunami happened because He was disgusted with nude Australian sunbathers. If gods are tweaking natural events, then we want to curry their favor. Around the world, people make their special requests known to gods or spirits by talking to them and giving them gifts. Athletes huddle in prayer before a game, just in case those random bounces aren't random. After a good day at the casino, a thank-you tip may go into the offering basket. Or it may be that the offering goes into the basket beforehand.

All of this builds on the idea that supernatural beings are akin to us psychologically. They have emotions and preferences. They take action in response to things they like and dislike. They experience righteous indignation and crave retribution. They like some people better than others. They respond to our loyalty by being loyal to us. They can be placated or cajoled. They like praise, affirmation, and gratitude. They track favors and goodwill in a kind of tit-for-tat reciprocity.

Abstract theologies are a fairly recent invention in the history of human religion, and they tend not to govern religious behavior. Even people who describe their god as omniscient, or who insist that everything is predestined, often *behave* as if they need to communicate their desires and can influence future events by doing so. There are exceptions. An increasing number of Christians have moved beyond the concept of a person-god to a sense of mystical transcendence, participation in a divine reality that is made manifest in small particulars throughout the universe. They believe that God's power is brought into human lives more through our actions than through supernatural interventions. But most people prefer the tangible familiarity of a powerful *person* who watches over them and answers their prayers.[9]

An extraterrestrial anthropologist might look at Christianity's dogmas and think how beautifully they reflect the nature of our species as social information specialists. As we know, the social dimension of religion extends far beyond the doctrines, which would gain little traction if they were just dry ideas. Part of what keeps the doctrines alive is that they tap powerful emotions and relationships. Nowhere is this truer than in the experience of conversion and rebirth.

THE BORN-AGAIN EXPERIENCE

"I prayed harder and just then I felt like everything I was saying was being sucked into a vacuum. When I stood up, I felt like thin air; I had to brace myself. I felt this energy, it was a kind of an ecstasy."

—Cathy.[10]

"Something began to flow in me—a kind of energy.... Then came the strange sensation that water was not only running down my cheeks, but surging through my body as well, cleansing and cooling as it went."

—Colson.[11]

"It was a beautiful feeling of well-being, warmth, and loving...I went home and all night long these warm feelings kept coming up in my body."

—Jean.[12]

"I felt something real warm overwhelming me. It was in just a moment, yet it was like an eternity.... a joy, such a joy hit me with such a tremendous force that I jumped...and ran."

—Helen.[13]

For many Christians, being born again is unlike anything they have ever known. A sense of personal conviction, yielding, or release followed by indescribable peace and joy—this is the stuff of spiritual transformation. Once experienced it is unforgettable, and many people can recall small details years later. In the aftermath of such a moment, an alcoholic may stop drinking or a criminal fugitive may hand himself in to the authorities. A housewife may sail through her tasks for weeks, flooded by a sense of God's love flowing through her to her children. A normally introverted programmer may begin inviting his coworkers to church.

This experience, more than any other, creates a sense of certainty about Christian belief and so makes belief impervious to rational argumentation. What most Christians don't know is that these experiences are not unique to Christianity. In fact, the quotations that you just read come from two born-again Christians, a Moonie, and an encounter group participant. Their words are similar because the born-again experience doesn't require a specific set of beliefs. It requires a specific social/emotional process, and the dogmas or explanations are secondary.

Conversion is a process that begins with social influence. As sociologists like to say, our sense of reality is socially constructed. Missionary work typically begins with simple offers of friendship or conversations about shared interests. As prospective converts are drawn in, a group may envelope them in warmth, goodwill, thoughtful conversations, and playful activities, always with gentle pressure toward the group reality.

In revival meetings or retreats, semi-hypnotic processes draw a potential convert closer to the toggle point. These include repetition of words, repetition of rhythms, evocative music, and Barnum statements (messages that seem personal but apply to almost everyone—like horoscopes). Because of the positive energy created by the group, potential converts become unwitting participants in the influence process, actively seeking to make the group's ideas fit with their own life history and knowledge. Factors that can strengthen the effect include sleep deprivation or isolation from a person's normal social environment. An example would be a late-night campfire gathering with an inspirational storyteller and altar call at Child Evangelism's "Camp Good News."

These powerful social experiences culminate in conversion, a peak experience in which the new converts experience a flood of relief. Until that moment they have been consciously or unconsciously at odds with the group center of gravity. Now they may feel that their darkest secrets are known and forgiven. They may experience the kind of joy or transcendence normally reserved for mystics. And they are likely to be bathed in love and approval from the surrounding group, which mirrors their experience of God.

The otherworldly mental state that I refer to as the domain of mystics is known in clinical situations as a "transcendence hallucination," but this term fails to reflect how normal and profound the experience can be as a part of human spirituality. The transcendence hallucination is an acute sense of connection with a reality that lies beyond and behind this natural plane. It typically lasts for just a few seconds or minutes but may leave a profound impression that lasts a lifetime. Transcendence hallucination can be triggered by neurological events (like a seizure, stroke, or migraine aura) or by a drug (such as psilocybin), but it also can be triggered by overstimulation or understimulation of the brain.

Some mystics from the past have described or even drawn these events with such impressive detail that a diagnostic hypothesis is possible. Hildegard of Bingen, a medieval mystic, wrote of the intense pain accompanying her visions and created scores of drawings that show the visual field distorted in keeping with a migraine aura. In modern times, author Karen Armstrong describes the seizures that she first thought to be triggered spiritually.[14] In discussing an altered state known as Kundalini awakening, one migraine sufferer commented, "I usually don't follow any of the myotic/esoteric stuff, but I must say it is kind of strange to see all my symptoms lined up like that outside of a western/medical context."[15]

Let me emphasize, though, that these altered states don't depend on some kind of neurological damage or pathology. They can be unforgettable, peak experiences for normal people, long sought and hard won by those who care about the spiritual dimension of life. Sensory deprivation, fasting, meditation, rhythmic drumming, or crowd dynamics have all been used systematically to elicit altered states in normal people.[16]

Since we humans are meaning makers to the core, such a powerful experience demands an explanation. In an evangelical conversion context like a revival meeting or missionary work, religious interpretations of the snapping experience are provided both before and after it occurs. These explanations become the foundation stones on which whole castles of beliefs later will be constructed. The authorities who triggered the otherworldly experience are trusted implicitly, which gives them the power to now transform the convert's worldview in accordance with their own theology.

The conversion process as I have described it sounds sinister, as if manipulative groups and hypnotic leaders deliberately ply their trade to suck in the unsuspecting and take over their minds. I don't believe this is usually the case. Rather, natural selection is at play. Over millennia of human history, religious leaders have hit on social/emotional techniques that work to win converts, just as individual believers have hit on spiritual practices they find satisfying and belief systems that fit how we process information. Techniques that don't trigger powerful spiritual experiences simply die out. Those techniques that do trigger powerful spiritual experiences are refined and handed down.

With few exceptions the evangelists, from megachurch ministers to "friendship missionaries," are largely unaware of the powerful psychological tools they wield. They are persuasive in part because they genuinely believe they are doing good. After all, they have their own born-again experiences to convince them that they are promoting the Real Thing. Consider, for example, the apostle Paul, whose Damascus Road event (possibly a temporal lobe seizure) transformed his moral priorities and sustained a lifetime of missionary devotion. What decent person wouldn't want to share the secret to healing and happiness? The challenge is trying to figure out exactly what that secret is. As I say to my daughters, it is not enough to be well intentioned—even joyfully, generously so. We also have to be right.

CONCLUSION

Understanding the psychology of religion doesn't tell us whether any specific set of beliefs is true. I might believe in a pantheon of supernatural beings for all the wrong reasons (childhood credulity, hyperactive agency detection, theory of mind, group hypnotic processes, misattributed transcendence hallucination), and they still might exist. Social scientists can't address the truth value of otherworldly religious assertions or emotions, only the patterns, norms, and circumstances under which they occur. It remains the domain of philosophers and ethicists to examine the rational and moral qualities of religious beliefs—to examine internal coherence and virtue.

Despite these limitations, cognitive research does offer what is rapidly becoming a *sufficient* explanation for the phenomenon of belief. More and more, we can explain Christian belief with the same set of principles that explain supernaturalism generally. This is a serious blow to orthodoxy—to a religion based on right belief. In the past, one of the arguments put forward by believers was that there simply was no explanation for the "born-again" experience, the healing power of Christianity, the vast agreement among believers, or the joy and wonder of mysticism, save that these came from God Himself. We now know this not to be the case. Humans are capable of having transcendent, transformative experiences in the absence of any given dogma. We are capable of sustaining elaborate systems of false belief and transmitting them to our children. We are capable of feeling so certain about our false beliefs that we are willing to kill or die for them.

One general principle that has worked well for humans seeking to advance or refine our knowledge is called "parsimony," also known as Occam's Razor. It can be paraphrased thus: "*Usually the simplest explanation is the best one*" or "*Don't multiply entities unnecessarily.*" If we can predict storms by looking at barometric pressure and cloud formations, then there is no need to posit the existence of storm spirits or angry ancestors causing us trouble. If we can predict that an electric light will come on when a circuit is completed, we don't talk about the invisible parallel circuit that makes the whole thing work. When a scholar adheres to the principle of parsimony, explanatory factors get added only when they allow us to predict with greater accuracy, or explain things that previously were puzzling.

In fields of human knowledge other than theology, if we can find a sufficient explanation within nature's matrix, we don't look outside. We no longer, for example, posit that demons are involved in seizures or bubonic plague. It's not that we know for sure that the demon explanation is wrong, but simply that it is unnecessary for predicting or treating seizures.

What does all of this imply for the future of religious studies? Simply that supernatural explanations for religious experience are becoming unnecessary. Eighteenth-century French mathematician and astronomer Pierre Simone Laplace wrote a volume on the movements of the heavenly bodies. When asked by Emperor Napoleon I why he had not mentioned God in his treatise, he replied, "*Je n'ai pas eu besoin de cette hypothèse.*" ("I had no need of that hypothesis.") Modern scholars of religion, more and more, find themselves echoing the words of Laplace. We have no need of that hypothesis.

NOTES

1. Bootie Cosgrove-Mather, "Poll: Creationism Trumps Evolution," *CBS News*, November 22, 2004, http://www.cbsnews.com/stories/2004/11/22/opinion/polls/main657083.shtml; Pew Research Center Pollwatch, "Reading the

Polls on Evolution and Creationism," *Pew Research Center for the People and the Press*, September 28, 2005, http://people-press.org/commentary/?analysisid=118.

2. Bart Ehrman, *Lost Christianities: The Battles for Scripture and the Faiths We Never Knew* (New York: Oxford University Press, 2003).

3. Cordelia Fine, *A Mind of Its Own: How Your Brain Distorts and Deceives* (New York: Norton, 2006), p. 19. See also David Linden, *The Accidental Mind* (Cambridge, MA: Harvard University Press, 2008), and the entry for "self-deception" in Robter T. Caroll, "The Skeptic's Dictionary," http://www.skepdic.com/selfdeception.html.

4. For this and many more examples, see V. S. Ramachandran and Sandra Blakeslee, *Phantoms in the Brain* (New York: William Morrow, 1998); and hear V. S. Ramachandran, "A Journey to the Center of Your Mind," *Ted.com*, October 2007, http://www.ted.com/talks/vilayanur_ramachandran_on_your_mind.html.

5. Robert Burton, *On Being Certain: Believing You Are Right Even When You're Not* (New York: St. Martin's Press, 2008), p. xi.

6. Robert Jay Lifton, *Thought Reform and the Psychology of Totalism* (Chapel Hill: University of North Carolina Press, 1989).

7. See Richard Carrier, *Not the Impossible Faith* (Raleigh, NC: Lulu, 2009), pp. 17–20; and Samuel Noah Kramer, "The First Tale of Resurrection," *History Begins at Sumer*, 3rd ed. (Philadelphia: University of Pennsylvania Press, 1981), pp. 154–67; a connection between the two stories is even clearer in the ancient Christian redaction of the *The Ascension of Isaiah*, of which there is an English edition by R. H. Charles (New York: Macmillan, 1919).

8. Pascal Boyer, *Religion Explained* (New York: Basic Books, 2001), pp. 3, 4.

9. For more on this science of religious thought, see the video presentation of Dr. Andy Thomson, "Why We Believe in Gods," 2009 American Atheists Convention (Atlanta, Georgia), http://www.reasonproject.org/archive/item/why_we_believe_in_gods_-_dr_andy_thomson.

10. Flo Conway and Jim Siegelman, *Snapping: America's Epidemic of Sudden Personality Change*, 2nd ed. (New York: Stillpoint Press, 2005), p. 24.

11. Ibid., p. 32.

12. Ibid., p. 12.

13. Ibid., p. 31.

14. Karen Armstrong, *The Spiral Staircase* (New York: Anchor Books, 2004).

15. Iuris, "Visual Snow and Kundalini," *Migraine-Aura.org*, February 21, 2007, http://www.migraine-aura.org/content/e27891/e27265/e42285/e42419/e43344/index_en.html.

16. For more on this point, see Sharon Begley, "Your Brain on Religion: Mystic Visions or Brain Circuits at Work?" *Newsweek*, May 7, 2001, http://www.cognitiveliberty.org/neuro/neuronewswk.htm.

Chapter 3

THE MALLEABILITY
OF THE HUMAN MIND

Jason Long, PhD

I t is a curious thing that most of us ardently believe that we solved the ultimate question of the universe before we even learned how to tie our shoelaces. If philosophers, theologians, and scientists have struggled with the concept of existence for millennia without arriving at a definite solution, our naive assessment from childhood that a divine entity simply wished it were so certainly requires a reevaluation. It is nothing short of an incomprehensible tragedy that anyone in this age of reason would have to write a book debunking a collection of ridiculous fantasies from an era of rampant superstition.*[1]

Why do a majority of Americans believe in the ability to predict specific details in the distant future, the existence of winged messengers living in the sky, the worldwide Flood as told in Genesis, and the resurrection of a man who had been dead for over a day? How can these people believe they are enlightened enough to insist upon the veracity of these outlandish beliefs when studies show they know so little about them? They believe simply because they want to believe, they believe because they have always believed, and they believe because others around them believe. The vast majority of those who believe such things will stick to those beliefs

---

*Editor's note: This chapter is a brief summary of the first 95 pages of Jason Long's *The Religious Condition: Answering and Explaining Christian Reasoning* (New York: iUniverse, 2008).

65

throughout life despite overwhelming evidence to the contrary, as Dr. Eller and Dr. Tarico explained in the first two chapters of this collection.

While ideas from other religions might seem ridiculous to Christians, most of *them* believe in an omnipotent deity that will torture his underlings forever if we do not worship him. While God *could* choose any absurd method of interaction he wanted, people rarely stop to consider if God *would* manifest himself in that way. Sound reflection on this problem is not a matter of accepting that one method *must* be true and deciding that our hastily chosen belief sounds the least superstitious (or perhaps just as good as the next), but rather of determining if any suggestion can stand on its own as a sensible avenue for a god to take. The reasons given for belief are driven not by rational thought and reasoned argumentation, but by psychological factors that maintain what society has given the religious believer through indoctrination.

Some Muslims taught themselves it's normal to believe that Allah would provide a paradise for suicide bombers, and they are constantly able to recruit them. The Mormons taught themselves it's normal to believe in a prehistoric Jewish kingdom in America, and they are constantly able to find scholars who will attest to its existence. Christians taught themselves it's normal to pray to an earthly savior who miraculously rose from the dead, and they are constantly able to find "evidence" of his benevolence. Members of each group have their faiths because they are lifelong members of a society that has continually reinforced the "special" nature of their beliefs. What one society perceives as normal, another perceives as a collective delusion.

Explaining the various thought processes that place people in a certain religion is not intended to serve as proof that the belief system is wrong, but rather to demonstrate that devout observation of the system is typically void of rational and independent thought. In other words, the religion was offered, accepted, practiced, justified, and passed on; but it was *not* seriously questioned. This is hardly a coincidence.

It should not be a shocking discovery that parents pass on their religious beliefs through their children. Muslim parents tend to have Muslim children, Christian parents tend to have Christian children, Hindu parents tend to have Hindu children. Such consistent traditions simply cannot be maintained by chance alone. A child's environment must affect his religious affiliation to an extensive degree. In fact, all children are born without specific religious ideas and remain in a state of impressionability until influenced by the religious convictions of their parents or other similarly motivated individuals. Likewise, the parents are probably members of their religion because *their* parents were also members. How far back does this blind tradition continue? How do we know that the first person converted for an intellectually justifiable reason? Instead of initiating an honest and impartial analysis of the new evidence that science and enlightened thinking have provided, people simply bury their heads in the sand and continue to believe whatever religion their ancestors thought they needed, or were perhaps conquered with, centuries ago. They were instilled with the beliefs as children, and they will maintain them as adults.

Psychologists Richard Petty and John Cacioppo have explained how high-fear messages, such as the indoctrinated idea of a god who is always watching everyone's actions so as to later separate the righteous from the wicked, can be so upsetting that the audience engages in defensive avoidance and refuses to think critically about them.[2] The effectiveness of the message depends on three factors: the unfavorableness of the consequences that will occur if the recommended actions are not adopted, which is *absolute* because hell is complete (and often asserted to be eternal) agony;[3] the *likelihood* that unfavorable consequences will occur if the recommended actions are not adopted, which is *absolute* because the perfect Bible says so;[4] and the likelihood that unfavorable consequences will not occur if the recommended actions are adopted, which is *absolute* because, again, the perfect Bible says so.[5]

Hardly any conceivable message could be more motivating than the threat of hell, and we have good reason to conclude that such a message can be upsetting enough to deter critical thinking, especially when the message often begins at an age when the audience is too young to have developed a discipline that can challenge the validity of such assertions. Just the opposite, children habitually give benefit of the doubt to their parents and other role models. Religious indoctrination is firmly in place well before persuasability begins an established decline at the age of eight, making any subsequent attempts to remove the indoctrination extremely difficult.[6] Since parents tend to be correct on just about every other testable matter of importance, extending this pattern into the realm of the unfalsifiable seems unfortunately reasonable to a young child. And we must not forget about the ultimate reward for accepting Christianity: an eternal stay in heaven with infinite happiness. How can the young and impressionable refuse?

Psychologist Robert Cialdini has shown that people become more confident about their decisions as time progresses, even despite a complete lack of evidence to support the veracity of their choices.[7] As humans, we simply are not comfortable considering the notion that we might be wrong. We enjoy being right. Rather than entertaining the possibility that we might be wrong, we strive to convince ourselves that we have followed proper avenues of thought. This process is highly illogical, intellectually dishonest, and potentially dangerous. With enough exposure, people of deep religious faith become conditioned to avoid questioning their core beliefs.

While many think they have arrived at their Christian beliefs through logical deduction and not childhood indoctrination, prominent skeptic Michael Shermer demonstrates the existence of an *intellectual attribution bias* that helps dispel the claims of believers who think they are an exception to the indoctrination process. He shows that an individual is nearly nine times more likely to think he arrived at his religious position using reason than he is to think any other Christian did the same.[8] People are able to accept the fact that many religious believers have adopted their faiths because of societal influence, but they refuse to consider that the same might be true of themselves. Finding the gullibility of others is an easy task; finding it within ourselves can be a difficult and discomforting one.

Once indoctrination is firmly in place, and the children have become adults, we find that there are a number of factors in the very nature of skepticism that prevent it from winning a victory over thoughtless optimism. The first is that skeptics will explore many types of arguments, including both strong and moderate ones, that would debunk Christian preconceived notions. But the inclusion of the moderate arguments weakens the perceived credibility of the person presenting them. Petty and Cacioppo have found that providing a person with a few strong arguments provokes more attitude change than providing these arguments along with a number of moderate arguments.[9] People are prone to believing that if they think they can defeat a moderate argument, they would probably be able to spot the fallacies of the stronger arguments if they considered them long enough. This is an unfortunate mistake. The addition of moderate arguments onto a pile of already strong arguments should *add* credibility to the position, not diminish it.

Messages favoring the veracity of Christianity arrive through more convincing channels than those that support a nonreligious viewpoint.

Petty and Cacioppo report that face-to-face appeals repeatedly have a greater impact than appeals through mass media.[10] If the doubter wants to hear arguments from those with contrasting beliefs, where does he turn? To his atheist family members? To his atheist friends? To an atheist church group? These probably don't exist. Instead, he will likely rely on mass media, typically in the form of a book like this one. Thus the freethought literature must be superior enough to overcome not only the indoctrinated Christian message itself, but also the difference from the perceived level of superiority that's attributed to face-to-face communication.

Petty and Cacioppo also report that the likeability of the source of the message conveyed plays a major role in whether that message is capable of being persuasive.[11] The disparity in the amount of attitude change from identical messages provided by a likable source and an unlikable source is comparable to the disparity in the amount of change resultant from identical messages provided by an expert source and a nonexpert source. In short, you can obtain the same amount of perceived credibility by being likable as you can by becoming an expert! Unfortunately, society has painted a nasty picture of atheism and skepticism. People who do not believe in God are the least trusted minority in America.[12]

People are motivated to defend their beliefs from attacks, particularly when they are forewarned of a speaker's intent, and even more so when the belief is closely linked with identity.[13] Not only are religious beliefs synonymous with identity for a number of people, religious followers have been inoculated from skeptical arguments because they have been forewarned that skeptics are not trustworthy people. This "poisoning of the well" modifies individuals to be more resistant to attitude changes toward the position that they already believe to be fundamentally weak.

So there is no pressure from society to understand or defend itself against the true position of skeptics. This is unfortunate because Petty and Cacioppo report that subjects are often motivated to understand an issue when they are led to believe that they would have to later discuss the issue with someone who took a contrasting position.[14] Without this pressure, subjects are less likely to consider the position of the opponent. Since people do not have a real interest in evaluating their innermost beliefs, those who have been conditioned to believe in a book with a talking donkey will never actively seek out someone to challenge this position.

Human beings are surprisingly gullible creatures. The ability to think skeptically is not innate; it requires practice. One-half of America believes that a person can use extrasensory perception to read another person's mind.[15] Nearly the same amount believes we can communicate with the dead.[16] Otherwise sane individuals have been known to send death threats to meteorologists, not for inaccurate predictions, but for the actual weather conditions.[17] Among other feats of incredible sheepishness, Cialdini reports that people are more likely to buy unusual items when they are priced higher, buy items with coupons despite no price advantage, respond to requests when empty reasons are given, agree to absurd requests if they are preceded by ones of greater absurdity, and consider people intelligent and persuasive if they are attractive.[18] If people are so prone to following foolish patterns under such poor assumptions in order to help guide them through this complex world, we should not be at all surprised when people hypothesize the existence of a personal god in order to explain intelligent life, distant galaxies, childbirth, starvation, natural disasters, and suicide bombers.

The realization that rational skepticism is not as interesting, promising, or comforting as optimistic romanticism is perhaps more formidable than any other obstacle. It's only human to believe in things that make us happier. If you have admired a book since childhood because it says that your lost loved ones are waiting for you in heaven when you die, it's going to take an extraordinary amount of work to convince you that the talking donkey also found in the book might mean that the book is not proper evidence for such an optimistic idea.

Skepticism does not appeal to most people because humans have an innate tendency to search for patterns and simple explanations in order to make sense of the world. Such a practice results in an incorporation of elements that fit into an understandable answer and a neglect of elements that do not. Psychologists often use this phenomenon to explain the reason people believe in clairvoyance, horoscopes, prayer, and other such foolishness. Individuals remember when these methods "work" and forget when they do not. With respect to religion, people will often remember "answered" prayers but forget or rationalize the unanswered ones. Have you ever noticed how people will trumpet abundances of miracles when there are a few survivors of a catastrophe yet say nothing about the many people who died? It is also very easy to claim that prayer healed a person dying of a terrible disease, but quite another to prove it. Study after study demonstrates that prayer has no effect on patients when they are unaware that they are being prayed for.[19] Christians will avoid the rational conclusion that prayers are only "answered" by a placebo effect. They will avoid admitting that tragic events or unbelievable coincidences are the result of complex natural factors. They will avoid admitting that prayers have answers just as often as problems have solutions.

In addition to childhood indoctrination and the nature of skepticism itself, a specific psychological phenomenon prevents individuals from properly weighing the evidence on important decisions. Psychologist Leon Festinger established the presence of an innate tendency to rid oneself of uneasy feelings. He compared the psychological drive, later termed *cognitive dissonance*, to physiological hunger. Just as hunger is a motivation to eat and rid oneself of the hunger, dissonance is a motivation to explain inconsistency and rid oneself of the dissonance. Explanations, therefore, work toward satisfying dissonance just as nutrients work toward satisfying hunger. He suggested three modes that we use to rid ourselves of cognitive dissonance: altering the importance of the original belief or the new information, changing the original belief, or seeking evidence that is critical of the new information. Since religious people do not want to trivialize or change their beliefs, finding information that supports the original belief and/or information that brings the new evidence into question are the quickest methods to eliminate their cognitive dissonance.[20]

People simply become increasingly sure of their decisions after they have made them by rationalizing their choice of alternatives, which serves to reduce the cognitive dissonance produced by foregoing the good features of the unchosen alternative and accepting the bad features of the chosen alternative.[21] When it comes to religion, a believer will defend his faith and attack the alternatives in part simply because he has already rendered a decision on the matter. Furthermore— and this is where the strength of the motivation kicks into overdrive—Petty and Cacioppo explain that the effects of cognitive dissonance increase as the positions between the two beliefs diverge and the perceived importance of establishing a position grows.[22] Could any two positions be in sharper contrast than the existence and nonexistence of God? Could any dilemma be more important to the Christian than whether or not God exists? It naturally follows that questions on the issue of God's existence provoke the most cognitive dissonance within those who are deeply involved in the issue. As this debate generates the greatest amount of cognitive dissonance, it naturally follows that people are increasingly willing to accept explanations that alleviate the uncomfortable feelings and are decreasingly willing to consider disconfirming arguments. As the uneasiness becomes more powerful, people become more willing to surrender to whatever arguments are offered—just as when hunger becomes more powerful, people become more willing to eat whatever food is available. This will subsequently lead to accepting highly illogical justifications for maintaining highly important beliefs.

A troubled Christian might not peruse, comprehend, or even read an entire argument offered in defense of his belief, but the mere fact that a possible answer exists satisfies him that there is a reasonable answer to the skeptical objection. Never mind the fact that anyone can cite an authority who agrees with a particular position, especially when it comes to interpreting religion. Due to an innate bias to confirm what we already believe, the authority's position is not going to be scrutinized or tested against a rebuttal. The Christian is interested in feeling comfortable with his beliefs, not in dispassionately evaluating them. People want to feel reassured that they are correct in their beliefs, especially when there is a lot of emotion, personality, history, and identity at stake. If the Christian were genuinely interested in the truth, he would analyze the argument critically and thoroughly to see if it adequately addressed the points of the skeptical objection. But he is not questioning; he is defending.

There have been several prominent cases in which religious followers have manufactured outlandish explanations to relieve their cognitive dissonance. Members of a Southwestern United States evangelical cult who retreated into a bomb shelter to avoid a predicted imminent nuclear apocalypse went on to believe, after it didn't occur, that it did not take place because of their prayers![23] Members of the Keech cult, who were to be taken to the planet Clarion to avoid a global flood, went on to believe afterward, when it didn't happen, that aliens told their leader it was prevented by their faith.[24] Mormons believe Joseph Smith's unwillingness to retranslate the lost portions of the Book of Mormon was forbidden by God, even though it's crystal clear to the rest of us that Smith just couldn't remember verbatim what he had improvised and dictated. Christians believe that Jesus' failed prophecies of his return in his very near future aren't what they truly appear to be—failed predictions—as Loftus shows in chapter 12 of this book. These kinds of *post hoc* rationalistic justifications relieve the uncomfortable dissonance generated after external elements showed the facts were inconsistent with their beliefs.

In addition to *cognitive dissonance theory*, there are two complementary theories that help explain the reason why people provide illogical defenses for their beliefs. *Impression management theory* suggests that people increasingly stick by their decisions because consistency leads to social reward and inconsistency leads to social punishment.[25] *Psychological reactance theory* suggests that people increasingly stick by their decisions when others threaten their freedom to express their ideas.[26] It is my opinion that limited persecution in Rome during the infant years of Christianity may have dramatically increased its popularity. It's not difficult to imagine how people would become more dedicated to and firm in their beliefs when faced with opposition, especially when the opposition pushes a sharp reversal of current conditions.[27] People within the threatened group respond by dropping their differences to unite for a common cause, while people outside the group desire what the authorities forbade. There have been several historical instances in which the abolishment of certain products, services, and rights has led to an increase in the desire for those products, services, and rights.[28]

When religious believers are willing to admit that people often believe what they are raised to believe and that people are often incapable of rational thinking due to the effects of cognitive dissonance, they will often fall back to utilizing the arguments from experts who agree with them. However, if you wanted safety information on a used car, would it be wiser to trust the word of a used car salesperson or the findings of a consumer report? Similarly, if you wanted to obtain information on the historicity and veracity of Islam, would you ask only an Islamic scholar who has been taught about Islamic sanctity since childhood, or would you also ask a secular scholar with no emotional investment in Islam? Would you not also do the same for Hinduism, Mormonism, Buddhism, and so on? If you utilize the same reasoning and choose the unbiased scholar to help evaluate that position, as you very well should, why make an exception only for Christianity? People who study a concept in which they have no emotional investment are probably going to offer more reliable conclusions than those who want the concept to yield a specific result.

Scholars who begin with no emotional investment in Christianity probably present the most unbiased conclusions about it simply because they are more open during their studies to accept evidence that contradicts their tentative conclusions. Just as the used car salesperson will be hesitant to acknowledge and relay information that is damaging to the quality of his vehicles, the Christian scholar will be hesitant to acknowledge and relay information that is damaging to the veracity of his religion. We have no reason to think that belief in Christianity provides a special insight into the veracity of it, because every religion can make a parallel claim. The opinions of individuals with emotional involvement, personal attachments, or vested interests in the outcome of a debatable issue are less likely to change when confronted with new information because people have an innate inclination to seek evidence that confirms their preestablished beliefs and to ignore evidence that will not. Psychologists call this *confirmation bias*. We often do not weigh the facts before making judgments, but rather we believe in things based on our predispositions and influences. We then maintain these beliefs by ignoring and rationalizing away evidence that contradicts our preexisting conclusions. We believe in things for reasons other than logical reasoning and empirical evidence.

When subjects are given the task of solving a problem, most will immediately form a hypothesis and only look for examples to confirm it. They do not seek evidence to disprove the hypothesis, and they are very slow to change the hypothesis even when it is obviously wrong. Subjects also adopt overly simple hypotheses or strategies for solutions if the information is too complex, and form hypotheses about coincidental relationships they observe if there is no true solution.[29] By adopting these overly simple hypotheses and strategies for complex issues, individuals gain immediate gratification. Subjects will then ignore, distort, and eventually forget evidence for theories that they do not prefer. As the subjects spend more time focusing on internally justifying their beliefs, the confidence in their beliefs greatly increases.[30]

Psychologists Muzafer Sherif and Carl Hovland have demonstrated that a person's level of emotional involvement with an issue has an enormous impact on how new evidence is interpreted.[31] Involved persons have beliefs with greater specificity and therefore have larger latitudes of rejection for evidence that does not fit with those beliefs. People with a high involvement are more resistant to contrary persuasion than less involved persons because any given message has a greater probability of falling into the rejection region. Psychologist Drew Westen was among those who empirically demonstrated, using MRI scanning, that people who were strongly loyal to one candidate in presidential elections did not use areas of the brain associated with reasoning to resolve contradictory statements made by their candidate. The supporters instead relied upon regions of the brain associated with emotion to justify their personal allegiances.[32] I could cite numerous similar studies that demonstrate irrational behavior from highly involved individuals, but this is sufficient to establish my point that people shun dispassionate critical thought when justifying their most important beliefs and personal values.

Our analysis of emotionally involved people should lead us to an important question in desperate need of an answer. What good is a biblical scholar who refuses to consider that his point of view may simply be wrong? If past research tells us there are three scientific procedures capable of yielding a cure for a hypothetical disease, would we ever trust a scientist who was indoctrinated since childhood to believe that only one of those three procedures could produce a cure? Should we honestly believe that a biblical apologist who began with the notion of an inspired Bible would readily consider the possibility that his holy book is fundamentally flawed? Many of the top Christian apologists even admit that when the data conflicts with the text, we should trust the text. Prominent apologist William Lane Craig declares, "[S]hould a conflict arise between the witness of the Holy Spirit to the fundamental truth of the Christian faith and beliefs based on argument and evidence, then it is the former which must take precedence over the latter, not vice versa."[33] One of the most widely touted Young Earth Creationist Web sites, AnswersIn Genesis.org, even offers this in their statement of faith: "No apparent, perceived, or claimed evidence in any field, including history and chronology, can be valid if it contradicts the Scriptural record."[34] What's the point in listening to people like this? Such is the problem with all religious apologists, regardless of the specific belief. They will begin by presuming certain premises are true and mold explanations to patch the apparent problems, no matter how insulting the explanations are to common sense. This is how religions thrive in the age of scrutiny and reason. Apologists will find a "resolution" to every objection. No skeptical author can offer anything that Christian apologists think they cannot answer. After all, God wrote it, so it must be true—even if it violates science and common sense. Misguided believers often accomplish this intellectually dishonest defense by citing one of these biblical authorities who have also been indoctrinated, probably to an even greater degree.

The focus we need to place on apologetic defenses is the likelihood of the offered explanations and how an unbiased, dispassionate individual would rule on these explanations. Is the apologetic suggestion a likely solution to the problem, or is it a way of maintaining predetermined beliefs?

Since most staunch Bible defenders have already declared that nothing is going to change their minds (and the solutions to presented biblical complications often reflect this disposition), we must be highly suspicious of the intellectual honesty put forth toward apologetic solutions. After all, there are even apologists for contradictory schools of thought within Christianity itself. How can two groups of people consistently use two contradictory avenues of thought yet consistently arrive at the same answer, unless the conclusion itself consistently preceded the explanation? A dispassionate outlook is an indispensable necessity when in search of the truth. Religious scholars who began as religious believers lack this critical component. The practice of religion clouds judgment; understanding of religion does not.

People who have an interest in pursuing a career in Christianity are undoubtedly those who have already been indoctrinated with the importance of it. If they believe in Christianity ardently enough to pursue a career from it, they are unquestionably more likely to interpret evidence so that it is favorable to their preconceived notions. So it should come as no surprise that the vast majority of experts in *any* religion believe in the very religion that they study. A majority of experts in the history of the ancient Near East will defend positions that are beneficial to Christianity precisely because they were born in a Christian society. The majority of those who will back the Qur'an were born in an Islamic society. The majority of those who will back the Torah were born in a Jewish society. The opinions of these authorities, who began with a certain conclusion instead of analyzing the evidence to reach that conclusion, cannot be trusted merely because they are authorities. Conclusions based upon evidence are important. Conclusions based upon evidence that has been interpreted to support an a priori assumption are not. For these reasons, I put little stock in the opinions of people who began studying Christianity years after they settled on the existence of a talking donkey.

If an intelligent, rational group of people who were never exposed to the idea of religion were asked to become experts in the history of the ancient Near East, the *unanimous* consensus of the group would be that the Bible is bunk. They would reach this conclusion for two reasons: there is absolutely nothing in the book that would impress critically thinking dispassionate outsiders, and they would not have been exposed to the centuries of aura and mystique that society has placed on the Bible. To them, the Bible would not be a guide that billions have used for worship; it would be just another book in the mythology section of the library.

*   *   *

Are there some who are more likely than others to leave the comfortable confines of religious thought? Petty and Cacioppo point out that people with low self-esteem are more likely to accept messages that confirm an initial viewpoint, and less likely to be persuaded away from it.[35] The very foundation of Christianity is built upon the suggestion that we are insignificant creatures compared to the creator of the universe and that it is not possible to carry out a meaningful existence without accepting the biblical belief system.[36] However, once we accept the biblical teachings (and only after doing so), we become worthy of God's gift of eternal life. Such ideas are no doubt appealing to those with little or no self-esteem, but they carry less weight with someone confident of his own abilities and intelligence. Speaking of which, as Paul Bell of Mensa reports, "of 43 studies carried out since 1927, on the relationship between religious belief and one's intelligence or educational level, all but four found an inverse connection," and even of those four none indicated anything to the contrary. In other words, the higher your intelligence or educational level, the less likely you are to be religious.[37] Intelligence and educational achievement is therefore another factor affecting who will find religious belief unpersuasive.

Psychologist Frank Sulloway has shown that people with open minds also compose one group less likely to be religious.[38] This conclusion might seem counterintuitive, especially considering how mystical ideas are commonly purported to reveal themselves to those with "open minds," but the results make sense upon further reflection. Skeptics have their positions but are willing to consider other viewpoints; the religious are indoctrinated not to seriously question their beliefs. It does not take a willfully open mind to accept the existence of God because it is essentially the default position in our culture. It *does* take an open mind, however, to consider the possibility that one's most sacred beliefs might be false.

While it's true there are still plenty of highly intelligent people who are religious, we should ask ourselves why this is so. The best answer, in my opinion, comes from Shermer, within the very argument that he became famous for coining: "Smart people believe weird things because they are skilled at defending beliefs they arrived at for non-smart reasons."[39] Believing in otherwise absurd stories simply because they are part of a religion bestowed upon you obviously qualifies as believing in something for "non-smart reasons." The intellectual meltdown arrives from gifted people inventing extremely clever (but equally absurd) reasons why they think their beliefs are correct. Speaking from personal experience, I can say that even in the confines of solidarity, I could not be realistic about my former beliefs for one key reason: *It is never easy to be honest with yourself about the Bible when a mind-reading god is always present.* Simply *thinking* that God did something wrong might be as discomforting to someone as *saying* that a potentially abusive authority figure did the same. If God is perpetually monitoring us, knowing what we are thinking at every moment, objectivity certainly gives way to anxiety.

People who were never indoctrinated with religious beliefs often fail to appreciate the consequences of this dilemma. I'm afraid that I don't have much advice to give to those who are battling with intellectual self-honesty—other than to point out the inherent unfairness of a system in which an all-powerful being mistreats anyone who has the intellectual curiosity to arrive at its existence through reason rather than through faith. Perhaps you can tell God that you are going to set his existence aside for a moment in order to see what evidence would be most convincing to a non-believer. Or perhaps you can tell God that you want to make your faith stronger than ever by passing Loftus's *Outsider Test for Faith* (see chapter 4). Ask for forgiveness in advance if you feel you must, but if the evidence for God is as strong as the religious experts would have you believe, should it not find you rather easily?

NOTES

1. Michael Shermer, *Why People Believe Weird Things: Pseudoscience, Superstition, and Other Confusions of Our Time* (New York: Henry Holt, 2002), p. 258.

2. Richard Petty and John Cacioppo, *Attitudes and Persuasion: Classic and Contemporary Approaches* (Dubuque, IA: William C. Brown, 1981), pp. 72–73.

3. See Matthew 13:47–50, Mark 9:42–49, and Revelation 14:9–12.

4. See Matthew 13:41–50, 25:31–46; and Revelation 20:11–15.

5. See John 3:16.

6. Petty and Cacioppo, *Attitudes and Persuasion*, p. 80.

7. Robert Cialdini, *Influence: The Psychology of Persuasion* (New York: William Morrow, 1993), p. 57.

8. Shermer, *Why People Believe*, p. 296.

9. Petty and Cacioppo, *Attitudes and Persuasion*, p. 72.

10. Ibid., p. 85.

11. Ibid., pp. 259–60.

12. Johanna Olexy and Lee Herring, "Atheists Are Distrusted: Atheists Identified as America's Most Distrusted Minority, According to Sociological Study," *American Sociological Association News*, May 3, 2006, http://www.asanet.org/page.ww ?section=Press&name=Atheists+Are+Distrusted.

13. Petty and Cacioppo, *Attitudes and Persuasion*, pp. 228–29.

14. Ibid., p. 257.

15. Gallup poll, June 8, 2001, accessed from http://classes.skepdic.com/ gallup2001.pdf on July 18, 2009.

16. Shermer, *Why People Believe*, p. 26.

17. Cialdini, *Influence*, pp. 188–90.

18. Ibid., pp. 1, 4, 7, 29, 40, 172.

19. The three most definitive investigations are STEP from *American Heart Journal* 151, no. 4 (April 2006): 934–42; MANTRA from *Lancet* 366, no. 9499 (November 2005): 1769–70; and the 2001 Mayo Clinic coronary care unit trial in *Mayo Clinic Proceedings* 76, no. 12 (December 2001): 1192–98.

20. Festinger et al., *When Prophecy Fails: A Social and Psychological Study of a Modern Group That Predicted the Destruction of the World* (Minneapolis: University of Minnesota Press, 1956).

21. Petty and Cacioppo, *Attitudes and Persuasion*, pp. 141–42.

22. Ibid., p. 137.

23. J. A. Hardyck and M. Braden, "Prophecy Fails Again: A Report of a Failure to Replicate," *Journal of Abnormal and Social Psychology* 65, no. 2 (August 1962): 136–41.

24. Festinger et al., *When Prophecy Fails.*

25. Petty and Cacioppo, *Attitudes and Persuasion*, p. 152.

26. Ibid., p. 155.

27. Ibid., pp. 159–60.

28. Firearms, alcohol, pornography, speech, religion, and so on.

29. Shermer, *Why People Believe*, p. 59.

30. Ibid., pp. 299–300.

31. Muzafer Sherif and Carl Hovland, *Social Judgment: Assimilation and Contrast Effects in Communication and Attitude Change* (New Haven, CT: Yale University Press, 1961).

32. Drew Westen et al., "The Neural Basis of Motivated Reasoning: An fMRI Study of Emotional Constraints on Political Judgment during the US Presidential Election of 2004," *Journal of Cognitive Neuroscience* 18 (2006): 1947–58. See also Drew Westen, *The Political Brain: The Role of Emotion in Deciding the Fate of the Nation* (New York: PublicAffairs, 2007).

33. William Lane Craig, *Reasonable Faith: Christian Truth and Apologetics*, 3rd ed. (Wheaton, IL: Crossway Books, 2008), p. 48.

34. Answers in Genesis, "The AiG Statement of Faith," section 4, article 6, http://www.answersingenesis.org/home/area/about/faith.asp.

35. Petty and Cacioppo, *Attitudes and Persuasion*, p. 82.

36. See Matthew 10:37–39; Luke 18:9–14; Romans 3:9–28; and so on. See also Craig, *Reasonable Faith*, pp. 46–47, 65–86.

37. Paul Bell, "Would You Believe It?" *Mensa Magazine* (February 2002): 12–13.

38. Shermer, *Why People Believe*, p. 292.

39. Ibid., p. 297.

Chapter 4

THE OUTSIDER TEST FOR FAITH
REVISITED

John W. Loftus

*W*hat I intend to do in this chapter is to further argue for and defend my Outsider Test for Faith *(OTF) from initial feedback I received about it. This is just one of several arguments I use in my book* Why I Became An Atheist *(WIBA) to demonstrate that the predisposition of skepticism is warranted when examining the evidence for a religious faith. This feedback came from several sources including the Midwest regional meeting of the Evangelical Philosophical Society, where I presented a paper on this topic in March 2009 at Ashland Theological Seminary.*

The most important question of all when it comes to assessing the truth claims of Christian theism (or religion in general) is whether we should approach the available evidence through the eyes of faith or with skepticism. Complete neutrality as sort of a blank-slate type of condition, while desirable, is practically impossible, since the cultural worldview we use to evaluate the available evidence is already there prior to looking at the evidence. With the OTF I'll argue that we should adopt a skeptical predisposition as best as possible prior to examining the evidence, if we adopt any predisposition at all.

My argument is as follows:

1) Rational people in distinct geographical locations around the globe overwhelmingly adopt and defend a wide diversity of religious faiths due to their upbringing and cultural heritage. This is the *religious diversity thesis*.

2) Consequently, it seems very likely that adopting one's religious faith is not merely a matter of independent rational judgment but is causally dependent on cultural conditions to an overwhelming degree.[1] This is the *religious dependency thesis*.

3) Hence the odds are highly likely that any given adopted religious faith is false.

4) So the best way to test one's adopted religious faith is from the perspective of an outsider with the same level of skepticism used to evaluate other religious faiths. This expresses the OTF.

The OTF is primarily a test to examine religious faiths. When I refer to religious faith here, I'm primarily referring to beliefs that are essential for a member to be accepted in a particular religious community of faith who worship together and/or accept the same divinely inspired prophetic revelations whereby one's position in the afterlife depends. The OTF is no different than the prince in the Cinderella story who must question forty-five thousand people to see which girl lost the glass slipper at the ball the previous night. They all claim to have done so. Therefore, skepticism is definitely warranted. This is especially true when an empirical foot-match cannot solve the religious questions we're asking.

There are at least three legs supportive of the first three premises of my argument: anthropological studies, psychological studies, and sociological (or demographic) data. The first two legs have been sufficiently argued for by David Eller, Valerie Tarico, and Jason Long in their earlier chapters. Daniel Dennett sums up the psychological data in these words: "One of the surprising discoveries of modern psychology is how easy it is to be ignorant of your own ignorance."[2] Cultural anthropology shows us that we don't see culture so much as we see *with* culture. We swim in a Christian culture. It's hard to argue Christians out of their faith because they were never argued into it in the first place. Elsewhere, Eller has argued that "nothing is more destructive to religion than other religions; it is like meeting one's own anti-matter twin ... other religions represent *alternatives* to one's own religion: other people believe in them just as fervently as we do, and they live their lives just as successfully as we do ... the diversity of religions forces us to see religion as a culturally relative phenomenon; different groups have different religions that appear adapted to their unique social and even environmental conditions. But if *their* religion is relative, then why is *ours* not?"[3]

The third leg of sociological data is easy to come by. For instance, 95 percent of people born and raised in Saudi Arabia are Muslim, while 95 percent of the people born and raised in Thailand are Buddhist. If you were born in India, you'd likely be a Hindu. If you were born in Mexico, you'd likely be a Catholic. In fact, we were all raised as believers, to a large extent. We were taught to believe whatever our parents told us. If they said there is a Santa Claus, then he existed until they said otherwise. If we were told there was a god named Zeus, we would've believed it. The sociological data is vast, and I've already documented some of it in *WIBA*.[4] All three legs converge to provide overwhelming, undeniable, and noncontroversial support for the OTF by showing that when it comes to religious faith, an overwhelming number of believers adopt and defend what they were raised to believe by their parents in their respective cultures.[5]

Religious faiths are not chosen by us. They are given to us. We inherit them. They are caught—not taught. In most cases we rarely stray far from what we were raised in but merely move around among versions of the same general religion, and even when we make a more radical change, we rarely do so after conducting a thorough study of the comparative evidence. So the question the OTF addresses is how we should test the faith given to us, or any new faith we may be considering instead. The problem is that social conditions provide us with the initial control beliefs we use from that moment onward to incorporate all known facts and experiences. That's why they're called control beliefs. They are like blinders. From the moment they are put on, we pretty much see only what our blinders will let us see. What else can best explain why there is still a Mormon church even though DNA evidence now shows us that Native Americans did not come from the Middle East, as the Mormon Bible claims?[6]

Valerie Tarico describes the process of adopting and following blinding-beliefs that are subsequently defended by intelligent people. She claims, "It doesn't take very many false assumptions to send us on a long goose chase." To illustrate this, in *The Dark Side: How Evangelical Teachings Corrupt Love and Truth* she tells us about the mental world of a paranoid schizophrenic. To such a person the perceived persecution by the CIA sounds real:

You can sit, as a psychiatrist, with a diagnostic manual next to you, and think: as bizarre as it sounds, the CIA really is bugging this guy. The arguments are tight, the logic persuasive, the evidence organized into neat files. All that is needed to build such an impressive house of illusion is a clear, well-organized mind and a few false assumptions. Paranoid individuals can be very credible.[7]

Given these facts, the central thesis of the OTF is a challenge to believers to test or examine their own religious faith as if they were outsiders with the same presumption of skepticism they use to test or examine other religious faiths. Its presumption is that when examining one's own religious faith, skepticism is warranted, since the odds are good that it is false. Remember, *brainwashed people do not know that they have been brainwashed*. We know that billions of people have been brainwashed to believe, if you grant that they have been misled by their parents and culture. So you must take seriously the real possibility that you are one of them. If you really want know if you've been brainwashed to believe, then taking the OTF is the best and probably the only way to know the truth about your own religious faith, since there seems to be no reasonable alternative.

If believers refuse to take the OTF, then they must justify having such a double standard. Why are they more critical of other religious beliefs than they are their own? For believers to object that what I'm asking is unfair, they have the burden of proof to show why their inconsistent approach to religious faith is justified in the first place.

If after having investigated one's own religious faith with the presumption of skepticism it passes intellectual muster, then the believer can have his or her religious faith. It's that simple. If not, abandon it. I suspect that if believers are willing to take the challenge of the OTF, they will find that their faith fails the test; consequently they will abandon it, along with all other religious faiths, like I did. Any loving god who requires us to believe correctly, when instead we have this extremely strong tendency to accept what we were raised to believe, especially if he'll punish us if we end up being wrong, should surely make the correct religious faith pass the OTF. If God exists and he doesn't care which religion we accept, that kind of god might survive the OTF, but then we would end up believing in a nebulous god with no definable characteristics, perhaps a deistic god or the "god of the philosophers." But this god is much too different from the God of any full-blown Christianity or any specific revealed religion though, and can be safely ignored.

In a way, adopting the OTF is like following the Golden Rule, or so argues Dr. James McGrath, associate professor of religion at Butler University, Indianapolis, IN. He claims this is the way to assess the likelihood of Christian miracles in history:

> One doesn't have to be committed in advance to history's inability to deal with miracles in order to begin to realize that one cannot claim Christianity is grounded purely in history while other traditions are at best shrouded in myth. One simply has to apply the most basic Christian principle to one's investigation of the competing claims: *The Golden Rule.* And so what does it mean to do history from a Christian perspective? It means doing to the claims of others what you would want done to your claims. And perhaps also the reverse: doing to your own claims, views and presuppositions that which you have been willing to do to the claims, views and presuppositions of others. Once one begins to attempt to examine the evidence not in an unbiased way, but simply *fairly*, one cannot but acknowledge that there are elements of the Christian tradition which, if they were in your opponent's tradition, you would reject, debunk, discount, and otherwise find unpersuasive or at least not decisive or compelling.[8]

I've investigated my faith as an insider with the presumption that it was true. Even from an insider's perspective with the Christian set of control beliefs, I couldn't continue to believe.[9] Now, from the outside, it makes no sense at all. Christians are on the inside. I am now on the outside. Christians see things from the inside. I see things from the outside. From the inside, it seems true. From the outside, it seems bizarre. As Stephen Roberts quipped: "When you understand why you dismiss all the other possible gods, you will understand why I dismiss yours."[10]

WHAT DOES THE OTF REQUIRE OF BELIEVERS?

Believers should approach all religious faiths equally with the same level of skepticism. Look closely at how evangelical Christians, for instance, dismiss the distinctive beliefs of Muslims or Mormons and with it their religious worldviews. They use two different methods. One faulty method is to argue that since what they believe is true the other religious faiths are false. Other faiths either don't address the right questions or the questions they do address are not answered satisfactorily when compared to their own answers. Such a method is faulty. It first presumes what they believe based on what they were raised to believe, so it begs the question.

The other method Christians use is on much firmer ground. They use David Hume's evidentiary standards for examining miraculous claims to the faiths they reject. They also deconstruct these other religious texts by assuming human rather than divine authors. They adopt a methodological naturalist viewpoint to test these other extraordinary claims and find them wanting. That best represents the skepticism from the outside using tests that are very well defended as not being sociologically dependent but rather scientifically dependent. I'm arguing that Christians should transfer that same skepticism toward Trinitarian, incarnational, resurrection faith and see what they get. I argue they won't get much.

To the Christian theist the challenge of the OTF means there would be no more quoting the Bible to defend the claim that Jesus' death on the cross saves them from sins. As an outsider you wouldn't believe such a claim just because you read it in some ancient text. The Christian theist must now try to rationally explain it. No more quoting the Bible to show how it's possible for Jesus to be 100 percent God and 100 percent man with nothing left over. The Christian theist must now try to make sense of this claim, coming as it does from an ancient superstitious people who didn't have trouble believing Paul and Barnabas were "gods in human form" (Acts 14:11, 28:6). The Christian theist must not assume prior to examining the evidence that there is an answer to the problem of horrendous suffering in our world, either. And she'd be skeptical of believing in any of the miracles in the Bible, just as she would be skeptical of any miraculous claim in today's world supporting other religious faiths. Why? Because she cannot start out by first believing the Bible, nor can she trust the people close to her who are Christian theists to know the truth, nor can she trust her own anecdotal religious experiences. She would want independent evidence and reasons for these beliefs.

At the very minimum, a believer should be willing to subject her faith to rigorous scrutiny by reading many of the best-recognized critiques of her faith. And she should look at Christian arguments the same way others do—as an outsider. Whether it comes to Plantinga's *Reformed Epistemology*, William Lane Craig's argument for the "inner witness of the Spirit," divine hiddenness arguments, Pascal's Wager, or William James's argument for faith, the Christian believer must think of them just as an outsider would. Just think how it would sound to evangelical Christians if Mormons claimed their faith was "properly basic," or that the inner witness of the Spirit self-authenticates their faith? Just think how it would sound to Christians if Muslims explained the lack of belief in Allah because Allah was a hidden God? The "many gods" objection to Pascal's Wager destroys the wager's force since we must first decide among the various gods which one to wager on. And William James's argument for faith can be used to justify any religion at all. Many of these types of arguments can be easily dismissed if you evaluate them as an outsider would.

The OTF also challenges believers to critically examine the social conditions of how they came to adopt their particular religious faith in the first place. That is, believers must consider who or what influenced them to believe and whether those initial reasons were good ones. Would they have become Mormons instead, had a joyous, friendly Mormon group approached them at that same vulnerable time in their lives? Most of us do not have good initial reasons to accept a religious faith.

Take for example Dr. William Lane Craig's conversion testimony as presented on his Web site ReasonableFaith.org (Question 78: "Your Personal Testimony"). Craig is considered the leading Christian apologist in our generation by many people today. Craig tells us he felt "empty" inside with no purpose and he didn't see anyone as "genuine," even himself. Yet he really did want meaning in his life. And he wanted to love and to be loved by others. One day he met a girl who "was always so happy it just makes you sick!" She told him she was happy because Jesus saved her and that Jesus loved him too. This hit him "like a ton of bricks." That "thought just staggered me," he wrote, "to think that the God of the universe should love me, Bill Craig, that worm down there on that speck of dust called planet Earth! I just couldn't take it in." So he began reading the New Testament from cover to cover and was "absolutely captivated by the person Jesus of Nazareth." And he began worshipping with other people who were happy just like this girl. In that group he found the meaning and love that he craved. So he cried out to God in prayer and found what he was looking for. He looked up at the Milky Way and thought, "God! I've come to know God!"

From reading his story I don't think Bill had good initial reasons to believe, just like I didn't. His personal story stresses his need for happiness, love, significance, and meaning. And he found these things simply because of a wonderful story that was told to him by a happy person during a vulnerable time in his life. He initially read the Bible uncritically along with some other Christian books. But how does someone properly investigate whether a claim is true or not? He or she doesn't do it by only reading the literature of the people who advocate it. He or she does it by also reading the best critiques of the people who disagree with it, and Dr. Craig now knows this. By now he also knows there is a lot of hypocrisy and unhappiness among church people. Bill has had problems with church people by now and he surely suffers like most of us do from bouts of anger toward others and unhappiness. Does this subsequent experience cause him to doubt the initial youthful rush of friends and the happiness he felt at the time? I suspect so, or it should. By now he also knows that the need for significance and meaning isn't a good reason for accepting a religious story, since there are many to choose from. I'll bet he can also pick up those very same Christian books he first read and find several large holes in their arguments.

So would Bill have believed in the first place if he knew then what he does now? Remember, back then he didn't believe. He was an "outsider." I dare say that if he knew what he does now and hadn't already chosen to adopt his faith, he would not have believed in the first place.

I'm asking believers to change their assumptions and/or become agnostics. This is what I call the "default position." If someone claims he or she cannot do this, then do what René Descartes did with a methodological or hypothetical doubt (although I'm not suggesting his extreme type of doubt). Hypothetically consider that you believe mainly for emotional and not intellectual reasons, just like people who have the fear of heights are afraid to stand at the edge of a precipice for emotional, not intellectual, reasons. They intellectually know people go up to the top of skyscrapers and come down safely. So they must face their fears. They must get to the first floor and look around. When comfortable they must go up to the second floor, and so on until they get to the top.[11] This may take some time. Julia Sweeney, a former *Saturday Night Live* comedian, faced her fears when she put on her "No God Glasses" for a moment to look around at the world as if God did not exist. Then she put them on for an hour a day. Try this. As she faced her fears, she "began to see the world completely differently." Eventually she was "able to say good-bye to God."[12]

ANSWERING SEVEN OBJECTIONS

I've already answered several objections to the OTF in *WIBA* (pp. 72–77), so I don't need to answer them again, except as different ways of stating those same objections that have come to my attention, or as I've come up with additional answers to them.

ONE

Do I consider myself "lucky" to have been born in an era and in a place in which the rise of modern science and rational inquiry has progressed to the point where I have the necessary critical-thinking tools to argue for the OTF? Can I offer a "rational justification" for this luck? If not, why am I justified in advocating the OTF based upon this privileged position in time?

In answer I would have to say that yes, I was indeed lucky to have been born when and where I was born to know what I do in order to offer the OTF as a critique of religious faith. We have experienced an explosive growth of scientific knowledge that produced the modern world. Unless I could have come up with this vast amount of knowledge myself, then I wouldn't know any different than others if I was born in 1000 BCE. So the rational justification for this luck is to be found in the solid advancement of science itself.

The only thing we can and should trust is the sciences. Science alone produces consistently excellent results that cannot be denied, which are continually retested for validity. I'm claiming religious beliefs learned on our mama's knees are in a different category than the results of repeatable scientific experiments, and that this claim is both obvious and noncontroversial. We can personally do the experiments ourselves. When it comes to religious faiths, there are no mutually agreed upon reliable tests to decide between them, and this makes all the difference in the world. Besides, as David Eller has argued, Christians are not opposed to modern science anyway.[13] They adopt its methods and conclusions in a vast majority of areas except a few limited ones concerning their faith. So the question is why they adopt such a double standard with regard to science. Why do they accept the results of science the vast majority of the time but subsequently reject them with regard to their faith?

TWO

It's objected that there are people, lots of them, who choose to be Christian theists who were born and raised in parts of Asia and the Southern

Hemisphere, where Christianity is growing phenomenally.[14] These people are ousiders who can and do escape their culturally adopted faith.

When it comes to these converts, however, my opinion is that most of them do not objectively weigh the evidence when making their initial religious commitments. They mainly change their minds due to the influence and believability of the evangelist and/or the wondrous nature of the religious story itself, just like Bill Craig did. In these parts of the globe, people already share much of the same social, economical, political, and superstitious viewpoints that the ancient biblical people shared anyway, so it should be no surprise that the Gospel is being accepted there.[15]

These new converts in different cultural contexts have no initial way of truly investigating the proffered faith. Which evangelist will objectively tell the ugly side of the Bible and of the church while preaching the good news? None that I know of. Which evangelist will tell a prospect about the innumerable problems Christian scholars must solve? None that I know of. Which evangelist will give potential prospects a copy of a book like this one to read along with a copy of a Christian apologetics book and ask them to truly examine it before deciding? Again, none that I know of. Only if they do will I sit up and take notice. Until then I am not impressed.

THREE

Related to objection two above are recent polls showing many Americans are leaving the faith of their parents. If correct, this is supposed to undermine the sociological basis for the OTF somehow. The 2008 Pew Forum Poll tells us that "28 percent of American adults have left the faith of their childhood for another one. When we include people who switched from one Protestant denomination to another the number would jump to 44 percent."[16]

But this poll data does not undermine the sociological data at all. Americans are embracing syncretism, pluralism, and pragmatism when it comes to religion. American culture is changing, so it should not surprise us in the least that they are also changing their religious faiths. If someone lives and breathes in a pluralistic culture then he or she will be a pluralist, you see, even if raised otherwise by his or her parents. More and more believers are treating religion like they do diet and sex. Variety is the spice of life when it comes to these things. So also is religion to them. Americans don't think there is much of a difference between many of the sects within Christianity, and some think that way about religions in general. So it stands to reason believers will switch church affiliations to attend where their friends do in churches that have more to offer them with programs that meet their practical needs. They'll switch churches for a warmer pew with a better church building to hear better music and a better sermon. After all, the moral message still seems to be the same, and that's what more and more Americans think the value of religion provides anyway.[17]

In any case, the fact is that these newly chosen faiths are still not passing the OTF. So this is just another instance of unwarranted conversion to what happens to be culturally available.

FOUR

It's objected that just because rational people disagree about an issue, that does not justify skepticism about any particular opinion of it. In other words, it has been argued that the mere existence of disagreement between rational people does not automatically lead us to be skeptical about that which we think is true.

On the contrary, I think it can and it does. The amount of skepticism warranted depends not only on the number of rational people who disagree, but also whether the people who disagree are separated into distinct geographical locations, the nature of their beliefs, how their beliefs originated, under what circumstances their beliefs were personally adopted in the first place, and the kinds of evidence that can possibly be used to decide between the differing beliefs. My claim is that when it comes to religious faiths, a high degree of skepticism is warranted precisely because of these factors.

Richard Feldman, professor of philosophy at the University of Rochester, NY, argues that when there are two "epistemic peers" who have a "genuine disagreement" about "shared evidence," the reasonable thing to do is to "suspend judgment" about the issue. Under these conditions "one should give up one's beliefs in the light of the sort of disagreement under discussion." If, however, "one's conviction survives the 'confrontation with the other'... this seems more a sign of tenacity and stubbornness than anything else."[18] By contrast, the more that rational people agree on an issue then the more probable their shared opinion is true. Even though we know that everyone can be wrong, this is still the best we can do. No one bets against gravity, for instance, because there is evidence for it that was learned apart from what we were taught to believe in our separate, geographically distinct locations.

This is why I liked Bill Maher's movie *Religulous*.[19] It's obvious from watching the many different (and even bizarre) religious opinions expressed in it, that any given one of them is false. By putting them on an equal playing field they all appear to be false, which is what the OTF is meant to force us to consider. How do you know your religion isn't the false one and theirs the true one? Only by passing the OTF can you know.

FIVE

Believers may object that the skepticism required of the OTF is self-defeating. A self-defeating argument is one that is internally inconsistent with itself and, therefore, is by definition false. They'll rhetorically ask as does Alvin Plantinga: "If the pluralist had been born in (say, Morocco) he probably wouldn't be a pluralist. Does it follow that... his pluralist beliefs are produced in him by an unreliable belief-producing process" too?[20] If not, why does the pluralist (or skeptic) think he can transcend his culture but a Christian theist cannot?

In answer I think it's extremely difficult to transcend our culture because it provides us with the very eyes we use to see with, as Eller argued in chapter 1. But precisely because we know from anthropology, psychology, and the demographic data that this is what cultures do to us, it's possible for us to transcend the culture we were raised in. *What we've learned is that we should be skeptical about that which we were led to believe even though we can't actually see anything about our beliefs to be skeptical about.*

And so it's not self-defeating to argue on behalf of skepticism. Not by a long shot. Skepticism is not a belief system. It's an approach to truth claims, and a reasonable one at that. Skepticism is the hallmark of an adult who thinks for herself. I see nothing self-defeating about this at all. If after approaching a truth claim with skepticism it passes muster, then the skeptic has good reasons to accept it. And so the reasonable skeptic does indeed accept many claims to be true. No one can be skeptical of everything. It's just that we should be skeptical to some degree about everything we were taught to accept unless we can confirm it for ourselves. That confirmation process is not Cartesian though, and we cannot confirm everything we accept as true.

Skepticism is best expressed on a continuum, anyway. Some claims will warrant more skepticism than others. Some claims we should be extremely skeptical about ("I saw a pink elephant;" "the CIA is dogging my steps"), while others on the opposite side will not require much skepticism at all ("there is a material world," "if you drop a book it will fall to the ground," "George Washington was the first president of the United States of America"). I'm arguing that religious faiths warrant the same level of skepticism that other similar beliefs require, like beliefs in the elves of Iceland, the trolls of Norway, and the power of witches in Africa. They must all be subjected to the same levels of skepticism given both the extraordinary nature of these claims and how some of these beliefs were adopted in the first place.

Consider some odd sort of phenomena, and let's say there are only seven known theories to explain it, some more probable than others. Skeptics may deny outright three of them and weigh the others in the balance. Then they might conclude one theory is the best explanation for it. But they also acknowledge they could be wrong, and even that there might appear an eighth theory to explain it that no one has thought of yet. Believers may only consider one particular theory, the one they were taught to believe, and they may pronounce it to be true beyond what the evidence calls for, even though there are other theories that have some degree of probability to them as well. True believers act with a high degree of certainty that they are correct, as Valerie Tarico has argued in chapter 2. They may not even consider the other theories at all, or if they do, they do so to refute them.

That's the difference. There is a huge difference between affirming a truth claim and denying one. The hard part, as someone quipped, isn't in smelling a rotten egg, it's in laying a good one. The OTF calls us to be egg smellers with the same level of critical olfactory senses that we use to detect other rotten religious eggs. The denial is the easy part, since there are many possible theories to explain a phenomenon. The hard part is to affirm which one of them is the correct one.

The skeptic has the more reasonable position, by far, and it simply is not self-defeating at all. There are just too many ways to be wrong. Simply trusting in what you were taught is a method we know to be unreliable, especially since so many sincere people in the world believe in different religions. Since you came to believe the same way they did, you should be skeptical that you've made the right choice, precisely because you are skeptical that they did.

Furthermore, when it comes to the OTF someone cannot say I ought to be just as skeptical of it as I am about the conclusions I arrive at when I apply the test, since I have justified this test independently of my conclusions. From what we know is the case, the three legs that support the OTF more than justify it.

SIX

A similar objection to the one above is that all of us have a set of presuppositions that provides a framework for seeing the world as a whole, called a worldview. In other words, there isn't a presuppositionless way of looking at the world from a neutral, "outside" standpoint. In this sense, it's argued, atheism is a worldview based on faith, and therefore atheists should take the OTF too, or as Pastor Timothy Keller argues, they "must doubt [their] doubts." He claims: "All doubts, however skeptical and cynical they may seem, are really a set of alternative beliefs. You cannot doubt Belief A except from a position of faith in Belief B." Writing to skeptics, he proclaims: "The reason you doubt Christianity's Belief A is because you hold unprovable Belief B. Every doubt, therefore, is based on a leap of faith."[21] Skeptics have faith, he opines, whenever they accept something that is "unprovable," and all of us "have fundamental, unprovable faith commitments that we think are superior to those of others."[22] So this is why he thinks atheists likewise "must doubt [their] doubts."[23] What can we make of this?

In the first place, even if I grant for the sake of argument that skeptics have faith assumptions when they cannot prove something they believe, then what method does Keller propose to distinguish between that which is provable from that which is unprovable? Surely he doesn't mean to say that if we cannot be absolutely certain of something all we have left is blind faith, or that everything that is unprovable has an equal epistemological merit. Christians like him want to claim that skeptics have unproven beliefs, and then they try to drive a whole truckload of Christian assumptions and beliefs through that small crevice. If that's what he's doing, then Mormons and Muslims could write the same things he did, and then drive their own truckload of assumptions and beliefs through that small crevice too. And then we would still be in no better position to judge between faiths. What I'm proposing with the *Outsider Test for Faith* is a way to distinguish between what we should accept from what we should not. I'm arguing there isn't a better test when it comes to religious beliefs. So again, what better method is there?

In the second place, I do not accept Keller's definition of faith. He's manipulating the debate by using a language game in his favor. I reject his game. I know as sure as I can know anything that there is a material world, and that I can reasonably trust my senses. And I conclude that the scientific method is our only sure way for assessing truth claims. These things I know to be the case. They are not beliefs of mine. William Lane Craig objects by using hypothetical conjectures to show otherwise—that scientifically minded skeptics have an equivalent kind of faith. Dr. Craig wrote:

> [M]ost of our beliefs cannot be evidentially justified. Take, for example, the belief that the world was not created five minutes ago with built-in memory traces, food in our stomachs from meals we never really ate, and other appearances of age. Or the belief that the external world around us is real rather than a computer-generated virtual reality. Anyone who has seen a film like *The Matrix* realizes that the person living in such a virtual reality has no evidence that he is not in such an illusory world. But surely we're rational in believing that the world around us is real and has existed longer than five minutes, even though we have no evidence for this.... Many of the things we know are not based on evidence. So why must belief in God be so based?[24]

But there is no epistemic parity here at all! For example, when it comes to the possibility that I'm presently living in a virtual, Matrix world, rather than the real world, that scenario cannot be taken seriously by any intelligent person. The story is extremely implausible. I see no reason why there would be any knowledge of the Matrix by people living in it, since the Matrix determines all of their experiences...all of them. So how could taking a virtual red pill while in the Matrix get someone out of it and into the real world in the first place? As far as Neo knows the red pill could have been nothing more than a hallucinogenic drug anyway. And even if Neo came to believe a real world lies beyond his own virtual, Matrix world, how could he know that the so-called real world isn't just another Matrix beyond the one he experienced? Neo would have no good reason for concluding he knows which world is the *really* real world at that point. The *really* real world could be beyond the one he experienced after taking the red pill, or beyond that one, or beyond that one, and so forth.

If all we need to be concerned with is what is possible rather than what is probable we couldn't claim to know anything at all. We would end up as "epistemological solipsists." So as David Mitsuo Nixon has argued with respect to the Matrix: "The proper response to someone's telling me that my belief *could* be false is, 'So what?' It's not *possibility* that matters, it's *probability*. So until you give me a good reason to think that my belief is not just *possibly* false, but *probably* false, I'm not changing anything about what I believe or what I think I know."[25]

In fact, believing we're in a Matrix would be a much closer parallel for believing in God than Craig may realize. Craig is actually giving us a reason to *doubt* an ad hoc, unevidenced assumption like God. For if it's silly to believe in the Matrix, it should be silly to believe in God. As I've argued before, Christians repeatedly retreat to the position that what they believe is "possible," or "not impossible," rather than what is probable. Just because all of these things are a remote theoretical possibility doesn't mean he can conclude that what he believes is probable. A possibility is not a probability. The inference does not follow. It's a huge non sequitur.

So words like *faith* and *belief* just don't do justice to the things we reasonably accept. David Eller has argued, "knowing is not believing." He claims that if believers "can drag down real knowledge to their level and erase any distinctions between the true and the false, the known and the merely felt or believed or guessed, they can rest comfortably in their own undeserved self-certainty." According to him "knowledge is about reason" while "belief is about faith." He says, "the two are logically and psychologically utterly different and even incompatible."[26] He simply refuses to play this religious language game, and a game it is. Given his argument, the usual philosophical definition of "knowledge" as "justified true belief" should be discarded in favor of "justified true conclusions," or "justified true acceptances." The word *faith* must be reserved to apply in this context to beliefs that cannot be empirically tested and aren't needed to explain anything, like ghosts, angels, demons, and gods.

In the third place, it's patently false to say atheism is a religion or a worldview, which Keller and other Christians do. "If atheism is a religion" as David Eller quips, "then not collecting stamps is a hobby."[27] The fact is that no one can predict in advance what atheists think about politics, economics, environmental issues, or social ethics. In fact, not much can be said about all atheists just because they're atheists. There are Marxists, Freudians, existentialists, and the "New Atheists" of our generation. There are even atheistic religions, like Buddhism, Jainism, Daoism, Confucianism, and yes, even a religionless Christian atheism.

If a worldview encompasses everything someone claims to know and/or believe, as it does, then atheism is no more a worldview than is Christian theism, since Christians themselves have a wide variety of opinions about a wide variety of issues down through the centuries. Bare-bones creeds like the Apostles Creed or the Nicene Creed are not in themselves expressions of a worldview. They say little about how Christians should interpret those creeds, whether they can still be Christians if they reject portions of those creeds, how Christians should think about economic and political issues outside of those creeds, and how to behave based on those creeds.

Worldviews are dynamic rather than static things, anyway. They are constantly changing with additional education and experience. Some of the ideas once adhered to as part of a total worldview have been rejected upon further investigation, while others have become firmly grounded as the evidence confirms them. Since worldviews are dynamic rather than static, one need not be a total "outsider" to test his or her faith. Believers merely have to take seriously the real possibility they are wrong and then subject a few minor beliefs of theirs to skepticism. Successfully doing so may subsequently lead to being skeptical about some of their major beliefs until they end up rejecting their religious faith as a whole. An outsider perspective then is one that can be described as a place just a bit outside one's present total perspective.

Fourthly, even if it's true that an atheist should take the OTF, this doesn't give believers any excuse to avoid taking the OTF themselves. All of us should at least start by standing on the minimal common ground that we share. We can agree on some rock-solid conclusions impervious to doubt, like the *cogito* of Descartes ("I think therefore I am") and/or logical laws and mathematical truths. We can agree on the evidence of the senses, and the scientific conclusions based upon the evidence of the senses, like gravity. Beyond that are such things as a small core of solid ethical and historical conclusions we can accept. This minimal common ground is what I consider the "outside" standing place for us to test the many other ideas we were raised to believe. From this common ground we can all proceed to take the OTF.[28]

Finally, atheists do indeed take the OTF. That's why atheists are atheists in the first place. An atheist is someone who merely rejects the claim that supernatural entities exist, whether it's a god, or gods. Atheists do not think believers have produced enough evidence for their extraordinary supernatural claims. It's widely accepted that extraordinary claims demand extraordinary evidence to support them, especially when the evidence should be there and is not. And religious claims are indeed extraordinary, since believers accept at least one thing more than the atheist does: that a god exists in addition to the universe. Such an additional claim requires more by way of justification due to Ockham's razor.

Keep in mind that when it comes to the religious or nonreligious options in front of us, the choices are emphatically *not* between any one particular situated cultural form of Christianity and atheism. The choices are myriad. This fact makes agnosticism the default position. The odds of just happening to have the correct worldview are no better than one in the total number of available worldviews accepted by people around the globe. So the odds are that we are wrong. When we all equally apply an outsider test to our own answers to existence every one of us should be agnostics about all such metaphysical affirmative claims—all of us. We should all doubt our doubts. But agnostics already do this. The double negative way Keller expresses these things does not lead to faith. It leads to agnosticism. Therefore, anyone, and I mean anyone including myself, who leaves the default agnostic position and affirms an answer, any answer, has the practical burden of proof, especially in our religiously diverse world where people disagree with each other.

By contrast, what extraordinary claims are *atheists* making? Is it an extraordinary claim for atheists to say with Carl Sagan that, "the cosmos is all that is or ever was or ever will be"? It may seem that way to believers, and so this must still be shown to be the best explanation of the available evidence in discussions with them. But it's not an extraordinary claim at all. Atheism is a reasonable conclusion arrived at by the process of elimination due to taking the OTF. By finding the evidence lacking for the extraordinary claims that supernatural entities exist, the atheist simply concludes these claims are false. And if these entities don't exist, then Carl Sagan's conclusion is all that remains. I am an atheist because that's the direction agnosticism pushed me. I rejected one supernatural entity after another, leaving the only reasonable answer: atheism.

SEVEN

One last objection is that I'm committing the informal genetic fallacy of irrelevance. This fallacy is committed whenever it's argued that a belief is false because of the origination of the belief.

But this charge is irrelevant and false. In the first place it's irrelevant since the origination of certain kinds of beliefs is indeed a relevant factor when assessing if those beliefs are probable. Take for example a person who has a paranoid belief about the CIA spying on him, and let's say we find that it originated from taking a hallucinogenic drug like LSD. Since we have linked his belief to a drug that creates many other false beliefs, we have some really good evidence to be skeptical of it, *even though we have not actually shown his belief to be false in any other way.* So when many false beliefs are produced at a very high rate by the same source we have a good reason to doubt any beliefs arising out of that same source. I'm arguing that the source of most people's religious faith is an unreliable one, coming as it does from the geographical accidents of birth. It produces many different and irreconcilable religious faiths that cannot all be true.

This charge is also *false.* I allow that a religion could still pass the OTF even despite its unreliable origins, so I'm committing no fallacy by arguing correctly that those origins are demonstrably unreliable. At best there can only be one true religion in what we observe to be a sea of hundreds of false ones, which entails a very high rate of error for how believers first adopt a religion. Hence, believers need some further test to be sure their faith is the correct one. That is not a fallacious conclusion, nor is the skepticism that it entails. I'm not arguing that religious faiths are necessarily false because of how believers originally adopt them. I'm merely arguing that believers should be skeptical of their culturally adopted religious faith because of it.

VICTOR REPPERT'S OBJECTIONS

Christian philosopher Victor Reppert has offered some initial criticisms of the OTF.[29] He claimed it would be cheating "to have a test and just mark our religious beliefs as the beliefs to be tested," so he offered other examples that I might consider testing in the same way. Reppert first objected that since we were brought up in the West to accept an external material world, should we also subject what we were taught about this to the OTF too? After all, if someone born in India should take the OTF who was brought up believing the world of experience is *maya*, or an illusion, then why shouldn't Westerners do likewise?

I must admit this is an interesting suggestion. However there is a distinction here that makes all the difference. I was not just taught to think there is an external world. I experience it daily. In fact, to deny this would require denying everything I personally experience throughout every single day of my life. And denying this would deny science—the very thing that has produced the modern world through testable experience. I think it's a categorical mistake to equate the nonverifiable religious view that there is no external world with the scientific view that there is one. (George Berkeley's similar view was inspired by his religious commitment to solve the mind/brain problem). So I would argue that people born in India would have to subject their own religious upbringing to the OTF, whereas the consensus of scientists has already passed the OTF, in that it has survived the scientific method. After all, in the face of all the evidence we've accumulated, saying there is an external world causing our experiences is not an extraordinary claim. But denying it is.

Reppert further asks whether any moral and political beliefs would survive an outsider test: "I think that rape is wrong. If I had been brought up in a certain culture, I'm told, I would believe that rape is okay if you do it in the evening, because a woman's place is at home under her husband's protection, and if she is gone she's asking for it. So my belief that rape is wrong flunks the outsider test." He also thinks that "representative democracy is a better form of government than monarchy." He wrote: "If I lived in sixteenth-century Europe, or in other parts of the globe, I probably would not believe that. So my belief in democratic government flunks the outsider test." And yet, he claims, just because they both flunk the test, he still has no reason to think differently than he does.

My argument is that we must examine any belief learned on our mama's knees with the skepticism of outsiders, unless we can verify it for ourselves. The amount of skepticism warranted depends on several factors, as I previously mentioned. So Reppert is correct to apply the OTF to ethics and politics as well, although we might better call this the *Outsider Test for Beliefs* (or OTB) at this point. Indeed, one of the principle causes of social strife, confusion, and misery is a failure to examine our own moral and political beliefs skeptically and critically. That includes the rightness of democracy or the wrongness of rape.

But I know of no skeptical person in today's world who would ever want to morally justify rape. Beliefs like the acceptability of rape (and honor killings) are based on religious faiths and ancient texts, so they must be scrutinized with the skepticism of the OTB because the nature and origin of those beliefs are religious in nature. The same thing goes for claims that challenge democracy. Only religious believers in today's world are defending the notion of a theocracy, both in Muslim countries and the Christian Reconstructionists in America. So subjecting such a theocratical political system to the OTB would be to undercut such a belief, especially when we consider the harm it does to human beings.

The truth is that there are a great many political and moral beliefs we think are essential to a human society but are not necessary at all. Democracy is one of them. People have done fairly well without democracy from the beginning when a dominant male lion or ape had free reign with a harem of females and ruled over the others, although we've subsequently learned democracy is much better. That being said, Richard Carrier countered Reppert's conclusions (via e-mail):

> Reppert's error appears to lie in neglecting the role of information in decision making: any rational sixteenth-century man who was given all the information we now have (of the different outcomes of democratic vs. nondemocratic nations over a long period of time) would agree with us that democracy is better. Hence, democracy passes the OTB. Similarly any rational would-be rapist who acquired full and correct information about how raped women feel, and what sort of person he becomes if he ignores a person's feelings and welfare, and all of the actual consequences of such behavior to himself and his society, then he would agree that raping such a woman is wrong. Hence, our ethic against rape will also pass the OTB. It's just that people in those societies haven't subjected their ethical and political views to an adequate application of the OTB, which is a fact that actually discredits their views, not the OTB.

Reppert finally argued that "a certain natural conservatism with respect to changing our minds about matters of worldview, or any other issue for that matter, is both natural and rational.... If we have to be skeptics about all of our sociologically conditioned beliefs, I am afraid we are going to be skeptics about a lot more than just religion."

Well, it's certainly the case that accepting epistemic conservatism is natural with respect to us not wanting to change our traditionally handed-down beliefs. It's so natural that we will go to some extreme lengths to defend what we were led to believe. But we should *only* accept what we were led to believe if what we believe has been derived by a highly reliable method for grasping the truth. Only then is epistemic conservatism warranted. Conversely, when our traditionally handed-down beliefs have not been derived by a reliable method, then epistemic conservatism has no demonstrable warrant. In short, religious traditions that have never passed any measure of the OTF deserve no conservative respect at all. So I see nothing about this conservatism that is justified, otherwise at some extreme level we'd still believe in Santa Claus or tooth fairies. The rational thing to do is to grow and learn and think and investigate and follow the arguments and evidence wherever they lead. This is what we should do despite wanting to cling to traditionally accepted beliefs that cannot be reasonably justified.

My Final Argument

In the end, Reppert wrote: "If what it is to be skeptical is just to entertain skeptical questions about one's beliefs, to subject them to scrutiny, to take seriously possible evidence against them and to ask what reasons can be given for them, then I have been performing the outsider test since 1972." But has he? I don't think so at all. I don't think any revealed religion can pass the OTF.

Just review with me what Eller, Tarico, and Long have argued in their earlier chapters. Eller argued from cultural anthropology: "Christians are not easily argued out of their religion because, since it is culture, they are not ordinarily argued *into it* in the first place." "Christians," he continues, "like other religionists, are not so much convinced by arguments and proofs as colonized by assumptions and premises. As a form of culture, it seems self-evident to them; they are not so much indoctrinated as enculturated."

Tarico argued from the findings of psychology: "It is easy for us to distort the evidence in our own favor, in part because we aren't so great with evidence in general. One of the strongest built-in mental distortions we have is called *confirmation bias*." She argues that "Once we have a hunch about how things work, we seek information that fits what we already think."

Long argued that "we humans are only partly rational. Bias is our default setting, and most of the distortions happen below the level of conscious awareness." And Long refers us to Michael Shermer's extensive research on why people believe in God and weird things. Nine out of ten people say that other people are influenced by nonrational factors to believe in weird things, and yet these same respondents turn around and say that they are the exceptions to this. How is it possible for nine out of ten respondents to be the exceptions to what nine out of ten of them recognize to be the rule? Logically they cannot all be correct about this. Either 90 percent of them came to their conclusions rationally, which we KNOW is not the case from psychological studies, or the respondents are simply deceiving themselves and are no different than other people. As human beings we have what Shermer calls an *intellectual attribution bias,* "where we consider our own actions as being rationally motivated, whereas we see those of others as more emotionally driven. Our commitment to a belief is attributed to a rational decision and intellectual choice; whereas the other person's is attributed to need and emotion."[30] And Shermer goes on to explain that "[s]mart people, because they are more intelligent and better educated, are better able to give intellectual reasons justifying their beliefs that they arrived at for non-intelligent reasons," even though "smart people, like everyone else, recognize that emotional needs and being raised to believe something are how most of us most of the time come to our beliefs."[31]

So upon what basis do nearly all believers around the world, including Reppert, think they are the exceptions if this is the case? They *cannot* all be the exceptions! Believers are simply in denial when they claim their religious faith passes the OTF. Psychology has repeatedly shown us that people, all people, seek to confirm what they believe, and we also have an intellectual attribution bias to explain away what we intuitively know to be true. We do not come to our conclusions based solely on rational considerations. Because of these biases, *believers should be just as skeptical that their particular religious faith passes the OTF as they are when other believers in other different religions claim the same thing.*

So rather than subjecting his own religious faith "to scrutiny" as Reppert claims to have done, if he had instead subjected his own faith to the same level of skepticism he subjects the other religious faiths he rejects, that would be more impressive to me. Instead, Reppert, like most all Christians, has adopted St. Anselm's motto, "faith seeking understanding" (*fides quaerens intellectum*). Theirs is a faith that calls upon believers to subsequently understand, confirm, and defend what they believe. But such a faith attitude is not conducive to testing what one believes, so long as he or she has faith in the first place. In fact, most Christian thinkers from Tertullian to Luther to William Lane Craig have all disparaged reason in favor of faith. Faith is the warp and woof of Christian theology and apologetics, and it can *only* increase the level of confirmation bias people already have. Maintaining faith is the antithesis to examining whether or not one's faith is true. Until believers repudiate such a faith stance, they cannot claim with a straight face that their faith has passed the OTF. Let me express this same thought within the language game of Christianity: *Faith is not some-*

thing Christians can have while seeking to examine the religion that was given to them, since that is not how they approach any of the other religions they reject.

NOTES

1. It might be that our religious, moral, and political beliefs are culturally relative, which is something David Eller's argument leads us to think in chapter 13 of this collection. But one need not go this far to make this case, since even if humans can and do rationally transcend their respective cultures, it changes very little about the odds of doing so.

2. Daniel Clement Dennett, *Breaking the Spell: Religion as a Natural Phenomenon* (New York: Viking, 2006), p. 32.

3. David Eller, *Atheism Advanced: Further Thoughts of a Freethinker* (Cranford, NJ: American Atheist Press, 2007), p. 233.

4. See *Why I Became an Atheist* (Amherst, NY: Prometheus Books, 2008) pages 67–69. Some sociologists even go so far as to make the claim that reality itself is a social construct in what is called the "Sociology of Knowledge" thesis. There is a great amount of literature on this subject, but one place to start is the classic by Peter L. Berger and Thomas Luckmann, *The Social Construction of Reality: A Treatise in the Sociology of Knowledge* (Garden City, NY: Anchor Books, 1966). See also Peter L. Berger, *The Sacred Canopy: Elements of a Sociological Theory of Religion* (Garden City, NY: Anchor Books, 1990).

5. Stephen Maitzen uses the "uneven distribution of theistic belief around the world" against Christians who argue on behalf of divine hiddenness. In arguing for the best explanation of this data he claims theistic answers to this problem "are less plausible" than naturalistic ones: "[E]ven judged on their own terms, theistic explanations of the geographic lopsidedness of belief look far-fetched compared to naturalistic explanations." See Stephen Maitzen, "Divine Hiddenness and the Demographics of Theism," *Religious Studies* 42 (2006): 177–91, and Stephen Maitzen, "Does Molinism Explain the Demographics of Theism," *Religious Studies* 44 (2008): 473–77. But I'm making a different case with regard to global religious diversity itself. I'm arguing that because of it we should approach all religious faiths with the skepticism of an outsider.

6. I thank William Lobdell for pointing this out to me in his book *Losing My Religion* (New York: Collins, 2009), pp. 280–82. For this evidence, see Simon G. Southerton, *Losing a Lost Tribe: Native Americans, DNA, and the Mormon Church* (Salt Lake City, UT: Signature Books, 2004).

7. Valerie Tarico, *The Dark Side: How Evangelical Teachings Corrupt Love and Truth* (Seattle: Dea, 2006), pp. 221–22.

8. See his blog post: "Miracles and the Golden Rule" at http://exploringourmatrix.blogspot.com.

9. As such, I also maintain Christian theism also fails the *Insider Test for Faith*, since even as an insider I couldn't continue to believe. On this, see the blog http://failingtheinsidertest.blogspot.com/.

10. Found on Common Sense Atheism's Web site, http://commonsense atheism.com/.

11. For this I thank Jason Long's work in *The Religious Condition* (New York: iUniverse, 2008), pp. 74–77.

12. Julia Sweeney, *Letting Go of God*, Disc 2, Track 6, "What If It's True?" Indefatigable, 2006.

13. Eller, *Atheism Advanced*, pp. 202–207.

14. Philip Jenkins, professor of history and religious studies at Pennsylvania State University, tells us of this explosive growth in his book *The Next Christendom: The Coming of Global Christianity*, 2nd ed. (Oxford: Oxford University Press, 2007).

15. See Philip Jenkins, *The New Faces of Christianity: Believing the Bible in the Global South* (Oxford: Oxford University Press, 2006). This is something Eller's first chapter in this book, "The Cultures of Christianities," shows: missionaries actually modify their marketing specifically to exploit local cultural assumptions to leverage belief, so their success elsewhere is more about the religious dependency thesis, and is not evidence against it.

16. See the Pew Forum on Religion and Public Life, "US Religious Landscape Survey," http://religions.pewforum.org/.

17. See Michael Horton, *Christless Christianity: The Alternative Gospel of the American Church* (Grand Rapids, MI: Baker Books, 2008); Roger Finke and Rodney Stark, *The Churching of America, 1776–1990: Winners and Losers in Our Religious Economy* (New Brunswick: Rutgers University Press, 1992); and Rodney Stark and William Sims Bainbridge, *The Future of Religion: Secularization, Revival, and Cult Formation* (Berkeley: University of California Press, 1985).

18. See Richard Feldman, "Reasonable Religious Disagreements," in *Philosophers without Gods*, ed. Louise M. Antony (Oxford: Oxford University Press, 2007).

19. I was a respondent on a panel at the annual meeting of the Society of Biblical Literature in November of 2009 concerning Bill Maher's movie *Religulous*. To read my paper, run a search on my blog for "My Comments at The SBL on Bill Maher's Movie *Religulous*," to be found here: http://debunkingchristianity .blogspot.com/2009/11/my-comments-at-sbl-today.html.

20. In James F. Sennett, ed., *The Analytic Theist: An Alvin Plantinga Reader* (Grand Rapids, MI: Eerdmans, 1998), p. 206.

21. Timothy Keller, *The Reason for God: Belief in an Age of Skepticism* (New York: Riverhead Books, 2008), p. xviii.

22. Ibid., p. 20.

23. Ibid., p. xix.

24. Quoted from William Lane Craig, "Reasonable Faith: Question 68, Subject: The Witness of the Holy Spirit," http://www.reasonablefaith.org/site/.

25. William Irwin, ed., "The Matrix Possibility," in *The Matrix and Philosophy: Welcome to the Desert of the Real* (Chicago: Open Court, 2002), p. 30. For the demon and dream conjectures and more about the Matrix possibility, see my blog post "Is It Faith? The Demon, Dream, and Matrix Conjectures," www.debunkingchristianity .blogspot.com.

26. David Eller, *Natural Atheism*, pp. 132–33. For more, read chapters 5 and 11 in his book *Atheism Advanced*.

27. *Atheism Advanced*, p. xvi.

28. On this, see Richard Carrier, "Defending Naturalism as a Worldview: A Rebuttal to Michael Rea's World without Design," the Secular Web, 2003, http://www.infidels.org/library/modern/richard_carrier/rea.html.

29. Reppert's aims were to help me clarify it, for which I'm thankful, and to also offer some criticisms of it. See his blog, http://dangerousidea.blogspot.com, and run a search for "outsider test," which will produce several posts devoted to it (in reverse chronological order). We also interacted via e-mail.

30. Michael Shermer, *How We Believe: The Search for God in an Age of Science* (New York: W. H. Freeman, 2000), pp. 85–86.

31. Michael Shermer, *Why People Believe Weird Things: Pseudoscience, Superstition, and Other Confusions of Our Time* (New York: A.W.H. Freeman, 2002), p. 299.

Part 2

WHY THE BIBLE IS NOT GOD'S WORD

Chapter 5

THE COSMOLOGY OF THE BIBLE

Edward T. Babinski

U ntil the middle of the nineteenth century most biblical scholars maintained that the religious literature of ancient Israel was unique. However, as the nineteenth century progressed into the twentieth it brought with it increasing knowledge of ancient Near Eastern languages and literature that led biblical scholars to acknowledge that Israel's religion, scriptures, and view of the cosmos mirrored those of her neighbors.

This change came about because of discoveries that revealed what time had kept hidden for thousands of years, namely, the meanings of ancient Egyptian hieroglyphics (etched on walls, stelas, and coffins) and Mesopotamian cuneiform scripts (baked on clay tablets). Their meanings were unknown until archeological discoveries and linguistic breakthroughs revealed them in the 1820s and 1850s respectively.[1] Moreover, from the 1800s until today, archeologists have uncovered tens of thousands of cuneiform tablets that are older than the oldest surviving texts of the Hebrew Bible. George Smith, a pioneer in the study of Mesopotamian myths, published *The Chaldean Account of Genesis* in 1876. Today, scholars from both Catholic and Evangelical Protestant backgrounds agree that ancient Near Eastern views of creation shed considerable light on descriptions of creation found in the Bible. One need only point to the recent spate of books that discuss the many ways Genesis 1 fits into its ancient milieu.[2]

Typically, ancient Near Eastern cosmological writings depict heaven (or sky) and earth (dry, flat land) as the two halves of creation, and they describe ways in which the sky came to be held securely above the earth. They also demonstrate concern that the boundaries of the sea be "set" securely to maintain the dry land, and they imagine what may lie above the sky, beneath the earth, and at its "ends."

The ancients also expressed concern that their particular kingdom and way of life be established forever and as firmly as heaven and earth. For instance, the prologue to the code of laws of a famed king of Babylon, states: "Marduk [high god of Babylon] ... founded an everlasting kingdom, whose foundations are laid as solidly as those of heaven and earth."[3] It is not difficult to see why such a concern proved central in the ancient Near East, where kingdoms of divine (or divinely appointed) kings competed for supremacy. In like manner, some of their myths involved gods competing for supremacy, resulting in the winner(s) creating the world over which he (they) ruled. In contrast, other myths involved no conflict, but depicted a high god acting like a king, simply commanding creation to arise. As Mark S. Smith points out:

> We may identify three major models of creation [creating by divine power, creating with divine wisdom, or creating with some form of the divine presence] all related to kingship.... Power, wisdom, and presence (especially in the palace) are all attributes associated with kings. In addition, the king is responsible for building temples. In accordance with these ideas, various creation accounts present God as a warrior-king, as a wise ruler, or as the great monarchic presence in his palace or builder of his sanctuary space. *All of these were old ideas in the ancient world well before the historical emergence of Israel around 1200 BCE* [emphasis added].[4]

Since the king's power was associated with the power of god(s), it was essential for the king to maintain divine approval. So as kingdom succeeded kingdom, sacred myths were recycled, re-edited, or combined with others.[5] And the names of the winners in these myths were changed to match the names of the gods worshiped by the new regimes. This was only fitting, since the new regimes believed their gods had helped them conquer the old regimes. And to their gods the kings and priests built temples and performed sacred rituals. For they must not risk angering the gods, otherwise the gods could dissolve creation in whole or in part by sending floods (as in *The Epic of Gilgamesh* and Noah's Flood) earthquakes (by shaking heaven and earth), lightning (by casting down fire from heaven), volcanic eruptions (by casting down fire and brimstone), plagues, famines, or invading armies. (Interestingly, ancient texts reveal that the Hebrews employed the same rationalization as their neighbors when it came to explaining why bad things happened to them. It was "divine punishment" due to immorality and lack of proper worship.)[6]

In short, ancient Near Eastern kings, priests, and people were concerned with making sure that their kingdoms—as well as the earth beneath their feet, the waters on their shores, and the sky above their heads—were secure and stable. And they believed the best way to keep things that way was to curry the favor of gods.

With that in mind, let's take a look at the creation and cosmological myths of Egypt and Mesopotamia—civilizations older than Israel—before looking at "biblical cosmology."

EGYPTIAN COSMOLOGY

According to John A. Wilson in *Before Philosophy*, Egyptian concepts of earth and sky/heaven changed slowly over a period of about three thousand years, "with vestiges of prehistoric development partially visible."[7] But their representations left no doubt as to how important the sky's *support* was to them. In one image, heaven was represented as the underbelly of a star-studded celestial cow whose legs were planted firmly on the earth below. They also wrote about "four posts" (not unlike the four legs of the celestial cow) holding up heaven. Wilson adds, "The great distance of the posts was asserted by such expressions as 'I have set ... the terror of thee as far as the four pillars of heaven.' That the posts were four in number suggests they were placed at the limits of the four cardinal directions ... an arrangement that appealed to the Egyptian as being both strong and permanent: '(As firm) as heaven resting upon its four posts' is a simile used more than once."[8]

Heaven was also depicted as an inverted pan with stars on it—and there is an image of a divine Egyptian king holding up the inverted pan of heaven.[9] Another image has the inverted pan of heaven being held up by a semicircle directly beneath it, a semicircle that stretches over a flat earth, reaching from one distant mountain at one horizon to another distant mountain at the opposite horizon, looking like a dome above the earth—such a "wall-ring" representation may have made heaven appear doubly secure and solidly upheld.[10]

Yet another image depicts heaven as a star-studded goddess whose body is arched in a semicircle above a prone earth-god. The goddess's fingers and toes touch the earth's far horizons and support her. Such an image was derived from the idea that heaven and earth arose from two deities (a goddess, named Nut, and a male god) whose bodies were locked in a passionate embrace, but one day they separated (or were separated by a third god), creating enough space between them for heaven and earth to arise. Some images depict this third god, Shu, with his arms raised beneath the goddess of heaven. In the Pyramid Texts, circa 3000 BCE, it says, "The arms of Shu are under Nut, that he may carry her" (utterance 506, 1101c). This third god, Shu, added assurance that heaven would remain securely in place.[11] Some images depict Shu standing on the flat earth with the symbol for mountains on his head, and the mountains are in direct contact with the belly of the sky goddess, which illustrates the idea that "mountains of the horizon provide immediate support of the sky."[12]

Egyptian tales of creation begin with divinities of water, darkness, formlessness and emptiness, as well as air and wind. Creation takes place via a regal command either of the heart or the spoken word. According to the Egyptian *Book of the Dead*, every act of creation represented a thought of a high creator god and its expression in "words." A host of Egyptian creation myths agreed that the agency of creation was the god's "word." They also depicted primeval waters being divided and a primeval hill (the earth) emerging out of those waters. So the earth was understood to be dry land encompassed above, below, and at the furthest horizon by primeval waters.

Lastly, it is important to note that Egyptian ideas of god(s), ranged from crude polytheistic notions to ideas of a most high divinity. Egyptians employed such exalted notions as "The Ancient of Heaven . . . Supporter of the Heavens, Founder of the Earth, Lord of Days, Maker of Light . . . whose eye subdues the wicked, sending forth its darts to the roof of the firmament."[13] "Hail to Thee . . . to the height of the heavens, to the breadth of the earth, to the depths of the sea [compare Job 11:8, 9] . . . who raises the heavens and fixes the earth [compare Job 26:7] . . . causing all things which are to exist."[14] "Who suspended or raised the heaven, who laid down the ground, Father of the fathers of all the gods"[15] or the high god is "one and alone, and none other exists with him—he existed when nothing else existed—he is a spirit—no man knows his form. No man has been able to seek out his likeness—He has stretched out the heavens and founded the earth ... He fashioned men and formed the gods—he gives life to man, he breathes the breath of life into his nostrils...."[16]

In conclusion, ancient Egyptians depicted the earth as the foundation of creation with heaven stretched out above it. Furthermore, they believed a high god or gods made everything, held it firmly in place, and kept at bay primeval waters. As we shall see, this view was common in the ancient Near East.

MESOPOTAMIAN COSMOLOGY

Over the centuries, Mesopotamian kingdoms included those of the Sumerians, Akkadians, Babylonians, Kassites, Hittites, Assyrians, and Chaldeans/Neo-Babylonians, as well as the city-states of Ebla, Ugarit and Emar (to name a few). In general, Mesopotamian and Egyptian tales of creation involved the same basic "elements," that is, darkness and light, wind and water, and a separation of heaven from earth. For instance, a Sumerian myth depicts a single mountain rising out of a primeval sea and an air-god dividing the mountain in two to form heaven and earth, lifting heaven on high. In a Hittite version of the separation of heaven and earth, a saw, or divine cleaver, does the dividing. In Phoenician cosmology, a "world egg" cracks into two equal halves, heaven above and earth below. And in Babylonian and Hebrew versions waters are divided.

The Mesopotamians, like the Egyptians, also placed a high, even magical value, upon "words," and the necessity of obeying spoken commands from kings, priests, and, of course, gods. The pre-Babylonian civilization of Sumeria believed that all things existed and were made by the "word" of a high god named Enki. In fact, they viewed the "word" of all their gods as a definite and real thing—a divine entity or agent. Even Sumerian personal names reflected their belief in the power of the "word," including names like, "The word of the wise one is eternal," "His word is true," and, "The word which he spoke shakes the heavens."[17] A very early Sumerian prayer to a god states, "Thy word upon the sea has been projected and returns not [void]."[18] Compare subsequent Hebrew usage, "So shall my [the Lord's] word be which goeth up from my mouth; it shall not return unto me void; For it shall have done that which I desired" (Isaiah 55:11).

The Babylonian creation epic, *Enuma Elish*, begins, "When on high no name was given to heaven, Nor below was the netherworld called by name. … When no gods at all had been brought forth, None called by names, no destinies ordained,"[19] and adds that before all else there existed primeval waters in the form of two deities, male and female, "their waters comingling." Later in the story, Marduk leads the fight against Tiamat, the female water-deity, depicted as a raging monster. He subdues her and splits her open like a fish for drying (or an opened clamshell) making heaven out of her (as a cover above the watery deep below—for the earth has not yet been made). Marduk stretches out her skin and assigns watchmen, ordering them not to let Tiamat's waters escape, thus allaying ancient fears that creation might be washed away by the waters above. Such a scene may be compared with Genesis 1, where primeval waters are divided by a firmament with the upper waters positioned above the firmament.[20] A Babylonian tablet fragment even mentions a *Tiamat eliti* and a *Tiamat sapliti*, that is an Upper Tiamat (or ocean) and a Lower Tiamat (or ocean), that correspond to the waters above and below the firmament in Genesis 1:7.[21]

Ancient concern over how heaven was secured can also be seen in the depiction of Marduk twisting Tiamat's tail into something he uses to "keep the heavens in place over the earth's surface, and then using Tiamat's crotch as a wedge to hoist the heavens upward and keep them from falling."[22] Heaven and earth are also joined together: "A number of texts refer to cosmic bonds, including 'bonds,' 'lead-ropes,' and 'the great bond,' which secure the heavens in place. (Another text speaks of 'seams' of heaven and earth.)"[23]

According to Wayne Horowitz, author of *Mesopotamian Cosmic Geography*, "Ancient Mesopotamian understandings [of the general shape of the cosmos] remained remarkably constant over the 2,500 years or so from the earliest evidence for cosmography in literary materials through the end of the cuneiform writing.[24] … Heaven is the upper of the two halves of the universe. In ancient Mesopotamia, as in Judeo-Christian tradition, the heavens include both the visible areas [clouds, sun, moon, stars] … and higher regions above the sky, where gods of heaven dwell."[25]

Mesopotamian myths describe the higher regions of the sky as having a stone floor. According to Horowitz, "The floors of each level of the heavens were composed of a different type of stone … These assumptions find support in a parallel from Exodus, where the floor of heaven is apparently built of blue-sapphire brick (Exodus 24:9–10; Ezekiel 1:26–28, 10:1).

... The gods Anu and Igigi apparently stand on stone floors of the Upper and Middle Heavens, just as the God of Israel is apparently standing on a blue 'sapphire' brick heavenly floor in Exodus."[26] Horowitz adds, "The interior of Marduk's cella in the Middle Heavens cannot be seen from earth, but its blue stone floor may be visible as the blue sky. Marduk drew stars on the Lower Heavens."[27] And this heaven was not light-years away, for in the tale of *Etana*, Etana and the eagle are able to fly to the Heaven of Anu.[28]

How were the heavens shaped? Horowitz explains, "Mesopotamians believed that the heavens were extremely broad and high... a number of texts make it clear that the heavens extend over the entire earth's surface."[29] An ancient Near Eastern poem contains the phrase, "Wherever the earth is laid, and the heavens are stretched out."[30] Compare this to Hebrew proclamations concerning how the Lord has stretched out the heavens above the earth: Psalms 33:14, 144:5; Isaiah 40:22, 45:12. It may run counter to today's astronomical wisdom to marvel at the mere fact that the heavens cover the earth below, but to flat-earth-minded ancients, the creation of heaven and its maintenance above the earth, stretched out and covering the entire earth below was indeed an architectural marvel.

Horowitz adds: "The visible heavens were thought to be circular in shape, since the clear sky appears to be a giant circle. Textual evidence for this belief is found in the terms 'circle of the sky,' and 'circle of heaven.'"[31] The word for horizon expressed this boundary between earth and heaven, as it meant "heaven's base," "the base of heaven," or "heaven's edge."[32] Horowitz continues, "... all of the available evidence [among ancient Mesopotamian literature] agrees that the earth's surface ends at the horizon, the place where heaven and earth meet. Yet there is widespread disagreement about the topography of the ends of the earth's surface. Some texts suggest that the ends of the earth's surface are marked by cosmic mountains, while others suggest that the cosmic ocean extends to the ends of the earth. Still others are ambiguous."[33] Such ambiguity demonstrates the ancients' lack of knowledge of the geography of the earth beyond a certain distance. Certainly they knew of mountain ranges at their borders as well as the waters of the Mediterranean Sea, Red Sea, Black Sea, Arabian Sea, and Persian Gulf. But they blended such knowledge into a mythically enhanced geography of the world, which featured far-off cosmic mountains and/or an encircling cosmic ocean. Such haziness concerning what lay at the horizons, combined with the clarity of the divine centrality of their own civilization was a view common to Egyptians, Mesopotamians, and Hebrews, each of whom also believed that their nation lay at the "center of the world."[34]

And just as Mesopotamians spoke of the "circle of the sky," or "circle of heaven," Horowitz adds that they spoke in a similar fashion concerning the flat earth disk, calling it the "circle of the earth" or "circle of the lands," "circle of the four corners," "circle of the four winds," and "circle of the four (regions)." The author of the Babylonian "map of the world" even drew "the limit of the earth's surface as two concentric circles."[35] And as we shall see, such phrases as "the circle of the earth" and the "circle of heaven" are just as much a part of biblical cosmology as they are Mesopotamian cosmology.

Lastly, the Mesopotamians, like the Egyptians, held high-god notions alongside crude polytheistic ones. For instance, consider this prayer exalting a Mesopotamian moon-god, "Merciful, gracious father, who holds all the life of the land in your hand! Lord, your divinity is like the distant heaven, like the broad sea, full of fearfulness... whose deep mind no god penetrates... the source of all things, who sees and protects all creatures! Lord, who determines the destiny of heaven and earth, whose command no one can alter... In the heavens—who is high? You alone are high. On earth—who is high? You alone are high."[36]

In Babylon, Marduk, instead of the moon-god, attained top-god status. In a ritual for the New Year festival, Marduk was invoked in this fashion: "My lord is my god, my lord is my ruler, is there any lord apart from him?"[37] And Nebuchadnezzar II prayed at his accession to Marduk: "Everlasting lord, master of all that exists, grant to the king, whom you love, and whose name you name, all that is pleasant to you. Keep him on the right way... You have created me and entrusted to me the dominion over all peoples. O lord, let me according to your grace, which you pour over them all, love your exalted might, and create in my heart fear of your divinity."[38] And in *Enuma Elish* Marduk is: "The trust of the land, city and people. The people shall praise him forever.... At his name the gods shall tremble and quake.... Who administers justice, uproots twisted testimony, In whose place falsehood and truth are distinguished.... Who uprooted all enemies. ...snuffed out all wicked ones... his name shall be the truth!" (Tablet VI:135–36, 146 and VII:39–40, 43, 45, 54)

After reading such language one cannot help but notice how people of the ancient Near East all attempted to make their high god(s) sound more "supreme" than the rest. Below is a chart comparing accolades bestowed on Marduk (Mesopotamian) with those bestowed on Yahweh/El (Israelite):

[Marduk] shall be 'Lord of All the Gods'.... No one among the gods shall [make himself equal] to him. —*Enuma Elish* Tablet VI:141 and VII:14	Our God is above all gods... God of gods... Lord of lords. —Psalm 135:5 and 136:2, 3
[Marduk] established the holy heavens.... Creator of the earth above the waters, establisher of things on high... who made the world's regions.... He created "places" and fashioned the netherworld. —*Enuma Elish* Tablet VII:16, 83, 89, 135	[God] established the heavens... inscribed a circle on the face of the deep... made firm the skies above... marked out the foundations of the earth. —Proverbs 8:27–28 [God] stretched out the earth above the waters. Psalm 136:6
[Marduk] patterned the days of the year... established the positions of Enlil and Ea [referring to the rotation of stars in the sky]... made the moon appear, entrusted (to him) the night... assigned to the crown jewel of nighttime to mark the day (of the month).... [Marduk] d[efined?] the celestial signs [for religious festivals]... the doorbolt of sunrise... the watches of night and day. —*Enuma Elish* Tablet V:3, 5, 8, 12–13, 23, 44, 46	God said, Let there be lights in the firmament of the heaven to divide the day from the night; and let them be for signs, and for seasons [the literal Hebrew means religious festivals], and for days, and years.... And God made two great lights; the greater light to rule the day, and the lesser light to rule the night: he made the stars also. And God set them in the firmament of the heaven to give light upon the earth. —Genesis 1:14, 16–17
[Marduk] made mankind... creatures with the breath of life... creator of all people. —*Enuma Elish* Tablet VI:33,129 & VII:89	God formed man of the dust of the ground, and breathed into his nostrils the breath of life; and man became a living soul. —Genesis 2:7

[Marduk] shall be the shepherd of…his creatures. —*Enuma Elish* Tablet VI:107	The Lord is my shepherd. —Psalm 23:1
Creation, destruction, absolution, punishment: Each shall be at [Marduk's] command. —*Enuma Elish* Tablet VI:131-32	The One forming light and creating darkness, causing well-being and creating calamity. —Isaiah 45:7
[Marduk's] word is truth, what he says is not changed, Not one god has annulled his utterance. —*Enuma Elish* Tablet VII:151–52	Has [God] said, and will he not do it? Or has he spoken, and will he not make it good? —Numbers 23:19
Word of [Marduk] shall endure, not to be forgotten. —*Enuma Elish* Tablet VII:31–2	The word of our God shall stand forever. —Isaiah 40:8
Let them ever speak of [Marduk's] exaltation, let them sing his praises! —*Enuma Elish* Tablet VII:24	Be exalted, O Lord, in your strength; we will sing and praise your might. —Psalm 21:13
[Marduk's] beneficent roar shall thunder over the earth. —*Enuma Elish* Tablet VII:120	[God's] mighty thunder… rumbles from his mouth…under the whole heaven, and his lightning to the ends of the earth. —Job 26:14 and 37:2–3
[Marduk] crossed vast Tiamat [sea goddess] back and forth in his wrath, Spanning her like a bridge at the place of single combat. —*Enuma Elish* Tablet VII:74	[God] tramples down the waves of the sea. —Job 9:8 [God's] way was in the sea, and his paths in the mighty waters. —Psalm 77:19
[Marduk,] profound of wisdom, ingenious in perception, Whose heart is so deep that none of the gods can comprehend it. —*Enuma Elish* Tablet VII:117–18	[God] does great things, unfathomable, and wondrous works. —Job 9:10 Among the gods there is none like unto thee, O Lord. —Psalm 86:8

Biblical Cosmology

It is apparent from the foregoing that both the Egyptians and Mesopotamians imagined the cosmos as requiring divine support, especially the heavens/sky above a flat earth. They also shared the concept of a cosmic ocean that existed before creation.

And, just as the Egyptians and Mesopotamians told different stories about creation, there is evidence of more than one creation story in the Bible. Mark S. Smith in *The Priestly Vision of Genesis 1* points out that the book of Psalms includes some creation hymns that were probably composed earlier than Genesis 1 and adds that those hymns and other creation passages in the Bible may represent some of the earliest beliefs of the Israelites about creation. However, because Genesis 1 was composed with greater sweep, significance, and priestly precision, and placed at the beginning of the Hebrew Scriptures, those other creation passages lost the prominence they once held.

Some of the earliest creation passages in the Bible depict Yahweh in conflict with watery foes, not unlike Marduk's battle with the primeval water goddess Tiamat, or Baal's battle with the sea god, Yam. Professor Smith has an excellent discussion of such biblical passages in a section of his book subtitled, "Creation as Divine Might." Concerning Psalm 74:12–17, for example, he says that it "makes the divine conflict over the cosmic enemies of the water the basis for the establishment of the sun, moon, and stars as well as the boundaries of the earth."[39] Smith adds that other texts, "such as Psalm 89:9–11, Job 26:7–13, *and* 38:1–11 [also] refer to a divine conflict at the beginning of creation."[40]

Though the Lord's defeat of cosmic foes was sometimes applied metaphorically to the Hebrew defeat of the Egyptians (as in the book of Exodus story about Yahweh splitting the waters of the sea in half and then closing them to smash the Egyptians), the names of the sea monsters defeated by Yahweh in Psalm 74 are found in texts from ancient Ugarit where they are identified as foes whom Baal defeated. Mythical tales of Baal's conquests of sea gods and monsters also parallel those of Marduk, who conquered Tiamat (an ocean goddess and monster), subduing her with his mighty wind and then piercing her. Compare such tales with the image in Job 26:12–13 (from the Jewish Publication Society Hebrew Bible or Tanakh): "By His power He stilled the sea; By His skill He struck down Rahab. By His wind the heavens were calmed; His hand pierced the Elusive Serpent."

Smith goes on to explain the evolving nature of the creation story in the Bible:

Genesis 1 built on and supplanted other Israelite versions of creation that understood the primordial universe as a field of battle between two divine wills. It envisions instead a royal-priestly power beyond all powers, enthroned over the world understood as a holy place similar to a sanctuary.... The royal politics of creation expressed in texts such as *Enuma Elish* and Psalm 74 were replaced partially in Genesis 1 with a priestly order imbued with the proper religious life of the Sabbath ["rest on the seventh day"], and festivals of the priestly calendar [the "appointed times" of Gen. 1:14].[41]

Genesis 1:1 (KJV) states, "In the beginning God created the heaven and the earth."[42] This is a summary of the story that follows, which takes place via steps, not all at once. Another way of translating Genesis 1:1 is "In the beginning when God began to create heaven and earth" (see Smith's discussion and other translations of the Bible).

Genesis 1:2 states, like *Enuma Elish*, that in the beginning nothing had yet been formed/named, "And the earth was without form, and void; and darkness was upon the face of the deep. And the Spirit of God moved upon the face of the waters." Creation stories told by Israel's neighbors start in a similar manner—with a Big Splash rather than a Big Bang—out of which heaven and earth are eventually made (cf. 2 Peter 3:5 in the NT).

The "deep" is mentioned not only in Genesis 1:2 but also in Genesis 49:25, which, according to Smith, "lists blessings of various divine figures, including the 'blessing of Heaven above, blessings of Deep crouching below' (see also Deuteronomy 33:13), and 'Deep' in this passage is feminine [as was the Babylonian sea goddess, Tiamat].... [Moreover,] Heaven and Deep are both divinities related to cosmic origins in earlier West Semitic tradition."[43] Smith adds, "It is not necessary to see a particular Mesopotamian background at work behind Genesis 1 in order to compare *tehom* [the Hebrew "deep"] with Tiamat. This word for ocean occurs in the Ugaritic texts not only in the god-lists, but also in mythological contexts. ...[And,] *tehom* in a battle context is an old West Semitic idea and not just a Mesopotamian one."[44] Nor do all creation stories employ battle contexts. Some are as serene as Genesis 1. One Babylonian story that was recited during the building of temples and that featured Marduk as creator began,

"All lands were sea. Then there was a movement in the midst of the sea." Some Egyptian stories began with a god (Amon) moving over the face of divine waters (Nu).

Continuing, we find that Genesis 1:3–5 describes the first act of creation: "And God said, Let there be light: and there was light. And God saw the light, that it was good: and God divided the light from the darkness. And God called the light Day, and the darkness he called Night. And the evening and the morning were the first day."

God names the first light, "Day," meaning the light of daytime, and sets up a numbered sequence of earth-days. Naturally, if one is writing a story in which every act is performed so that the earth may appear and become the lower half of creation, then there's nothing odd about beginning by creating "earth time." But modern astronomers know the earth is not the lower half of creation, it's a planet, and each planet and moon keep their own unique time, "earth time" is not universal.

At this point in Genesis 1 the "sun, moon, and stars" have not been "made" nor "set in the firmament of heaven," yet daylight exists. The sun was not "made" yet? That is what the text says. Therefore, the daylight of the first three days of creation is a form of light that does not depend on the sun. (In a similar vein, texts from ancient Ugarit, Israel's West Semitic neighbor, mention gods of light, as well as gods of Dawn and Dusk that are separate from gods of Sun and Moon.) Saint Ambrose, an early church father, noted the way daylight preceded sunlight in Genesis 1, and wrote, "Three days [of creation] have passed. No one, meanwhile, has looked for the sun, yet the brilliance of light has been in evidence everywhere.... The light of day is one thing and the light of the sun and moon and stars another.... The day ... has its light ... a serener light.... The sun adds its brilliance to the light of day. This can be seen at the dawn of day or at its setting. There is daylight before the rising of the sun, but it is far from being brilliant."[45]

The above distinction brings to mind another Bible verse, Ecclesiastes 12:2, that says, "... the sun, *or the light*, or the moon, or the stars, be not darkened..." [emphasis added]. The Hebrew word translated as "light" in this passage is *'or*, which is the same word that occurs in the original Hebrew of Genesis 1:3–5, and is there called the light of day. "The light" [of day] is thus placed between "the sun" and "the moon" in order of diminishing brightness, exactly where Ambrose would have agreed it belonged. "Light" is also spoken of as existing by itself in Job 38:19, which asks, "Where is the way where light dwelleth? And as for darkness, where is the place thereof?"

Having compared the events of the first day of creation with the fourth, we now examine the days that lay in between:

> God said, Let there be a firmament in the midst of the waters, and let it divide the waters from the waters. And God made the firmament, and divided the waters which were under the firmament from the waters which were above the firmament; and it was so. And God called the firmament Heaven. And the evening and the morning were the second day. And God said, Let the waters under the heaven be gathered together unto one place, and let the dry land appear: and it was so. And God called the dry land Earth; and the gathering together of the waters called he Seas...and the evening and the morning were the third day. (Genesis 1:6–10, 13 KJV)

Primeval waters are divided by a firmament, creating heaven, after which God commands "waters" to be "gathered together" under the newly created heaven. God names the waters "seas" (thus setting boundaries for the sea, a common ancient Near Eastern concern) and names the dry land "earth." Both halves of creation (sky and dry land) are now made, but are bare and have to be accessorized in the days that follow, adding plants to the earth, adding sun, moon, and stars above the earth, and finally adding animals and humans, a process of filling creation that resembles other creation myths.

One should also note the difference between the words heaven and firmament in the Bible. The Hebrew word for heaven (*shamayin*) appears more than 400 times in the Bible and applies to a wide variety of things, from "birds of heaven, angels of heaven, foundations of heaven, pillars of heaven, to the firmament of heaven" (Genesis 1:14). In contrast, firmament (*raqia'*) only appears 17 times in the Bible. According to Luis I. J. Stadelmann in *The Hebrew Conception of the World*, "*Shamayin* (heaven) designates the space above the earth, including the atmosphere, the region of the clouds, the firmament and God's abode above the firmament," places both seen and unseen overhead. Other Hebrew words translated as "heaven" or "sky" function in a similar, broad manner. But not the Hebrew word for "firmament." The author of Genesis 1 makes clear that it was the creation of a "firmament" in the midst of primeval waters that made heaven/sky possible, as well as earth/dry land.

As Denis Lamoureux, himself an Evangelical Christian, admits in a book review (see note 2), "Scripture clearly states that the firmament was under 'the waters above,' not in them or part of them. Second, if the writer of Genesis 1 had intended 'the waters above' to mean clouds, vapor, or mist 'from which rain comes,' then there were three well-known Hebrew words he could have used (*'anan*, *'ed*, and *nasiy'*; Genesis 9:13, Jeremiah 10:13, and Genesis 2:6, respectively). Instead, he employed the common term for water (*mayim*) five times in Genesis 1:6–8.... Third, the sun, moon, and stars are placed *in* (Hebrew *b*) the firmament on the fourth day of creation, above which lay 'the waters.'"

Additional references to heavenly waters include Psalm 148:3–4, "Praise him, sun, moon, and stars, Praise him, highest heavens, and ye waters that be above the heavens" and Psalm 104:1–3, "O Lord . . . who stretches out the heavens like a curtain: who lays the beams of his chambers in the waters...." The Hebrew word translated as "beams" is *qarah*, which refers to structural beams or timbers for a building. The Hebrew word translated as "chambers" is `aliyah* and specifically means "roof room" or "roof chamber." The passage therefore indicates that the God of the Bible built his heavenly chambers in the cosmic waters above the "roof" of the world (i.e., the firmament of heaven).

Just as there are vast waters above, there are also vast waters beneath the earth. A passage mentioning them is Genesis 7:11–12 concerning the biblical Flood: ". . . on that day all the fountains of the great deep burst forth, and the windows of the heavens were opened" (NRSV). Thus, the waters of the abyss, or the great deep "burst forth" from beneath the earth to inundate the land. And according to the same story, such waters remained in abundance, enough to flood the earth again should God desire, because the Flood ended only after God "closed" the floodgates of the sky and the fountains of the deep, and "promised" not to do such a thing again. So the author presumably thought that such waters—located beneath and above the earth—were without limit and that God was relied upon to set their boundaries, as stated elsewhere in the Bible. In that respect, the story of the Flood agrees with Genesis 1 and with the psalmists who stated that such waters continued to exist "above the highest heavens," near God's own "chambers."

But what is a "firmament"? What does the word mean in the original Hebrew? The Hebrew word *raqia'* (translated as "firmament") means "that which is firmly hammered, beaten out, or stamped (as of metal)."[46] According to Gerhard von Rad in *Genesis: A Commentary*, another word of the same root in Phoenician means "tin dish,"[47] and the Paleo-Hebrew alphabet, used to write early Hebrew, was a regional offshoot of Phoenician.

Even the *Theological Word Book of the Old Testament*, authored by conservative Evangelical Christian scholars R. Laird Harris, Gleason L. Archer, and Bruce K. Waltke, and published by Moody Press, agreed that the Bible verses in which the root of *raqia'* (i.e., *raqa'*) appeared were all related to something solid being spread out, stamped, or pounded down; the following list provides examples of this translation:

Isaiah 42:5 "'spread out' the earth,"
Isaiah 44:24 "'spreading out' the earth"
Psalm 136:6 "'spread out' the earth"
Ezekiel 6:11 "'stamp' your foot"
Ezekiel 25:6 "'stamped' your feet"
II Samuel 22:43 "I 'stamped' them"
Jeremiah 10:9 "'beaten' silver"
Isaiah 40:19 "'plates it' with gold"
Exodus 39:3 "'hammer out' gold leaf"
Numbers 16:39 "'hammered (bronze censers) out' as a plating for the altar"

Note the description in Job 37:18 where we read the following in the KJV: "Hast thou with him spread out the sky, which is strong, and as a molten looking glass?" The Hebrew word translated as "spread out" is *raqa'*, as in the cases already mentioned. In addition, the Hebrew word translated as "strong" is *chazaq*, which means "strong," "hard," or "firm." In ancient times, mirrors were made of polished metal, not glass, as they were during the time of King James. The NEB translation of the verse follows the meanings of the key Hebrew words more closely and is clearer than is the version in the KJV: "Can you beat out the vault of the skies, as he does, hard as a mirror of cast metal?" T. H. Gaster in his article on "Heaven" for *The Interpreter's Dictionary of the Bible* comments: "Job's expression finds a parallel in the 'brazen heaven' of the ancient Greeks, while, somewhat similarly, heaven is described in ancient Egyptian sources and occasionally by Homer as made of iron."[48]

Another example of the idea that something firm lay overhead is found in Proverbs 8:27–28 (NRSV): "When [God] established the heavens, [wisdom] was there, when he drew a circle on the face of the deep, when he made firm the skies above, when he established the fountains of the deep." The Hebrew word translated as "firm" is *'amats*, which, according to the authoritative *Brown Driver Briggs Hebrew and English Lexicon*, has a specific meaning of "be stout, strong..." and also "to make firm, strengthen."[49] According to *The Hebrew and Aramaic Lexicon of the Old Testament* (Koehler/ Baumgartner), the meaning of *'amats* is "be hard" and "to make firm."[50]

Therefore, three different passages in the Bible, Genesis 1:6–8, Job 37:18, and Proverbs 8:27–28, use three different words to indicate (with remarkable unanimity) that the biblical sky, or heaven, is strong, hard, or firm. (Speaking of firmness, Genesis 1 is not the only place in the Bible that mentions a firmament. Ezekiel 1:22, 26 describes one with the Lord's throne above it, and the wings of angels "stretched out straight" beneath it, a firmament of "crystal," literally, the "eye of awesome ice.")

What was the shape of the earth according to the Bible? Isaiah 40:22 provides the answer: "It is he that sitteth upon the circle (Hebrew, *chug*) of the earth, and the inhabitants thereof are as grasshoppers; that stretcheth out the heavens as a curtain, and spreadeth them out as a tent to dwell in." Because this passage mentions "the circle of the earth," some people interpret it as a description of a spherical earth. But they are ignoring the context of the verse that has nothing in it implying sphericity, only "*tent*-icity," since God "sits upon the circle" and spreads heaven out like a "tent to dwell in." The Hebrew word *chug* has a primary meaning of "circle" and no lexicon of ancient Hebrew offers "sphere" as a meaning for *chug*. Moreover, see the previous section on Mesopotamian cosmology for references to "circle of the earth," and other phrases they employed with "circle" in them to depict the earth, including the Babylonian map of the world that depicts the limits of the flat earth's surface as two concentric circles. Therefore, the phrase "circle of the earth" is not unique at all and was already in use by flat-earth-believing Mesopotamians long before the book of Isaiah was written. Elsewhere in Isaiah, the most the author says of the earth is that God "spread it out" (literally pounded or flattened it out) at creation (Isaiah 42:5 and 44:24). So there does not appear to be a single verse in the Bible that depicts the earth as a sphere.[51]

On the other hand, there are numerous incidental phrases as well as entire passages in the Bible that support the conclusion that its authors believed the earth to be flat. Take the phrase "the ends of the earth," which arose among people whose creation stories easily illustrate their flat-earth beliefs, a phrase just as ubiquitous in the Bible as it is in Mesopotamian literature. Deuteronomy 13:7 speaks of "the people that are round about you... from one end of the earth even unto the other end of the earth." Isaiah 40:28

says, "[the Lord is] the Creator of the ends of the earth." Job 28:24 states, "He looks to the ends of the earth, and sees everything under the heavens." Also note the use of "the ends of the earth" in Job 38:12–13, in which God asks Job: "Hast thou commanded the morning… that it might take hold of the ends of the earth, that the wicked might be shaken out of it?" God is comparing the earth to a blanket or garment picked up at one end and shaken. The dawn grasps the earth by its "extremity or hem" (Hebrew, *kanap*; see Numbers 15:38 and 1 Samuel 15:27) and shakes the wicked out of it. This is immediately followed in the same chapter of Job by the depiction of the earth as a piece of clay (presumably a clay tablet, something flat and stationary) whose surface is changed by the impression of a seal (the sun) pressed or rolled across it, after which, the earth's "features stand out like those of a garment."[52] Those two verses in Job employ at least two flat metaphors for the earth in a row: (1) grabbing the "ends of the earth" like a blanket or garment to shake out, (2) a [flat] clay tablet, and end with the echo of a third flat metaphor since the author returns to comparing the earth to a "garment." Neither does Job refrain from implying the earth's flatness in other passages. For instance, Job 11:9, "[God's] measure is longer than the earth, and broader than the sea" and Job 38:5, "Who stretched the line on [the earth]?" and Job 38:4, 6, in which God asks Job, "Where were you when I laid the foundation of the earth?… On what were its bases sunk? Or who laid its cornerstone?"

The Bible not only speaks of the "the ends of the earth," but also mentions "the ends of heaven" (compare "heaven's edge" in Mesopotamian cosmology). In Psalm 19:1–6 we find: "The heavens declare the glory of God; and the firmament shows his handiwork…. In them he set a tabernacle for the sun…. [The sun's] going forth is from the end of the heaven, and his circuit unto the ends of it" (KJV). The phrase "from the one side of heaven unto the other" also occurs in Deuteronomy 4:32. And in Deuteronomy 30:3–4 (NJB) Yahweh says, "Should you [my people] have been banished to the very sky's end [the outmost parts of heaven], Yahweh your God will gather you again even from there, will come there to reclaim you." The Hebrew word translated as "outmost" is *qatseh*, which has the meaning of "end" or "extremity," and is the same Hebrew word used in the phrase "end of the earth" in most occurrences. The NT (Matthew 24:31) echoes the same phrase, "His angels… shall gather together his elect from the four winds, from one end of heaven to the other." So the "ends of heaven" parallel the "ends of the earth" in the Bible just as they did in ancient Mesopotamian cosmology.

Flat-earth beliefs remained popular between the time of the last book of the OT and the first book of the NT, also called the intertestamental period. One book composed during that period says, "I went to the ends of the earth...and...I saw the ends of the earth whereon the heaven rests" (*The Book of Enoch* 33:1–2).[53]

The book of Daniel, a late addition to the OT (and a book that scholars argue was probably produced during the intertestamental period like the *Book of Enoch*), provides a further example of how biblical authors took for granted the flatness of the earth. In Daniel 4:10–11, Nebuchadnezzar has a dream and asks Daniel to interpret it: "I saw, and behold, a tree in the midst of the earth, and the height thereof was great. The tree grew, and was strong, and the height thereof reached unto heaven, and the sight thereof to the end of all the earth." If a tree's height was indeed so "great" that it "reached unto heaven" then it might very well be seen to the "ends of the earth" on a flat earth. But the same does not apply to a sphere. Another verse parallels the one in Daniel, and is found in the NT, where Jesus is taken by the devil to the top of a "very high" mountain and there shown "all the kingdoms of the world (literally, 'cosmos')" (Matthew 4:8). Both cases speak of something "very high" or of "great height that reaches unto heaven," which allows the entire world to see it (or allows the whole world to be seen from it), which is true on a flat earth, but not on a spherical one.

What supported the flat earth securely in the midst of primordial waters? The ancients could only guess, and they relied heavily upon a belief that the earth was kept safe and secure due to the unsearchable wisdom and magical might of the god(s). For instance, an Egyptian drawing of the earth disc found in Othmar Keel's *Symbolism of the Biblical World*, shows a deity with long arms that extend from one end of the earth disc to the other holding it in place from below. There is also an Egyptian story about the creator god Kephra whose first act of conquering primordial disarray was to conceive a secure place on which to stand. One Babylonian story has Marduk establish the earth as a floating reed mat above primeval waters. The authors of the Bible were equally in the dark when it came to knowing how the earth was established/fixed or what lay beneath it. The prophet Jeremiah exclaims in effect that "the foundations of the earth can [never] be searched out below," for it is more likely that they will be searched out than that God will cast off Israel, which is another way of saying, "never" (31:37). There are also plenty of Bible passages about how Yahweh established, fixed, founded, and continuously preserves the world via his wisdom and might (Psalm 102:25, Proverbs 3:19, Jeremiah 51:15). Consider Isaiah 48:13, "Mine hand also hath laid the foundation of the earth, and my right hand hath spanned the heavens: when I call unto them, they stand up together." Or Isaiah 44:24, "[He] stretched out the heavens and spread out the earth." Sometimes a verse will say that God established or founded the earth "upon the seas, waters, rivers, deeps" (Psalm 24:2). In all such cases, the ancients explained the earth's support by handing out accolades to their respective god(s)' miraculous, mysterious might.

Sometimes "pillars" were suggested as supports for the earth, as in 1 Samuel 2:8, "... for the pillars of the earth are the Lord's, and he hath set the world upon them." Job 9:6 states: "[God] shaketh the earth out of her place [earthquake], and the pillars thereof tremble." The Hebrew word translated as "pillars" here is `ammud, which has the meaning of "pillar" or "column." Also see Job 38:4–6, "Where were you when I laid the earth's foundations? Tell me, since you are so well-informed! ... What supports its pillars at their bases? Who laid its cornerstone?" (NJB) and Psalm 75:3, "The earth and all the inhabitants thereof are dissolved: I bear up the pillars of it."

Regardless of how the biblical earth is held in place;[54] verses throughout the Bible agree that the earth is immovable, moving only in the case of earthquakes—again, something only God can produce. Psalm 93:1 states, "the world also is established [or fixed] that it cannot be moved." Psalm 96:10 makes a similar statement: "the world also shall be established that it shall not be moved." Another such statement is found in 1 Chronicles 16:30: "the world also shall be stable, that it be not moved." And Psalm 104:5 states "[God] laid the foundations of the earth, that it should not be removed for ever."

The Bible confirms this depiction by stating that everything moves *but* the earth. Take Ecclesiastes 1:5: "The sun rises and the sun sets, and *hurries back to where it rises*" (NIV) [emphasis added]. Compare Psalm 19:4–6, "In [the heavens] He [God] has placed a tent for the sun, which is as a bridegroom coming out of his chamber; it rejoices like a strong man to run its course, its rising from one end of the heavens, and its circuit to the other end of them." Such a depiction is reminiscent of ancient Mesopotamian beliefs. In *The Shamash Hymn*, the Sun-god is said to "continuously cross the heavens, daily ... pass over the vast earth," and in a different text the sun is described as moving, "as far as the edge of heaven, as far as the edge of earth, from the mountain of sunrise to the mountain of sunset."[55]

Bible verses that further illustrate their authors' belief in the movement of the sun include Job 9:7, "He [God] can command the sun not to rise." That God would direct his command at the sun rather than the earth implies a belief in a stationary earth. Likewise, Joshua directed his commands at both the sun and moon, even commanding the sun to stand still "over Gibeon," and the moon "over the valley of Aijalon" (Joshua 10:12).

The Bible also teaches that stars "course" through the sky each night (Judges 5:20), and God "brings them out one by one" and "because of His great power not one of them is missing" (Isaiah 40:26). Compare *Enuma Elish* VII:130, which states, "He [Marduk] shall maintain the motions of the stars of heaven." In addition, Job 38:31–33 (NASB) states that constellations are "led forth" by God, as when God asks Job rhetorically, "Can you lead forth a constellation in its season, And guide the Bear with her satellites? Do you know the ordinances of the heavens, Or fix their rule over the earth?"

But anyone with knowledge of astronomy knows that the reverse is true of all the biblical truths above. The sun does not "hurry back to where it rises," the earth spins. Commanding "the sun" not to move, makes as little sense as someone in a moving car commanding the scenery not to move. The stars do not have "courses," they only *appear* to move in a large circle round the pole star each night due to the earth's rotation. God does not "bring the stars out one by one by His great power," there is no "great power" involved, it is the diminishing intensity of the sun's rays reflecting off the atmosphere that "brings out the stars." (Though to St. Philastrius in the fourth century CE the words of Scripture were irrefutable divine teachings, including those about God bringing out the stars from his treasure-house and hanging them in the sky every evening, to deny which was heresy and "false to the Catholic faith.") Neither do "none of the stars go missing" when God "by His great power brings them out" because sometimes stars explode into dust.[56] Neither does God "lead forth," and "guide" constellations, they only *appear* to twirl around nightly (and dip high, low, or vanish for months beneath the horizon) due to the earth's rotation and its revolution around the Sun.

Some Christians and conservative Jews continue to defend geocentrism, asking their brethren, "Does the Bible depict God 'commanding,' 'leading forth,' and 'stopping' things that don't really move?" They add that "God's might is evidenced in His ability to shake an otherwise immovable earth (Job 9:6; 2 Samuel 22:8; Joel 2:10; Isaiah 13:13; Revelation 6:12–13), and in His ability to lead forth and guide constellations, and direct His command at the sun to make it stop moving. Such actions are either demonstrations of God's might, or, mighty deceptive language for God to have inspired." Therefore, they say, "If you take the Bible at its word you ought to be a geocentrist!" Ironically, the same point is made by creationists, "If you take the Bible at its word you ought to be a creationist!" But, as we have seen in this chapter, taking the Bible at its word also means thinking in terms of a flat earth.

Another aspect of the biblical cosmos to consider is that God's abode in heaven was not imagined to lay light-years away. The author of Psalm 103:11–12 drew a parallel between "as high as heaven is above the earth" and the distance "from the east to west" on the earth. And the author of Psalm 139:8–9 drew a parallel between the distance from heaven to Sheol (beneath the earth) and the distance from the light of dawn to the remotest part of the sea. So in the mind of the psalmists, distances from one part of the earth to another part of the earth paralleled the distance to heaven above.

We read in the Tower of Babel story that the Lord "came down [from heaven] to see the city and the tower that the men were building…the tower whose top may reach unto heaven" (Genesis 11:4–5—and see Psalm 144:5 and 2 Samuel 22:10 for added examples of Yahweh "coming down from heaven"). After taking a peek at what the builders were doing, the Lord felt the need to scatter them over the face of the earth, perhaps because, "The heavens are the heavens of the Lord's, but the earth He has given to man" (Psalm 115:16). The Lord also "stretches out the heavens like a tent and lays the beams of his upper chambers on their waters. He makes the clouds his chariot and rides on the wings of the wind" (Psalm 104:2–3). In Isaiah 14:12–17 the king of Babylon is depicted as a Canaanite deity, the "Morning Star, son of Dawn," and declares, "I will ascend to heaven; I will raise my throne above the stars of God, and I will sit on the mount of assembly in the recesses of the north. I will ascend above the heights of the clouds; I will make myself like the Most High" (Isaiah 14:13–14, NASB). The Lord "treads upon the high places of the earth" (Amos 4:13). High-flying birds are thought to fly across the face of the firmament (Genesis 1:20). Angels (cherubim and seraphim) are depicted with bird-like wings. People like Elijah and Jesus ascend from the earth to heaven (2 Kings 2:11; Acts 1:9–11, 7:56). Stories of ascents and descents from heaven appear throughout the Bible (Genesis 28:12; Proverbs 30:4; Luke 2:15; John 1:51; Acts 10:11; 1 Thessalonians 4:16, 17). "Manna," a type of food, falls from heaven (Exodus 16, Numbers 11, Deuteronomy 8). Fire and lightning also fall from heaven, parceled out at the Lord's discretion (on par with other ancient deities). Even a city is depicted as descending from heaven to earth (Revelation 3:12, 21:2).[57] If the ancients did not believe heaven was so near, and heavenly beings so attentive and active, they wouldn't have been as concerned with appeasing them or seeking their blessings—yet these were universal concerns in the ancient Near East.

The god(s) were perched on a celestial balcony, so to speak, gazing at the drama below, handing out blessings and curses to individuals and nations alike; at least that's what the people believed who built the temples, founded the priesthoods, invented holy rituals, and performed burnt offerings (so the smoke would ascend to heaven as a "soothing aroma"—see Genesis 8:21; Exodus 29:18, 25; Leviticus 3:16, 6:21 and Numbers 15:3, 10). Moreover, the Israelites shared with their neighbors the eastward orientation of their tabernacle and temple, the placement of important cultic objects within them, the designation of areas of increasing holiness, rules for access to the Holy Place and Holy of Holies, as well as practices like circumcision and sacrificial offerings.[58] Like other nations, they feared the anger of their god and subsequent punishment if attention was denied him. The duty of kings and priests was to ensure such attention was maintained, for the safety and security of the nation.

Do we feel the coziness or the peculiar dread of such a cosmos anymore, one in which god(s) live overhead? Such feelings have diminished greatly since the invention of the telescope that allowed humans to peer more deeply into the "heavens of the Lord." Its invention signaled the beginning of the end of belief in both a stationary earth and in a starry firmament with waters above it—beliefs held by Christians for fifteen hundred years.[59]

Today, even conservative Christians, such as John Walton, professor of Old Testament at Wheaton College, find that they cannot deny the relevance of studying ancient cosmologies when it comes to understanding Genesis 1:

The Israelites [like the nations around them] did not know that stars were suns; they did not know that the earth was spherical and moving through space; they did not know that the sun was much further away than the moon, or even further than the clouds or high-flying birds. They believed that the sky was material (not vaporous), solid enough to support the residence of the deity as well as hold back waters.[60]

But Walton's admission is just the tip of the iceberg. What about the news that Genesis 1 is probably not the earliest Mesopotamian creation story, nor even the earliest Hebrew creation story? What about the news that Hebrew conceptions of their cosmos, their god, and their religious rituals all owe a great deal to their cultural milieu? What about the fact that flat-earth themes run through the entire Bible (i.e., the creation of the firmament, God "coming down" to see the Tower of Babel, Elijah's ascension into heaven, Jesus' ascension, and the New Jerusalem descending from heaven)? Today the first eleven chapters of Genesis are commonly conceded to be mythological tales of "primeval history" composed by people who deemed their founding myths, high god(s), and places of worship "central."

In light of the preponderance of evidence presented here, it's clear the Bible is a product of the prescientific period in which it originated. Furthermore, if there are any "words of God" in the Bible it appears that human beings are the ones picking and choosing among them as to which those might be, which to emphasize, which to deemphasize, which to praise, which to question, and how to interpret them.

Lastly, the cosmos that telescopes and space probes have revealed is not nearly as cozy a place as the ancient one we have examined, though it does feature a peculiar dread all its own, namely that our planet is a tiny life raft bobbing in space with far less fortunate rafts bobbing over to our left and right. Neither does our world appear to be inhabited by heavenly beings above and shades in Sheol below. Instead we live on the thin outer layer of our planet's shifting surface. Moving just five miles beyond that layer up or down we would die from lack of oxygen or boil from the heat. And our world remains vulnerable to solar flares, collisions with other objects, nearby novas, or to any star sailing close enough to disrupt planetary orbits. So any number of probable catastrophes from space could cripple or annihilate human civilization. And none of these inherent dangers seem to have anything to do with whether or not gods are appeased. Neither does our cosmos show any evidence that dire events on Earth must entail the destruction and recreation of a "new heaven and earth," as the author of the last book in the Bible appears to presume. If our planet was obliterated tomorrow, the stars of over 100 billion galaxies would continue to shine for billions of years. And there are planets aplenty in this cosmos if one judges by the over four hundred detected around nearby stars. Maybe elsewhere in this cosmos there are even sentient beings, lacking telescopes, who are beginning to compose their own creation myths?

NOTES

1. Discoveries such as the Rosetta Stone and the Behistun Inscription revolutionized studies of hieroglyphs and cuneiform, respectively. The Rosetta Stone is inscribed with the same declaration written in three different scripts: Egyptian hieroglyphics, Egyptian demotic, and classical Greek. Using the Greek inscription as a guide, scholars were able to decipher hieroglyphs by 1822. The Behistun Inscription is similar to the Rosetta Stone in that it also featured a declaration in three different scripts that enabled cuneiform to be deciphered in the 1850s.

2. Mark S. Smith, Othmar Keel, John H. Walton, and Kenton L. Sparks (respectively, two Catholic and two Evangelical Protestant scholars) are the authors of some superb books on the meaning of Genesis 1 in its cultural context. See the following works:

Mark S. Smith, *The Priestly Vision of Genesis 1* (Minneapolis, MN: Fortress Press, 2009).

Othmar Keel and Silvia Schroer, *Creation: Biblical Theology in the Context of Ancient Near Eastern Religion* (Winona Lake, IN: Eisenbrauns, Forthcoming, Spring 2010).

Othmar Keel, *The Symbolism of the Biblical World: Ancient Near Eastern Iconography and the Book of Psalms* (Winona Lake, IN: Eisenbrauns, 1997).

John H. Walton, *The Lost World of Genesis One: Ancient Cosmology and the Origins Debate* (Downers Grove, IL: IVP Academic, 2009).

Walton, "Interpreting the Bible as an Ancient Near Eastern Document," in *Israel: Ancient Kingdom or Late Invention? Archaeology, Ancient Civilizations, and the Bible*, pp. 298–327, ed. D. Block (Nashville, TN: Broadman/Holman, 2008).

Walton, *Ancient Near Eastern Thought and the Old Testament: Introducing the Conceptual World of the Hebrew Bible* (Grand Rapids, MI: Baker Academic, 2006).

Walton, "Ancient Near Eastern Background Studies," in *Dictionary for Theological Interpretation of Scripture*, eds. K. Vanhoozer et al. (Grand Rapids, MI: Baker, 2005).

Walton, *New International Version Application Commentary: Genesis* (Grand Rapids, MI: Zondervan, 2001).

Kenton L. Sparks, *God's Word in Human Words: An Evangelical Appropriation of Critical Biblical Scholarship* (Grand Rapids, MI: Baker Academic, 2008).

Sparks, "*Enuma Elish* and Priestly Mimesis: Elite Emulation in Nascent Judaism," *Journal of Biblical Literature* 126, no. 4 (2007): 625–48.

Sparks, *Ancient Texts for the Study of the Hebrew Bible: A Guide to the Background Literature* (Peabody, MA: Hendrickson, 2005).

G. K. Beale and John N. Oswalt (Evangelical Christian professors of NT and OT, respectively) agree with their brethren above that Genesis 1 should not be used as the basis for "creation science." Neither should isolated verses be plucked from the Bible and treated as evidence of divine foreknowledge of modern science [my summation of e-mail communications with both professors]. On the other hand, both agree that the wealth of parallels between the Bible and ancient Near Eastern myths are impinging uncomfortably on a belief in the "inerrancy of Scripture," so they each offer slightly different means by which to try to defend the Bible's uniqueness. [Beale, *The Erosion of Inerrancy in Evangelicalism: Responding to New Challenges to Biblical Authority* (Wheaton, IL: Crossway Books, 2008); Oswalt, *The Bible among the Myths: Unique Revelation or Just Ancient Literature?* (Grand Rapids, MI: Zondervan, 2009).] Two Evangelicals have reviewed Beale's book and explained why Genesis 1 and other parts of the Bible present falsifiable statements regarding cosmology that cannot be explained away solely as "temple imagery" (as Beale had hoped): Peter Enns, the *Bulletin for Biblical Research* 19, no. 4 (2009): 628–31, http://aboulet.files.wordpress .com/2010/01/ennsbbrreview.pdf; and Denis O. Lamoureux, "The Erosion of Biblical Inerrancy, or Toward a More Biblical View of the Inerrant Word of God?" http://www.asa3.org/asa/PSCF/2010/ PSCF6-10Lamoureux.pdf.

The following are additional works by Evangelical Christians who agree that the ancient Near Eastern milieu of Genesis 1 needs to be taken more seriously by their fellow Evangelicals:

Paul H. Seely, "The Firmament and the Water Above, Part I: The Meaning of *Raqia'* in Gen 1:6–8" *Westminster Theological Journal* 53 (1991): 227–40, http://faculty.gordon.edu/hu/bi/Ted_Hildebrandt/OTeSources/ 01-Genesis/Text/Articles-Books/Seely-Firmament-WTJ.pdf;

Seely, "The Firmament and the Water Above, Part II: The Meaning of 'The Water above the Firmament' in Gen 1:6–8," *Westminster Theological Journal* 54 (1992): 31–46," http://www.thedivinecouncil.com/seely pt2.pdf;

Seely, "The Geographical Meaning of 'Earth' and 'Seas' in Genesis 1:10," *Westminster Theological Journal* 59 (1997): 231–55, http://faculty

.gordon.edu/hu/bi/Ted_Hildebrandt/OTeSources/01-Genesis/
Text/Articles-Books/Seely_EarthSeas_WTJ.pdf;

Seely, "The Date of the Tower of Babel and Some Theological Implications," *Westminster Theological Journal* 63, no. 1 (2001): 15–38, http://
faculty.gordon.edu/hu/bi/Ted_Hildebrandt/OTeSources/01
-Genesis/Text/Articles-Books/Seely_Babel_WTJ.pdf;

Seely, "The Three-Storied Universe," *American Scientific Affiliation* 21, no. 18
(March 1969): 18–22, http://www.asa3.org/ASA/PSCF/1969/JASA3
-69Seely.html;

Seely, "The First Four Days of Genesis in Concordist Theory and in Biblical Context," *American Scientific Affiliation: Perspectives on Science & Christian Faith* 49 (June 1997): 85–95, http://www.asa3.org/ASA/
PSCF/1997/PSCF6-97Seely.html;

Denis O. Lamoureux, *Evolutionary Creation: A Christian Approach to Evolution*
(Eugene, OR: Wipf & Stock, 2008);

Lamoureux, "Lessons from the Heavens: On Scripture, Science and Inerrancy,"
Perspectives on Science and Christian Faith 60, no. 1 (March 2008): 4–15,
http://www.asa3.org/ASA/PSCF/2008/PSCF3-08Lamoureux.pdf;

Gordon J. Glover, *Beyond the Firmament: Understanding Science and the Theology
of Creation* (Chesapeake, VA: Watertree Press, 2007), http://www.blog
.beyondthefirmament.com/;

Stephen C. Meyers, *A Biblical Cosmology* (master's thesis at Westminster Theological Seminary, 1989), http://www.bibleandscience.com/bible/
books/genesis/genesis1_toc.htm;

Meyers, "The Bible and Science: Do the Bible and Science Agree?" http://
www.bibleandscience.com/science/bibleandscience.htm;

Robert J. Schneider, "Does the Bible Teach a Spherical Earth?" *Perspectives
on Science and Christian Faith* 53 (September 2001): 159–69, http://
www.asa3.org/ASA/PSCF/2001/PSCF9-01Schneider.html;

R. Christopher Heard, "Why I Am Not a Creationist," *Higgaion*, November
18, 2005, http://www.heardworld.com/higgaion/2005/11/why-i-am-
not-creationist.html.

Essential works include Wayne Horowitz, *Mesopotamian Cosmic Geography*
(Winona Lake, IN: Eisenbrauns, 1998); Luis I. J. Stadelmann, *The Hebrew Conception
of the World: A Philological and Literary Study* (Rome: Pontifical Biblical Institute,
1970); and Richard J. Clifford, *Catholic Biblical Quarterly Monograph Series: Creation
Accounts in the Ancient Near East and in the Bible* 26 (Washington, DC: The Catholic
Biblical Association of America, 1994).

3. *Hammurabi's Code of Laws*, translated into English by L. W. King in 1910
[available online]. The stela containing the Code of Hammurabi was discovered

in 1901. The Code of Hammurabi was one of several sets of laws in the ancient Near East. Earlier collections of laws include the *Code of Ur-Nammu*, king of Ur (ca. 2050 BCE); the *Laws of Eshnunna* (ca. 1930 BCE); the codex of *Lipit-Ishtar of Isin* (ca. 1870 BCE); Hittite laws, and Assyrian laws. These codes come from similar cultures in a relatively small geographical area, and they have passages that resemble each other. The text of the Code of Hammurabi was redacted for 1,500 years, and is considered the predecessor of Jewish and Islamic legal systems. See David P. Wright, *Inventing God's Law: How the Covenant Code of the Bible Used and Revised the Laws of Hammurabi* (London: Oxford University Press, 2009).

4. Smith, *Priestly Vision*, pp. 11–12.

5. Victor Hurowitz, "The Genesis of Genesis: Is the Creation Story Babylonian?" *Bible Review* 21 (2005): 52: "The author of *Enuma Elish* is deliberately attributing to Marduk and Babylon acts ascribed to other gods and cities in other myths. The author is stealing the thunder of these gods, undermining them in favor of Marduk. When Marduk receives Ellil's fifty names, he in effect becomes Ellil. When the gods build Babylon instead of Nippur, Babylon becomes the new religious capital.... *Enuma Elish* is a story about Marduk that challenges a[n earlier] story about Ninurta. It reflects a political-theological competition over primacy in the pantheon and supremacy of the capital city.... These tales of Marduk's [supremacy] spawned debate. An ancient Babylonian commentary praises Marduk; an Assyrian commentary satirizes him.... The ancient Near East was full of conflicting claims to supremacy of this or that god or city over all others. The Bible is part of this polemic." For more on the historical development of both Mesopotamian and Hebrew creation myths see Smith, *Priestly Vision*, pp. 18–21, 136–37, 150, 182–83.

6. For example, after Babylon had been plundered by the king of Assyria, the next king of Babylon interpreted that invasion as a punishment sent by Babylon's high god who had been angered by his own people: "[The citizens of Babylon] had oppressed the weak, and handed the weak into the power of the strong. Inside the city there was tyranny, receiving of bribes, people plundering each other's things, sons cursing fathers in the street, slaves cursing masters, they put an end to offerings [to the gods], they laid hands on the property of the temple of the gods, and sold silver, gold and precious stones.... Marduk [the high god of Babylon] grew angry and devised evil to overwhelm the land and destroy the peoples," cf. W. G. Lambert, *Babylonian Wisdom Literature* (London: Oxford University Press, 1960), p. 5.

7. John A. Wilson, "Egypt," *Before Philosophy*, ed. H. Frankfort (Baltimore, MD: Penguin Books, 1967), p. 53.

8. Ibid., pp. 54–55.

9. Keel, *Symbolism*, p. 28.

10. Ibid., pp. 26, 37.

11. Wilson, "Egypt," pp. 55–56. Paul Seely adds, "A number of texts speak of the time when the sky was literally separated from the earth. Pyramid Text 1208c specifically mentions the time 'when the sky was separated from the earth.' Text 1156c mentions that 'his (Shu's) right arm supports the sky;' and 2013a says, 'Thou art a god who supports the sky.' Coffin Texts (ca. 2050 to 1800 BC) reiterate these ideas of the sky needing support, for example, spells 160, 366, 378, and 664. And Text 299a implies that if the supporting arms of Shu were hacked off, the sky would fall." ["The Firmament and the Water Above, Part I," p. 231.]

12. Keel, *Symbolism*, pp. 31, 33, 36.

13. Raymond van Over, ed., "Egyptian Hymns to the Creator," in *Sun Songs: Creation Myths from around the World* (New York: New American Library, 1980), pp. 286–88, 289–91.

14. Raymond van Over, ed., "Hymn to Amen-Ra," in *Sun Songs: Creation Myths from around the World* (New York: New American Library, 1980), pp. 289–91.

15. *The Context of Scripture: Canonical Compositions from the Biblical World*, vol. 1, ed. William Hallo (Leiden: Brill, 1997), pp. 38–39; Walter Beyerlin, ed., John Bowden, trans., in collaboration with Hellmutt Brunner et al., *Ancient Near Eastern Texts Relating to the Old Testament* (Princeton: Princeton University Press, 1969), p 365

16. E. A. Wallis Budge, *The Egyptian Book of the Dead: The Papyrus of Ani* (New York: Dover, 1967, a reprint of the 1895 edition), pp. xcii–xciii.

17. Stephen Herbert Landgon, "Word (Sumerian and Babylonian)," *The Encyclopedia of Religion and Ethics*, vol. 12, ed. James Hastings (New York: Charles Scribner's Sons, 1922), pp. 749–52.

See also, Helmer Ringgren, *Word and Wisdom: Studies in the Hypostatization of Divine Qualities and Functions in the Ancient Near East* (Lund, Germany: H. Ohlssons boktr., 1947).

And Frederick L. Moriarty, "Word as Power in the Ancient Near East," in *Light Unto My Path: Old Testament Studies in Honor of Jacob M. Myers*, eds. Howard N. Bream and Carey A. Moore (Philadelphia: Temple University, 1974), pp. 345–62, http://www.biblicalstudies.org.uk/pdf/myers/moriarty.pdf.

18. Ibid.

19. *Enuma Elish*, Tablet I:1–2, 7–8 (Foster translation). Benjamin R. Foster, *From Distant Days: Myths, Tales and Poetry of Ancient Mesopotamia* (Bethesda: CDL Press, 1995), p. 11. All quotations from *Enuma Elish* in this chapter are from Foster's translation.

20. Wayne Horowitz, *Mesopotamian Cosmic Geography* (Winona Lake, IN: Eisenbrauns, 1988), p. xii.

21. L. W. King, ed., *Enuma Elish: The Seven Tablets of Creation*, vol. 1 (New York: AMS Press, 1976, a reprint of the 1902 edition), p. LXXXIII.

22. Horowitz, *Mesopotamian Cosmic Geography*, p. 243.

23. Ibid., p. 262.

24. Ibid., p. 265.

25. Ibid.

26. Ibid., p. 9.

27. Ibid., p. 243.

28. Ibid., p. 250.

29. Ibid., p. 264.

30. From the Akkadian "Poem of the Righteous Sufferer," W. G. Lambert, *Babylonian Wisdom Literature* (Oxford: Clarendon Press, 1960), pp. 58–59.

31. Horowitz, p. 264.

32. Ibid., pp. 233–35.

33. Ibid., p. 330.

34. Each ancient nation portrayed both its god(s) and its nation as if they were "central" to the "world"—and in more than just a figurative fashion. An ancient Babylonian map of the world depicts Babylon in the center of the circle of the earth. Similarly, an Egyptian image of the circle of the earth shows Egypt lying at the center of the earth (Keel, *Symbolism*, pp. 37–39). And according to Andrew Dickson White, *A History of the Warfare of Science with Technology*, vol. 1, (New York: Dover, 1960, reprint of original 1896 work), pp. 98–99: "Every great people of antiquity, as a rule, regarded its own central city or most holy place as necessarily the center of the earth. The Chaldeans held that their 'holy house of the gods' was the center. The Egyptians sketched the world under the form of a human figure in which Egypt was the heart, and the center of it Thebes. For the Assyrians, it was Babylon; for the Hindus, it was Mount Meru; for the Greeks, so far as the civilized world was concerned, Mount Olympus or the temple in the city of Delphi.... It was in accordance, then, with a simple tendency of human thought that the Hebrews believed the center of the world to be Jerusalem." For example, "This is Jerusalem; I (God) have set her at the center of the nations, with lands around her" (Ezekiel 5:5); "the people (of Israel)... live at the center of the world" (Ezekiel 38:11, 12). In addition, the Samaritans, an ancient Jewish sect, believe to this day that their holy mountain, Gerizim, lay at the center of the earth. They quote Judges 9:37, "Look, men are coming down from tabbur haares (navel of the earth)," cf. Robert T. Anderson, "Mount Gerizim: Navel of the World," *Biblical Archeologist* (Fall 1980): 217.

35. Horowitz, p. 334. See also Gaalyah Cornfield, ed., *Adam to Daniel* (New York: Macmillan, 1962), p. 41, which features a labeled depiction of the Babylonian map of the world.

36. Helmer Ringgren, *Religions of the Ancient Near East*, trans. John Sturdy (Philadelphia: Westminster Press, 1973), p. 57.

37. Ibid., p. 110.

38. Ibid., p. 67.

39. Smith, *Priestly Vision*, p. 17.

40. Ibid., p. 185.

41. Ibid.

42. David Presutta, author of *The Biblical Cosmos versus Modern Cosmology* (Tamarac, FL: Llumina Press, 2007), edited one of the earliest drafts of this chapter and also provided the initial outline for the "Biblical Cosmology" section. I appreciate greatly his assistance and his permission to include portions of his work.

43. Smith, p. 59.

44. Ibid., pp. 69, 239 n.185.

45. Saint Ambrose, *Hexameron, Paradise, and Cain and Abel*, trans. J. J. Savage (New York: Fathers of the Church, 1961), pp. 126, 130, 132 (Hexaemeron, Lib., 4, Cap. III).

46. Gunther Plaut, Bernard J. Baumberger, and William W. Hallo, eds., *The Torah: A Modern Commentary* (New York: Union of American Hebrew Congregations, 1981), p. 18 n. 6; E. A. Speiser, *Genesis: The Anchor Bible Commentary* (New York: Doubleday, 1964), p. 6 n. 6; Robert Davidson, *Genesis: 1–11: The Cambridge Bible Commentary* (New York: Cambridge University Press, 1973), p. 18.

47. Gerhard von Rad, *Genesis: A Commentary*, trans. John H. Marks (Philadelphia: Westminster Press, 1961), p. 51.

48. T. H. Gaster, "Heaven," *The Interpreter's Dictionary of the Bible*, vol. 2, E–J (New York, Abingdon Press, 1969), p. 551.

49. Francis Brown, ed., Edward Robinson, trans., with the cooperation of S. R. Driver and Charles A. Briggs, *The New Brown, Driver, Briggs, Gesenius Hebrew and English Lexicon: With an Appendix Containing the Biblical Aramaic* (Peabody, MA: Hendrickson, 1996 reprint).

50. Ludwig Koehler, Walter Baumgartner, *The Hebrew and Aramaic Lexicon of the Old Testament*, trans. M. E. Richardson (Boston: Brill Academic, 2002 reprint).

51. One curious attempt to argue that the Bible depicts the sphericity and rotation of the earth is based on a passage found in the NT, Luke 17:34–36, which speaks of the coming of the Son of Man, "In that night, there shall be two men in one bed; the one shall be taken, and the other shall be left. Two women will be grinding together.... Two men shall be in the field." "In other words," wrote Henry Morris, the founder of the Institute for Creation Research, "this great event will take place instantaneously at night, in the morning, and in the afternoon. Such a combination would be possible only on an earth in which day and night could be occurring simultaneously, and that means a rotating earth."

Contra Morris, there is nothing in the verse about the earth "rotating," and in fact a stationary earth with a circling sun, as in a geocentric cosmos, could explain such a verse just as well. Morris also fails to note that Jesus' dictum, "No one knows the day or the hour," inspired Luke's multiple illustrations, including a bedtime illustration. Luke has simply mixed together three distinct possibilities and is not stressing their simultaneity. Luke is saying one must be ready at all times for the coming of the Son of Man, no matter what you may be doing—working in the field, sleeping in bed, or grinding meal. For the Son of Man might arrive at an early hour of the day, a later hour of the day, or at night. *No one knows the day or the hour.*

The passage in Luke is repeated almost identically in Matthew 24:40–41, which mentions only men in the field and women grinding, that is, activities that may be performed at the same hour of the day when the Son of Man comes. The point that the two gospel authors are trying to make is not in reference to astronomy but to apocalyptic expectations. According to them, the coming of the Son of Man will reveal a wide separation between hearts joined together by toil or friendship: two men may share a bed together, two women work as closely as at the handle of one hand mill, and one shall be taken, the other left. Certainly no more can be made of Luke's inclusion of a bedtime illustration than Matthew's exclusion of one. Was Luke's Gospel more astronomically inspired than Matthew's?

Lastly, one may note that according to some ancient Mesopotamian writings, at least one region of the flat earth's surface lay in perpetual darkness. So the ancients believed that even a flat earth could have darkness and light on it at the same time. Moreover, the sun is relatively small in a flat-earth cosmos and only sails directly above one part of the earth at a time, so even flat-earthers would not have expected every region of the earth to be lit at the same time with equal brightness. The Bible even states in the story of Joshua that he commanded the sun and moon to halt over specific regions, "Sun, stand still over Gibeon; and Moon, over the valley of Aijalon" (Joshua 10:12). And if I may paraphrase famed nineteenth-century freethinker, George William Foote, "When the Greek philosopher Anaxagoras dared to suggest that the sun was far larger than the Peloponnesos (the southern peninsula of Greece) he startled his contemporaries. What must have been the notions of a grossly unscientific people like the Jews? For them it was easy to regard the sun, moon, and 'the stars also,' as mere satellites of the earth, as lanterns for the human race."

52. "The cylinder was rolled on the wet clay of the tablet being sealed" [David Maltsberger, "Late Bronze Age Seals," in *Field Notes: The Newsletter of Archaeology in Israel and the Near East* 2, no. 1 (1994)]. See also, *Ancient Seals and the Bible*, eds., L. Gorelick and Elizabeth Williams-Forte (Malibu: Undena, 1983).

Note, some King James Bible followers, like Henry Morris (mentioned in the previous note), claim the seal in this verse in Job remains stationary and is applied to a wet piece of clay being "turned" on a potter's wheel. In other words, Morris claims this verse depicts the earth as spinning! But no such potter's wheel is mentioned in the verse in Job, and Morris misunderstands the meaning of the Elizabethan English word "turned," which was being used in the sense of "the milk *turned* sour," instead of depicting a spinning motion. Modern Bibles use the word "changed" instead of "turned." So this verse in Job compares the earth to a clay tablet, and compares the imprint of a cylinder seal rolled on its surface to the sun's rays changing the appearance of the earth's surface.

53. R. H. Charles, *The Apocrypha and Pseudepigrapha of the Old Testament in English*, vol. 2, *Pseudepigrapha* (London: Oxford University Press, 1969, a reprint of the 1913 edition), p. 208.

54. There is a curious verse in the book of Job that states God "hangs" the earth "over nothing," "on nothing," "on nothing whatsoever," or "without anything" (Job 26:7). Those who believe the Bible contains hidden nuggets of modern astronomical wisdom sometimes point to this verse as an illustration of the principle of gravity. But there is nothing in this verse about the shape of the earth, about the earth's position relative to an object in, say, outer space, or about the earth moving.

As pointed out by Lamoureux in *Evolutionary Creation: A Christian Approach to Evolution*, the Hebrew word *talah*, which is translated "suspends" or "hangs," appears in contexts of hanging up an object like a utensil on a peg (Isaiah 22:24), weapons on a wall (Ezekiel 27:10), or a lyre on a tree (Psalm 137:2). It does not refer to hovering in empty space, but to hanging something from some perch. Job 26:7 simply states that the earth is not hanging from anything in the three-tier cosmos of heaven above, earth below, and the deep/Sheol under the earth. The primary point of the verse is that "He" (Yahweh) is displaying his might by hanging the earth miraculously, securely, safely in the midst of such a three-tier cosmos.

Take a closer look at the entire verse, Job 26:7 (NASB), and note that it reads:

He stretched out the north [Hebrew *saphon*]
over empty space [Hebrew, *tohu*],
and hangs the earth on nothing [Hebrew *beli-mah*].

The verse contains two parts that parallel one another. The first part features the word *saphon*, which was originally the name of a mountain in "the north" where the Canaanites believed their gods assembled—a cosmic mountain connected with heaven or the sky. The "north/heaven" is stretched over *tohu*, which is the same word that appears in Genesis 1:2 and describes the "formless, pre-created stuff" that would later become the earth. In other parts of the Bible *tohu* is used to express "confusion, unreality, wasteland, desolation," something a bit grittier than just "empty space." In fact, *tohu* is translated as "chaos" in this verse in both the New Jewish Publication Society translation of the Hebrew Bible and in *The Book of Job: The Cambridge Bible Commentary*.

The second part of the verse says God hangs the earth *beli-mah*, a compound word that appears only once in the Bible, so linguists do not know its range of use, or its meaning in different contexts. According to Smith in *The Priestly Vision of Genesis 1* (p. 58) *beli-mah* means literally "without-what," and since it appears in parallel with *tohu* most likely refers to a type of "emptiness" that is "quite literally a terra incognita [unknown land]." Other translations for *beli-mah* include "nothing," "nothingness," "without anything," and "what (not)." Used as a parallel for *tohu* in this verse, *beli-mah*'s "nothingness," "emptiness," may be referring to the primeval, watery deep and shadowy land of death/destruction, all of which lay beneath the earth in biblical cosmology. The context of Job 26:7 agrees with such an interpretation, since Job says that God sees right down to the watery depths and the lands of death (Sheol) and destruction (Abaddon) over which (it was believed) lay the expanse of the earth: "The departed spirits tremble under the waters and their inhabitants. Naked is Sheol before Him, and Abaddon has no covering. He stretches out the north over empty space and hangs the earth on nothing.... He has inscribed a circle on the surface of the waters at the boundary of light and darkness. The pillars of heaven tremble and are amazed at His rebuke. He quieted the sea with His power, and by His understanding He shattered Rahab. By His breath the heavens are cleared; His hand has pierced the fleeing serpent," Job 26:5–7, 10–13 (NASB).

Further support for such an understanding of Job 26:7 can be found in God's point-by-point reply to Job in chapter 38: "Where were you when I laid the foundation of the earth?... Who set its measurements?... Or who stretched the line on it? On what were its bases sunk? Or who laid its cornerstone?...I placed boundaries on [the sea] and set a bolt and doors, and I said, 'Thus far you shall come, but no farther; and here shall your proud waves stop.'...Have you entered into the springs of the sea or walked in the recesses of the deep? Have the gates of death been revealed to you, or have you seen the gates of deep darkness? Have you understood the expanse of the earth?" Job 38:4–6, 10–11, 16–18 (NASB).

Lastly, as a side note, there's at least one curious Mesopotamian hymn of creation that stands out among Mesopotamian literature in a way similar to how Job 26:7 stands out among Hebrew literature. I am speaking of *The Samas Hymn*, which states, "You (Samas, the sun god) climb to the mountains surveying the earth. You suspend from the heavens the circle of the lands [the earth]" [W. G. Lambert, *Babylonian Wisdom Literature* (Oxford: Clarendon Press, 1960), ll. 21–22].

55. Horowitz, pp. 331, 333.

56. The fact that some stars explode is not in doubt, neither is the fact that new ones continue to be born. Yet according to Genesis 1, God "made the stars" on the fourth day of creation, and the author leaves it at that, with no mention of the remarkable fact that God is creating them still. To read about the birth of new stars see *Astronomy, Sky & Telescope* and *Astrophysical Journal*. Newborn stars also have rings of matter circling them in which new planets may be forming. As of January 2010, astronomers have discovered 424 known extrasolar planets, ranging

from the size of gas giants to that of terrestrial planets. And speaking of ongoing creation, inside each star, the simplest of atoms, hydrogen, is fusing with other such atoms to give birth to heavier elements.

57. The last book of the Bible mentions a city that descends from heaven, the New Jerusalem: "And the city lieth foursquare, and the length is as large as the breadth...twelve thousand furlongs [about 1,500 miles, according to most commentaries, which is also the distance from the earthly city of Jerusalem to the city of Rome, the capital of the Roman Empire]. The length and the breadth and the height of it are equal" (Revelation 21:16). Some Christians believe this is a literal city that shall descend from heaven, but wouldn't a cube that size seesaw on the earth's surface, since the earth is not flat, but a sphere? An object that massive would also trigger earthquakes, eruptions, and make a planet wobble on its axis. (Try gluing a small cafeteria-sized carton of milk to a large bowling ball and spin the bowling ball to see what I mean.) How could the New Jerusalem maintain its cubic shape since asteroids of far smaller widths collapse into sphere-shaped objects due to the force of their own gravity? And what would prevent the city, after it landed, from growing as wide and flat as any mountain range due to its mutual attraction with the earth's gravity? The height of the New Jerusalem is so great that it would extend 1,300 miles further into space than the International Space Station (which is situated only 200 miles above the earth). The New Jerusalem would also block jet streams in the upper atmosphere and be pummeled by natural and manmade objects orbiting the earth, as well as by solar winds and radiation. If you happen to live in the New Jerusalem on a floor higher than 100 miles above sea level, I would not suggest opening your windows without first donning a space suit.

The author of the book of Revelation also wrote that the "twelve gates" of the New Jerusalem are "twelve pearls; every gate is of one pearl" (21:21), hence the slang expression for heaven, "the pearly gates." But where can you find "one pearl" as large as a city gate? However, Christian apologist Grant R. Jeffrey turns all such questions on their heads, and asserts the literal truth of everything written in the Bible about the "New Jerusalem," by asking, "What reason would God have for describing such details so precisely unless they were true?" [*Apocalypse: The Coming Judgment of the Nations* (Toronto: Bantam Books, 1994), p. 351] But who knows whether it is *God* who is describing such details?

The author of the book of Revelation probably envisioned the New Jerusalem as a cube because that was the shape of the holy of holies of Solomon's temple—and he assumed this super massive cube did not have to travel light-years to get here, but would descend from God's heaven directly above the earth and rest securely, as cubes do, on a flat surface, that of the flat earth. In a similar vein, the book of Revelation mentions that its author passed through a "door to heaven" (Revelation 4:1) and was shown things "in the spirit." "I saw four angels standing on the four corners of the earth, holding the four winds of the earth" (Revelation 7:1). Another verse in Revelation says that "every eye" will see Jesus when he returns from heaven to earth "on clouds" (Revelation 1:7). "And I saw a new heaven and a new earth: for the first heaven and the first earth were passed away; and there was no more sea" (Revelation 21:1).

Final question: if the Bible begins and ends with a mythical view of the cosmos, then what other myths might not lay between its pages?

58. G. K. Beale, *The Erosion of Inerrancy in Evangelicalism: Responding to New Challenges to Biblical Authority* (Wheaton, IL: Crossway Books, 2008), pp. 216–17.

59. **A Chronology of the *Raqia'* and, "Waters above the *Raqia'*"**:

• The Hebrew Past
Raqia' is solid throughout the OT.

• Fourth or Third Century BCE
The *Book of Enoch* (in one of its oldest sections, "The Book of Watchers") affirms a solid firmament.

• Second Century BCE:
Hebrew scholars translate their Scriptures into Greek (the Septuagint or LXX version of the Hebrew Bible) and employ the Greek word *stereoma*, based on *stereos*, which means "firm/hard," as the closest equivalent to the Hebrew word, *raqia'*. And the *Song of the Three Holy Children* [found in some copies of the Book of Daniel after 3:23], says that "waters be above the heavens" and are called upon to bless the Lord, but after the reader is brought closer to the things of the earth, clouds are called upon to bless the Lord, thus distinguishing between the two.

• First Century CE:
The authors of the NT assume a three-tier cosmos, consisting of God in heaven above, a flat earth below, and people/beings "under the earth" (Philippians 2:10; Revelation 5:3, 5:13; see also Ephesians 4:9–10).

• Second to Fifth Century CE:
Origen, a second-century church father, calls the firmament, "without doubt firm and solid; and it is this which 'divides the water which is above heaven from the water which is below heaven.'" Ambrose, a fourth-century church father, comments, "the specific solidity of this exterior firmament is meant." Jerome, a fourth–fifth-century church father, and translator of Genesis from Hebrew into Latin, translates *raqia'* as *firmamentum*, based on *firmus*, which means "firm/hard." Augustine, a fourth–fifth-century church father, says, "the term 'firmament' does not compel us to imagine a stationary heaven: we may understand this name as

given to indicate not that it is motionless but that it is solid and that it constitutes an impassable boundary between the water above and the waters below." Augustine adds, "Whatever the nature of the waters [above the firmament], we must believe in them, for the authority of Scripture is greater than the capacity of man's mind," a phrase echoed by Martin Luther as late as the fifteenth century.

Jewish writings agree with those of the Christian fathers: In *2 Enoch* [dated by some to the first century CE] Enoch is placed on a cloud, transported above the first heaven, and shown "a very great Sea, greater than the earthly Sea." The *Testament of Adam* says, "waters [mighty waves] are above heaven" and praise God in the fifth hour, while clouds are distinguished from such waters by being made in the sixth hour. Rabbinical works mention the firmament and the waters above it, and speculate as to the firmament's composition and thickness. [For citations to statements made in the preceding two paragraphs, see Paul H. Seely, "The Firmament and the Water Above," Parts I and II, listed in note 2.]

• Fifth to Fifteenth Century CE:

Most medieval theologians follow the lead of the Bible and church fathers and claim with certainty that waters lay above the planets and stars. But what kind of waters? Thomas Aquinas says such waters must be material, but he adds that their nature depends on the composition of the firmament—as is his custom, he describes various possibilities. But the most popular view of the firmament is as a "sphere of fixed stars" above which lay a "sphere of water" in liquid or crystalline form, and by "crystalline" most mean "liquid." Indeed, in the twelfth century, Bartholomew the Englishman explains that the waters above the starry firmament are called "crystalline, not because they are hard like a crystal but because they are uniformly luminous and transparent." Such waters are said to reflect downward the light of the luminaries and to prevent the melting of the firmament. [Edward Grant, *Planets, Stars, and Orbs: The Medieval Cosmos, 1200–1687*, first paperback ed. (Cambridge, England: Cambridge University Press), 1996, p. 103; and Grant, "Journey Through the Spheres: The Cosmos in the Middle Ages," lecture delivered at Rice University, Houston, Texas on Friday, March 14, 1997, https://scholarworks.iu.edu/dspace/handle/2022/101]

• Sixteenth Century:

Martin Luther, in his *Lectures on Genesis*, writes of "this marvelous expansion of thick mist Moses calls a firmament...(whose) Maker gave solidity to this fluid material."

John Calvin, unlike Luther, is more influenced by astronomy than the Bible, and he writes: "Things that we observe plainly show the fixed stars are above the planets, and that the planets themselves are placed in different orbits...the sun, moon, and stars are not confusedly mixed together, but each has its own position and station assigned to it" [John Calvin, *Commentary on the Book of Psalms*, trans. James Anderson (Grand Rapids, MI: Eerdmans, 1949), Psalm CXLVIII, p. 305]. Calvin also admits that the biblical description of the moon as one of only "two great lights" is at odds with astronomy: "If the astronomer inquires respecting the actual dimensions of the planets, he will find the moon to be less than Saturn"; but Calvin excuses such a gaffe by claiming Genesis 1 features a "gross method of instruction." [*Commentary on Genesis*, trans. John King (Grand Rapids, MI: Eerdmans, 1948), pp. 79, 87; see also Scott M. Manetsch, "Problems with the Patriarchs: John Calvin's Interpretation of Difficult Passages in Genesis," *Westminster Theological Journal* 67 (2005): 13–15.]

I'm willing to bet that the ancients, not having the benefit of Calvin's astronomical knowledge, held a more Lutheran view of the cosmos; compare their opinions below:

"Moses describes the special use of this *raqia'*, 'to divide the waters from the waters,' from which words arise a great difficulty. For it appears opposed to common sense, and quite incredible, that there should be waters above the heaven" [Calvin, *Commentary on Genesis*, trans. John King (Grand Rapids, MI: Eerdmans, 1948) pp. 79, 87].

"Scripture simply says that the moon, the sun, and the stars were placed in the firmament of the heaven, below and above which ... are the waters. ... We Christians must be different from the philosophers in the way we think about the causes of things. And if some are beyond our comprehension like those before us concerning the waters above the heavens, we must believe them rather than wickedly deny them or presumptuously interpret them in conformity with our understanding" [Martin Luther, *Luther's Works*, vol. 1, *Lectures on Genesis*, ed. Janoslaw Pelikan (St. Louis, MI: Concordia, 1958), pp. 30, 42, 43].

• Nineteenth Century:

Anglican theologians and scholars contribute to a book that sums up the growing challenge to interpreting Genesis and other parts of the Bible in a literal fashion. One contributor writes, "The root [of *raqia'*] is generally applied to express the hammering or beating out of metal plates; hence something beaten or spread out. It has been pretended that the word *raqia'* may be translated 'expanse' so as merely to mean empty space. The context sufficiently rebuts this" [C. W. Goodwin, "On the Mosaic Cosmology," *Essays and Reviews* (West Strand, London: John W. Parker and Son, 1860), p. 220 n. 1]. Two contributors to *Essays* are indicted for heresy and lose their jobs, but are reinstated later. Published four months after

Darwin's *On the Origin of Species*, more copies of *Essays* are sold in two years than of Darwin's *Origin* in its first twenty.

60. John H. Walton, *The Lost World of Genesis One: Ancient Cosmology and the Origins Debate* (Downers Grove, IL: IVP Academic, 2009), p. 16.

Chapter 6

THE BIBLE AND MODERN SCHOLARSHIP

Paul Tobin

Most Christians claim they have a *reasoned* faith. This faith claim is based on the Bible being the word of God in some meaningful sense. But modern scholarship has shown us that the canonical Bible:

1. is inconsistent with itself,
2. is not supported by archaeology,
3. contains fairy tales,
4. contains failed prophecies, and
5. contains many forgeries.

Given all this, the Bible cannot be considered an inspired—"God breathed" —document. Rather it seems to be written by a superstitious people who were creating God in their image, as Ludwig Feuerbach charged. Therefore Christianity is not a reasoned faith. It cannot stand up to critical scrutiny.[1]

THE INCONSISTENT BIBLE

That the Bible contains verses that stand in direct opposition to each other has been known for a long time. Pagan critics of Christianity such as

Celsus (second century CE) and Porphyry (third century CE) already noted the discrepancies between the Old and New Testaments and between the various books of the New Testament.[2] We find Augustine (354–430 CE) trying to defend the Bible against such accusations in one of his letters to Jerome (347–420 CE), by claiming "...if in these writings I am perplexed by anything which appears to me opposed to truth, I do not hesitate to suppose that either the manuscript is faulty, or the translator has not caught the meaning of what was said, or I myself have failed to understand it."[3] The problem with such an apologetic strategy is obvious: it's a circular argument. This explanation is based on the prior assumption that the Bible is divinely inspired, or inerrant, in the first place. An in-depth analysis of the inherent problems with such a stance taken by evangelicals today can be found in Robert Price's books, *Inerrant the Wind: The Evangelical Crisis of Biblical Authority*, and in *Beyond Born Again*.[4]

These errors begin in the first few chapters of Genesis with the creation accounts. In Genesis 1:12 we read that the land had produced vegetation on the third day before the creation of Adam. Yet we read later in Genesis 2:5 that there was no vegetation until after Adam was created. In Genesis 1:20–25 we read that the animals were created on the fifth and sixth days of creation, all before Adam. Yet in Genesis 2:18–19 we're told they were created after Adam, when seeking to find him a companion. In a rather desperate attempt to "cover up" this obvious fact, the evangelical translation of the Bible, the *New International Version* (NIV) translates Genesis 2:18–19 as follows:

> The LORD God said, "It is not good for the man to be alone. I will make a helper suitable for him." Now the LORD God *had formed* out of the ground all the beasts of the field and all the birds of the air. He brought them to the man to see what he would name them; and whatever the man called each living creature, that was its name. [emphasis added]

The NIV translators changed the simple past ("formed") into the perfect past ("*had* formed"). Translating it this way has the effect of obscuring the difficulty in this passage. By using the perfect past, the passage could now be read to mean that animals had already been created prior to Adam. But as Hector Avalos points out in *The End of Biblical Studies*, such a translation is inconsistent, for earlier in Genesis 2:7, the NIV translates the same form of the Hebrew verb using a simple past tense (i.e., Genesis 2:7 —"and

the Lord God *formed* the man from the dust of the living ground...").
Fudging the translation to get rid of difficulties in the biblical accounts is
a common tactic of many evangelical versions of the Bible.[5]

There are similar errors in the story of Noah's ark and the Flood. In
Genesis 6:19–20 we read that Noah brought two of every kind of animal into
the ark, and that no separation is made between clean and unclean animals
(the word "every" before the kind of animal excludes the possibility). Then
just a few verses later in Genesis 7:2–3, we read where Noah brought even
more animals into the ark. There we read that Noah brought into the ark
seven pairs of every kind of clean animal along with two pairs of every kind
of unclean animal. These are just a few initial examples that have led
scholars to discover that what is normally called the *Five Books of Moses* is
actually an ancient compilation of many different documents written by different people and at different times and in various different locations.[6]

But all of those kinds of errors are just the tip of the iceberg. Biblical
scholar Randel Helms, in his book *The Bible against Itself*, argues that "[t]he
Bible is a war zone, and its authors are the combatants."[7] Let's list just a few
examples here. We find discrepancies over the issue of racism in the Bible.
God decreed that neither the Ammonites nor Moabites shall be welcomed
"into the assembly of Yahweh; even to the tenth generation...forever"
(Deuteronomy 23:3). Later we see Nehemiah (13:1–3) and Ezra (10:14–44)
both deny mixed marriages because of this. Such racist viewpoints against
foreigners stand in stark opposition to the story of Ruth though, who was
a Moabite (Ruth 1:22) and married a Jew, Boaz. She became the great-
grandmother of king David (Ruth 4:13–4:17). It seems that, depending on
which prophet he is speaking to, God could either be a proponent of racial
harmony or of racial hatred.

The differences between the authors of Proverbs and Ecclesiastes
cannot be reasonably reconciled either. Proverbs extols wisdom and
knowledge, telling its readers that "a wise son makes a glad father"
(Proverbs 10:1), while Ecclesiastes disparages all kinds of wisdom and
knowledge, stating that it only gives the wise person "grief" and "sorrow"
(Ecclesiastes 1:18).[8] In Proverbs one is called to help the poor. In Ecclesiastes one is simply told "not to be amazed" at poverty, as it is a natural state
of things (Proverbs 14:31; Ecclesiastes 5:8). In general, Proverbs has a
sunny outlook on life, stating that by keeping sound wisdom, one can "walk
securely" in life and sleep peacefully (Proverbs 3:21–26). Ecclesiastes,
however, extols no such thing. It says that "all is vanity" and that it does not

matter whether you are wise or strong or knowledgeable, because "time and chance happens" to everyone (Ecclesiastes 1:2; 9:11).

In the New Testament (NT), we find a difference in views as well.[9] The apostle Paul called the Law of Moses "a curse" (Galatians 3:13), and in one unguarded moment compared it to "dung" (Philippians 3:8). Yet we find in the Epistle attributed to James (supposedly the brother of Jesus) a very high regard for the same Law calling it "the Law of liberty," "the perfect Law" and "the royal Law" (James 1:25; 2:8). Indeed what can be more contradictory than these two verses: "[A] man is justified by faith apart from the works of the law" (Romans 3:28), and "[A] man is justified by works and not by faith alone" (James 2:24)?

Suffice it to say that the number of errors in the Bible is massive.[10] The doctrine of biblical inerrancy cannot be defended given what we find there. This is not for want of trying. Evangelicals have expended countless hours and published entire encyclopedias trying to reconcile these "difficulties" in the Bible, which only ends up proving how many difficulties there are, and how elaborately one must labor to explain them away.[11]

DIGGING THE GRAVE OF "BIBLICAL ARCHAEOLOGY"

Prior to the 1970s one can be forgiven for thinking that archaeology is the handmaid of the Bible—for one archaeological dig after another seemed to confirm it.[12] But this is no longer true. Scholars are questioning the whole paradigm of "biblical archaeology," which starts with the assumption that the Bible is a reliable guide for field research.[13] Indeed, there is now so much contrary evidence against the historical accuracy of the Bible that the term "biblical archaeology" has been discarded by professional archaeologists and *Syro-Palestinian archaeology* has been suggested by some practicing in the field as a more appropriate term.[14]

It has long been known that the story of the great Flood told in Genesis chapters 6–9 is a scientific impossibility. Ian Plimer, professor of geology at the University of Melbourne, gives a thorough listing of these problems in his book *Telling Lies for God: Reason versus Creationism*. Among the evidence he cites is the pattern of sedimentary rocks. High energy sediments, such as gravel, are deposited during the height of floods, while low energy sediments such as siltstone, mudstone and claystone, are deposited during the waning of floods. If there was once a worldwide flood, we would expect a uniform worldwide sedimentary formation with the high-energy sediments (ancient gravel, sands) at the bottom and the low-energy sediments at the top. Yet, this is not what we find. It's not even close on a global scale. As Plimer pointed out, if this were seen on a global scale, oilfield geologists would have an easy job, since all sedimentary formation would invariably have sandstone at the bottom and siltstones, mudstones, and claystones at the top.[15]

Archaeological discoveries have shown that the story of Noah's ark and the Flood wasn't even an original Hebrew tale. In the nineteenth century archaeologists unearthed twelve ancient clay tablets in an excavation on the banks of the River Tigris in modern-day Iraq. Contained within the tablets is an ancient tale known as *The Epic of Gilgamesh*. This epic tells the story of Gilgamesh, a Sumerian king who purportedly lived around the middle of the third millennium BCE. Gilgamesh, in his quest for immortality, set out on a long journey to look for his ancestor, Utnapishtim. Utnapishtim was already bestowed with eternal life by the gods. Upon reaching the island of Utnapishtim's abode, Gilgamesh was told a story by his ancestor of a great flood that once swept the world. The similarities between this story and that of Genesis (6:5–9:19) are astounding. Just as in the Genesis story of Noah, the Gilgamesh epic tells how the gods wanted to destroy the world with a worldwide flood (cf. Genesis 6:11–13). Likewise, a single man, Utnapishtim, was called by the gods to build an ark to save himself, his family, and all kinds of animals (cf. Genesis 6:14–19). Just as Noah's ark came to rest on "the mountains of Ararat" when the waters subsided, Utnapishtim's ship came to rest on top of the "Mountain of Nisir" (cf. Genesis 8:4). After the flood, like Noah, Utnapishtim released a few birds. When the last bird did not return, he knew the waters had abated (compare Genesis 8:6–12).[16]

As the famed archaeologist Cyrus Gordon (1908–2001) showed us in *The Bible and the Ancient Near East*, the scholarly consensus holds that the Genesis story is dependent on the Gilgamesh epic.[17] This consensus is reached mainly by considering the following facts:

• Floods are a common occurrence in ancient Mesopotamia, while Israel is, in general, an arid land. We would expect stories of floods to be told by people who are familiar with floods.
• The geographical setting of Noah's story—having the ark rest on a mountain at the source of the Tigris and Euphrates—points toward Mesopotamia as its origin.

- The Gilgamesh epic was very well known throughout the ancient Near East, a fragment was even found in ancient Israel.
- Babylonia was the dominant civilization of that time, while Israel was a "backwater of sorts." The general historical trend is for a dominant culture to influence a lesser one through its culture and myths.[18]

Turning next to the *Patriarchal Narratives*, the stories in Genesis about Abraham, Isaac, Jacob, and Joseph are also no longer considered historical by most scholars competent in the field.[19] The reasons are compelling:

- Genesis 11:26–28 says that Abraham came from "Ur of the Chaldees." Estimates of Abraham's lifetime fall anywhere between the twenty-third century BCE and the sixteenth century BCE, yet the Chaldeans as a people only came into existence around the eighth to seventh century BCE—long after the time of Abraham.[20]
- Genesis 26:1 relates a story about Isaac going to Gerar to meet with "Abimelech, king of the Philistines." Archaeological finds tell us that there was *no city of Gerar* and *no king of the Philistines* to meet with Isaac during the historical period in which he would have lived.[21]
- Genesis 12:14–16, 24:10–11, and 37:25–28 include the use of *domesticated camels* in the story of Abraham and of Joseph. The archaeological evidence shows us that camels did not become domesticated until the eleventh century BCE, well after the time of Abraham and Joseph. Camels could not have been used during the time of the patriarchs.[22]
- Genesis 17: 9–11 tells of the covenant between God and Abraham, which was sealed by the act of circumcision. We know that circumcision was widely practiced in ancient times in the Fertile Crescent. In particular, the Egyptians and the Canaanites practiced the rite, the very people with whom Abraham would have had the most contact. How could the act of circumcision be "a sign of the covenant" between God and Abraham when everyone else was doing it? It was only during the time of the Babylonian captivity, during the sixth century, that this custom could have set the Jews apart. For the Babylonians of that time did not practice circumcision.[23]

Thomas Thompson, professor of Old Testament at the University of Copenhagen, noted with iron-clad logic, that *if* these and other specific references in the patriarchal narratives have been shown to be anachronistic, *then* they add nothing to the story; *but* these very references were the *historical anchors* that supposedly rooted the narratives into history in the first place. Without them how are we to distinguish these narratives from other completely mythical folk tales?[24]

Since the last decade of the twentieth century there is a growing consensus in modern scholarship that the major elements of the Exodus tale (the Israelites living in Egypt for 430 years, the exodus of this large group out of Egypt into Canaan, and the intervening forty years of wandering in the Sinai Peninsula) are also myths, not history.[25] Let us review the evidence. The existence of Moses, the main protagonist of the Exodus account, as a historical person is not proven either way, but certainly many elements are legendary. The story of Moses' birth, his escape from harm by being put in a papyrus basket and left to drift on the river before being discovered (Exodus 2:2–10) parallels closely the nativity story of the legendary Akkadian king Sargon, who was also placed inside a basket to escape dire circumstances and left to drift on the river before being rescued by someone. The general flow of cultural influence and the antiquity of the Akkadian legend make it seem likely that the Exodus account is based on the Akkadian legend.[26]

Other details add to our doubt regarding the historicity of the story. We have at least three names for Moses' father-in-law—Reuel (Exodus 2:18), Jethro (Exodus 3:1), and Hobab (Numbers 10:29; Judges 4:11).[27] Even the name "Moses" itself was originally Egyptian, not Hebrew.[28]

The date of the Exodus is also plagued with uncertainty. According to 1 Kings 6:1, the Exodus happened 480 years before Solomon built the temple. This places the event somewhere around 1495–1440 BCE. Yet the Israelites were forced to build the cities of Pithom and Ramses, according to Exodus 1:8–11. Now, there are only two possible pharaohs who might have had a role to play in the building of the city of Ramses, since a city with that name could not have been built by anyone else but by the pharaoh whose name it reflects, and both of them reigned too late for biblical chronology to be accurate. The first Egyptian pharaoh named Ramses came to power in 1320 BCE. This is a century too late to be harmonized with biblical chronology. There is evidence from Egyptian sources that a city called Pi-Ramses was built under a pharaoh named Ramses II, who reigned over Egypt from 1279–1213 BCE. But the story of Israelite slaves building Pi-Ramses could only have happened during his reign—more than two hundred years after the time calculated by the biblical chronology.[29] Any attempt to equate the Hyksos—a line of Semitic kings who ruled Egypt from the mid-seventeenth to the mid-sixteenth centuries BCE—with the Israelites fail, too. For the Hyksos were expelled from Egypt into Canaan by Pharaoh Amose around 1570 BCE, which is too early for any of the biblical chronology to work. It's simply more probable that the violent expulsion of the Hyksos became embedded in the folktales of the Canaanite people, which forms the basis for the oral tales that eventually became the Exodus narrative. But the main details of the Exodus (Moses, the forty-year trek in Sinai, and the locations the Israelites went through) must all be pieces of historical fiction.[30]

Now, according to Exodus 12:40, the Israelites lived in Egypt for 430 years. Yet for all this time, there is simply no literary and archaeological evidence outside the Hebrew Bible that records the sojourn of the Israelites in Egypt.[31] A similar problem exists with the number of people claimed to have left Egypt. According to Exodus 12:37, there were six hundred thousand men, not counting the women and children, who left with Moses. We are also told this one-million-plus nation wandered for forty years in the wilderness in Sinai (Joshua 5:6). Surely more than a million people wandering around for forty years would have left some traces for archaeologists to find. Yet not a single piece of archeological evidence has been found. This is not for want of trying, either.[32]

William Dever, an archaeologist normally associated with the more conservative end of Syro-Palestinian archaeology, has labeled the question of the historicity of Exodus "dead."[33] Israeli archaeologist Ze'ev Herzog, provides the current consensus view on the historicity of the Exodus: "The Israelites never were in Egypt. They never came from abroad. This whole chain is broken. It is not a historical one. It is a later legendary reconstruction—made in the seventh century [BCE]—of a history that never happened."[34]

The story of the conquest of Canaan told in the book of Joshua has suffered much the same fate as the Exodus—archaeological discoveries have shown that it simply did not happen the way the Bible describes. One of the most memorable stories in the Bible is that of the conquest of Jericho by Joshua and the Israelites (Joshua 6:1–21). We are told that on the seventh day of the siege, the Israelites shouted and the priests blew the trumpets, which brought the walls of Jericho tumbling down. Unfortunately, archaeological digs led by Kathleen Kenyon in the 1950s showed that in the period most likely for this event (1550 to 1200 BCE), Jericho was either uninhabited or a small village with just a few huts. There was certainly no fortified wall that could have dramatically came tumbling down![35] The same negative results greet excavations at Ai (Joshua 8:21–29),[36] Gibeon (Joshua 10:1–2),[37] Lachish (10:32),[38] and other cities.[39] Indeed, according to archaeologists William Dever and Lawrence Stager, almost all of the roughly thirty cities Joshua was supposed to have conquered were either uninhabited at that time or destroyed by other means, or never even destroyed.[40]

The story of the united kingdom of Israel under David and Solomon also seems to be unraveled by archaeology. According to the Bible, David's kingdom consisted of a united Israel and Judah along with other kingdoms he conquered—Syria and Hamath to the north; Moab, Ammon to the east; Philistine to the west; and Edom to the south (2 Samuel 8: 3–13; 10). Surely such a vast empire would have left immense archaeological evidence of its existence. The date normally ascribed to King David's reign is 1005–970 BCE. And although no one doubts the *existence* of King David,[41] there is no archaeological evidence for his kingdom beyond his existence. As archaeologist John Laughlin noted: "[T]here is little in the overall archaeological picture of the tenth century BC that can be connected with David."[42] Whatever evidence there is points to the fact that the story about the grandeur of David's empire is a myth of a fictional golden age created by later writers. David's "vast" empire is a myth.[43] If David was indeed king, he never ruled over the vast regions described in the Bible.[44]

David's son Solomon has not fared much better. According to the Bible, Solomon, who was king around 970–931 BCE, ruled over an even larger empire than his father did. His vast kingdom supposedly spanned from the Euphrates River to the border of Egypt (1 Kings 4:21). Solomon's fame and influence spread far and wide (1 Kings 10:1). His diplomatic skills were proven by his securing alliances with other nations such as Egypt (1 Kings 3:1) and Tyre (1 Kings 5). He was also known for his massive architectural projects, including the Temple in Jerusalem (1 Kings 6) and the royal palace on Ophel (1 Kings 7). He also improved on the fortifications of Jerusalem, Hazor, Megiddo, and Gezer (1 Kings 9:15). He also built forty thousand stalls of horses for his fourteen thousand chariots and twelve thousand horsemen (1 Kings 4:26).

And yet, as in the case with his father David, modern archaeology simply finds no evidence for this empire or for any of his supposed architectural undertakings. Solomon's temple is described in detail in 1 Kings 6, yet despite the extensive archaeological digs in the city, in the words of archaeologist John Laughlin, "not a single piece of this building has been found."[45] There is also no sign of any of the other grand architectural works that he supposedly built; his palace, or the fortifications at Jerusalem, Hazor, Megiddo, and Gezer.[46]

The archeological evidence for the population, settlement patterns, and economic resources of Judah turns out to be the same for the time of Solomon as for the time of David. But as archaeologists Finkelstein and Silberman succinctly put it: "As far as we can see on the basis of archaeological surveys, Judah remained relatively empty of permanent population, quite isolated and very marginal right up to and past the presumed time of David and Solomon, with no major urban centers and with no pronounced hierarchy of hamlets, villages and towns."[47]

Modern archaeology is no friend of the Bible.

MYTHS, LEGENDS, AND FAIRY TALES IN THE BIBLE

We are all familiar with stories of talking animals in Aesop's Fables—the hare and the tortoise and the fox who cried "sour grapes" are just two of the many endearing tales we treasure from our childhood. Aesop's fables came from around the sixth century BCE and are therefore near contemporaries of stories told in the Pentateuch.[48] While we cannot say one directly influenced the other, we can safely say that telling tales like these is how ancient storytelling cultures conveyed moral lessons. In the Old Testament (OT), something evangelicals would like us to believe is a purely historical document, we find the same kinds of themes. Genesis 2 introduces us to a talking snake who urged Eve to partake of the forbidden fruit. In Numbers 22 we find the story of Balaam and his talking donkey.

We find parallels in myths, legends, and religious fairy tales that were contemporaneous with the authors of the canonical Bible in every stage of its development. Here I can only devote space to one such myth concerning the similarities in the stories of the virgin birth, found in Matthew and Luke, with those found in Greco-Roman culture.

First, let's look at the birth stories of clearly mythical gods of the Mediterranean world. Many of the popular deities were born of virgins. For example, in the Greek myth, Perseus was born of the virgin Danae, by Zeus who took the form of a shower of gold to impregnate her. Phoenician mythology claimed Adonis to be born of the virgin Myrrh. *Parthenogenesis* was also the explanation for the birth of the Phrygian deity Attis from his mother Cybele.[49] Similarly, even in stories told about historical figures we find common themes. Great men must have their greatness injected into their DNA from the time they were conceived. Thus the idea of conception by gods, either virginally or via some form of unusual intercourse was a common element in the stories told about them. Alexander the Great (356–323 BCE) was conceived when his mother-to-be dreamed of a bolt of lightning—a symbol of Zeus—entering her womb. The Roman emperor Augustus Caesar (63 BCE–14 CE) was conceived when Apollo, in the form of a snake, had intercourse with Augustus's mother, who was sleeping in the temple. Apollo was also implicated in the conception of the Greek philosopher Plato (ca. 427 BCE–ca. 347 BCE) and the Greek mathematician Pythagoras (sixth century BCE).[50] It is not just Zeus or Apollo that did all the impregnating in the ancient world. In the Roman legend of Romulus and Remus, we are told they were conceived when Mars, the god of war, impregnated their mother, Rhea Silvea, the vestal virgin.[51]

So it should not come as a surprise that the early Christians came up with similar stories about Jesus. He was born of a virgin mother, Mary, who was impregnated by an act of the Holy Spirit (Matthew 1:20; Luke 1:35). Evangelicals protest that the stories about those other gods and Greco-Roman heroes are mere myths and legends, whereas the story of Jesus' conception and birth is grounded in world history. In the nativity stories of Matthew and Luke, we find references to historical figures, such as King Herod the Great (ca. 74–4 BC) and the Roman governor of Syria, Quirinius (ca. 51 BCE–21 CE). Herod tried to have Jesus murdered by ordering the killing of all male infants aged two and below, while the reason we're told Joseph and Mary had to go to Bethlehem from Nazareth was due to the census conducted by Quirinius.

These figures do not just form a backdrop to the stories but were integral to the plot. Yet, rather ironically, it's these very figures that when laid bare show us how the nativity stories are merely ancient fairy tales historicized. The story of Herod's involvement in the nativity is told in chapter 2 of Matthew. There we read that after Jesus was born, "wise men from the east" (Matthew 2:2) came to Jerusalem to look for the newborn "king of the Jews." They had seen a star in the east that led them to Judea. Their enquiries reached the ears of Herod. He was worried about this possible threat to his throne and summoned the chief priests and the teachers of the law to inquire from them where the Messiah would be born. They told him Bethlehem was the ordained place for his birth since it was prophesied in the OT (Micah 5:2). Herod then told the wise men to look for the newborn and to inform him of the baby's whereabouts on the pretext that he, too, would want to worship the new "king of the Jews." The star then led the wise men to Bethlehem until it "stood over where the young child was" (Matthew 2:9). Upon seeing the baby Jesus, the wise men gave him gifts of gold, incense, and myrrh and worshipped him. Then they went back to their own country by another route, having been warned by an angel in a dream not to go back to Herod. Then an angel appeared to Joseph, again in a dream, telling him to take his family to Egypt for fear of King Herod, which he did. So Herod, realizing the wise men had outwitted him, had given orders to slaughter all the baby boys less than two years of age in and around Bethlehem (Matthew 2:16). After Herod died, Joseph took his family from Egypt back to Judea. But when he heard that Archelaus was reigning in his father's stead, they went to live in Nazareth of Galilee instead.

Now we know Herod was the sort of fellow who could have gone around killing babies. We know from the Jewish historian Josephus (37–100 CE) that, among other things, he murdered his wife, had his brother-in-law and three of his sons executed, and had the Jewish high priest Aristobolus III and forty-five members of the Jewish religious council (the Sanhedrin) killed for supporting the Hasmoneans. The most dramatic point in Matthew's nativity story was when Herod was said to have ordered the slaughtering of all the male children "in Bethlehem and all the surrounding countryside" (Matthew 2:16). Herein lies a major problem: there is no other account of this massive slaughter in any other source—neither in the rest of the NT nor in any other secular records. Josephus's account of Herod and his exploits spanned four books in his *Jewish Antiquities* (books 14–17). From his description of Herod, it is quite obvious that Josephus hated him. He laid out in detail the crimes committed by Herod, many of which were of a lesser kind than the slaughter of the children. Yet nowhere in Josephus's work do we find any mention of this massacre. This silence speaks volumes, for he should have been in a position to know, and he would have had every reason to tell the story if he had known about it. But he said nothing. Most scholars have correctly interpreted this to mean that the incident never happened and was just an invention of Matthew.[52]

As an aside, it is also interesting to consider this story from the framework of the problem of evil. Note that God intervened by revealing to the wise men in a dream not to go back to Jerusalem so Herod would not know exactly where the baby Jesus was to kill him. It was because of not knowing this that Herod had *all* the male babies below two years of age in Bethlehem slaughtered. It was also revealed to Joseph in a dream to take Mary and Jesus and flee to Egypt to avoid this massacre. As the critical nineteenth-century historical scholar David Strauss (1808–1874) pointed out, if God wanted to avoid the massacre of the innocents, he could easily have intervened supernaturally at the *beginning* by making the wise men avoid Jerusalem altogether and head on to Bethlehem directly. That way Herod would never have heard of the birth of the Messiah.[53]

There are other reasons to doubt the historicity of Matthew's account. As many scholars have noted, Matthew's account of this section—including the flight from Egypt and slaughter of male children—parallels the story of Moses found in Exodus. In Exodus 1:22 we're told that the pharaoh ordered that every male baby born shall be killed by being thrown into the river. That Moses' flight from Egypt is so obviously in Matthew's mind when he wrote this account can also be seen from the fact that he used a passage from Hosea (11:1–2), which actually referred to the original Exodus, as a prophetic passage about the return to Judea of Joseph, Mary, and Jesus. The Exodus story was the source that provided Matthew with the base material with which to construct the story.[54] The author of Matthew would not have considered this method unusual, since it is a well-known Jewish exegetical method known as *aggadic midrash*. This involves recasting older stories into newer ones and thereby reading "deeper" meanings into old text. This can be seen even in the OT where Moses' parting of the Red Sea (Exodus 14:2–31) is recast as the story of Joshua parting the River Jordan (Joshua 3:14–17). Likewise, the historical connection between Herod and Jesus is an invention of the Gospel of Matthew.

According to the Gospel of Luke, and in contradiction to Matthew, it was the census called by Quirinius that compelled Joseph and the pregnant Mary to travel *from* Nazareth *to* Bethlehem (Luke 2:1), rather than (as in Matthew) the other way around (and for a different reason: fear of Herod's successor, Archelaus). The census is undoubtedly a historical event. But unfortunately, the problems begin to pile up the moment we consider the whole story in more detail.[55]

- According to Luke 2:3–4, Joseph had to go to Bethlehem because he was a descendent of David, who was from that town. Apart from being a logistical nightmare, this method of going to one's ancestral hometown to register for the census is unheard of in other historical sources. Evangelicals refer to a papyrus dated to 104 CE where the prefect of Egypt ordered all "to return to their own homes" to register for the census, as supporting evidence for such a requirement.[56] But such an interpretation is incorrect. Many scholars have pointed out that Roman censuses were done for taxation purposes. This means that the "homes" being referred to in the order above is to where one's properties are. In other words, the location of registration is at one's *permanent residence* not their *ancestral hometown*.

- Luke 2:1 states Caesar Augustus ordered a census for "all the world." Yet historians know of no such worldwide census. While the Romans did periodically conduct censuses at different times in various locations, there is simply no evidence that there was ever a simultaneous worldwide census under Caesar Augustus.
- According to Luke (1:26) Joseph and Mary lived in Nazareth. But the area under the jurisdiction of Quirinius covered only Judaea, where Bethlehem was, not Nazareth. Nazareth in Galilee was under the rule of Herod Antipas (d. ca. 40 CE) and would not have been under the control of Quirinius. Given what Luke says, there is no way a census under the supervision of this Roman governor could have applied to Joseph and Mary who supposedly lived in Nazareth.
- Finally, the clincher. Both Matthew and Luke said Jesus was born during the time of Herod the Great (Matthew 2:1, Luke 1:5). Herod's date of death is unassailable—it was 4 BCE. The date of Quirinius's census is also firmly established—6 CE. In other words, there is a discrepancy of about ten years between the two events—the death of Herod and the Quirinius census.[57]

The last point has been doggedly attacked by evangelicals. The reason for such determined apologetics is understandable. If the above is unassailable, then the case is settled: the Bible contains fiction, and biblical inerrancy is confined to the scrap heap of human history. Let us look in detail at some of these apologetic attempts.

The first step is to claim that there was an earlier census under Quirinius that was done during the reign of Herod the Great. This means that Quirinius was twice governor of Syria, once between 6 CE and 12 CE and another earlier tenure during the reign of Herod the Great. As "evidence" to prop up this, the British archaeologist Sir William Ramsay (1851–1939) is normally invoked, together with the inscription Sir Ramsey interpreted to mean that Quirinius was governor of Syria not once, but twice, separated by a few years on both of the occasions mentioned above.[58] This argument is obsolete, as it has been *proven* false. The reasons are as follows:

- The inscription found by Ramsey simply mentioned that Quirinius was honored for his role in achieving a military victory. It was Ramsey who *guessed* that Quirinius's reward for his role was an earlier appointment, prior to 6 CE, as governor of Syria. Nothing in the inscription even suggests this. It is not surprising that most historians are of the opinion that the inscription *does not* provide any evidence to support the assertion that Quirinius was governor of Syria earlier than 6 CE.[59]
- From Josephus we know most of the Roman governors of Syria around that time. Table 6.1 below shows the governors of Syria from 23 BCE to 7 CE. The two Roman governors of Syria during the last years of Herod's reign were Gaius Sentius Saturninus, who held the post from 9 to 6 BCE, and Publius Quintilius Varus, who was his successor from 6 to 4 BCE. It was Varus who, as governor, suppressed the uprising that occurred *after* the death of Herod (Antiquities 17:10:1). There are only two "blanks" in the list of governors between 23 BCE to 7 CE; once between 13–11 BCE and another time between 3–2 BCE. The latter gap is of no consequence, since by then Herod was already dead, and the former gap was probably filled by Marcus Titius, from 12 to 9 BCE, as we know he was governor sometime in that period, and a three-year term was typical.[60]

TABLE 6.1 THE GOVERNORS OF SYRIA BETWEEN 23 BCE AND 7 CE[61]

Years of Governorship	Name of Governor
23–13 BCE	M. Agrippa
13–11 BCE	?
ca. 10 BCE	M. Titius
9–6 BCE	C. Sentius Saturninus
6–4 BCE [*after* Herod's death]	P. Quintilius Varus
ca. 4–2 BCE	?
1 BCE to 4 CE	Gauis Caesar (?)
4–5 CE	L. Volusius Saturninus
6 CE–after 7 CE	P. Sulpicius Quirinius

- Quirinius's career is relatively well documented in our primary sources. Tacitus's *Annals of Imperial Rome* (3:22–23, 3:48), Suetonius's *Tiberius* (49), Strabo's *Geography* (12:6:5) and Josephus's *Antiquities of the Jews* (17:13:5, 18:1:1) all mention aspects of his career. From these accounts we know that he was born sometime before 50 BCE and that he died in 22 CE. We know that he was consul of Rome by 12 BCE. He was in Asia Minor between 12 and 6 BCE, where he fought the war against the Homonadenses. He was the governor of Pamphylia-Galatia between 6 to 1 BCE. And he was serving as the adviser for Gauis Caesar for several years before 4 CE. Josephus mentioned Quirinius several times when he became governor of Syria in 6 CE (Antiquities 17:13:5, 18:1:1). So we read of Quirinius's career spanning twenty years from 12 BCE to 6 CE, yet not once was he mentioned as taking over the governorship of Syria at any time during the reign of Herod.[62]

The conclusion is inescapable—Quirinius could not have been governor of Syria twice.[63]

To add on to this insurmountable difficulty there are still others concerning the suggestion of an earlier census. For instance, there is no historical evidence for any Roman census in Judea before 6 CE. The Romans took direct control of Judaea only after that time. Prior to this time the province was a "client kingdom"—under Roman domination but not direct Roman rule. The Romans have never been known to initiate any census in their client kingdoms. As mentioned above, the Roman census is taken primarily for taxation purposes. By all accounts Herod the Great was an obedient subject of Rome who paid his dues properly. There was no need for Rome to intervene directly with any kind of census in Judea prior to 6 CE.[64]

With the links now completely severed between the nativity and world history, we can now see the rest of the nativity accounts for what they really are—the mysterious "wise men from the east" who followed a magical star that could "stand above" where the baby Jesus was (Matthew 2:9), the angels who spoke to Mary (Luke 1:26–37), to Joseph (Matthew 1:20) and the shepherds (Luke 2:15), people who could burst into spontaneous songs of praise (Luke 1:46–55; 1:68–79)—are not historical details but elements of a fairy tale. Removed from the anchors of history provided by Herod and Quirinius, the nativity accounts drift into the realm of myths and legends.

FAILED PROPHECIES AND FAKED PROPHECIES

We have all heard evangelical claims about fulfilled prophecies, especially messianic prophecies of the OT supposedly fulfilled in Jesus. Yet such a view is erroneous and involves interpreting passages as prophecy that are not prophetic at all, or reinterpreting prophetic passages that had nothing to do with the Messiah. Modern scholarship has shown that most of these so-called messianic prophecies in the OT do not refer to Jesus or the Messiah.[65] Critical historical scholars identify fewer than half a dozen passages in the OT as genuinely messianic. Yet even in these cases, they refer to people and events of their own time, not to the distant future.[66]

The author of the Gospel of Matthew, for instance, interpreted Hosea 11:1–2 as a prophecy of the holy family's return from after the death of Herod (Matthew 2:14–15). But that passage was actually about the return of the Israelites during the Exodus. In Matthew 1:22–23, Isaiah 7:14 is cited as a prophecy of Jesus' miraculous birth to a virgin, yet that passage has nothing to do with the virgin birth—since the Hebrew word used (*almah*) did not refer to "virgin" but merely to a "young woman." Matthew had used the Greek translation of the Bible, which had erroneously translated the Hebrew "young woman" (*almah*) into "virgin" (*parthenos*).[67] Furthermore, the whole context of the prophecy in Isaiah 7:10–17 refers to events during the time of that prophet and had nothing to do with events of the distant future.[68]

More damning to the whole idea of prophecy in the Bible is the presence of prophecies we know to have failed. Here are just a few:[69]

- Isaiah 19:5–7 claims the river Nile will dry up. The passage was written almost three thousand years ago and was clearly meant for his time. Yet to this date, the Nile has yet to dry up.
- Isaiah 17:1–2 asserts Damascus will cease to be a city forever. I think most people living today in Damascus, the capital city of Syria, would find such a prophecy rather funny.
- Ezekiel predicted (26:7–14) that Nebuchadnezzar will destroy the city of Tyre. Yet even by the prophet's own later admission, the prophecy failed (Ezekiel 29:17–20).
- Ezekiel tried his hand again at prophecy when he predicted that Egypt will become desolate, completely uninhabited, and that

Egyptians will be scattered to other countries (Ezekiel 29:8–12). Yet Egypt has never been desolate, or completely uninhabited, and there never was an Egyptian diaspora.

- Hoping for a third time, Ezekiel tried again. He predicted that Nebuchadnezzar will conquer Egypt (29:19–20). Nebuchadnezzar never did this.
- Jeremiah 36:30 prophesied that Jehoiakim, the king of Judah, shall have no successor. Yet 2 Kings 24:6 says he was succeeded by his son, Jehoiachin.

One of the techniques modern psychics use in their continuing effort to fleece the public is called "postdiction." This involves claiming *after* the occurrence of something sensational that you predicted the event before it happened, but for some reason the prediction had been ignored or missed. We find such a method distasteful, yet some biblical authors were not above such tactics. A case in point is the author of the book attributed to Daniel. That book presents itself as being written by the prophet around the sixth century BCE.[70] Even as early as the third century, pagan critics such as Porphyry (234–ca. 305) had already pointed out that Daniel's prophecy was remarkably accurate for events leading up to the desecration of the temple in Jerusalem in 167 BCE, but totally off for events following that. Modern scholars are now in agreement that Daniel was written a year or two after 167 BCE.[71] Why did the author of Daniel do this? Obviously the answer is that if he could present some of his "postdictions" as accurate, people would give more credence to his book and to its predictions of the future. The one "real" prediction in it that could be verified—the location of the death of Antiochus IV—has been shown to be completely off the mark. Daniel 11:45 predicted that Antiochus IV (ca. 215–164 BCE) would die in a location between Jerusalem and the Mediterranean Sea, but he uncooperatively died in Persia.[72] One wonders how different such authors were from the likes of modern-day "psychics" who fleece the gullible in order to enrich themselves.

INERRANT FORGERIES

There is a class of books called by scholars *pseudepigraphy* (literally "false writing") characterized by *pseudonymity* ("false name") in which the author *deliberately* tries to present his writing as originating from someone else.[73] We all know there are many religious writings outside the Jewish and Christian canon that are pseudepigraphical. Jewish writings such as the books of *Enoch*, the *Assumption of Moses, Wisdom of Solomon,* and the *Psalms of Solomon* are all well known to have been written much later than the time of their supposed authors. Christian pseudepigraphy outside the canon includes works such as Paul's third letter to the Corinthians (*3 Corinthians*), the *Gospel of Thomas*, and the *Letter of Peter to James* (found in the *Pseudo-Clementine Homilies*). All are falsely attributed to the various apostles by their actual authors.[74]

Are there pseudepigraphical works even in the canonical Bible? The answer is something critical scholars have known for years—an unequivocal "Yes." In the OT, the book of Daniel,[75] some portions of Psalms,[76] and the later part of Isaiah[77] are all known to be pseudonymous. In the NT, the Pastoral Epistles (1 Timothy, 2 Timothy, and Titus) are considered by a vast majority of critical scholars *not* to have been written by Paul.[78] As a summary, the lines of evidence that point to the fact that these Epistles were not written by Paul but by someone else around 100 CE or later includes all of the following points:

- The pastoral Epistles were not attested in any early works until the end of the second century. They were first mentioned by Irenaeus around 185 BCE. The arch-Paulinist Marcion (d. ca.160) did not seem to have been aware of the pastorals. When we contrast this to, say, 1 Corinthians, which was quoted as early as 95 CE by Clement (1 Clement 47), we can see how late the attestation is for the pastorals.[79]
- Paul, in the authentic Epistles, always refers to the Gentiles in the second-person "you" (e.g., Romans 11:13; 1 Corinthians 12:2), but in Titus the first-person plural "we" is used (Titus 3:3) when speaking about Gentiles. This inclusion of himself in the same group as Gentiles ("we" instead of "you") is not a characteristic of the historical Paul.[80]
- A highly organized church simply did not exist in Paul's time. In the genuine Pauline Epistles we find that there were many different kinds of believers, such as prophets, apostles, and miracle workers, among others. These speak whenever they want to and there was no one truly in charge (1 Corinthians 11:33; 12:28; 14:26–33). In the pastorals, this chaotic structure no longer exists. Instead we find a hier-

archical structure of *paid* and *formally appointed* offices for bishops, presbyters and deacons (1 Timothy 3:1–7; 4:14; 5:27; Titus 1:5–9).[81]

- In the authentic Epistles of Paul, he expected the apocalyptic end of the world within his own lifetime, or at least the lifetime of most of his flock (1 Corinthians 7:29–21; 1 Thessalonians 4:15–17). In the pastorals, we find "Paul" making provisions for the death of *his* followers by commanding them to pass his teachings on (2 Timothy 2:1–14).[82]

- Of the 848 different words used in the Pastorals, 306 (or 36 percent) are not found anywhere else in the other ten letters of the Pauline corpus. Furthermore, of this unique vocabulary, 211 words are very commonly used by *second-century* writers.[83]

- Even the words that are shared between the pastorals and genuine Pauline Epistles have markedly different meanings. "Faith" for Paul meant a sense of trust one has in the redeeming feature of Jesus' death (e.g., Romans 1:16–17). However, in the Pastorals the word is used to mean the body of teachings of the church (e.g., Titus 1:13).[84]

Three other Pauline Epistles (Colossians, Ephesians, and 2 Thessalonians) are also considered by a majority of scholars to be pseudonymous.[85] 2 Peter is unanimously considered to be pseudonymous,[86] with most scholars also lumping 1 Peter into the same category.[87] James and Jude are also generally considered to be pseudepigraphical works.[88]

It is now time to point out the elephant in the room, standing quietly by the corner: *pseudepigraphs are forgeries*! Many critical historical scholars are Christians, however nominally. While it is easy for them to explain away the inconsistencies and mythological elements present in the Bible as conveyors of some "higher truth,"[89] forgery is another matter. For it implies a conscious attempt to deceive. To prevent such a stigma, they have tried a three-step approach. The first is to avoid using the word "forgery" at all cost and use abstruse words like "pseudepigraphy" and "pseudynomity" instead. The second step is to claim that the disciples of Paul (or Peter or James or Jude) wrote under their master's name because the letter "was intended as an extension of his thought—an assumption of the great apostle's mantle to continue his work."[90] The final step is to then say that the ancients accepted pseudepigraphy as something normal and would not consider it negatively as we would today. Seeing pseudepigraphy as a form of deception "represents a great misunderstanding of the ancient world, imposing our modern concepts of authorship and copyright most inappropriately," we're told.[91]

Do pseudepigraphers (i.e., forgers!) merely try to reflect or extend the thoughts and teachings of the one they are pretending to be? The answer to this question is no, not always. Just compare the "pseudepigraphically written" 2 Thessalonians with what we find in the genuine Pauline Epistles. The real Paul in 1 Thessalonians expected the world as we know it to end very soon, during his lifetime, as Loftus explains in chapter 12 of this book. Far from carrying the mantle of Paul, 2 Thessalonians substantially alters what the self-proclaimed apostle to the Gentiles taught. 2 Thessalonians warns its readers "not to be deceived" by a "letter as from us" which claims that the return of Christ is imminent (2:2–3). Since 1 Thessalonians 1:1 claims to be from Paul, 2 Thessalonians is in fact calling 1 Thessalonians a deceptive forgery.[92] The irony of ironies, the forger is calling the original a fake!

Did the ancients view pseudepigraphy differently from us today? This, too, can be shown to be false. Greek and Roman authors warned their audience about forgeries written in their names. The famous Greek doctor Galen (ca. 129–ca. 200 CE) actually wrote a whole book telling his audience how to distinguish his work from forgeries. Even among the early Christians such practice was frowned upon. The church father Tertullian (ca. 160–ca. 225) told the story of how the forger of 3 Corinthians, a Christian presbyter, was duly convicted by the ecclesiastical authority for composing this letter and falsely attributing it to Paul.[93]

As Bart Ehrman pointed out in his recent book, *Jesus Interrupted*,[94] the ancients used words such as *pseudon* (a lie) and *nothon* (a bastard child) to describe forgeries. Pseudepigraphy was not considered "okay" by the ancients and anyone who wrote such a piece of work must have been aware of the morally repugnant nature of what he was doing. Yet the works of such people as these made it into the NT. We end this section on an ironical note. One of the most commonly used passages by evangelicals to "prove" biblical inspiration is this one: "Every Scripture is God-breathed and profitable for teaching, for reproof, for correction, and for instruction in righteousness" (2 Timothy 3:16). Yet this passage is almost certainly the work of a forger.

CONCLUSIONS

Let's recap what modern scholars have found. The Bible is filled with so many diametrically opposite viewpoints that if they were present in a human being we would probably label that person bipolar or, even worse, schizophrenic. We have seen that the pillars of biblical archaeology—the Patriarchal Narratives, the Exodus, and the Conquest—events once thought to have been historical, are now shown to be made up almost completely of myths and legends. In the NT we find that critical historical research has relegated the nativity accounts in Matthew and Luke to the realm of myths, legends, and fairy tales. Prophecy, far from being strong evidence for the divine authority of the Bible, is actually an Achilles' heel. The Bible contains prophecies that were faked (i.e., made after the fact) and prophecies that failed. We also find that the verse most often used by evangelicals to support their doctrine of biblical inerrancy, 2 Timothy 3:16, comes from the pen of a forger.

The Bible cannot be considered inspired by God in any meaningful sense at all.

ADDENDUM: THE LIBERALS AND THE BIBLE

I have argued that the evangelical belief in biblical inspiration cannot be defended in the light of modern scholarship. However, there are many Christians who are not evangelicals, members of the mainline Protestant churches, such as Lutheran, Anglican, and Methodist churches, who do not accept the evangelical position. These churches subscribe to some forms of liberal-modernist theology. Liberal or modernist theologians would happily admit to all of the findings mentioned in this chapter but would dismiss them as "insignificant" objections to their faith. Yet, strange as it may seem to the average person, these theologians still consider themselves Christians.

Liberal modernist theology has its roots in the Enlightenment—an intellectual movement that started in the eighteenth century—which placed reason above all else. The skepticism of philosophers such as David Hume (1711–1776) and to a certain extent, Immanuel Kant (1724–1804) presented many difficulties for Christian theologians. Even more troubling to theology than philosophy was *natural* philosophy, or, as it eventually became known, science. The Copernican revolution, which showed that the sun, not the earth, was the center upon which everything in the then-known universe revolves, took away the earth's, and thus man's, place from the center of the universe. It became harder to believe how man could be the crowning glory of creation when he is placed in an insignificant corner of the universe.[95] The plight of the theologians continued to pile up in the nineteenth century. The publishing of Charles Darwin's (1809–1882) treatise on evolution, *On The Origin of Species* (1859), meant that science had gone one step further against the theologian. The theory of evolution presented by Darwin showed that man is an evolved animal, no more and no less. If evolution is true, and the evidence marshaled by Darwin in his book is compelling, then Genesis is false; far from being created in God's image, humankind bore all the marks of an animal ancestry.

Within Christendom, the development of biblical criticism, especially in its "higher" form, began to show that the Bible was not a unique document (as we've shown). Christian theology bifurcated into fundamentalist/conservatism on one side and liberal/modernism on the other.[96] While the fundamentalist side rejected the assured results of science and biblical criticism, the liberal side embraced them and subsequently reinvented their Christian faith. Thus the liberals did not reach their position by abstruse theological reasoning. Instead they were *forced* into it by external circumstances—the findings of science, comparative religions, enlightenment philosophies, and textual and historical criticism.

The position of the liberals on the Bible can be divided into two broad, not necessarily mutually exclusive, positions. The first is that the biblical myths convey symbolic truths, as expressed in a report published by the Anglican Church Commission on Christian Doctrine in 1938: "Statements affirming particular facts may be found to have value as pictorial expressions of spiritual truths, even though the supposed facts themselves did not actually happen. In that case such statements must be called symbolically true. …It is not therefore of necessity illegitimate to accept and affirm particular clauses in the Creeds while understanding them in this symbolic sense."[97] This report, probably on purpose, never made it clear which clauses of the Anglican creeds were to be understood in this symbolic sense.

The second position asserts that the Bible, while being fallible, is in general the inspired word of God, as Carl Lofmark summed up the views of liberal R. P. C. Hanson and A. T. Hanson:

> They recognized that the Bible contains errors and cannot be divinely inspired, that its world view is "pre-scientific" and its accounts of history mainly myths, legend, or fiction, that its miracles never happened and that parts of it are unedifying if not disgusting…. They agree that the

Bible text is unreliable and the original words (including the words of Jesus) have often been altered. Yet they still believe that the Bible's "general drift" or "impression" is a "true witness to the nature of God." The unedifying texts are "balanced" by others, which reveal the truth. Deep significance is not found everywhere in the Bible, but only in its "high spots."... This approach is eclectic: they select from the Bible those passages which they find edifying and construct from those passages their own impression of the Bible's "general drift," while rejecting the bulk of what the Bible contains. Only the better parts are a true witness to the nature and purpose of God.[98]

The first problem to note is that if modern liberals are right about the Bible, then most Christians have failed to understand God's true message throughout church history until recent time. Put in this way, the liberal position sounds smug and pretentious.

The second problem is that the question remains as to *which* passages are to be taken literally and which are to be taken symbolically. If the intent of the biblical authors is rejected by the method of selection, then this leaves the door wide open for selecting which passages should be symbolic and which should not. Thirdly, *how* are those passages to be interpreted symbolically? There is no guide or generally accepted method of symbolic interpretation. How does one know which symbolic interpretation is correct? Fourthly, just because the stories are *defined* as symbolic by the liberals, it does not mean that the issue of the criterion of truth has been successfully avoided. What happens when two liberal theologians come up with two mutually exclusive symbolic truths from the same biblical passage? And finally, many so-called interpretations of the symbolic truths of the Bible are actually *devoid of any cognitive meaning.*

Take for instance an Ascension Day sermon written for an English newspaper by an Anglican bishop: "[The ascension of Jesus is] not a primitive essay in astrophysics, but the symbol of creative intuition...into the abiding significance of Jesus and his place in the destiny of man. It might be called a pictorial presentation of the earliest creed, Jesus is Lord.... Creed and scripture are saying in their own language that here is something final and decisive, the truth and the meaning of man's life and destiny—truth not in theory but in a person-life in its ultimate quality, that is God's life."[99] From what he said only one thing is clear: the good bishop does not believe that the ascension story is to be taken literally. Apart from this, it is very difficult to fathom what it is he is trying to say and how what he is trying to say is derived from that story told in three verses in Acts, if it is not grounded in an actual historical event. While we can forgive the author of Acts for his lack of knowledge of astrophysics, it is hard to know what to do with the bishop.

As for the "take some and leave some" approach to the Bible, the central question remains: if some parts of the Bible are false or unacceptable, what guarantee do we have that the other parts are true, or are of any special value? Thus the moment one admits that some parts of the Bible are untrue or unacceptable, the position of the Bible as the inspired word of God becomes very difficult to objectively defend.

Take for instance this passage from American liberal theologian Leslie Weatherhead: "[W]hen Jesus is reported as consigning to everlasting torture those who displease him or do not 'believe' what he says, I know in my heart that there is something wrong somewhere. Either he is misrepresented or misunderstood.... So I put his alleged saying in my mental drawer awaiting further light. By the judgment of the court within my own breast...I reject such sayings."[100] The question here is simple: if he could use his own judgment to accept and reject biblical passages, why rely on the Bible at all?

This leads us into the liberal theologians' views of Jesus. It is obvious that since the late nineteenth century these theologians have ceased to believe that the main events of the Gospels are historical, especially the virgin birth, the associated nativity stories, the miracles, and the bodily resurrection of Jesus. The liberals trip all over themselves trying to avoid saying the actual truth: *if the bodily resurrection of Jesus is not historical then traditional Christianity, in any form, is no longer valid.* This is the skeptic's position, of course. But the liberals added that the resurrection is to be understood in a different sense, but just exactly what sense is not clear. Their writings contain so much garbled speech that it is difficult to even see if they agree with one another. Most of the liberal interpretation involves accepting the resurrection as some kind of internal revelation of the disciples. This experience, they proclaim, is what really matters, not the actual historical fact of resurrection. But why should it, we ask? Why should the visions or dreams of a few ill-educated, first-century Galilean peasants be of any significance and be treated any differently from others all over the world and throughout history? Because it is about Jesus? But take away the historical claims about his supposed supernatural powers, his miracles, and his bodily resurrection, and what do we have? A first-century, xenophobic, ignorant Galilean peasant who thought the world was going to end (as Loftus proves in chapter 12). If this is so, why not just dispense with it altogether? It's high time they did. As Hector Avalos has argued very effectively in *The End of Biblical Studies*, it's time that biblical studies as we know them should end.

NOTES

1. Editor's note: This chapter sums up only a few sections of Paul Tobin's far more extensive book, *The Rejection of Pascal's Wager: A Skeptic's Guide to the Bible and the Historical Jesus* (Bedfordshire, England: Authors Online, 2009). Good summaries of what scholars now widely conclude about the Bible, fully in accord with Tobin's account, can be found in Israel Finkelstein and Neil Silberman, *The Bible Unearthed: Archaeology's New Vision of Ancient Israel and the Origins of Its Sacred Texts* (New York: Free Press, 2001) and Bart Ehrman, *Jesus Interrupted: Revealing the Hidden Contradictions in the Bible* (New York: HarperOne, 2009) (for the OT and NT, respectively). All three books should be required reading for any actual or prospective Christian.

2. Robert L. Wilken, *The Christians as the Romans See Them* (New Haven, CT: Yale University Press, 1984).

3. See "The Confessions and Letters of Saint Augustin, with a Sketch of His Life and Work: Letter 82," Christian Classics Ethereal Library, http://www.ccel .org/ccel/schaff/npnf101.vii.1.LXXXII.html.

4. Robert Price, *Inerrant the Wind: The Evangelical Crisis of Biblical Authority* (Amherst, NY: Prometheus Books, 2009) and *Beyond Born Again: Towards Evangelical Maturity*, http://www.infidels.org/library/modern/robert_price/beyond _born _again/index.shtml.

5. The reader is encouraged to consult the following works for further information: Hector Avalos, *The End of Biblical Studies* (Amherst, NY: Prometheus Books, 2007), pp. 37–53; Dan Barker, *Godless: How an Evangelical Preacher Became One of America's Leading Atheists* (Berkeley, CA: Ulysses Press, 1992), pp. 222–50; Rod Evans and Irwin Berent, *Fundamentalism: Hazards and Heartbreaks* (LaSalle, IL: Open Court, 1988), pp. 89–94; Bruce Metzger, *The Bible in Translation* (Grand Rapids, MI: Baker Academic, 2001), pp. 140–41; and my own *Rejection of Pascal's Wager*, pp. 197–204.

6. On this see Richard Elliott Friedman's two books, *Who Wrote the Bible?* (New York: Perennial Library, 1989) and *The Bible with Sources Revealed: A New View into the Five Books of Moses* (San Francisco: HarperSanFrancisco, 2003). Friedman is

a premier critical historical scholar and a professor of Hebrew and comparative literature. He outlines how scholars discovered the source documents of the Pentateuch when they realized that different accounts actually come from different sources that the editors of the Pentateuch tried to cobble together.

7. Randel McGraw Helms, *The Bible against Itself: Why the Bible Seems to Contradict Itself* (Altadena, CA: Millennium Press, 2006).

8. Compare also: Proverbs 1:13–17 versus Ecclesiastes 7:15–17; and Proverbs 1:7 and 2:5 versus Ecclesiastes 7:23 and 8:1, 17–18. See Helms, *Bible against Itself*, pp. 60–63.

9. Helms, *Bible against Itself*, pp. 115–33.

10. C. Dennis McKinsey has written a book of more than five hundred pages cataloging these errors, *The Encyclopedia of Biblical Errancy* (Amherst, NY: Prometheus Books, 1995).

11. Some examples: Gleason Archer, *Encyclopedia of Bible Difficulties* (Grand Rapids, MI: Zondervan 1982), in 476 pages; Norman Geisler and Thomas Howe, *The Big Book of Bible Difficulties* (Grand Rapids, MI: Baker Books, 1992), in 615 pages; and R. A. Torrey, *Difficulties in the Bible* (Chicago: Moody Press 1972), in 159 pages.

12. For example, the book by the German journalist Werner Keller, *The Bible as History* (1956), has the subtitle "Archaeology Confirms the Book of Books!"

13. See chapter 4, "Collapse of the Paradigm," in Thomas W. Davis, *Shifting Sands: The Rise and Fall of Biblical Archaeology* (Oxford: Oxford University Press 2004).

14. Davis, *Shifting Sands*, p. 145; P. R. S. Moorey, *A Century of Biblical Archaeology* (Louisville, KY: Westminster John Knox Press, 1992), pp. 173–75.

15. Ian Plimer, *Telling Lies for God: Reason versus Creationism* (Milsons Point, NSW: Random House Australia, 1994), p. 75.

16. For the full text of the epic of Gilgamesh, see: http://www.ancient texts.org/library/mesopotamian/gilgamesh/.

17. Cyrus Gordon and Gary Rendsburg, *The Bible and the Ancient Near East* (New York: W.W. Norton, 1997), p. 50.

18. Archaeologists have discovered two even earlier versions of flood myths—the Sumerian epic of Ziusudra (ca. 2600 BCE) and the Akkadian epic of Atrahasis (ca. 1900 BCE). Together with the epic of Gilgamesh, these myths involve the gods causing a worldwide flood and a hero who builds an ark to save himself, his family, and some animals. The epics of Ziusudra and Atrahasis do not survive in their complete forms and are today extant only in fragments. For a thorough analysis of the relationship between these various flood myths, see Jeffrey Tigay's monograph *The Evolution of the Gilgamesh Epic* (Philadelphia: University of Pennsylvania Press, 1982).

19. See Finkelstein and Silberman, *Bible Unearthed*, pp. 27–47; Niels Peter Lemche, *Prelude to Israel's Past: Background and Beginnings of Israelite History and Iden-*

tity (Peabody, MA: Hendrickson, 1998), pp. 12–44; John Van Seters, *Abraham in History and Tradition* (New Haven, CT: Yale University Press, 1975); Thomas Thompson, *The Historicity of the Patriarchal Narratives: The Quest for the Historical Abraham* (Harrisburg, PA: Trinity Press International, 2002).

20. Eric Cline, *From Eden to Exile: Unraveling the Mysteries of the Bible* (Washington, DC: National Geographic, 2007), pp. 56–57; Lemche, *Prelude to Israel's Past*, pp. 39, 62.

21. Finkelstein and Silberman, *Bible Unearthed*, p. 37.

22. Manfred Barthel, *What the Bible Really Says* (New York: Wings, 1980), p. 79; Michael D. Coogan, ed., *The Oxford History of the Biblical World* (London: Oxford University Press, 1998), pp. 28, 109; Finkelstein and Silberman, *Bible Unearthed*, p. 37; Lemche, *Prelude to Israel's Past*, p. 64. A contrary claim that camels were already domesticated in the Levant during the time of Abraham is based solely on drawings of camels and the finding of camel bones in archaeological sites dated to the second and third millennia BCE. But as Israel Finkelstein explains in his paper "Arabian Trade and Socio-Political Conditions in the Negev in the Twelfth–Eleventh Centuries BCE" for the *Journal of Near Eastern Studies* 47, no. 4 (October 1988): pp. 241–52, these findings only show that the people of that time were familiar with *wild* camels (and may have eaten their meat?!).

23. Coogan, *Oxford History of the Biblical World*, p. 271; Barthel, *What the Bible Really Says*, pp. 77–78.

24. Thompson, *Historicity of the Patriarchal Narratives*, pp. 324–26; Finkelstein and Silberman, *Bible Unearthed*, p. 38.

25. See Cline, *From Eden to Exile*, pp. 61–92; William Dever, *Who Were the Early Israelites and Where Did They Come From?* (Grand Rapids, MI: Eerdmans, 2003), pp. 4–21; Finkelstein and Silberman, *Bible Unearthed*, pp. 48–71; John C. H. Laughlin, *Archaeology and the Bible* (New York: Routledge, 2000), pp. 86–92; Lemche, *Prelude to Israel's Past*, pp. 44–61; Amy Marcus, *The View from Nebo: How Archaeology Is Rewriting the Bible and Reshaping the Middle East* (Boston: Little, Brown, 2000), pp. 51–77; William H. Stiebing, *Out of the Desert? Archaeology and the Exodus/Conquest Narratives* (Amherst, NY: Prometheus Books, 1989).

26. Cline, *From Eden to Exile*, pp. 70–71; Keller, *Bible as History*, pp. 122–23; Lemche, *Prelude to Israel's Past*, pp. 49–50; E. Riedel, T. Tracy, and B. Moskowitz, *The Book of the Bible* (New York: Bantam, 1981), pp. 27–28.

27. Lemche, *Prelude to Israel's Past*, p. 50 n. 49; Stiebing, *Out of the Desert*, p. 20.

28. As Lemche noted, in Egyptian the name appears in compound form for various Egyptian pharaohs, for example, Kamose, Tuthmosis, and Ramose (Rammesses), compare *Prelude to Israel's Past*, p. 52 n. 50; see also Stiebing, *Out of the Desert*, p. 198.

29. Cline, *From Eden to Exile*, pp. 71–73; Finkelstein and Silberman, *Bible Unearthed*, pp. 56–57.

30. See Finkelstein and Silberman, *Bible Unearthed*, pp. 54–57.

31. Ibid., p. 60.

32. Ibid., pp. 61–63, and appendix B, pp. 326–28; Marcus, *View from Nebo*, p. 75; Laughlin, *Archaeology and the Bible*, p. 91; and Matthew Sturgis, *It Ain't Necessarily So: Investigating the Truth of the Biblical Past* (London: Headline Book, 2001), p. 72.

33. Quoted in Laughlin, *Archaeology and the Bible*, p. 92.

34. Quoted in Sturgis, *It Ain't Necessarily So*, p. 74.

35. Cline, *From Eden to Exile*, pp. 100–101; R. Davidson and A. R. C. Leaney, *Biblical Criticism* (Harmondsworth, England: Penguin, 1970), p. 46; Dever, *Who Were the Early Israelites?* pp. 45–46; Finkelstein and Silberman, *Bible Unearthed*, pp. 81–82; Robin Lane Fox, *The Unauthorized Version: Truth and Fiction in the Bible* (London: Penguin, 1992), pp. 226–27; Stiebing, *Out of the Desert*, pp. 46–47; Sturgis, *It Ain't Necessarily So*, pp. 58–59.

36. Cline, *From Eden to Exile*, p. 109; Dever, *Who Were the Early Israelites?* pp. 46–47; Finkelstein and Silberman, *Bible Unearthed*, p. 82; Sturgis, *It Ain't Necessarily So*, p. 61. Indeed, the very name "Ai" means "ruin." This suggests the Israelites knew the place only as the ruins of an old settlement (Sturgis, *It Ain't Necessarily So*, p. 65).

37. Finkelstein and Silberman, *The Bible Unearthed*, p. 82; Fox, *The Unauthorized Version*, pp. 226–28; Stiebing, *Out of the Desert*, pp. 84–87.

38. Although Lachish shows signs of being destroyed, the archaeological evidence is conclusive that it was destroyed around 1160 BCE, much too late for Joshua and his men. See Cline, *From Eden to Exile*, pp. 111–12; Dever, *Who Were the Early Israelites?* pp. 64–65; Fox, *Unauthorized Version*, p. 228.

39. Only with Hazor (Joshua 11:10) is there any disagreement between scholars. Some scholars date its destruction to the last quarter of the thirteenth century and attribute this to Joshua while others remain unconvinced and either date the destruction later and/or attribute the destruction to non-Israelites. See Cline, *From Eden to Exile*, pp 112–14; Fox, *Unauthorized Version*, p. 228; Finkelstein and Silberman, *Bible Unearthed*, p. 83; Sturgis, *It Ain't Necessarily So*, pp. 80–83.

40. Sturgis, *It Ain't Necessarily So*, p. 66.

41. The discovery of the "Tel Dan Stela" in 1993, a ninth-century BCE inscription, seems to clinch this. The inscriptions tell of the invasion of Israel by Hazael, king of Damascus, around 835 BCE. In the inscription is written how this king slew the king who was of "The House of David" (see Finkelstein and Silberman, *Bible Unearthed*, pp. 128–29; Laughlin, *Archaeology and the Bible*, p. 122; and Sturgis, *It Ain't Necessarily So*, pp. 162–64). Although for a skeptical evaluation of the Tel Dan Stela and its use as evidence for David's historicity, see Hector Avalos, *End of Biblical Studies*, pp. 127–30.

42. Laughlin, *Archaeology and the Bible*, p. 124.

43. Finkelstein and Silberman, *Bible Unearthed*, pp. 32, 142–43; Marcus, *The View from Nebo*, p. 125.

44. Finkelstein and Silberman, *Bible Unearthed*, pp. 132, 142–43.

45. Laughlin, *Archaeology and the Bible*, p. 127.

46. Finkelstein and Silberman, *Bible Unearthed*, pp. 131–35.

47. Ibid., p. 132.

48. Aesop was a Phrygian slave who (probably) lived around 620–560 BCE. That he was a "fabulist" was mentioned in all the earliest sources that mentioned him: Herodotus (ca. 484–ca. 425 BCE) in his *Histories* (2:134) calling him "the writer Aesop," Plato (427–348 BCE) wrote in Phaedo that Socrates was "putting Aesop into verse," Aristotle (384–322 BC) in his *Rhetoric* (2:20) talks about the "fables of Aesop." See chapter 8, "Aesop the Fabulist," in Page DuBois's *Slaves and Other Objects* (Chicago: University of Chicago Press, 2008) pp. 170–88.

49. Marcello Craveri, *The Life of Jesus* (London: Panther, 1969), pp. 33–34.

50. Robert J. Miller, *Born Divine: The Births of Jesus & Other Sons of God* (Santa Rosa, CA: Polebridge, 2003), pp. 133–53. See also Price, *The Incredible Shrinking Son of Man* (Amherst, NY: Prometheus Books, 2003).

51. Moses Hadas, *Imperial Rome* (Amsterdam, Netherlands: Time Life Books, 1966).

52. Raymond Brown, *The Birth of the Messiah* (New York: Doubleday, 1993), pp. 226–27; Don Cupitt and Peter Armstrong, *Who Was Jesus?* (London: BBC, 1977), p. 46; Edwin Freed, *The Stories of Jesus' Birth: A Critical Introduction* (Sheffield, England: Sheffield Academic, 2001), p. 102; Gerd Lüdemann, *Virgin Birth? The Real Story of Mary and Her Son Jesus* (Harrisburg, PA: Trinity Press, 1998), p. 83.

53. See Lüdemann, *Virgin Birth?* pp. 81–84.

54. Brown, *Birth of the Messiah*, pp. 227–30, Cuppitt and Armstrong, *Who Was Jesus?* p. 46; Freed, *Stories of Jesus' Birth*, p. 102; Miller, *Born Divine*, p. 184.

55. See the summary of the issues (and attempts to resolve them) in Richard Carrier, "Luke vs. Matthew on the Year of Christ's Birth," Errancy Wiki, http://www.errancywiki.com/?title=Legends&rcid=41896.

56. Strobel, *The Case for Christ: A Journalist's Personal Investigation of the Evidence for Jesus* (Grand Rapids, MI: Zondervan, 1998), p. 135.

57. Brown, *Birth of the Messiah*, p. 549–50; Craveri, *Life of Jesus*, p. 44; John Dominic Crossan, *Who Is Jesus?* (New York: HarperCollins, 1996), p. 23; Freed, *Stories of Jesus' Birth*, p. 119; Charles Guignebert, *Jesus* (New York: University Books, 1956), pp. 30–32; Miller, *Born Divine*, pp. 180–81; Price, *Incredible Shrinking Son of Man*, pp. 65–66.

58. Strobel, *Case for Christ*, p. 136.

59. Brown, *Birth of the Messiah*, pp. 550–51; M. Cary and H. H. Scullard, *A History of Rome* (New York: St. Martin's, 1979), p. 630; Price, *Incredible Shrinking Son of Man*, p. 61.

60. Brown, *Birth of the Messiah*, p. 550; G. B. Caird, *Saint Luke* (Harmondsworth, England: Penguin, 1963), p. 28; Guignebert, *Jesus*, pp. 100–101.

61. Adapted from Brown, *Birth of the Messiah*, p. 550.

62. Brown, *Birth of the Messiah*, p. 550; L. Michael White, *From Jesus to Christianity* (San Francisco: HarperSanFrancisco, 2004), pp. 33–34.

63. In a sign of evangelical desperation, there is now a suggestion that there were two different Quiriniuses: see Strobel, *Case for Christ*, p. 136.

64. Guignebert, *Jesus*, p. 100.

65. Two good references on the issue of messianic prophecies are: Tim Callahan, "'And the Word Became Flesh and Dwelt among Us': Do the Old Testament Prophecies Foretell the Life of Jesus?" in *Bible Prophecy: Failure or Fulfillment?* (Altadena, CA: Millennium Press, 1997), pp. 111–32; McKinsey, "Second Coming and Messianic Age, Messianic Prophecies," in *Encyclopedia of Biblical Errancy*, pp. 149–68.

66. J. Alberto Soggin, *Introduction to the Old Testament* (Louisville, KY: Westminster John Knox, 1987), p. 257.

67. Lüdemann, *Virgin Birth?* p. 70.

68. Miller, *Born Divine*, pp. 93–94.

69. A. D. Howell Smith, *In Search of the Real Bible* (London: Watts, 1943), pp. 40–41; McKinsey, *Encyclopedia of Biblical Errancy*, p. 304.

70. Although in the first half of the book Daniel is spoken of in the third person, later portions of the book clearly present itself as being composed by Daniel (see Daniel 7:1, 28; 8:2; 9:2; 10:1, 2; 12: 4, 5).

71. Anderson, *A Critical Introduction to the Old Testament* (London: Duckworth, 1979), p. 211; Soggin, *Introduction to the Old Testament*, p. 477.

72. A detailed treatment of Daniel's prophesies can be found in chapter 7 of Tim Callahan's book, *Bible Prophecy: Failure or Fulfillment?* pp. 149–77.

73. For a good but brief discussion of pseudonymity in the Bible, see John W. Loftus, *Why I Became an Atheist: A Former Preacher Rejects Christianity* (Amherst, NY: Prometheus Books, 2008), pp. 167–76.

74. Good introductory works on Jewish and Christian pseudepigrapha and other noncanonical writings include Bart Ehrman, *Lost Scriptures: Books That Did Not Make It into the New Testament* (London: Oxford University Press, 2003) and Willis Barnstone, *The Other Bible* (San Francisco: HarperSanFrancisco, 2005).

75. Anderson, *Critical Introduction*, pp. 209–12; Soggin, *Introduction to the Old Testament*, pp. 475–78.

76. Anderson, *Critical Introduction*, pp. 179–80.

77. Ibid., pp. 113, 119–20; Soggin, *Introduction to the Old Testament*, p. 299.

78. The late Catholic NT scholar Raymond Brown (1928–1998) estimated the percentage of scholars who rejected the authenticity of the pastorals at around 80 to 90 percent. See Brown, *Introduction to the New Testament* (New York: Doubleday, 1997), pp. 639, 654, 673.

79. Barr, *New Testament Story*, p. 169; G. A. Wells, *The Jesus Myth* (New York: Open Court, 1999), pp. 79, 270 n32.

80. Barr, *New Testament Story*, p. 171.

81. Ibid., p. 170; Udo Schnelle, *The History and Theology of the New Testament Writings* (Minneapolis: Fortress Press, 1994), p. 170.

82. Werner G. Kümmel, *Introduction to the New Testament* (Nashville, TN: Abingdon Press, 1973), p. 382.

83. Barr, *New Testament Story*, p. 169; Ehrman, *New Testament*, p. 357.

84. Barr, *New Testament Story*, p. 169; Ehrman, *New Testament*, p. 358.

85. Brown, *Introduction to the New Testament*, pp. 591, 600, 621.

86. Ibid., p. 762.

87. According to L. Michael White, who is Ronald Nelson Smith Chair in Classics and Christian Origins at the University of Texas at Austin and director of the Institute for the Study of Antiquity and Christian Origins, the authenticity of 1 Peter "is now doubted by almost all modern scholars" (*From Jesus to Christianity*, p. 272).

88. Brown, *Introduction to the New Testament*, p. 726; Schnelle, *History and Theology*, p. 417.

89. See the addendum at the end of this chapter and my book *Rejection of Pascal's Wager*, pp. 187–96, on how liberal Christians trip all over themselves trying to make some sense of what they believe.

90. Brown, *Introduction to the New Testament*, p. 586.

91. David L. Barr, *New Testament Story: An Introduction* (Belmont, CA: Wadsworth, 1995), p. 158.

92. A more thorough analysis of this relationship between 1 and 2 Thessalonians can be found in Gerd Ludemann's *Heretics: The Other Side of Early Christianity* (Louisville, KY: Westminster John Knox 1996), pp. 108–19.

93. Ehrman, *Lost Christianities: The Battles for Scriptures and Faith We Never Knew* (London: Oxford University Press, 2003), pp. 30–32, 210; Ehrman, *The New Testament: A History Introduction to the Early Christian Writings* (Oxford: Oxford University Press, 2000), pp. 341–44.

94. Bart Ehrman, *Jesus Interrupted*, p. 116.

95. William Hordern, *A Layman's Guide to Protestant Theology* (New York: Macmillan, 1968), pp. 31–33.

96. While this section concerns mainly Protestant liberal theology, it should be mentioned that there was a similar movement in the Roman Catholic Church toward the end of the nineteenth and early twentieth century, which was also called "Modernism." Its advocates openly accepted the findings of biblical criticism and generally rejected the traditional Catholic scholastic theology. This group was eventually suppressed by an encyclical in 1907 by Pope Pius X. See Alan Bullock, *Dictionary of Modern Thought* (London: Fontana, 1977), p. 540; and F. L. Cross and E. A. Livingstone, eds., *Oxford Dictionary of the Christian Church* (Oxford: Oxford University Press, 1997), p. 341. Although Roman Catholic scholarship is nowadays

quite "liberal," its scholars tend to treat central Roman Catholic dogma (e.g., Mary's perpetual virginity, Jesus' resurrection) with kid gloves or tend not to study these critically.

97. Quoted in Margaret Knight, *Honest to Man: Christian Ethics Re-examined* (London: Pemberton, 1974), p. 172.

98. Carl Lofmark, *What Is the Bible?* (Amherst, NY: Prometheus Books, 1989), pp. 138, 61–62.

99. Quoted in Knight, *Honest to Man*, p. 173.

100. Leslie Weatherhead, *The Christian Agnostic* (Nashville, TN: Abingdon Press, 1965), quoted in George H. Smith, *Atheism: The Case against God* (Amherst, NY: Prometheus Books, 1989), p. 79.

Chapter 7

WHAT WE'VE GOT HERE IS A
FAILURE TO COMMUNICATE

John W. Loftus

I t has been said that the Bible debunks itself, and I agree wholeheartedly. Isaac Asimov wrote, "Properly read, the Bible is the most potent
force for atheism ever conceived."[1] When atheist Christopher Hallquist
was asked in a debate on Christianity which books he would recommend
for further reading, he said, "The Bible. Read the Bible."[2]

One approach to seeing this is to simply look at the many barbarisms
in the Bible.[3] There are moral problems to be found in almost every
chapter. Some of them do not need comment because they go against every
decent moral standard civilized people accept in today's world, despite
several Christian rationalizations for them. Nearly every book contains at
least some good moral teachings. So it should surprise none of us that
there is good in the Bible. But the barbaric things in the Bible need to be
examined and explained, not explained away.

There is another approach I'll take in this chapter. I'm going to take
readers on a brief romp through the Bible with an eye on the failure of a
perfectly good omniscient God to communicate (or reveal) his perfect will
to believers. Dispensing with higher critical studies and just taking the Bible
at face value, what are we to make of the way God communicated, given the
final canonical Bible? My claim is that God did a woefully inadequate job,
especially since he's supposedly omniscient and knows how "sinful" people

such as us could misunderstand his words. Because God did not communicate clearly, believers who thought they were doing his will caused a great deal of suffering. Add to this the failure of the Holy Spirit to "illuminate" believers to know the will of God and there is a very serious problem here. I call it the *Problem of Miscommunication*. I don't think Christians can completely exonerate an omniscient God from being at least partially to blame for the miscommunication that was used by sincere believers to commit so many horrendous acts.

The famous American agnostic of the nineteenth century, Robert G. Ingersoll, introduces much of what I will argue for in this chapter: "Every [Christian] sect is a certificate that God has not plainly revealed His will to man. To each reader the Bible conveys a different meaning. About the meaning of this book, called a revelation, there have been ages of war and centuries of sword and flame. If written by an infinite God, He must have known that these results must follow; and thus knowing, He must be responsible for all."[4] I'll not argue God is responsible for it all though. I need only to establish God is at least partially to blame.

Friedrich Nietzsche likewise noted this problem when it came to why people cannot understand God's supposed warnings:

> A god who is all-knowing and all-powerful and who does not even make sure his creatures understand his intention—could that be a god of goodness? Who allows countless doubts and dubieties to persist, for thousands of years, as though the salvation of mankind were unaffected by them, and who on the other hand holds out the prospect of frightful consequences if any mistake is made as to the nature of truth?...Did he perhaps lack intelligence to do so? Or the eloquence? Must he not then...be able to help and counsel [his creatures], except in the manner of a deaf man making all kinds of ambiguous signs when the most fearful danger is about to befall on his child or dog?[5]

Communication is a two-way street. Both the one doing the communicating and the one listening must do his or her best in facilitating a correct understanding. My dentist is one of the best communicators I know. He makes sure I understand what my problem is, what he intends to do about it, and what I should do after my visit. He tells me in two or three different ways. There is no mistaking what he wants me to know. Ronald Reagan was considered the "Great Communicator," "because of his skill at talking evocatively and using folksy anecdotes that ordinary people could understand."[6] I consider Christian philosopher Richard Swinburne to be a superior communicator as well. When he's done talking or writing, you know what he meant to say, even if you disagree.

In any business the CEO must effectively communicate to his people. If any company is in disarray or pursuing dead ends, then the buck stops with the CEO. He isn't communicating very well. The blame is laid squarely at the top. This is obvious and noncontroversial. So I'm going to apply this same line of thought to the God who supposedly revealed himself in the Bible, especially since he knew how certain texts would be misused by the faithful. Then I'll examine several Christian attempts to deal with this problem and conclude that the evidence strongly suggests there is no divine mind behind the human authors.

Just imagine if we were to help God in the production of his book given what we know today. What things would we change, knowing the history of the church like we do? If God has omniscience, then he knows us intimately. If God has foreknowledge then he had our present-day perspective in mind when he revealed himself in the Bible. Remember, we're talking about a perfectly good God unblemished by the hint of even so much as an impropriety. You'll need your Bible if you want to read along.

THE OLD TESTAMENT

THE GENESIS CREATION ACCOUNT. GENESIS 1

This whole passage is contrary to modern science in so many ways, as Ed Babinski has pointed out in chapter 5. I've already suggested a different way for God to have begun the first few sentences in Genesis 1: "In the beginning God created an immeasurable universe of billions of stars, some of which are billions and billions of miles away, through a process that took billions of years out of which he finally created the sun, moon, and a spherical earth which revolves around the sun. On it he created water, land, the beasts of the sea, and eventually every living thing on it through stages as one species evolved into the next one. Finally he created human beings to rule over everything he created."[7]

See how easy that was? In the passages that follow I won't always suggest how I would change the wording, because it would quickly become repetitive. I think intelligent readers can do that for themselves. For now, I just want to highlight several biblical texts that created conflict, violence, murder, and mayhem because the divine communicator did not effectively communicate his perfect will to his so-called fallen human beings.

THE DOMINION (OR CULTURAL) MANDATE. GENESIS 1:26–28

This passage has been used in opposition to the care of our planet and of the animals on it. It tells us that since we have been given dominion over it we can do what we want to with it. The words "to rule over" and "to dominate" are extremely harsh.[8]

God also commands human beings to populate the world with children, which has been used against contraception and family planning in an era where overpopulation is a problem with the earth's limited resources. It is also being used by Christian Reconstructionists in advocating a theocracy where the church rules over the nations. Been there. Done that.

THE INFERIORITY OF WOMEN AND HOMOSEXUALS. GENESIS 2:18–25

This passage has been used to denigrate women since Eve was made from man as a "helpmate" to help him, and because Adam named her, which makes him an authority over her. Also, since another man was not made as a helpmate for Adam this text is used as a justification for condemning loving homosexual relationships.[9]

WOMEN BLAMED FOR THE SIN OF MAN. GENESIS 3:13–14

Because Eve was used to tempt Adam, women have been blamed for Adam's sin. Because of this women are seen as the weaker sex, and as such, man is told to "rule over" her (verse 16). Somewhere along the line God should've said: "Thou shalt not treat women as inferior persons, nor shall you rape them nor force them to marry a man they do not want to marry."

THE CURSE AND MARK OF CAIN, THE FIRST MURDER. GENESIS 4:8–17

Here is recorded a horrible act. One brother kills another. This passage has been used to support racism and slavery. Christians have falsely interpreted the "curse" and the "mark" on Cain to mean that his skin was turned black and his descendants were cursed. As such it was also used to justify a ban on interracial marriage.

DIVINE GENOCIDE: THE FLOOD. GENESIS 6–9

This is the first of many stories showing us a God who sends natural disasters upon human beings because of their sins, which is a dominant explanation for such things as droughts and plagues of locusts, and one reason why natural scientific explanations for these phenomena were not pursued.

A REAFFIRMATION OF THE DOMINION MANDATE. GENESIS 9:1–3

Notice here God is understood to authorize the meat-eating industry, since God tells Noah that "everything that lives and moves will be food for you." And once again God commands mankind to have children, which has been used against contraception and family planning.

THE "DIVINE" AUTHORIZATION OF CAPITAL PUNISHMENT. GENESIS 9:6–7

This practice is being rejected by more and more civilized people. It has condemned a lot of innocent people and has been disproportionately applied against black people in America. There are many barbaric capital punishment laws found in the Old Testament (OT), including having extramarital sex (Deuteronomy 22:13–30), homosexuality (Leviticus 20:13), and engaging in other deeds that democratic, free-loving people would not think deserve such a punishment, to say the very least (Exodus 21–22, 31:14–15, 35:2; Numbers 15:32–36; Deuteronomy 13:1–18, 17:2–5, 21–22, 24:5; Leviticus 20–21, 21:9, 24:10–16).

THE CURSE OF HAM. GENESIS 9:20–27

This passage has been notoriously used to justify racism and the brutal enslavement of Africans and to condemn interracial marriage. It says Canaan was cursed to be the lowest of slaves to his brothers, and the proslavery faction used it to justify that Canaan's curse was the black man's curse.[10]

POLYGAMY: ABRAHAM'S WIVES AND CONCUBINES. GENESIS 16:1–3

Not only does Abraham take Sarah and Hagar as his wives, he also had many concubines (Genesis 25:6). This has been used to justify polygamy. Jacob (Genesis 29:15–30; 30:1–12) and Solomon (1 Kings 11:1–3) followed the same practices, as did many kings.

THE PALESTINIAN LAND PROMISE. GENESIS 17:1–8

This grant by God has been the source of conflict over the land of Palestine from the beginning. It was reiterated to Jacob (Genesis 28:1–15) who was renamed Israel and known as the father of the Jews. Today this conflict is still seen between Arabs and Jews.

THE DESTRUCTION OF SODOM AND GOMORRAH. GENESIS 19:1–28

More divine genocide! This passage has been used to label gay people as "Sodomites" and is the source of the oppression, beating, and killing of them.[11] Notice also how cavalierly Lot is willing to hand his daughters over to be raped by the men of Sodom and how a slighted God turns Lot's wife into a pillar of salt.

ABRAHAM'S ATTEMPTED SACRIFICE OF ISAAC. GENESIS 22:1–12

For no reason at all God commands Abraham to sacrifice his only son. The silence of God about child sacrifice here is appalling. God never says child sacrifice is abhorrent to him in this passage.

ONAN'S SIN AND DEATH. GENESIS 38:7–10

Onan was slain by God because he did not fulfill his duties to help produce an heir for his brother. The sin of Onanism has been used to prohibit masturbation, *coitus interruptus*, and contraception.

NO GRAVEN IMAGES. EXODUS 20:4

This second commandment was used to prohibit and destroy some great artwork of the past. During and after the Protestant Reformation, as but one instance, there were several outbreaks of iconoclasm, with Protestants destroying both Catholic and sometimes even Protestant religious artwork and statues.

RELIGIOUS FREEDOM AND SPEECH IS CONDEMNED BY DEATH.

Anyone who accepts a different religion and/or seeks to convert others is to be put to death (Deuteronomy 12:1–13:16). Anyone who curses God is to be put to death (Leviticus 24:11–16). Witches are also condemned to death (Exodus 22:18, Deuteronomy 18:10). This is very significant when it comes to democratic, free-loving people, and it was the impetus for a great many killings and wars, as we shall see when it comes to the Thirty Years' War. What would have been so wrong for God to have said, "Thou shalt not kill anyone under any circumstances simply because of what he or she believes"?

THE ATROCIOUS LAWS ABOUT SLAVERY.
EXODUS 21:1–32 (CF. LUKE 12:47–48)

Surely no civilized person should accept indentured servitude or slavery of any kind, nor any of these specific laws. I know of no ethical code or civilized law where one person can strike or beat another person so long as that person doesn't die within two days. But that's what we find a supposedly perfectly good God saying. Leviticus 25:44–46 tells us that slaves could be bought from foreign nations. They are considered to be "property." They can be bequeathed to children. They are to be slaves for life with no hope of personal freedom. What did the southern states do that isn't found here? Just picture yourself as a slave who was forcibly ripped from her homeland, stripped naked on the auction block and "inspected," sold independently of her family, brutally broken to obey if disobedient, and forced against her will to be lifelong servant. Would you really want to say that a perfectly good God: (a) could not have said anything different or (b) that this expresses God's complete and utter love toward you as an individual? I don't think so. Not at all. Not by a long shot. It can't. On this rock the Christian faith dies.

"EYE FOR AN EYE" PASSAGES (I.E., LAW OF RETRIBUTION). LEVITICUS 24:18–20, EXODUS 21:22–25

This is barbaric justice, period, and is still practiced in some cultures to this day. We also read that a woman's hand should be cut off if she tried to rescue her husband in a fight by grabbing the other man's private (literally, "shameful") parts (Deuteronomy 25:11–12). This Exodus passage is also used by antiabortionists to deny women the right to choose. This in turn has caused many women to die from "back alley" abortions and has been used to justify the actions of terrorist abortion clinic bombers. However, they are wrong to use this text to justify antiabortionist views.[12]

USURY LAWS. EXODUS 22:25; LEVITICUS 25:35–37; DEUTERONOMY 23:20–21; PSALM 15:5; JEREMIAH 15:10; EZEKIEL 18:8–9, 13, 17

These laws prohibiting the charging of interest on a loan in the OT demanded a sophisticated level of gerrymandering to get around them. They didn't prevent investment, but made the lender a joint-venturer such that he or she would have to share the risk. The rise of modern democratic capitalism by contrast, has raised the standard of living in countries that have rejected these specific laws. In Dante's *The Divine Comedy* we read that the usurers are in the inner ring of the seventh circle of hell.

"LIFE IS IN THE BLOOD." LEVITICUS 17:10

Regardless of the many unnecessary dietary laws themselves, this verse was (and is being) used to deny blood transfusions, which are now necessary for performing some surgeries and to sustain injured people.

HOLY WAR

Even though the phrase "holy war" is not mentioned in the OT, divinely sanctioned wars are frequently mentioned (Joshua 8:1, Judges 4:14–15, 1 Samuel 17:45, 1 Samuel 23:4, 2 Kings 3:18), including genocide against the Canaanites (Deuteronomy 7:1–3; Joshua 10:40, 11:19–20), the Amalekites (1 Samuel 15:2–3) and others (Deuteronomy 2:31–34; 3:1–6). Many wars in the history of Christendom were justified by claims that God demanded it, as in the Crusades. In most wars fought between Christian nations both sides claimed God was on their side, even the Nazis who wore belts that said *Gott mit Uns* (God with Us).

A LEVITE AND HIS CONCUBINE: MORE RAPE, MORE SLAUGHTER, AND MORE KIDNAPPING. JUDGES 19–21

These few chapters in the Bible describe incredible horrors. They must be read in their entirety to see how barbaric God's people were. It is one thing for God to have commanded genocide against foreigners, as utterly appalling as that is. It's quite another thing to see the near genocide that takes place between the tribes of Israel. According to the Bible, God sanctioned the near genocide of the Benjamites (Judges 20:18, 23, 28, 35), leaving only six hundred men who escaped. And since the people of Israel didn't want to exterminate the Benjamites, they felt obligated to keep an inalterable vow they made about not giving their own women to them as wives (on vows see Numbers 30:3; Deuteronomy 23:21–23). So they slaughtered every man, woman, and child of the inhabitants of Jabesh-gilead, except for four hundred virgins, and gave these virgins to the remaining Benjamites. But they still needed two hundred more virgins, so the "elders of the congregation" encouraged the kidnapping of two hundred virgins of Shiloh to be their wives (Judges 21:5–7). This is absolutely stunning and hideous. Where was God? Why didn't he tell them not to do this? Most important, why should we trust the writings of people who saw nothing wrong with this? In other passages women are considered booty for the victors as sex slaves (Deuteronomy 21:10–12, Numbers 31:15–18).

SAUL CONSULTS THE WITCH OF ENDOR. 1 SAMUEL 28:3–19

This text was understood by the witch hunters (from 1450–1750 CE) to say that witches really do have power over other people, and should be killed. We also read where God's people were not to allow a witch to live (Exodus 22:18).[13]

THE NONBELIEVER IS A "FOOL." PSALM 14:1, 53:1

The use of the word "fool" here generally means a person who conducts his life as if God and his will are of no consequence. This has been used to berate and discriminate against nonbelievers, and even persecute them.

BEATING AND SPANKING CHILDREN. PROVERBS 13:24, 22:15

These verses have been used by abusive fathers who were justified in using a "rod" to beat their children because they were "loved." We now have more enlightened ways of disciplining children.[14]

"I WILL MAKE THEM EAT THE FLESH OF THEIR CHILDREN."
JEREMIAH 19:3–9

As you read this passage consider both the morality and the intelligence of Jeremiah's God. A few children were being sacrificed to other gods, so God gets angry with the adults who were doing this, and arranges for them to eat their children. As a result of God's judgment more children will die, and/or be eaten, and/or be fatherless. This does not make any sense at all. What difference does it make to God whether parents sacrifice their children or they eat them? In either case innocent children are still being killed!

Besides, there are much better ways to handle such things. Merely send them a prophet who can do great miracles in their midst to tell them the sacrificing of children is plainly forbidden. Better yet, why not just make one of the Ten Commandments: "Thou shalt not sacrifice any man, woman, or child to me or to the many other false gods"? The God of Jeremiah is nothing more than the reflections and musings of an ancient, superstitious, barbaric people—plain and simple. This is the best and simplest explanation for what we find in the Bible.

THE HEALTH AND WEALTH GOSPEL.

Prosperity for obedience to God is promised and/or given in several OT passages. God will bless his people if they obey him (Genesis 33:11, 49:24–26; 2 Chronicles 7:14; Psalms 127:1, 128:1–2). In Malachi 3:8–12 we read where God will bless people if they tithe (meaning, provide a payment of one-tenth of one's income). Televangelist preachers use these verses to bilk their followers out of any and all money they can. Most theologians do not think the tithing laws apply to Christians. They think the "health and wealth gospel" is neither healthy, nor biblical. There are some serious problems in trying to harmonize the biblical passages themselves on this subject.

THE NEW TESTAMENT

Let me deal briefly with some of the texts in the New Testament. In it there are texts that speak of cutting off body parts if they cause someone to sin, rather than being cast into hell (Matthew 5:29–30, 18:8–9). Origen of Alexandria (ca. 185–254 CE) took this literally and had himself castrated so he could tutor women without suspicion.[15] There are harsh demands when it comes to the conditions allowable for divorce, which say nothing about divorcing a spouse for verbal and/or physical abuse (Matthew 5:31–32, 19:3–9; Mark 10:2–12; 1 Corinthians 7:8–17). There are harsh sayings about hating one's parents that cultists have used in brainwashing their young converts, since they seek to separate rebellious youths from parental oversight (Matthew 10:34–39, 12:46–50; Luke 14:26). There are guilt-producing texts like the unforgivable speaking sin of blasphemy (Matthew 12:31–32), which has forced many believers to wonder if they had committed this sin prior to converting.[16] Expressed in the NT we find racism (Matthew 15:21–28) and even anti-Semitism (Matthew 27:21–36; John 8:44–45; Revelation 2:9–10, something that Hector Avalos argues in chapter 14 was influential in justifying the Holocaust). In it we find asceticism and the denial of the value of this world (Matthew 16:24–26, 19:29; Romans 7; 1 John 2:15–17); even to the point of selling everything and giving it to the poor (Luke 12:33, 18:22), like Francis of Assisi, the founder of the Franciscan Monks is known to have done.

We find the virtues of faith to be more important than reason in the NT too (Mark 9:23, 1 Corinthians 1:18–2:16), which has led many believers into some bizarre fatal doomsday cults. We find texts on prayer that have led Christians to pray in faith to be healed rather than go to the hospital (Mark 11:22–24, James 5:14–15). Many children have died because their parents refused to take them to a doctor for easily treatable medical problems. We find texts that offer sexually repressing advice (1 Corinthians 7)—including what many Christians see as the denigration of homosexuality (Romans 1:18–32). We find chauvinistic passages that tell us women are to be silent in the churches (1 Corinthians 14, 1 Timothy 2:8–14), and that they should submit to and obey their husbands (Ephesians 5:22–24, 1 Peter 3:1–6). We find disturbing passages that slaves are supposed to obey their masters, which helped sustain the status quo (Ephesians 6:5–8, Titus 2:9–10, 1 Peter 2:18–20). Then there's the church's ultimate threat of hell in the lake of fire (Revelation 20:11–15), the most terrifying cradle-to-grave threat of all.

Taking these biblical passages at face value is no longer an option for most Christians. Instead, Christians find other passages that can be used to interpret them in a gerrymandering fashion by finding the "canon within the canon," so they are more palatable to their modern consciences. But at face value they have caused harm, and in some cases a great deal of harm, for an unconscionably long time. Even if Christians reinterpret such passages to mean something other than what they appear to say, God is still proven to be one of the worst communicators in history. All of this could have been prevented and clarified right from the start, and to the benefit of countless people, by even an average communicator, much less one with the alleged talents of a god.

DOCTRINAL DISPUTES AND CHRISTIAN VIOLENCE

Not only is there divine miscommunication about morals, which has led to a great deal of suffering at the hands of believers, but there is also the problem of doctrinal disputes Christians have had between themselves. If God had done a better job communicating what he wanted the faithful to believe, there wouldn't have been as much bloodshed, even between Christians themselves, nor would there be as many splintered groups, all calling themselves Christians. Could an omniscient God have foreseen this and communicated better? I see no reason why not.

During the decades of conflict between the Arians and the followers of Athanasius, Christian people were strong-armed and killed on both sides of their debate over who Jesus was.[17] I'm pretty sure that if God had been clearer about whether Jesus was the second person of the Trinity, God the Son, "fully God and fully man in every respect," this debate and the suffering incurred would not have happened.

Moving on, centuries later the angelic doctor Thomas Aquinas had argued that heresy was a "leavening influence" upon the minds of the weak, and as such, heretics and infidels should be killed. Since heretical ideas could inflict the greatest possible harm upon other human beings, it was the greatest crime of all. Heretical ideas could send people to an eternally conscious torment in hell. So, he argued, logic demands that the church must get rid of this heretical leavening influence. It was indeed the greatest crime of them all, given this logic and the biblical passages that supported it (Exodus 22:20; Numbers 25:2–8; Deuteronomy 13:1–15 and 17:2–5, 20). So, beginning in the thirteenth century and carrying on for three hundred years, the rallying call of the Inquisition was "convert or die!"

Protestantism's founders were not exempt from this same logic. They killed thousands of Anabaptists, known as rebaptizers, often by burning them at the stake or by drowning, which was a parody of baptism.[18] Martin Luther and John Calvin both believed heretics like these should be punished and even killed by the state, as did some other reformers.[19] Martin Luther wrote:

> There are others who teach in opposition to some recognized article of faith which is manifestly grounded on Scripture and is believed by good Christians all over the world, such as are taught to children in the Creed.... Heretics of this sort must not be tolerated, but punished as open blasphemers...If anyone wishes to preach or to teach, let him make known the call or the command which impels him to do so, or else let him keep silence. If he will not keep quiet, then let the civil authorities command the scoundrel to his rightful master—namely, Master Hans [i.e., the hangman].[20]

But the number of deaths during the Inquisition pale by comparison to the religious wars fought between Christians themselves. Bryan Moynahan, in his balanced treatment of the history of the church, tells us that the "twenty-five thousand" victims from the Inquisition "bear no comparison to the eight million or more who died in the swill of religious wars that devastated other parts of Europe."[21] These religious wars were an outgrowth of inquisitional thinking applied to whole groups of people who were thought of as heretics. The mentality expressed in the phrase "Heretics Must Die" was transformed into: "Heretics Must *All* Die." While it's true that wars almost always have a multifaceted number of causes, religious differences were certainly among the causes of these wars. And people probably never kill with more passion than when they do so because of religious reasons. Without these religious differences one wonders whether there would even be the conflict in the first place. At the very least we could say that religious differences exacerbated and intensified the conflict.[22]

In sixteenth-century France (1562–1598) there were a series of eight wars between Roman Catholics and Protestants (primarily Calvinist Huguenots), known as the "French Wars of Religion." The infamous St.

Bartholomew's Day Massacre took place during one of them. Starting on the eve of the feast of Bartholomew, August 23, 1572, a group of Huguenot leaders were slaughtered by Catholics. Lasting several weeks, the massacre extended across the countryside where as many as ten thousand Protestants were slaughtered (see note).[23]

The Thirty Years' War (1618–1648) was one of the most destructive wars in European history that pitted Christians against each other. This war was fought primarily in Germany, but other countries got involved as well. Roman Catholicism and Protestant Calvinism figured prominently in the opposing sides of this conflict. So great was the loss of life from this war that estimates show one-third of the entire population of Germany was killed. Württemberg lost three-quarters of its entire population. Brandenburg suffered the loss of half of its population, as did Marburg and Augsburg, while Magdeburg was reduced to rubble. Outside of Germany nearly one-third of the Czech population died as well.[24] Christian apologist Paul Copan admits: "Denominational differences were a matter of life and death."[25] That's an understatement. We're talking about a Christian bloodbath. From this conflict the idea of religious tolerance was born, and with it the basis for modern democracy, something we find precursors of in ancient Greece.

The main doctrinal disputes between Catholics and Protestants were over the means of salvation, the importance of biblical authority, and the priesthood of all believers. When it came to the Catholic claims of authority, a disputed text in Matthew's Gospel was unclear to them. After Simon Peter confessed Jesus was "the Christ, the Son of the living God," Matthew's Jesus replied: "Blessed are you, Simon son of Jonah, for this was not revealed to you by man, but by my Father in heaven. And I tell you that you are Peter, and on this rock I will build my church, and the gates of Hades will not overcome it. I will give you the keys of the kingdom of heaven; whatever you bind on earth will be bound in heaven, and whatever you loose on earth will be loosed in heaven" (Matthew 16:16–19).

The Catholic Church claimed a succession of popes stemming from Peter, the first Pope. What is the "rock" that Jesus was to build his church upon? Did Jesus mean to say he would build his church on Peter, or on his confession of faith? Knowing church history as we do, if a perfectly good, omniscient God were involved we would certainly want Matthew's Jesus to be very clear here, but he wasn't. Because he wasn't, a massive number of Christians were killed by their brothers in the faith.

Protestants themselves fought over the nature of the Eucharistic wafer.

At the last supper before being crucified Jesus is reported to say: "Truly, truly, I say to you, unless you eat the flesh of the Son of man and drink his blood, you have no life in you; he who eats my flesh and drinks my blood has eternal life, and I will raise him up at the last day. For my flesh is food indeed, and my blood is drink indeed. He who eats my flesh and drinks my blood abides in me, and I in him" (John 6:53–56).

Was Jesus speaking metaphorically with regard to the Eucharist, or literally? It wasn't that clear to the church in those days. Knowing the history of the church like we do, why wasn't John's Jesus clear? He could have used different words or said plainly "I'm speaking metaphorically." That would have saved Christians from spilling a massive amount of blood between themselves—the very people whom Jesus prayed should be unified as one (John 17:20–23).

Skipping ahead in history, the American Civil War was due, in part, to religious conflict. While the war concerned state's rights, the principle cause for the conflict had to do with the right of Southern states to own slaves. Historians agree that abolitionist John Brown played a major role in starting the Civil War with his failed terrorist raid on Harper's Ferry, (West) Virginia, in 1859. Brown was a deeply religious Calvinist his whole life.[26] Equally religious were his opponents, and equally passionate. Biblical passages supporting and opposing slavery were bandied back and forth on this issue from pulpits and essayists like weapons of war. The issue really isn't that clear at all in the Bible. In fact, it appears to me that when the Bible is taken at face value, the proslavery arguments were stronger than the abolitionist ones.[27] These disputes were settled when the North won the war. But 620,000 Christian people on both sides lost their lives to settle it. Had God been very clear on this issue from the beginning, no Christian believer could ever biblically justify such a cruel and barbaric institution. God would certainly have known this would cause such a war, including the horrific suffering of the slaves themselves, and simply said over and over, "Thou shalt not buy, beat, or own slaves as property" and left out the other texts supportive of slavery.

CHRISTIAN ATTEMPTS TO EXPLAIN GOD'S FAILURE TO COMMUNICATE

Christian thinkers are not unaware of these problems. Several attempts have been made to explain them away. Let me offer eight of the most serious attempts to do this, along with some brief objections to them:

1. *The people who committed these terrible acts were not true Christians.*[28] The problem with this attempted answer is that there is no such thing as Christianity. There are only Christianities, as David Eller argued in chapter 1. Christianity reinvents itself in every generation and in every culture as it's forced to adjust to its historical and cultural environment. Such an answer presupposes that the Christianity in any given local culture of today is true while all of the others in the past, present, and future are false. That's a huge presumption! I tell people who make this argument to start a blog or Web site titled *True Christianity* and invite all professing Christians—the only kind we ever see—to try to come to a consensus. We know that will never happen. If instead, Christians want to argue that good morals are what define a Christian, the same thing applies. The history of Christian morality itself is fraught with the same kinds of disputes.[29] Besides, if having good morals defines a Christian (rather than correct doctrinal beliefs), then not only does this debunk those Christianities who think otherwise, but even atheists can be Christians by being good. Not only this, such an answer presumes that the people who killed one another over correct doctrinal beliefs were extremely insincere, stupid, and/or evil, and that too is nonsense. This brings me to the next attempted answer.

2. *Sinful fallen humans committed these atrocities in disobedience to God despite what God clearly communicated.* But I find this almost ludicrous. God would know in advance that we are fallen human beings, so he would know that he *must* communicate better to us. And if he also had foreknowledge of what believers would do, God would also know what to say so that the historic Church as an institution could not biblically justify so many horrendous deeds. It's one thing for individual believers to justify wrongdoing. It's another thing entirely for the Church as an institution to justify wrongdoing, for this requires a number of church leaders to agree with each other and the willing compliance of the people in the pew.

3. *God in his revelation was accommodating his commands to their hardened hearts.* But why should God have to do so? Doesn't the law have an educating effect? Then why not educate his people from the very beginning with Adam and Eve, or Moses, by communicating better than he did? What could possibly morally justify leaving people in the dark about his will, knowing full well that the Church would do the things she has done?

4. *Even though the Israelites and Christians committed atrocities, they were still morally better than the surrounding cultures.* Any believer who reads Judges 19–21 or Psalm 137 and concludes the Israelites were better than their sur-

rounding cultures is simply fooling himself.[30] Even if so, and I doubt this, being "better" doesn't cut it. Who cares if they were better, if they did the horrendous things we read about in the Bible? And who cares if the church was better than the secular governments of her day if she did the horrendous things she did? The fact is they did horrendous things! In many ways believers today are better people than the believers of the past. So at the very least God could have brought the believers of the past up to speed with today's moral understandings.

5. *The Bible does indeed contain a lot of barbarisms, but through it all God was progressively leading believers to civilized notions about morality, which were either finally realized in Jesus, or later in the Church down through the centuries.* But what can morally justify how long it took God to do this, given the massive amount of carnage that took place in the meantime? All he had to do from the very beginning was to give them the correct morals the first time around. And all he had to do in Jesus was to be clearer to the church who even misunderstood him.

6. *The Old Testament covenant was different, containing civil, ceremonial, and moral laws, most of which don't apply to believers who are under a new covenant of love by a loving God, expressed in Jesus.*[31] But Christians in prior generations had not yet come to this conclusion, even if it's correct. And if it is, then why didn't God tell them about this clearly? That he didn't do so is evidenced by the fact that Christians are still debating whether or not there is a difference between the two Covenants—between the law and the Gospel.[32]

7. *Calvinists claim God has at least two wills, one revealed in the Bible and a secretive one only he knows. The revealed will is not his true will. But it can be used to get people to do his true secretive will. His secretive will sometimes sovereignly decrees that people will commit horrendous acts against others for higher purposes.* In the Calvinist sense then, God didn't communicate his true will on purpose. But if this view is correct, then as I've argued elsewhere, Calvinists have no reason whatsoever to trust the Bible about anything at all.[33] It also means everyone eventually does what God wants them to do, including me. You see, I'm doing God's secretive will by editing this book, which will lead people astray. Maybe his secretive will is to save all skeptics and damn all Calvinists to hell? On Calvinistic grounds there can be no reasonable objection to this possibility because Calvinism leads to a complete and utter skepticism with regard to what God really wants us to do and to believe.

8. *What God does is a mystery. We are not in a position to question his actions. God's ways are above our ways.* But if we cannot understand his ways, when

his ways of communicating have caused so much bloodshed, then why should we believe that his ways are perfectly good? The evidence from the *Problem of Miscommunication* says otherwise. The only way to know whether God exists and his ways are good is to understand enough of his ways to know that he exists and that his ways are good! There is no other way. And if God supposedly created us with minds, then he also expects us to use them. That's what we read in various passages of the Bible (Deuteronomy 6:5; Isaiah 1:18; Matthew 22:37; 2 Corinthians 10:5). But when we use them to think about these questions, rather than to defend the beliefs we were raised with, it causes us to think differently. Christians will further argue that we are fallen human beings and as such we cannot think properly about these issues. But if so, how can God reasonably expect us to come to the right conclusions and be saved? Besides, the fact remains that only if some of us would *not* have sinned in the Garden of Eden as the first human pair did, is it possible to view that test as a fair one, rather than a sham? For if we all would have sinned, then the test was a sham. But if some of us would not have sinned under the same initial test conditions, then there are human beings who have been punished for something they would never have done.

I don't have the space to deal in any greater depth with each one of these *post hoc* rationalizations, but that's what they are. They fall on deaf ears. It takes more faith than I could ever possibly muster to believe that Christians simply did not want to properly understand God's will so they knowingly distorted it for their own selfish ends, or that God's purposes are higher, more mysterious ones, or that he didn't even try to reveal his real will. The overwhelming numbers of Christian believers are sincere people who want to please God and understand his will. As a former preacher, people would ask me all of the time what God's will is for their lives. Many believers agonized over it. But as we look back in history many Christians "misunderstood" it, and many still do today. I don't even doubt the sincerity of the Inquisition.

Christians just want to blame human beings, not God, no matter what the problem is. But communication is a two-way street. If there is any miscommunication, then both sides involved are probably at fault to some degree. Today we know that effective communication between persons is problematic, to say the least. We don't always understand what people say. We disagree about everything and we are constantly correcting misunderstandings about what we have said. Sometimes we hear what we want others to have said. In Plato's dialogues Cratylus didn't even think communication was possible. So in response to any question he would merely wiggle his finger. I'm not that skeptical. But if Cratylus has any point to make at all, then God should have known this and communicated his will much more clearly than he did. He should have at least created us so that we can better understand that which is being communicated. And even if not, the Holy Spirit should be doing his job much better than he is.

This is especially the case in the *high context*, ancient society of the Bible. High-context societies are what sociologists describe as those societies where there is a "broadly shared, well-understood knowledge of the context of anything referred to in conversation or in writing."[34] Communication in these societies didn't require the blanks to be filled in, so to speak. The details were already understood. By contrast, *low-context* societies are ones where there are "highly specific and detailed documents that leave little for the readers to fill in or supply."[35] Communication in these societies requires highly specific, detailed knowledge to fill in the blanks. One must spell the details out to be properly understood.

For example, the title to this chapter, "What We've Got Here Is a Failure to Communicate," comes from a line in the movie *Cool Hand Luke*, starring Paul Newman. In a high-context society I would not need to tell readers where it came from because it would be understood. But in a low-context society I need to tell my readers where it came from if I expect them to understand where I got this line. I use that line to show we live in a low-context society, and to illustrate that by revealing himself in a high-context society, God made it extremely difficult to understand what he meant.

The conservative publisher InterVarsity Press has published books on various doctrinal and ethical disputes among Christian authors who offer different views. There are books like: *Two Views of Hell: A Biblical and Theological Dialog, What about Those Who Have Never Heard? Three Views on the Destiny of the Unevangelized; In Search of the Soul: Four Views of the Mind-Body Problem; Divine Foreknowledge: Four Views; Four Views on Divine Sovereignty and Human Freedom; Four Christian Views of Economics; Four Theologians Debate the Major Millennial Views; The Meaning of the Millennium: Four Views; God & Time: Four Views; Science & Christianity: Four Views; Psychology & Christianity: Four Views; Women in Ministry: Four Views; Divorce and Remarriage: Four Christian Views; Theologians and Philosophers Examine Four Approaches to War*, and others.

Another conservative publishing company, Zondervan Press, as part of their Counterpoints Series, has produced similar kinds of books: *Two Views on Women in Ministry; How Jewish Is Christianity? Two Views on the Messianic Movement; Three Views on the Rapture; Three Views on the Millennium and Beyond; Three Views on Creation and Evolution; Three Views on Eastern Orthodoxy and Evangelicalism; Remarriage after Divorce in Today's Church: Three Views; Are Miraculous Gifts for Today: Four Views; Show Them No Mercy: Four Views on God and Canaanite Genocide; Understanding Four Views on Baptism; Who Runs the Church? Four Views on Church Government; Four Views on Salvation in a Pluralistic World; Four Views on the Book of Revelation; Four Views on Eternal Security; Four Views on Hell; Evaluating the Church Growth Movement: Five Views; Five Views of Law and Gospel; Five Views on Sanctification; Five Views on Apologetics; Exploring the Worship Spectrum: Six Views,* and more.

Neither series from either publisher is finished. Maybe they'll each do one on why there is doctrinal disagreement among Christians? Christian theologians cannot come to a consensus on what the Bible requires them to believe[36]—that's why there are so many denominations and "cults." They cannot even come to a consensus on how to interpret the Bible in the first place.[37] What is the best explanation for this? In light of such confusion and disagreement, can anyone take seriously the idea that God communicated his perfect will to his believers?

C. Michael Patton, a graduate from Dallas Theological Seminary with a Th.M in New Testament, and founder of "Reclaiming the Mind Ministries," wrote a blog post titled "Doctrinal Disagreement to the Glory of God." In it he outlined various answers for why there is doctrinal disagreement, including ignorance, sin, or that people who disagree aren't even Christians. While Patton does not default to these answers he does think they are "possibilities." And he humbly acknowledges he might be wrong. Then he suggests a more likely possibility. He suggests that Christians don't agree with each other because "God does not want us to agree, irrespective of who is right." He claims: "God does not want absolute doctrinal unity. In fact, practically speaking...I believe that doctrinal disagreements are healthy for the church....Conflict, in the end, can bring about a deeper conviction of the truth....It is often said that heresy is God's gift to the church. Why? Because when a false option is presented the truth becomes much clearer. In contrast there is clarity. In clarity there is conviction."[38]

Patton adequately expresses what Christians have been forced into accepting by the violent conflicts of the past. But his view is a hindsight conclusion learned from this conflict. The believers who were killing each other in the name of Jesus did not share this conclusion. That's why they killed one another. The thought never occurs to Patton that if this is the lesson God wanted Christians to learn he could've just said so. He could've said that the only thing important to him is that Christians agree on several essential matters of faith and then specifically named them and articulated them. Then God could've said the rest is nonessential, a matter for opinion and speculation, that other things don't matter much to him or to their salvation. Instead we have the Apostle Paul saying this: "I appeal to you, brothers, in the name of our Lord Jesus Christ, that all of you agree with one another so that there may be no divisions among you and that you may be perfectly united in mind and thought" (1 Corinthians 1:10; see also John 17:21, Ephesians 4:4–6).

Christians might finally respond by claiming that no matter what God revealed it would still be misunderstood by the Church to some extent and used to justify harming other people. Maybe this would be true in some respect, if I grant for the moment that God created us like he did, which I don't. But even if he did, God created us with the very propensities we have for misunderstanding and violence, otherwise we wouldn't be in this mess in the first place (think Adam and Eve if you want to). Nonetheless, if God had clearly revealed his will in the Bible, then the kind of violence resulting from it would not have taken place. It's this very violence that allows me to make this argument. There would be no way the historic church could biblically justify religiously motivated crusades, wars, heresy trials, witch hunts, or slavery—just for starters.

For Christians to argue that the church would still have done harm to others because she is made up of sinful human beings, then what kind of wrongs would she have done? Certainly, whatever evils would remain, they would have been far fewer and less awful than what we have been witnesses to. And even if I grant there would still be some leftover misunderstandings and harm done had God been clearer in his revelation, the Christian must still explain why the Holy Spirit has not done his job by illuminating the faithful with the proper understandings. The Christian claims about such things are all very improbable.

The real reason why Christians don't agree is because of a multifaceted set of problems including the problems of language, and the fact that God supposedly revealed himself in a high-context, superstitious society of the ancient past. My contention is that if God revealed his will to believers, he chose a poor medium and a poor era to do so, and that makes an omniscient Christian God look stupid as well as uncaring.

One would think with very good reasons that an omniscient God like that would be the best communicator in all of history. One would expect he would express his will in a crystal clear fashion with an eye on how believers might misunderstand it. Or, he would have created us so that we could understand what is being communicated. Even if not, one would expect that the Holy Spirit would do his job better. That God did not do this strongly disconfirms the hypothesis that the Bible was inspired by him.

Today's Christians say the churches of the past that committed atrocities were wrong. And that's correct. They were wrong. But not for the reasons stated. They claim the Christians of the past were wrong because they misinterpreted the Bible. The truth is that they were wrong to believe the Bible in the first place. They were wrong just like Christians of today are wrong, and just like the Christians of the future will be, too. My contention is that there is not a single statement in the Bible that reveals a divine mind behind the human authors. Everything in it can be more credibly explained by the hypothesis that it's just the musings of an ancient, superstitious, barbaric people—period.

NOTES

1. Isaac Asimov, Feb. 22, 1966, letter, *A Lifetime of Letters*, ed. Stanley Asimov (New York: Main Street Books, 1996), p. 316.

2. Hallquist said this in debate between himself and Campus Crusade staff member Tim Leisz on April 25, 2007, at the University of Wisconsin–Madison.

3. For examples of this see chapter 8 in this book, "Yahweh Is a Moral Monster," by Hector Avalos. See also the additional chapter on this topic posted online by Richard Carrier, "The Will of God," to be found on our official Web site: http://sites.google.com/site/thechristiandelusion/Home/the-will-of-god.

4. "The Lectures of R. G. Ingersol" (New York: Globusz Publishing, n.d.), http://www.globusz.com/ebooks/Ingersoll/00000026.htm.

5. Friedrich Nietzsche, *Daybreak*, trans. R. J. Hollingsdale (Cambridge: Cambridge University Press, 1982), pp. 89–90.

6. Lou Cannon, "Why Reagan Was the 'Great Communicator'" *USA Today*, June 6, 2004.

7. John W. Loftus, *Why I Became an Atheist: A Former Preacher Rejects Christianity* (Amherst, NY: Prometheus Books), pp. 276–77.

8. On this, see my extensive documentation in a blog post, "The Bible and the Treatment of Animals," The Christian Delusion, http://sites.google.com/site/thechristiandelusion/, which I consider a chapter for this book in and of itself.

9. After a survey of the biblical texts on homosexuality, evangelical expositor John R. W. Stott finds that the one lone, "essential" scriptural text that shows homosexuality is wrong is this one. See chapter 16, "Homosexual Partnerships?" in his book *Decisive Issues Facing Christians Today* (Old Tappan, NJ: Fleming R. Revel, 1990), pp. 336–64.

10. For two book-length treatments on this topic, see Stephen R. Haynes, *Noah's Curse: The Biblical Justification of American Slavery* (Oxford: Oxford University Press, 2002), and David M. Goldenberg, *The Curse of Ham: Race and Slavery in Early Judaism, Christianity, and Islam* (Princeton: Princeton University Press, 2003).

11. This passage does not support the claim that God condemns homosexuality per se, since any forceful rape of another human being is wrong. Besides, according to Ezekiel their sin was that they did not help the poor and needy (16:48–50). A classic liberal Christian statement about homosexuality and the Bible can be found in John J. McNeill, *The Church and the Homosexual* (New York: Pocket Books, 1976), pp. 48–98.

12. The text cannot apply to abortion since the related incident is about an accidental injury and not an intentional abortion. The law does not require the death penalty for an accidental death (Exodus 21:13–14, 20–21; Numbers 35:10–34; Deuteronomy 19:1–13). The concern expressed is for the husband's loss of property, both his wife and his child to be. If antiabortionists want to use this text, then let them also embrace the property status of the woman to her husband, and let them also embrace a barbaric "eye for an eye" justice.

13. See Brian Levack's books *The Witch-Hunt in Early Modern Europe*, 3rd ed., (Harlow, England: Longman, 2006), and *The Witchcraft Sourcebook* (New York: Routledge, 2003).

14. See, for instance, Thomas Gordon, *Parent Effectiveness Training: The Proven Program for Raising Responsible Children* (New York: Three Rivers Press, 2000).

15. "Origen of Alexandria," Religion Facts, http://www.religionfacts.com/christianity/people/origen.htm.

16. To see what this sin is, read my blog post "The Blasphemy Challenge: Is It What Jesus Meant?" at www.debunkingchristianity.blogspot.com.

17. See Richard Rubenstein, *When Jesus Became God: The Struggle to Define Christianity During the Last Days of Rome* (Orlando: Harvest Books, 1999).

18. For an account of the history of Anabaptists in the sixteenth century, see William Roscoe Estep, *The Anabaptist Story: An Introduction to Sixteenth-Century Anabaptism*, 3rd ed. (Grand Rapids, MI: Eerdmans, 1996). See also Thieleman van Bragt, *Martyrs Mirror: The Story of Seventeen Centuries of Christian Martyrdom from the Time of Christ to AD 1660*, trans. Joseph F. Sohm (Scottsdale, PA: Herald Press, 2001).

19. For a list of quotes from the Protestant reformers, see Catholic apologist Dave Armstrong's Web site, http://socrates58.blogspot.com/2007/03/protestant -inquisition-reformation.html. For an overview of this period, see Diarmaid MacCulloch, *The Reformation* (New York: Penguin Books, 2005). On Luther, see Heiko A. Oberman, *Luther: Man Between God and the Devil*, trans. Eileen Walliser-Schwarzbart (New Haven, CT: Yale University Press, 2006). To read a fair and balanced account of John Calvin's involvement in the trial and condemnation of Michael Servetus, see Bernard Cottret, *Calvin: A Biography* (Grand Rapids, MI: Eerdmans, 2000), pp. 205–33, and then read "John Calvin: His Life in Geneva" at http://www.biblestudying.net/johncalvin.html.

20. Luther, "Commentary on Psalm 82," *Luther's Works, The American Edition*, eds. Jaroslav Pelikan and Helmut Lehmann (St. Louis, MI: Concordia and Fortress Press, 1955–1986), 13:54–55.

21. Bryan Moynahan, *The Faith: A History of Christianity* (New York: Doubleday, 2002), p. 455.

22. On this subject I recommend David Eller's "Religious Violence," in *Atheism Advanced* (Cranford, NJ: American Atheist Press, 2007), pp. 153–97, and Hector Avalos, *Fighting Words: The Origins of Religious Violence* (Amherst, NY: Prometheus Books, 2005).

23. Moynahan, *The Faith*, p. 456. William T. Cavanaugh has argued that religious wars were caused by the rise of the state in Europe during the sixteenth and seventeenth centuries, and that Queen Mother Catherine de Medici unleashed the Saint Bartholomew's Day massacre, which was entirely politically motivated. See Cavanaugh, "A Fire Strong Enough to Consume the House: The Wars of Religion and the Rise of the State," *Modern Theology* 11 (1995): 397–420. But Hector Avalos argues that the church was "deeply involved" in this massacre, in chapter 14 of his book *Fighting Words*. The Catholic Church produced the "rhetoric and policies that made such a massacre probable," and the church leadership celebrated this massacre afterward. Avalos writes: "If Catherine de Medici, or any other politician, was able to unleash anything, it is because religious hatred was already there to begin with. Had there been no steady drumbeat of violent anti-Protestant rhetoric and instructions from the Vatican and its allied institutions, there would have been no reason for Catholic populations to behave the way they did against their neighbors" (p. 341). Avalos concludes that Cavanaugh's analysis is "fatally flawed" and that "the massacre of the Hugenots was mostly the result of religious divisions and tensions" (p. 342).

24. To read about this devastating war, see C. V. Wedgwood, *The Thirty Years' War* (New York: New York Review Books Classics, 2005).

25. Copan, *When God Goes to Starbucks: A Guide to Everyday Apologetics* (Grand Rapids, MI: Baker Books, 2008), p. 192.

26. David S. Reynolds, *John Brown, Abolitionist: The Man Who Killed Slavery, Sparked the Civil War, and Seeded Civil Rights* (New York: Alfred A. Knopf, 2005).

27. To see what I mean, look at the collection of essays in *Cotton Is King and Pro-Slavery Arguments V2: The Bible Argument, in the Light of Social Ethics, and in the Light of Ethnology*, eds. Thornton Stringfellow, Chancellor Harper, et al. (Kessinger Publishing, 2007 reprint); Williard Swartley, *Slavery, Sabbath, War & Women: Case Studies in Biblical Interpretation* (Scottsdale, PA: Herald Press, 1983), pp. 31–64; and Paul Finkelman, ed., *Defending Slavery: Proslavery Thought in the Old South* (Boston: Bedford/St. Martin's, 2003).

28. Copan, in *When God Goes to Starbucks*, writes: "Not all professing Christians are genuinely or consistently Christian" (p. 201).

29. On this I recommend J. Philip Wogman, *Christian Ethics: A Historical Introduction* (Louisville, KY: Westminster/John Knox Press, 1993). There are many others.

30. On the subject of genocide, be sure to read my blog post "Psalm 137 Is a Genocidal Passage!" at www.debunkingchristianity.blogspot.com.

31. Gregory Boyd is writing a book tentatively titled *Jesus versus Jehovah: Understanding the Violent God of the Old Testament in Light of the God of the Cross*, where he will argue that "Jesus himself repudiated the violence of the OT—despite his belief that this collection of writings was inspired." Boyd continues, "In other words, if you obey Jehovah, you're not a child of God, according to Jesus." Boyd rhetorically asks: "Is it possible that some divinely inspired material is not supposed to reveal to us what God is like but what he is *not* like? Is it possible that some material is inspired precisely because God wants us to follow Jesus' example and repudiate it?" See "Jesus' Repudiation of Old Testament Violence," Christus Victor Ministries, http://www.gregboyd.org/. This is theological gerrymandering if I ever saw it!

32. See the book edited by Stanley N. Gundry, *Five Views on Law and Gospel* (Grand Rapids, MI: Zondervan, 1996).

33. See my blog "Calvinism Is Bullshit, and God Wanted Me to Say This," Debunking Christianity, January 31, 2009, http://debunkingchristianity.blogspot .com/2009/01/calvinism-is-bullshit-and-god-wanted-me.html. As I wrote on page 290 of my book *WIBA*: "If God decrees everything that happens, then he can know the future of every human action since he decrees each one of them. But there are serious problems with such a theology. It means God decrees every evil deed that we do. It also means that God decrees every evil desire that we have to do every evil deed that we do. We cannot do otherwise. We cannot even desire to do otherwise. It also means God decrees everything that we believe. None of us can believe other than that which God decrees. Therefore, God decrees people to hell, since those who end up there could not have believed differently. I only have the harshest kinds of comments for such a theology. That God is an evil monster requiring nothing but disgust and loathing. Such a theology creates atheists and motivates me like no other theology to attempt to demolish the Christian faith."

34. Bruce J. Malina and Richard L. Rohrbaugh, *Social-Science Commentary on the Synoptic Gospels* (Minneapolis, MN: Fortress Press, 2003), p. 11.

35. Ibid.

36. Two helpful books on these disagreements written by Roger E. Olson, an evangelical, are *The Story of Christian Theology: Twenty Centuries of Tradition and Reform* (Downers Grove, IL: InterVarsity Press Academic, 1999), and *The Mosaic of Christian Belief: Twenty Centuries of Unity and Diversity* (Downers Grove, IL: Inter-Varsity Press Academic, 2002).

37. See the book edited by Donald K. McKim, *Historical Handbook of Major Biblical Interpretations* (Downers Grove, IL: InterVarsity Press, 1998), which is composed of 643 pages.

38. "The Parchment and Pen."

Part 3

WHY THE CHRISTIAN GOD IS NOT PERFECTLY GOOD

Chapter 8

YAHWEH IS A
MORAL MONSTER

Hector Avalos, PhD

I n an essay titled "Is Yahweh a Moral Monster? The New Atheists and
Old Testament Ethics," Dr. Paul Copan, a well known Christian apologist and president of the Evangelical Philosophical Society, attempts to
combat the New Atheists and their dim view of biblical ethics. (If the
reader has not previously read his article, it might be best to do so now; it's
available online.)[1] However, it soon becomes apparent that his critique
repeats factual errors and biases found in earlier biblical apologists. Copan
reveals himself as just another Christian apologist who supports biblical
genocide and other injustices. He is definitely not successful in demonstrating the superiority of biblical ethics over those of other cultures in the
ancient Near East.

MISREPRESENTING NEAR EASTERN CULTURES

Copan begins by misrepresenting ancient Near Eastern legal materials in
at least three major ways:

1. The supposedly unique embedding of biblical laws in historical
   narratives,

2. The use of motive clauses in law, and
3. Distorted portrayal of ancient Near Eastern slavery laws.

NARRATIVES IN LEGAL MATERIALS AS SUPERIOR

According to Copan, the Bible is superior because it embeds its legal materials within a larger narrative that explains the history and principles behind the laws. He specifically states: "The absence of such narratives is glaringly apparent in cuneiform ANE [ancient Near Eastern] Mesopotamian law codes such as Hammurabi.... By contrast, cuneiform laws such as Hammurabi are never motivated by historical events: unlike biblical laws, no cuneiform law is ever motivated by reference to an historic event, a promise of well-being, or ... a divine will."

Copan does not show evidence of any complete reading of the Code of Hammurabi (CH). If Copan had read the entire CH, he would see that his statement is patently false. The CH does have both a very lengthy prologue and an epilogue, which are narratives that situate the CH in a claimed historical context. Consider the first paragraph, which is just a fragment of a much longer narrative prologue:

> When the august god Anu, king of the Anunnaku deities, and the god Enlil, lord of heaven and earth, who determines the destinies of the land, allotted supreme power over all the peoples to the god Marduk, the firstborn son of the god Ea, exalted him among the Igigu deities, named the city of Babylon with its august name and made it supreme within the regions of the world and established for him within it eternal kingship whose foundations are as fixed as heaven and earth, at that time, the gods Anu and Enlil, for the enhancement of the well-being of the people named me by my name: Hammurabi, the pious prince, who venerates the gods, to make justice prevail in the land, to abolish the wicked and the evil, to prevent the strong from oppressing the weak, to rise like the sun-god Shamash over all humankind, to illuminate the world.[2]

Maybe Copan does not regard this as "history," but it differs very little from the "history" given in Exodus, which also refers to a god (Yahweh) who called a man (Moses) through whom the law was given to the people. After all, there is much more evidence that Hammurabi was an actual historical figure, whereas we have nothing about Moses outside of biblical manuscripts that are no earlier than the first through the third centuries BCE in the Dead Sea Scrolls.

Moreover, the prologue and epilogue of the CH clearly enunciate principles for the laws. These principles can be summarized as follows:

1. to further the well-being of humanity;
2. to make justice prevail in the land;
3. to destroy the wicked and the evil-doers;
4. to prevent the strong from oppressing the weak;
5. to have as equal and as complete a rulership as the sun; and
6. to protect the orphan (or waif) and the widow.[3]

So, contrary to Copan's assertions, we do find in the CH the goal of bettering humankind and a reference to the divine will (Shamash's will). Clearly, Copan is simply wrong about the CH. That alone speaks volumes about how well he knows these ancient Near Eastern materials, and how fair he is in making comparisons.

MOTIVE CLAUSES AS SUPERIOR

Yet another misrepresentation of Near Eastern materials occurs in Copan's discussions of motive clauses, which explain the reasons for enacting or practicing a particular law. For example, the commandment to honor father and mother in Exodus 20:12 is accompanied by a motive clause ("that your days may be long in the land which the LORD your God gives you").

In the 1950s, a scholar named Berend Gemser argued that only biblical laws had motive clauses, and so biblical law was superior.[4] The supposed superiority of motive clauses is particularly ironic because another stream of apologetics, led by Albrecht Alt (1883–1956), the famous German biblical scholar, claimed that *apodictic* laws made the Bible unique and superior. Apodictic laws, such as "Thou shalt not kill," can be formulated without conditions or motive clauses. Even at the time of Gemser, scholars knew that many Near Eastern laws also had motive clauses, and so biblical apologetics eventually shifted to explaining how biblical motive clauses were superior.

Rifat Sonsino, author of *Motive Clauses in Hebrew Law*, thought he found what made biblical motive clauses superior. Copan relies heavily, and much too uncritically, on the work of Sonsino. In fact, the quote I highlighted above from Copan's essay derives almost directly from Sonsino, who wrote: "It is noteworthy that, unlike biblical laws, no cuneiform law is ever motivated by reference to an historic event, a promise of well-being or, for that matter, a divine will. In fact, in these laws the deity is completely silent, yielding its place to a human lawgiver whose main concern is economic rather than religious."[5]

Copan states, "Also unlike the Code of Hammurabi and other Mesopotamian law codes are the various 'motive clauses' in the Sinaitic legislation that ground divine commands in Yahweh's historical activity." Yet, as we have observed, it is simply not true that the CH does not view itself as grounded in historical events or in a narrative. The general motives are made explicit in the prologue, and so they do not need to be repeated in individual laws.

One has to go to footnote 23 of Copan's essay to see that Sonsino has a more nuanced position. While the main text of Copan's essay gives the misleading impression that the CH contained no motive clauses, Sonsino actually argues that the relative number of motive clauses is higher in the Bible. Sonsino further argues that that difference lies in the "form, content, and function" of motive clauses.[6] More important, Copan does not explain why we should accept laws with motive clauses as superior in any way. Can we say that the commandment to honor your father and mother is superior to the one forbidding killing (v. 13: "You shall not kill") because the former has a motive clause, while the latter does not?

If motive clauses make a law superior, then why are they not supplied for all biblical laws? Of course, Copan assumes that the motives should be deemed good in biblical law, where someone else could see some of them as appealing to self-interest. The motive for honoring one's father and mother in Exodus 20:12 is so that the Israelites can have a long life in the land. But is that sort of self-interest really a good motive to honor our father and mother?

If we regard the welfare of others, rather than self-interest, as the standard of a superior law, then I can find a much better motive clause in law 137 of the CH: "If a man should decide to divorce a priestess or a *shugitu* [priestess] who bore him children or a *naditu* [priestess] who provided him with children, then he shall return that woman her dowry, they shall give her half (of her husband's) field, orchard, and property, and she shall raise her children."[7] English translations do not reflect the fact that the last clause can function as a motive clause (i.e., it could be translated as "in order that she raise her children").[8] Here, a law is given for the good of the children, not for the self-interest of the man commanded to follow this law.

Copan shows his religionist biases when he assumes that having religious motivations is somehow superior to having economic motivations. But that also depends on how one sees economics. If the economic laws are supposed to protect the weak from the strong, as the CH asserts, then what is wrong with that? This fact must be considered in light of the types of laws that have motive clauses. Sonsino himself admits: "Most of the motivated laws deal with cultic/sacral sphere. Out of 375 motivated legal prescriptions, 271 can be assigned to this category. This represents ca. 72% of the motivated laws, but ca. 27% of the cultic/sacral instructions in the Pentateuchal legal corpora. The cultic sacral laws, in turn, constitute 78% of all the legal prescriptions in the Bible."[9]

In other words, many of the motivated laws have to do with why someone should sacrifice in a particular way, or not eat impure foods. Here is a typical cultic law with motive clauses (Leviticus 17:3–5):

> If any man of the house of Israel kills an ox or a lamb or a goat in the camp, or kills it outside the camp, and does not bring it to the door of the tent of meeting, to offer it as a gift to the LORD before the tabernacle of the LORD, bloodguilt shall be imputed to that man; he has shed blood; and that man shall be cut off from among his people. This is to the end that the people of Israel may bring their sacrifices which they slay in the open field, that they may bring them to the LORD, to the priest at the door of the tent of meeting, and slay them as sacrifices of peace offerings to the LORD.[10]

So how or why would the motive clause in verse 5 be superior to that of law 137 in the CH, which is motivated by the welfare of a divorced woman's children? Indeed, Sonsino calculates that there are only 51 "humanitarian admonitions," or 14 percent of all the motivated laws in the Hebrew Bible.[11] As we examine the specific list of so-called motive clauses by Sonsino, it also becomes dolorously apparent that many of these motives offer us nothing particularly more ethical than what could be offered by the laws of other religions.

Moreover, the impressively high counts of motive clauses in the Bible, relative to those of other ancient Near Eastern cultures, evaporate once you look at how those motive clauses are being counted. Consider the fact that Sonsino counts the statement, "I am Yahweh (your God)," as an entire motive clause in the following biblical passages: Leviticus 18:1, 22:8, 26:1–2.[12] Yet, is saying "I am Yahweh" really a better ethical motive than saying "I am Allah" or "I am Shamash"? One can see that the motive counts can rise dramatically in the Bible by defining these sorts of formulaic statements as motive clauses.

ADVANCES IN SLAVERY LAWS?

When comparing the Bible to Near Eastern cultures, Copan assures us that: "On the other hand, Israel's laws reveal a dramatic, humanizing improvement over the practices of the other ancient Near Eastern peoples." Within the Bible, he says we also find improvement: "What is more, the three main texts regarding slave legislation (Exod. 21; Lev. 25; Deut. 15) reveal a morally improved legislation as the text progresses." So, what was so improved in the Bible compared to Near Eastern laws? It is difficult to see, given that Copan admits that: "Pentateuch's legal code in places does differentiate between Israelite and non-Israelite slaves (for example, Exod. 12:43, where non-Israelites are not to partake in the Passover); it grants remitting loans to Israelites but not to foreigners (Deut. 15:3); it allows for exacting interest from a foreigner but not from a fellow Israelite (Deut. 23:20); Moabites and Ammonites are excluded from the sanctuary (Deut. 23:3)." Nonetheless, Copan offers us this reassurance: "To stop here, as the New Atheists do, is to overlook the Pentateuch's narrative indicating God's concern for bringing blessing to all humanity (Gen. 12:1–3). Even more fundamentally, human beings have been created in God's image as co-rulers with God over creation (Gen. 1:26–27; Ps. 8)."

If we used the intention to bring blessing to all humanity, then it is clear that the CH would also satisfy this requirement. Recall that the prologue to the CH includes this motive: "for the enhancement of the well-being of the people." In contrast to this more altruistic motive, if we look at what the "blessing" of humanity means in the Bible, then it is also not as benign as it appears. Copan quotes Genesis 12:1–3 for support. But Genesis 12 foreshadows the fact that the native population of Canaan mentioned in verse 6 eventually will be slaughtered to make way for the Israelites. Genesis 12:3 indicates that those who do not agree with the Abrahamic plan will be cursed. And it will eventually become clear that the ultimate goal is for Yahweh to be in full control of all humanity, and humanity will be his slaves, and slaves to his people (see Isaiah 14:1–2 discussed further below). In short, Copan is already working with a very biased view of "blessing."

When we examine more specific supposed improvements, Copan does not tell the whole story. For example, he says: "Hammurabi called for the death penalty to those helping runaway slaves [§16]. Israel, however, was to offer safe harbor to foreign runaway slaves (Deut. 23:15–16)." That may be true of the CH, but Copan does not cite Hittite law 24, which says: "If a male or female slave runs away, he/she at whose hearth his/her owner finds him/her shall pay one month's wages; 12 shekels of silver for a man, 6 shekels of silver for a woman."[13] So why aren't the Hittite laws characterized as a humanizing improvement? In the Hittite law, a slave runs away, and the person harboring the slave only pays a fine.

In fact, Hittite law systematically replaced death penalties with fines for many offenses. Thus, law 166 demanded the death penalty for appropriating another man's farmland (sowing seed upon previously sown land). But law 167 says: "But now they shall substitute one sheep for the man."[14] In other words, the very symbol of the Christian substitutionary atonement had a preceding parallel in Hittite law.

So the imposition of *Lex talionis* (eye-for-an-eye principle) in Pentateuchal laws, which are usually dated after the Hittite laws, even by Copan, should be seen as a regression. Yet Copan also says that these biblical laws: *"... are not taken literally. None of the examples illustrating 'an eye for an eye' calls for bodily mutilation, but rather just (monetary) compensation"* [emphasis added]. This is nothing more than mere assertion. No biblical text is offered to support this allegation, and several biblical texts clearly state the contrary (e.g., Exodus 21:22–25, Leviticus 24:19–21, Deuteronomy 19:18–21). In fact, Jesus seems to take this law very literally in Matthew 5:38–39: "You have heard that it was said, 'An eye for an eye and a tooth for a tooth.' But I say to you, Do not resist one who is evil. But if any one strikes you on the right cheek, turn to him the other also." Or are we to suppose that Jesus was merely doing away with monetary penalties?

Clearly, Copan must engage in special pleading to convince us that the Bible represents an advancement in *Lex talionis*. If one says that *Lex talionis* is an advancement, then this already had a precedent in the CH (law 196). If one says replacing *Lex talionis* with fines or sacrifices was an advancement, then the Hittites did this already. Pre-Hammurabi codes also can be found without the *Lex talionis* principle.

Copan sees as a moral advancement the releasing of Hebrew slaves in the seventh year. He remarks: "Indeed, Hebrew slaves were to be granted release in the seventh year (Leviticus 29 [*sic*]:35–43)—a notable improvement over other ancient Near Eastern law codes." Yet, this seems to contradict his own statement in footnote 52: "The Code of Hammurabi also makes provision for manumission." So why is the release of slaves ("manumission") in Leviticus an improvement over CH, which also had manumission? In fact, Leviticus 25 can be seen as worse than the CH when it comes to manumission. For example, the CH does not restrict manumission to "Babylonians," whereas Leviticus restricts manumission to Hebrews. Hammurabi's Code seems more open and without regard to ethnicity here.

Long before Leviticus 25, Mesopotamian kings promulgated so-called *misharum* ("equity") acts, which could include the release of whole classes of people. As Raymond Westbrook, one of the foremost biblical legal specialists, notes: "The proclamation of a *misharum* was an institution of the utmost significance in Old Babylonian society. It was originally thought that each king proclaimed a *misharum* as a once-only measure upon his accession to the throne, but J. Finkelstein has shown that *misharum* enactments might occur several times at intervals throughout a king's reign. For RimSin of Larsa there is a record of three such enactments falling at about the twenty-sixth, thirty-fifth, and forty-first years... Samsuiluna in his first and eighth year."[15]

These releases by RimSin and Samsuiluna (ca. eighteenth century BCE) were in intervals of nine, six, and seven years, respectively, and so quite comparable to the seven years of Leviticus. Therefore, there is really no advance on this issue in the Bible. In fact, we can just as well argue that some biblical improvements came about by imitating ancient Near Eastern institutions rather than by biblical innovation. We can find imitations of the *misharum* idea in Isaiah 61:1–2, which Jesus quotes in Luke 4:18–21 referring to himself.

Questionable exegesis is at the heart of some of Copan's examples of biblical improvements. He remarks, "The overriding goal in Deuteronomy 15 is that *there be no slavery in the land at all* (vv. 4, 11)" [emphasis added]. Yet, that is not really what Deuteronomy 15:4 and 11 say. Those verses actually say: "[4] But there will be no poor among you (for the LORD will bless you in the land which the LORD your God gives you for an inheritance to possess)... [11] For the poor will never cease out of the land; therefore I command you, You shall open wide your hand to your brother, to the needy and to the poor, in the land." Nothing is said about slavery ending. In fact, if anything it's the reverse, since verse 11 says: "For the poor will never cease out of the land." So even though Hebrew slaves were to be released seven years after being taken into service, there is nothing to prevent a new crop of Hebrew slaves from being taken into service all the time.

Note also how Copan places a positive spin on Exodus 21:20–21: "Another marked improvement is in the release of injured slaves themselves (Exod. 21:20–21). This is in contrast to their masters merely being compensated, which is typical in the ANE codes." Yet this is what Exodus 21:20–21 says: "When a man strikes his slave, male or female, with a rod and the slave dies under his hand, he shall be punished. But if the slave survives a day or two, he is not to be punished; for the slave is his money." So you can beat a slave nearly to death and the master will not be punished at all. The reason given is that a slave is "his money." The slave is property, not a human being.

The idea that a master has absolute control over his "money," regardless of any injustice to workers, is endorsed by Jesus' parable of the vineyard workers in Matthew 20:1–16. When workers complain that the master has paid those who worked all day exactly the same as those who worked only a fraction of that day, the master says: "Am I not allowed to do what I choose with what belongs to me?" Treating workers like the master did is an injustice. As far as labor laws are concerned, this is not an improvement, but rather a continuation of the idea of Exodus 21:21 ("for the slave is his money").

It is true that Exodus 21:26–27 allows a slave to go free if a slave's tooth or eye is damaged, but is that really better than other reasons for freeing slaves that we can find in the ancient Near East? Consider laws 170–71 of the CH, which, in the case of a master who has fathered children by slave-women, grants freedom to those slave-women and their children if the master did not adopt them formally. No beating is necessary to release these slaves.

If adopted, these children of slaves are not treated as property, but as an actual part of the master's family. Children of slave-women could be coinheritors with the children of the formal wife in the laws 170–71 of CH. This contrasts to the cruel attitude expressed by Sarah concerning Ishmael, Abraham's biological son by Hagar, a slave-woman in Genesis 21:10: "Cast out this slave-woman with her son; for the son of this slave-woman shall not be heir with my son Isaac." God tells Abraham to follow this injunction regardless of Abraham's sympathy for Ishmael (Genesis 21:12). So where Abraham might represent a humanizing tendency, God actually demands the more inhumane option. Paul repeats and endorses Sarah's cruel actions in Galatians 4:30, which should be counted as a regression relative to the rights of the children of slave-women in the CH.

Copan also claims that "Later in Amos (2:6, 8:6), slavery is again repudiated." But Amos 2:6 actually states: "Thus says the LORD: 'For three transgressions of Israel, and for four, I will not revoke the punishment; because they sell the righteous for silver, and the needy for a pair of shoes'" (see also Amos 8:6). Nothing is said here about the need for his people to repudiate slavery in order for Yahweh not to punish them. And there were other sources for slaves besides those being sold into bondage (Leviticus 25:44–45). For instance, one could still capture slaves in war (Numbers 31:25–47, Deuteronomy 21:10, and 1 Kings 9:21). Nor is it clear that non-Hebrew slaves were excluded from being sold in this manner. Isaiah 14:1–2, which is usually dated later than Amos, envisions a future with even more people enslaved: "But the LORD will have compassion on Jacob and will again choose Israel, and will set them in their own land; and aliens will join them and attach themselves to the house of Jacob. And the peoples will take them and bring them to their place, and the house of Israel will possess them in the LORD's land as male and female slaves; they will take captive those who were their captors, and rule over those who oppressed them."

Indeed, if we proceed to the New Testament (NT), slavery may have gotten even worse, not better, compared to Amos. In 1 Peter 2:18–20, we read: "Servants, be submissive to your masters with all respect, not only to the kind and gentle but also to the overbearing. For one is approved if, mindful of God, he endures pain while suffering unjustly. For what credit is it, if when you do wrong and are beaten for it you take it patiently? But if when you do right and suffer for it you take it patiently, you have God's approval." The word "overbearing" here is much too kind because the passage indicates that beatings might be part of being "overbearing." Thus, the word "cruel" or "brutal" would not be too far off the mark.

In any case, slaves are supposed to be in utter subjection to masters even if the masters beat them. It is deemed good to suffer pain and injustice. Moreover, the laws limiting service for Hebrew slaves were no longer applicable, since Christ is viewed as "abolishing in his flesh the law of commandments and ordinances" (Ephesians 2:15). So, if Copan sees a "humanizing" trajectory in the Old Testament (OT), it seems to have gone backward in the NT, which usually assumes slavery is acceptable, and where it is again deemed good to be treated in a dehumanizing way.

If harboring slaves was supposed to be an advance, in the NT we see Paul returning the slave named Onesimus, who has run away from Philemon, his master. In fact, Paul accepts that it is entirely Philemon's pre-rogative to retain Onesimus in slavery: "but I preferred to do nothing without your consent in order that your goodness might not be by compul-sion but of your own free will" (Philemon 14).[16] There is no reprimand of Philemon for having a slave. Slavery is not included in the list of sins, which includes drunkenness, that prevent entry into the kingdom of heaven (1 Corinthians 6:9–10). So why is drunkenness judged to be more sinful than slave owning? Are those really more advanced and humanizing values?

It was only after the secularization of the West, and after the erosion of biblical authority, that we moved away from slavery and toward greater civil rights for women.[17] If we followed Ephesians 6:5 or 1 Peter 2:18, we might still have slavery.

WHAT COUNTS AS CENTRAL BIBLICAL MORAL PRINCIPLES?

Copan unfortunately falls into the common trap that always besets biblical theologians. Historically, biblical theology has been preoccupied with finding "the central message" or the major principles of the Bible. This endeavor evaporates when we realize that the biblical materials have con-tradictory and complex principles that usually cannot be unified. Such tensions and contradictions are acknowledged by Copan himself when he recommends the approach of Christopher Wright in explaining contradic-tory slavery laws: "[Wright] goes so far as to say that while Exodus 21 emphasizes the humanness of slaves, even the ancient Israelite would rec-ognize that Deuteronomy 15 was in tension with earlier legislation. So, to obey Deuteronomy 'necessarily meant no longer complying with Exodus.'"

Yet how are we to know that Deuteronomy should reverse anything in Exodus? This is a faith claim. Even if we disregard the chronological prob-lems, contradictory texts usually mean that the interpreter ends up privileging one text over another and declaring that one "central." Yet an advocate of the Exodus slave legislation might declare Deuteronomy to be a corruption or deviation.

Because it is hard to erase all of the injustices found in biblical law, another favorite technique is the "trajectory" argument. Thus, apologists can argue that, while things may look bad, they are heading in the right direction. Of course, this already prejudges what the right direction is, and also plays pick-and-choose with what counts as a trajectory (e.g., why not say the trajectory is enslaving the entire world to Yahweh?).

Nonetheless, Copan believes that there is a "moral heart" to the OT in the following statement: "While acknowledging the drastically different mindset between ANE and modern societies, we can overcome a good deal of the force of the New Atheists' objections and discern the moral heart of the OT, which is a marked contrast to the New Atheists' portrayal." But Copan never establishes criteria for what constitutes "the moral heart" of the Bible. Is it a statistical criterion? That is to say, is it the number of times a specific concept or term is repeated? Or is it qualitative? That is to say, is it something believed to be the most important concept, regardless of how many times others are repeated?

Statistically, as we have already noted, cultic laws are an overwhelming majority of the laws. So shall we say that the moral heart is really about good cultic practices? Why should we accept that being good to one's neighbor is "the moral heart" when we also can find many instances of people destroying their Canaanite neighbors? Empirically and historically, what is identified as "the moral heart" differs sometimes by religious group or by scholar. Orthodox Jews obviously will not have a Christocentric approach to the Bible, and so a moral center must include maintaining food laws, which are intimately related to God's holiness, which does not change (see Leviticus 11:44). Jews chose death rather than violate food laws (1 Maccabees 1:62–63; Daniel 1:8). The food laws are just as much a part of the moral system for orthodox Jews as Jesus' injunctions are for Christians.

UNCLEAR CRITERIA FOR MORAL COMPARISONS

The religiocentric and ethnocentric biases of Copan play a fundamental role in how he evaluates other religions. Copan preselects the standards of his religion, and then just simply judges other religions by that standard. He is actually relying on a moral relativism that could be used to establish the superiority of any standard. For example, if we, as Americans, value freedom of religion, then it is clear that biblical law is inferior to that of other Near Eastern systems. One could easily argue that the denial of religious freedom is at the "moral heart" of the OT. It is the very first of the Ten Commandments in Exodus 20:3: "*You shall have no other gods before me.*"

The intolerance of other religions is found in every single biblical book. This includes:

1. commands to destroy the temples and property of other religions (e.g., Deuteronomy 7; 2 Kings 23),
2. destruction of the "clergy" of other religions (e.g., 1 Kings 18:40),
3. consistent commands not to worship other gods (e.g., Exodus 20:3), and
4. laws requiring the outright murder of any Hebrew exercising religious freedom (e.g., Deuteronomy 13:1–16, 17:2–5; Exodus 22:18).

Copan acknowledges this intolerance as well: "Yes, God prohibits the worship of other gods and the fashioning of graven images, but the ultimate desire is that Yahweh's people love him wholeheartedly."

In contrast, most Near Eastern religions valued religious diversity and allowed the worship of almost any god people chose. This freedom to worship would actually be more consistent with American ideals than with anything in the Bible. By the standard that attempts to maximize freedom of religion, the Bible is a setback for humanity, not an advance.

Moreover, Copan completely misunderstands the idea of "loving God." As has been pointed out by W. L. Moran, the "love of God" is simply another part of the slave-master rhetoric in the ancient Near East.[18] The slave was compelled to "love" the master or he would be punished (cf. Deuteronomy 28:15–68). Serving other slave masters could be a capital offense, and we see that Yahweh is simply envisioned as the ultimate slave master. "Love" (or even Christian *agape*) in the Bible is not necessarily the benign and mutual-respect idea that we value in the twenty-first century.

FAITH-BASED SPECIAL PLEADING

Copan's essay is thoroughly permeated with special pleading based on the faith claims of his religion. He uses faith claims that:

1. could easily be used by competing religions, and
2. are no more verifiable than the claims of competing religions.

CHRISTOCENTRIC BIASES

Let us begin with Copan's Christocentric theology. He excuses a lot of the violence and inequality in the OT because, "The Law—a temporary rather than permanent fixture—would give way to a new covenant under Christ." But a Muslim could just as well argue that anything Christ did was superseded by Muhammad's revelation. Both the Muslim and Christians faith claims are equally unverifiable.

Moreover, Copan's statement about the temporary nature of the law contradicts Deuteronomy 4:2: "You shall not add to the word which I command you, nor take from it; that you may keep the commandments of the LORD your God which I command you." If one does not add or subtract from these commandments, then they remain immutable. Copan may say that this is not what Deuteronomy 4:2 means, but that would only be because of yet other faith-based claims (e.g., the nature of a "New Covenant" in Jeremiah 31:31–40 is being interpreted correctly by the author of Hebrews 8:8–13, etc.).

Notice also how Copan simply assumes that Jesus' reasons for certain Mosaic laws are correct (e.g., Moses' law of divorce was given because of the obstinacy of the Hebrews). This also is a faith-based claim because it assumes that Jesus is correct about God's motives for that law. Throughout, Copan simply assumes that the rules given by his god are true, while those of other gods are not. But why couldn't we say that Shamash is the true god, and then judge biblical law with how it accords with Shamash's law?

JUSTIFYING GENOCIDE

Copan's arbitrary privileging of his faith claims devolves into a morass of moral relativism when he tries to justify the genocide of the Canaanites. First, the genocide of the Canaanites flies in the face of Copan's touting of the concept of humans being created in the image of god (*Imago Dei*) as a superior aspect of biblical ethics. He remarks:

> Even more fundamentally, human beings have been created in God's image as corulers with God over creation (Gen. 1:26–27; Ps. 8)—unlike the ANE mindset, in which the earthly king was the image-bearer of the gods. The *Imago Dei* establishes the fundamental equality of human beings, despite the ethnocentrism and practice of slavery within Israel.

Yet biblical narratives clearly show that the *Imago Dei* matters very little in ensuring human equality. There were many other events and reasons (e.g., birth order, gender) that could generate inequality. Sometimes it could simply be that Yahweh likes one person more than another, as in the case of Esau and Jacob. In no instance does God state that they are both equal because they were both created in his image (see Romans 9:13–16). After all, they are supposed to be twins.

Nor is it true that the Bible does not view the king as being in a unique image-bearing relation to Yahweh. In fact, there are passages that call only the human king the son of Yahweh: "I have set my king on Zion, my holy hill. I will tell of the decree of the LORD: He said to me, 'You are my son, today I have begotten you.'"(Psalm 2:6–7). In John 8:44, Jesus says that Jews are not sons of God, but rather of the devil: "You are of your father the devil, and your will is to do your father's desires. He was a murderer from the beginning, and has nothing to do with the truth, because there is no truth in him. When he lies, he speaks according to his own nature, for he is a liar and the father of lies." In my book *The End of Biblical Studies* I have explained how the effort to deny this anti-Judaism in the NT often relies on special pleading and arbitrary exegesis.[19]

Given the fact that Canaanite women and children are to be killed despite being made in the image of God, Copan's main defense is a faith claim. He remarks:

> First, Israel would not have been justified to attack the Canaanites without Yahweh's explicit command. Yahweh issued his command in light of a morally sufficient reason—the incorrigible wickedness of Canaanite culture…if God exists, does he have any prerogatives over human life? The New Atheists seem to think that if God existed, he should have a status no higher than any human being.

Of course, this assumes that Yahweh exists and has the authority to kill women and children. Copan is accepting the faith claim of the biblical author. By this logic, if Allah exists, does he have any prerogatives over human life? Indeed, a jihadist Muslim could say that Allah has the authority to wipe out all Americans because they are incorrigible and wicked. Of course, these jihadists might also feel entitled to use their own definition of "wicked" and "incorrigible" no less so than Copan.

As it is, Copan characterizes the Israelites as incorrigible ("Another dimension of this harshness seems to be a *response* to the rebellious, covenant-breaking propensity of the Israelites"). But this does not explain why Canaanite incorrigibility should be punished with genocide, while Israelite incorrigibility should be rewarded with mercy and patience. Consistent with my proposal that the "moral heart" of the Bible is religious intolerance, Copan tells us: "We see from this passage too that wiping out Canaanite *religion* was far more significant than wiping out the Canaanites themselves." So if jidahist Muslims kill millions of Americans in order to wipe out our supposedly corrupt religion, then I suppose that would be morally acceptable by Copan's logic. It all depends on whether you accept the faith claim that Allah is the true God. We must also recall that all the supposed crimes and wickedness of the Canaanite are narrated by their enemies, the biblical authors.

Over and over, we see Copan applying words such as "morally decadent" and "wicked" to Canaanites because he is accepting the judgments of biblical authors. In any case, Copan's procedure would be analogous to using only the pronouncements of Osama bin Laden to judge American culture.[20] In any event, for Copan, "idolatry" allows Israelites the right to kill women and children as long as the higher goal of wiping out idolatry is met. Of course, his view of idolatry is what counts. It really amounts to this: "Genocide is okay when my religion does it, but genocide is not okay if your religion does it."

But we could just as easily reverse this and say that, from the viewpoint of some mono-Baal worshipper, the worship of Yahweh is idolatry. That should give mono-Baalists the right to kill Yahweh worshippers if the higher goal is wiping out Yahweh worship. Moreover, we know that, even according to biblical materials, idolatry was not wiped out. Indeed, after all of the genocide carried out by Joshua and his successors, we still find idolatry being lamented in Jeremiah and other later prophets. Yahweh ends up killing women and children in vain. Yahweh apparently lacks the foresight to see that genocide will not work.

JUSTIFYING INFANTICIDE

To excuse the plain horror of infanticide, Copan offers this as comfort: "Death would be a mercy, as they would be ushered into the presence of God and spared the corrupting influences of a morally decadent culture." This rationale actually follows a long apologetic tradition, such as this one evinced by the famed fundamentalist apologist Reuben A. Torrey: "The extermination of the Canaanite children was not only an act of mercy and love to the world at large; it was an act of love and mercy to the children themselves."[21]

Copan does not seem to realize the theological implications of his own words. First, if it is true that killing infants ushers them immediately into the presence of God, and spares them corrupting influences, then this is a fantastic argument for abortion. Why allow any child to be born if we can send him or her straight to heaven? After all, isn't the salvation of souls more important than any human experience?

This is especially the case if we take literally the words of Jesus in Matthew 10:28: "And do not fear those who kill the body but cannot kill the soul; rather fear him who can destroy both soul and body in hell." If soul saving is the goal, then abortion provides a 100 percent salvation rate. Yahweh could also decriminalize killing infants today, since the goal of soul saving should be no less worthy today than it was in the time of the Canaanites.

One can see that Copan seems not to value life as much as he claims. Apparently, the value of practicing the right religion supersedes the value of life. Copan wants to kill women and children to save them from corrupt and wicked practices, but he does not see the killing of women and children as itself a "corrupt" or "wicked" practice. Nor does Copan explain why infants have to be killed for the sins of their parents. In fact, this contradicts God's own injunctions in Deuteronomy 24:16: "The fathers shall not be put to death for the children, nor shall the children be put to death for the fathers; every man shall be put to death for his own sin."

Moreover, Copan assumes that his omnipotent god could find no other alternative than to slaughter children to accomplish the purpose of preventing their corruption. Yet Yahweh was believed to cause sterility in women (see Genesis 20:17–18). So Yahweh could have sterilized Canaanite women supernaturally, and the problem would be solved in a generation or two. No need to kill children with this procedure.

A similar moral relativism and theological special pleading is at the heart of Copan's defense of biblical polygamy. He tells us: "Let us consider polygamy as an example: Why did God not ban polygamy outright in favor of monogamy? Why allow a double standard for men who can take multiple wives while a woman can only have one husband? For one thing, despite the practical problems of polygamy, Wenham suggests it was permitted perhaps because monogamy would have been *difficult to enforce.*"

But if God allows polygamy because monogamy is difficult to enforce, then why not do the same with idolatry, murder, and bestiality? The Bible itself tells us that idolatry never did completely die out, so why does that not qualify idolatry as a practice "difficult to enforce"? And by the same token, why should we judge other ancient Near Eastern cultures for allowing practices that their gods also might find "difficult to enforce"? If difficulty of enforcement is the criterion, then why are ancient Near Eastern cultures judged as inferior? And who decided that polygamy was a deviation from an ideal, original monogamy? The idea that monogamy was original is a faith-based claim—that is, based on accepting the word of the author of Genesis 2–3. After all, incest was also original, as you could not have reproduced from the first pair without incest at some level. So should we regard nonincestuous pairings as a deviation from the original ideal?

JUSTIFYING CHILD SACRIFICE

Copan mentions child sacrifice twice in his article. The first time he cited Richard Dawkins when he charged that Yahweh's commanding Abraham to sacrifice his son Isaac was "child abuse." The second time it's mentioned in his "Final Thoughts," where Copan wrote: "Genesis 1–2 undercuts ANE structures approving of racism, slavery, patriarchy, primogeniture, concubinage, prostitution, *infant sacrifice*, and the like."[22] [emphasis added].

But if Genesis 1–2 is intended as a cure for this horrible practice, it was not very effective, for child sacrifice may have been perfectly acceptable to Yahweh, something demonstrated in painstaking detail by Jon Levenson, the Albert A. List Professor of Jewish Studies at Harvard Divinity School. In his brilliant treatment, *The Death and Resurrection of the Beloved Son*, Levenson states, "only at a particular stage rather late in the history of Israel was child sacrifice branded as counter to the will of YHWH and thus ipso facto idolatrous."[23] He points to Ezekiel 20:25–26, as one example where Yahweh says: "Moreover I gave them statutes that were not good and ordinances by which they could not have life; and I defiled them through their very gifts in making them offer by fire all their first-born, that I might horrify them; I did it that they might know that I am the LORD."

But of which statutes is Yahweh speaking when referring the sacrifice of a first-born son? That statute may be the one in Exodus 22:29–30: "You shall not delay to offer from the fullness of your harvest and from the outflow of your presses. The first-born of your sons you shall give to me. You shall do likewise with your oxen and with your sheep: seven days it shall be with its dam; on the eighth day you shall give it to me." As Levenson observes, many Christian and Jewish scholars have tried to mitigate or eliminate the obvious meaning of these passages. But even Moshe Greenberg, author of a major commentary of Ezekiel, and who otherwise minimizes the idea that normative Yahwism engaged in child sacrifice, admits: "The polemic against child sacrifice (to YHWH) in Deuteronomy 12:29ff.; Jeremiah 7:31, 19:5, 32:35 indicates that at least from the time of the last kings of Judah it was popularly believed that YHWH accepted, perhaps even commanded, it."[24]

For Levenson, it was late texts that sought to substitute animals for actual human first-born sons. Genesis 22, which shows Yahweh substituting a ram for Isaac, is part of a late biblical tradition. Indeed, in Genesis 22, Abraham seems to presume that child sacrifice is not an impossible request, and it is the substitution of the ram that is unexpected. For most of biblical history, Yahweh was not against child sacrifice per se, but rather against child sacrifice to other gods.[25] Even the prophet Micah ponders whether he should sacrifice his oldest son "as a sin offering" to Yahweh, although he rejects doing so in the end (6:6–8).

And, of course, Copan forgets that sacrifice of a son is the foundation of Christianity. After all, Jesus Christ is viewed as the only-begotten son of God, who must be sacrificed to redeem the world because of "love" (John 3:16). Christ's sacrifice is premised on the sort of blood-magic inherited from the ancient Near East. This blood-magic is evident in Hebrews 9:22: "Indeed, under the law almost everything is purified with blood, and without the shedding of blood there is no forgiveness of sin." Christian apologists might claim that their god has the authority to order sacrifice, but this claim is no more verifiable than that of any other religion that practices human sacrifice.

MISCELLANEOUS ERRORS AND DISTORTIONS

Copan's essay literally contains dozens upon dozens of factual errors and half-truths that would take a book to correct. But here are brief responses to ten claims from Copan that have not been discussed above.

1. Copan claims: "These narratives also inform us that Israel's kings, no matter how powerful, are not above God's law: Nathan confronts David about his murder and adultery (2 Sam. 12)."

Actually, the narrative about David shows how much David is above the law. David committed at least two sins that demanded the death penalty. He committed adultery, and he committed murder (see 2 Samuel 12:9). A normal human being would be executed for adultery or murder (see Leviticus 20:10 and 24:17). God himself promised not to acquit a murderer in Exodus 23:7. But instead of David being put to death, it is David's son whom God kills (2 Samuel 12:14) in violation of his own law in Deuteronomy 24:16. Yahweh is the biggest moral relativist of all, especially since he seems to break his own moral promises.

2. Copan claims: "Furthermore, in Babylonian or Hittite law, status or social rank determined the kind of sanctions for a particular crime whereas biblical law holds kings and priests and those of social rank to the same standards as the common person. The informed inhabitant of the ANE would have thought, 'Quick, get me to Israel!'"

Copan ignores the numerous instances in which Israelite kings were treated differently from the common person. As I said before, a common person might be executed for committing adultery and murder, but David was not. Also, slaves did not have the same rights as their masters.

The idea that informed inhabitants of the ancient Near East were clamoring to get to Israel is contradicted by the story of Nabal, who alludes to David, when he exclaims "There are many servants nowadays who are breaking away from their masters" (1 Samuel 25:10). In fact, David flees to Philistine territory, where the Philistine king, Achish, gives him a whole town (1 Samuel 27:5–6).

3. Copan claims: "Even later on when the Jews returned from Babylon, Nehemiah was properly appalled by Jews opening themselves up to idolatry by marrying foreign wives (for example, Nehemiah. 13, esp. v. 25)."

Copan contradicts himself here because he also told us the following: "Because of Yahweh's covenant with Israel, laws intending to preserve both the family unit and Yahweh's unique covenant/marriage relationship to Israel were paramount." Yet the stories in Nehemiah and Ezra demonstrate that preserving the family unit *was not paramount*. Ezra, in fact, orders the break-up of families. Thus, Ezra 10:10–11 states: "And Ezra the priest stood up and said to them, 'You have trespassed and married foreign women, and so increased the guilt of Israel. Now then make confession to the LORD the God of your fathers, and do his will; separate yourselves from the peoples of the land and from the foreign wives.'"

Again, for Copan, religious intolerance is more important than family values. Ethnic values superseded family values. Rarely does one see families ordered to break up because people had different religions in the ancient Near East. Ezra and Nehemiah should count as a step backward for families.

Copan also claims "there are several disparities between ANE cuneiform laws versus biblical laws," which forms the basis of some more factual errors and half-truths listed below, numbered 4–8.

4. Copan claimed that cuneiform laws were made by kings (not gods) whereas biblical laws came from God as mediated through Moses.

This is patently false. Laws can also be attributed to a god in the ancient Near East, as in this Hittite text: "You (Sungod) establish the lands' customs and law."[26] Conversely, we can also find instances in the Bible where laws are made by human leaders:

> Then all the wicked and base fellows among the men who had gone with David said, "Because they did not go with us, we will not give them any of the spoil which we have recovered, except that each man may lead away his wife and children, and depart." But David said, "You shall not do so, my brothers, with what the LORD has given us; he has preserved us and given into our hand the band that came against us. Who would listen to you in this matter? For as his share is who goes down into the battle, so shall his share be who stays by the baggage; they shall share alike." And from that day forward he made it a statute and an ordinance for Israel to this day. (1 Samuel 30:22–25)

5. Copan claimed that cuneiform laws were to glorify kings whereas biblical laws were to glorify God and to instruct people, which shaped a national character.

The CH destroys this notion because the glory of the gods is paramount: "When the august god Anu, king of the Anunnaku deities, and the god Enlil, lord of heaven and earth, who determines the destinies of the land, allotted supreme power over all the peoples to the god Marduk, the firstborn son of the god Ea, exalted him among the Igigu deities...."[27]

Conversely, one can find the glory of the king comingled with praises for Yahweh, as in Psalm 89:1–4, 27: "I will sing of thy steadfast love, O

LORD, for ever; with my mouth I will proclaim thy faithfulness to all generations. For thy steadfast love was established for ever, thy faithfulness is firm as the heavens. Thou hast said, 'I have made a covenant with my chosen one, I have sworn to David my servant: I will establish your descendants for ever, and build your throne for all generations. . . . And I will make him the first-born, the highest of the kings of the earth.'"

As I have previously mentioned, the prologue of the CH states that laws are also meant to teach and build the character of the people of the kingdom.

6. Copan claimed that cuneiform laws reflected a king's unlimited authority whereas biblical laws limited the king's authority (as seen in Deuteronomy 17:14–20).

There are many instances where ancient Near Eastern law also limited royal authority. In certain periods of Hittite history, the *pankush*, a sort of broader council of nobles, acted to judge kings when they overstepped their boundaries.

7. Copan claimed that in cuneiform laws the offenses against slaves were on the same level as property crimes whereas in biblical law offenses were considered against slaves as persons of value.

I have already cited instances where slaves were given even better treatment in the ancient Near East (e.g., in case of providing for sons of slaves), and I can find instances of slaves being asked to submit to dehumanizing treatment in the NT (e.g., 1 Peter 2:18).

8. Copan claimed that in cuneiform laws religious sins were not typically capital offenses whereas in biblical law a number of religious sins were considered "capital offenses—idolatry (Deut. 13:6–9), false prophecy (Deut. 18:20), sorcery (Lev. 20:27), blasphemy (Lev. 24:10–23), Sabbath violations (Num. 15:32–36)."

Copan presumes that maintaining proper religious practices are worth more than human life. Why not count as abhorrent the thought that people could be killed for practicing a different religion?

Copan has failed to show these disparities between cuneiform laws versus biblical laws. But there are two more factual errors and half-truths left to point out.

9. Copan claimed: "Not only do we find morally inferior cuneiform legislation, but its attendant harsh, ruthless punishments. Commenting on the brutal and harsh Code of Hammurabi, historian Paul Johnson observes: 'These dreadful laws are notable for the ferocity of their physical punishments, in contrast to the restraint of the Mosaic Code and the enactments of Deuteronomy and Leviticus.'"

Copan ignores the replacement of many executions with fines or offerings in Hittite law. Moreover, he does not characterize as "ruthless" or as "brutal" the endorsement of drowning (Genesis 6), stoning (Leviticus 20:27), burning (Genesis 19), and slaughtering by the sword (1 Kings 18:40) those punished for various offenses in the Bible. Children are killed for the "crime" of being born a Canaanite.

It gets worse in the NT, as now we are to be burned eternally for not following the Christian religion (Matthew 25:41–46). I never see eternal torture by fire mentioned in the CH.

10. Finally, Copan claimed: "Babylon and Assyria (as well as Sumer) practiced the River Ordeal: when criminal evidence was inconclusive, the accused would be thrown into the river; if he drowned, he was guilty (the river god's judgment), but if he survived, he was innocent and the accuser was guilty of false accusation."

Copan forgets that, in contrast to Mesopotamia, not all Israelites lived near large and dependable rivers where such ordeals might work best. Geography can influence the types of resources and material available for punishment. Indeed, Israel did have another type of ordeal that was no less horrifying, and this one directed at women accused of adultery. The description of the ordeal is as follows in Numbers 5:16–22:

> And the priest shall bring her near, and set her before the LORD; and the priest shall take holy water in an earthen vessel, and take some of the dust that is on the floor of the tabernacle and put it into the water. And the priest shall set the woman before the LORD, and unbind the hair of the woman's head, and place in her hands the cereal offering of remembrance, which is the cereal offering of jealousy. And in his hand the priest shall have the water of bitterness that brings the curse. Then the priest shall make her take an oath, saying, "If no man has lain with you, and if you have not turned aside to uncleanness, while you were under your husband's authority, be free from this water of bitterness that brings the curse. But if you have gone astray, though you are under your husband's

authority, and if you have defiled yourself, and some man other than your husband has lain with you, then let the priest make the woman take the oath of the curse, and say to the woman 'the LORD make you an execration and an oath among your people, when the LORD makes your thigh fall away and your body swell; may this water that brings the curse pass into your bowels and make your body swell and your thigh fall away.' And the woman shall say, 'Amen, Amen.'"

Even the conservative commentator Philip Budd describes it as a "trial by ordeal."[28] Despite Budd's best efforts to say that the water was not very harmful, the text itself says that this water was meant to produce horrific results. Budd adds that "Modern practice of the ordeal would obviously be indefensible...."[29]

Having shown Copan's errors and Yahweh's supposed laws cruel and unjust, I want to end by comparing Copan's sense of morality with that of the atheist. He does not have a better morality. Atheism offers a much better way to construct moral rules.

ATHEISM'S MORALITY

Copan fundamentally misunderstands the New Atheism insofar as he believes that it cannot provide a sound moral ground for its judgments. For a Christian apologist to think he or she has triumphed by pointing out the moral relativism of the New Atheism is to miss the entire point.

As an atheist, I don't deny that I am a moral relativist. Rather, my aim is to expose the fact that Christians are also moral relativists. Indeed, when it comes to ethics, there are only two types of people in this world:

1. Those who admit they are moral relativists; and
2. Those who do not admit they are moral relativists.

Copan fails because he cannot admit that he is a moral relativist, and he thinks that God will solve the problem of moral relativism. But having a God in a moral system only creates a tautology. All we end up saying is: "X is bad because X is bad." Thus, if we say that we believe in God, and he says idolatry is evil, then that is a tautology: "God says idolatry is bad and

so idolatry is bad because God says it is bad." Or we end up using this tautology: "Whatever God says is good because whatever God says is good."

As Kai Nielsen deftly argues, human beings are always the ultimate
judges of morality even if we believe in God. After all, the very judgment
that God is good is a human judgment.[30] The judgment that what God
commands is good is also a human judgment. So Christians are not doing
anything different except mystifying and complicating morality. Christians
are simply projecting what they call "good" onto a supernatural being.
They offer us no evidence that their notion of good comes from outside of
themselves. And that is where the danger lies. Basing a moral system on
unverifiable supernatural beings only creates more violence and endangers
our species. I have already discussed this at length in my book, *Fighting
Words: The Origins of Religious Violence.*

Copan cites Dinesh D'Souza who repeats the oft-cited anecdote that
atheists have killed more people than religionists. Again, this is based on
the false idea that Nazis were atheistic Darwinists, and that Stalinist genocide was due to atheism rather than to forced collectivism (something I discuss in detail in chapter 14 of this book). Speaking only for myself here, I
can say that atheism offers a much better way to construct moral rules. We
can construct them on the basis of verifiable common interests, known
causes, and known consequences. There is an ironclad difference between
secular and faith-based morality, and we can illustrate it very simply with
these propositions:

A. I have to kill person X because Allah said so.
B. I have to kill person X because he is pointing a gun at me.

In case A, we commit violence on the basis of unverifiable premises. In
case B, we might commit violence on the basis of verifiable premises (I can
verify a gun exists, and that it is pointed at me). If I am going to kill or be
killed, I want it to be for a reason that I can verify to be true. If the word
"moral" describes the set of practices that accord with our values, and if
our highest value is life, then it is always immoral to trade real human lives
for something that does not exist or cannot be verified to exist.

What does not exist has no value relative to what does exist. What
cannot be proven to exist should never be placed above what does exist. If
we value life, then you should never trade something that exists, especially
life, for something that does not exist or cannot be proven to exist. That is

why it would always be immoral to ever take a human life on the basis of faith claims. It is that simple.

CONCLUSION

Copan's critique of the New Atheism fails philosophically and also in matters of simple factuality. First, his comparisons between ancient Near Eastern law and biblical law are devoid of a thorough reading of ancient Near Eastern legal materials. Talk of superiority or advancement in the Bible is illusory once Copan's ethnocentrism and religiocentrism are exposed. We can find dramatic regressions in biblical law (slavery is worse in the NT relative to Amos). If motive clauses are the standard, we can find self-interested ones in the Bible (Honor parents so that you live longer). If the welfare of children is the standard, then we can find the welfare of the children of slave-women was much more advanced in the CH than what we find in the case of Ishmael. Instead we find a God in the Bible who endorses slavery, genocide, infanticide, and child sacrifice—as only a moral monster could—and who apparently didn't have any new morals or laws to offer his chosen people that were all that innovative compared to other ancient Near Eastern cultures.

Finally, Copan misses the real threat of the New Atheism, if there is such a thing. The greatest threat will not be a Hitchens, a Dawkins, or a Harris. Rather, it will be highly trained biblical scholars who are former Christian apologists. It is they who know best where the rotting corpses of biblical ethics are buried.

What is tragic is that in the twenty-first century a Copan can still defend genocide and infanticide in any form. What is still unbelievable is that a Copan can say that killing women and children is sometimes good. It is that sort of frightening biblical moral ethos that makes the New Atheism more attractive all the time.

NOTES

1. See *Philosophia Christi* 10 (2008): 7–37, which can also be found online at http://www.epsociety.org/library/articles.asp?pid=45, from which I'll be quoting. This chapter is an edited version of my response to Copan. To read my complete

response see "Paul Copan's Moral Relativism: A Response from a Biblical Scholar of the New Atheism," found on Debunking Christianity, August 1, 2008, http:// debunkingchristianity.blogspot.com/2008/07/paul-copans-moral-relativism -response.html; as well as "Creationists for Genocide: Child Sacrifice Is Biblically Approved," Talk Reason, August 24, 2007, http://www.talkreason.org/articles/ Genocide.cfm#child. Paul Copan drew fire from critics such as Wesley Morriston and Randal Rauser in a symposium for *Philosophia Christi* 11 (2009): 7–92. Morriston's response can be found online at http://www.colorado.edu/philosophy/ wes/DidGodCommandGenocide.pdf and Copan's response to his critics can be found here: http://www.epsociety.org/library/articles.asp?pid=63. While Copan knew of my criticisms before writing a response to his other critics, he never addressed them. [Editor's note: See also the additional chapter on this topic posted online by Richard Carrier, "The Will of God," to be found on our official Web site: http://sites.google.com/site/thechristiandelusion/Home/the-will-of-god].

2. For the text of the Code of Hammurabi, I depend on Martha T. Roth, *Law Collections from Mesopotamia and Asia Minor* 2nd ed. (Atlanta: Scholars Press, 1997), pp. 76–77.

3. For the epilogue, see Roth, *Law Collections*, p. 133.

4. Berend Gemser, "The Importance of the Motive Clause in Old Testament Law," *Vetus Testamentum Supplements* 1 (1953): 50–66.

5. Rifat Sonsino, *Motive Clauses* (Chico, CA: Scholars Press, 1980), p. 174.

6. Ibid., p. 175.

7. Roth, *Law Collections*, p. 107 [My adapted translation; for better English understanding, I have added "priestess" in brackets to two terms (*shugitu* and *naditu*) that Roth leaves untranslated, and I have modified the spelling of those terms to suit English fonts].

8. On how translations sometimes do not reflect the more explicative form of some clauses that involve the particle -*ma* in the Code of Hammurabi, see Theophile Meek, "The Asyndeton Clause in the Code of Hammurabi," *Journal of Near Eastern Studies* 5, no. 1 (1946): 64–72.

9. Sonsino, *Motive Clauses*, p. 99.

10. Unless noted otherwise, all quotations of the Bible are from the RSV.

11. Sonsino, *Motive Clauses*, p. 99.

12. Ibid., pp. 241–48.

13. Harry A. Hoffner, *The Laws of the Hittites: A Critical Edition* (Leiden: Brill, 1997), p. 33.

14. Ibid., pp. 133–34.

15. Raymond Westbrook, *Property and the Family in Biblical Law* (Sheffield: Sheffield Academic Press, 1991), p. 45.

16. The idea that the book of Philemon has been misinterpreted to be too proslavery is advocated by Allen Dwight Callahan, *Embassy of Onesimus: The Letter*

of *Paul to Philemon* (Valley Forge, PA: Trinity Press International, 1997). I plan to respond to Callahan's flawed argument in the near future.

17. One of my forthcoming works will critique Rodney Stark, author of *For the Glory of God: How Monotheism Led to Reformations, Science, Witch-Hunts and the End of Slavery* (Princeton: Princeton University Press, 2003), who claims that Christianity, not secularization, was the main reason for the abolition of slavery. What I can say here is that Stark's misreadings of ancient Near Eastern materials are very similar to those of Copan.

18. William L. Moran, "The Ancient Near Eastern Background of the Love of God in Deuteronomy," *Catholic Biblical Quarterly* 25 (1963): 77–87.

19. Hector Avalos, *The End of Biblical Studies* (Amherst, NY: Prometheus Books, 2007), pp. 56–58.

20. I have addressed the supposed archaeological evidence for Canaanite wickedness in my essay, "Creationists for Genocide," Talk Reason, August 24, 2007, http://www.talkreason.org/articles/Genocide.cfm.

21. Reuben A. Torrey, *Difficulties in the Bible* (Chicago: Moody Press, n.d.), p. 60.

22. *Philosophia Christi* 10 (2008): pp. 7, 37 [emphasis added].

23. (New Haven, CT: Yale University Press, 1993), p. 5.

24. Moshe Greenberg, *Ezekiel 1–20* (Garden City, NY: Doubleday, 1983), p. 369.

25. Editor's Note: In *War in the Hebrew Bible: A Study in the Ethics of Violence* (New York: Oxford University Press, 1993) Susan Niditch tells us: "While there is considerable controversy about the matter, the consensus over the last decade concludes that child sacrifice was a part of ancient Israelite religion to large segments of Israelite communities of various periods" (p. 47). S. Ackerman argues in *Under Every Green Tree: Popular Religion in Sixth-Century Judah* (Atlanta: Scholars Press, 1992) that among the ancient Israelites, "the cult of child sacrifice was felt in some circles to be a legitimate expression of Yawistic faith" (p. 137). Francesca Stavrakopoulou concludes her book *King Manasseh and Child Sacrifice: Biblical Distortions of Historical Realities* (Berlin: Walter de Gruyter, 2004) by saying: "Despite the biblical exhortation that child sacrifice is alien to YHWH worship, practiced by the foreign and idolatrous, and consistently outlawed by YHWH, closer inspection of this biblical portrayal instead locates child sacrifice within the mainstream of its presentation of YHWH ... Child sacrifice appears to be a native and normative element of Judahite religious practice" (p. 318).

26. Quoted by Hoffner (*Laws of the Hittites*, p. 1).

27. Roth, *Law Collections*, pp. 76–77.

28. *Numbers: Word Biblical Commentary*, vol. 5 (Waco, TX: Word Publishers, 1984) p. 65.

29. Ibid, p. 67.

30. *Ethics without God* (Amherst, NY: Prometheus Books, 1992).

Chapter 9

THE DARWINIAN PROBLEM OF EVIL

John W. Loftus

T his chapter is about sentient nonhuman animals, all of them, both domesticated and those in the wild. Typically the animal kingdom in its most loosely stated definition includes every living thing in distinction from the plant kingdom.[1] In this world they suffer, sometimes horribly, because of the natural law of the jungle, as well as at the hands of human beings. Upon the supposition of Darwinian evolutionary biology, this suffering is natural. It's what we should expect to find. But upon the supposition of Christian theism, this is not what we should expect to find. I'll argue that the existence of animal suffering cannot be reconciled with the Christian faith and is one of the strongest reasons to reject it.

WHAT'S THE PROBLEM?

In 1859 when Charles Darwin published his work, *On the Origin of Species*, the world learned how all life is interconnected through the evolutionary process of natural selection, stretching back billions of years in time. From Darwin's detailed scientific investigations we learned that humans are directly related to other animals, especially to chimpanzees, who share 98.5 percent of our exact genetic makeup. We are not special to earth's ecosystem either. We depend on each other. It could no longer be said, except in the ignorant Bible-thumping pulpits of the world, that we were created instantaneously by divine fiat on one day of a divine workweek.

Rehearsing his own process from being a Christian to agnostic, Charles Darwin laid out what I'm calling the *Darwinian Problem of Evil*. In his autobiography he wrote:

> That there is much suffering in the world no one disputes. Some have attempted to explain this in reference to man by imagining that it serves for his moral improvement. But the number of men in the world is nothing compared with that of all other sentient beings, and these often suffer greatly without any moral improvement. A being so powerful and so full of knowledge as a God who could create this universe, is to our finite minds omnipotent and omniscient, and it revolts our understanding to suppose that his benevolence is not unbounded, for what advantage can there be in the suffering of millions of the lower animals throughout almost endless time? This very old argument from the existence of suffering against the existence of an intelligent First Cause seems to be a strong one; whereas...the presence of much suffering agrees well with the view that all organic beings have been developed through variation and natural selection.[2]

This argument is expanded upon by Christopher Hitchens, who states it with rhetorical flare. Based upon the claim that "at least 98% of all species on this tiny speck of a planet made only a few hesitant steps 'forward' before succumbing to extinction," Hitchens asks: "What kind of designer or creator is so wasteful and capricious and approximate? What kind of designer or creator is so cruel and indifferent?"[3] Hitchens also argues that we not only have the problem of nonhuman animal suffering up until to the first *Homo sapiens*. We also have the problem of human animal suffering up until God decides to reveal himself to them and/or to do something about it.[4] It's all part and parcel of the whole *Darwinian Problem of Evil*.

Richard Dawkins also reminds us that this problem does not just refer to the evolutionary past. The problem still faces us every single day; he writes:

> It is better for the genes of Darwin's ichneumon wasp that the caterpillar should be alive, and therefore fresh, when it is eaten, no matter what the

cost in suffering. Genes don't care about suffering because they don't care about anything. If Nature were kind, she would at least make the minor concession of anesthetizing caterpillars before they are eaten alive from within. But Nature is neither kind nor unkind. She is neither against suffering nor for it.... The total amount of suffering per year in the natural world is beyond all decent contemplation. During the minute it takes me to compose this sentence, thousands of animals are being eaten alive; others are running for their lives, whimpering with fear; others are being slowly devoured from within by rasping parasites; thousands of all kinds are dying of starvation, thirst and disease.... The universe we observe has precisely the properties we should expect if there is, at bottom, no design, no purpose, no evil and no good, nothing but blind, pitiless indifference.[5]

But there is even more. Human beings rule over the animal kingdom with an iron fist. Almost every kind of living creature is eaten as food by at least some of us on the planet. The history of the clash between the lower animals and us has been devastating to them. We have killed them just for the sake of hunting for sport. We've killed them for their trophy heads, hunted them for their ivory tusks, and/or trapped them for fur. We've experimented on them in grotesque ways, often even dissecting them while they were still alive. We've abused them for our own entertainment through cock fights, bull fights and dog fights. We have crammed them into small pens for what's called "intensive farming techniques." Some fish we like to eat so fresh that we cook their bodies and eat them while they are still alive and gasping for oxygen.

There is a new awareness in the last few decades that we shouldn't unnecessarily harm animals, even to the point where vegetarianism and veganism are becoming alternative lifestyles. With this new, humane awareness toward animals, Christian people must now come to grips with what their God purportedly said in the Bible about the relationship of man to beast. They must do this, according to Paul Waldau, the director of the Center for Animals and Public Policy at Tufts University School of Veterinary Medicine, because: "Treatment of nonhuman animals is a critical element in assessing any religious tradition's views of other animals."[6] If God is perfectly good, he should've been crystal clear that his followers must treat the lower animals kindly. But this is not what we find in the Bible. In fact, it's pretty much the reverse.[7]

THE PHILOSOPHICAL STANDARDS

The problem of such intense and ubiquitous animal suffering calls for a Christian answer. The kind of answer considered satisfactory will depend on what kind of standard of proof seems acceptable when answering it. What standard of proof should the theist meet in answering this problem? The most important standard is called a *theodicy*. Christian philosopher Alvin C. Plantinga describes a theodicy as an attempt "to tell us why God permits evil." This is a strong answer if satisfactory, for when the theodicist is done making her case there would be little left to explain. In contrast to a theodicy Plantinga argues for what he calls a *defense*. In a defense "the aim is not to say what God's reason *is*, but at most what God's reason *might possibly be*."[8]

I'm looking for an adequate theodicy, not a defense, when it comes to this problem, one that offers up rational explanations for why there is so much intense animal suffering if a perfectly good and omnipotent God exists. Such a theodicy need not explain everything, but it should explain a great deal. A defense merely suggests that something is possible. But that is too low to be accepted as any kind of standard at all. Christians continually want to talk about what is possible rather than what is probable, and they resort to this standard far too many times in defense of their faith to make their faith probable. But atheist philosopher Keith Parsons doesn't let this go unchallenged: "... for every evil that exists, a sufficiently clever theist might be able to imagine a scenario, no matter how farfetched, wildly implausible, or outrageously *ad hoc*, that if it were true, would justify God's permission of that evil." Continuing on, he argues that a Christian argument "must do more than show that the world's evils are *possibly* justified; it must give plausible grounds for thinking that in fact they *are* justified." Then with some flare Parsons concludes: "Without an adequate theodicy, arguing for God's existence will be like arguing that the earth is flat. Vast quantities of contrary data will either have to be ignored or dealt with in an arbitrary and *ad hoc* fashion."[9]

Michael J. Murray, a Christian professor of philosophy at Franklin and Marshall College, tries to steer a middle ground between a theodicy and a defense and offers a third kind of standard. He rejects the standard of a theodicy, because that standard is too high, which is par for the course. But he also rightly rejects the low standard of a defense. He wrote: "Defenses will be of little use in our context because...they do not aim to provide explanations that undercut the *evidential* value of evil."[10] Instead, Murray seeks "to find a middle way between a defense and a theodicy." He calls his standard *De Causa Dei*, meaning "on behalf of God," reminiscent of a juridical context about a legal case on behalf of a defendant in a trial, a phrase which comes from Leibniz, just like the word *theodicy* did. Such a standard might best be described by Murray: "[T]he theist may freely admit that she is not aware of any *plausible* hypotheses which turn back the evidential challenge. Still, there might be a variety of reasons which are, for example, *true for all she knows* and which are such that if they were true they would constitute good explanations for evil. Reasons like these would not fairly count as *plausible* (not *implausible*) but rather *as plausible as not, overall*."[11]

Murray claims there are theistic answers for the existence of animal suffering that can be warranted for theists based upon all that they know, even if the nontheistic critic doesn't share them. Whether the critic accepts the theistic answers or not, such answers "can still succeed for the theist."[12]

But what does Murray mean by the phrases, "true for all she knows," and "plausible as not, overall"? Two pages prior to the one upon which we find the above quote he mentioned how the death of Jesus was both evil and good. It was evil because Jesus suffered, he claims, but it was also good because it brought about the "great good of salvation for humanity." What Murray ends up proposing is that given everything a Christian believer accepts about a triune God who sent one third of himself (?) to become incarnate in Jesus, who subsequently died for our sins and rose from the grave, that he can offer some "plausible" answers with regard to the problem of animal suffering. Can he do this? I think not—not by a long shot. But even if he can, it still doesn't show that those background Christian beliefs, which form the basis *for all she or he knows*, are true. There are so many other undercutting defeaters to his collection of Christian beliefs that Murray shouldn't even be dealing with the problem of evil in the first place.

Peter van Inwagen offers a fourth kind of standard. He thinks he can convince us "that the argument from evil has not got the power to transform ideal (and hence neutral) agnostics into atheists," and therefore it's a "philosophical failure." *Neutral* agnostics, by his lights, are people who don't have an opinion either way on the matter, unlike so-called *weighted* agnostics, who think it's improbable that God exists. He calls this "the ideal debate test," which, if he's successful "will also show that the argument from evil is incapable of turning neutral agnostics into weighted agnostics." He acknowledges that the whole concept of an ideal test is problematic, but we'll leave that aside.[13] Nonetheless, I don't think he accomplishes what he proposes at all. If the argument from evil is successful, it doesn't lead someone to atheism or "weighted" agnosticism anyway. It could also lead a person to mysticism, or Deism, or panentheism (known as *process theism*). The argument from evil merely argues that if God exists, then he does not have one or more of the three attributes normally ascribed to him by Christian theism, namely, he might not be perfectly good, or all-powerful, or omniscient. That's all it can show. So what Van Inwagen should say instead is that the argument from evil will not be able to persuade neutral agnostics that this Christian kind of God doesn't exist. I think that it does, most definitely, and I hope to show this to be the case.

CHRISTIAN SOLUTIONS TO THE *DARWINIAN PROBLEM OF EVIL*

One thing is agreed upon when it comes to the *Darwinian Problem of Evil*, and that is a few of the usual Christian responses to this problem simply do not apply at all. Animals don't suffer because of their own sinful free-will choices to kill or be killed, so the free-will defense cannot be used to justify these sufferings. Nor are there any moral lessons animals can learn in response to their sufferings. Christian scholar Robert N. Wennberg, professor of philosophy at Westmont College, Santa Barbara, California, tells us:

> It is not that animal pain and suffering exacerbates the problem of evil by adding to the pain and suffering in the world. Rather, animal suffering intensifies the problem of evil.... [A]nimals suffer, innocent of sin and without guilt, who cannot be morally or spiritually benefited by the ravages of pain, who cannot place any meaningful or elevating interpretation upon their suffering, and who will not (according to most) be compensated for their suffering by another life beyond the grave. It would seem that some animals have been brought into existence only to suffer and die, and possibly along the way be put to use by humans: killed for food and clothing, harnessed as beasts of burden, hunted for sport, experimented upon, and in general valued only to the extent that they contribute one way or another to the satisfaction of human interests. And so the question emerges: how can we understand animal pain and suffering so as to make peace with a vision of a God whose compassion extends to all of his creatures?[14]

In what follows I'll describe and then criticize eight major options Christians have at their disposal in answering the *Darwinian Problem of Evil.* I'll argue that none of them succeed (see note).[15]

OPTION ONE

The traditional Christian answer is that animal predation and pain entered our world through the supposed fall of Adam and Eve in the Garden of Eden. There are two different ways of considering how such a fall into sin caused animal suffering and death. The first way is the traditional solution that a historical fall in the Garden subsequently caused human and animal suffering from that time forward. The second way is that God retroactively created these painful effects into creation from the very start, antecedently, because he foreknew a later fall would occur.

Standing squarely in the first traditional answer, young-earth creationists Henry Morris and Martin Clark claim that God cursed the whole earth and all of its inhabitants because Adam and Eve had sinned, who were his human vice-regents on earth. Before this time there were no carnivorous animals. All creatures ate fruits and herbs. With the fall of man things began to gradually change because of God's curse. There was now a hostile environment in a post-Edenic world (Genesis 3:17–19; Romans 8:21; 1 Corinthians 9:9), and later, even more so in a post-Flood world (Genesis 9:1–3). In their words:

> Pleasant flowering shrubs degenerated into noxious weeds. Many bacteria originally helpful in various organic processes became deadly disease-producing microorganisms. Certain organisms planned for symbiotic relationships with others declined in usefulness and became mere parasites. Certain plants actually became poisonous.... Similar changes began to take place among the animals, not immediately, but gradually.... As the plant kingdom began to suffer deteriorative changes, it became more and more difficult for the animals to derive their nourishment solely from the grasses and herbs. Gradually certain animals began to obtain some of their proteins and other needed foods by killing and eating animals smaller than themselves.... Eventually teeth and claws and other such characteristics (perhaps originally intended merely to tear and eat tough roots, bark, etc.) were modified and became established in certain varieties, and many species of animals thus became carnivores.

Morris and Clark tell us that the greatest modifications were "reserved for the drastic changes in the environment following the great Flood." After a supposed worldwide flood, "God even authorized man to eat animals (Genesis 9:3–4)."[16]

Of course, such an answer is simply no longer taken seriously by any scientifically literate person, even by many other Christians. C. S. Lewis admits: "Carnivorousness, with all that it entails, is older than humanity."[17] The consistent pattern in paleontology and in geology shows us that carnivorous, meat-eating animals did not arrive on the scene suddenly, but rather very slowly through millions and millions of years, which predates the arrival of human animals.

What Morris and Clark have done is to believe their literal interpretation of the Bible despite what we've learned from the sciences. This is evident from the title to their book: *The Bible Has the Answer*. But their answer is wildly implausible to modern, scientifically literate people. They must deny that the present laws of nature are the key to understanding the past without which paleontology and geology would be rendered null and void. And their answer still doesn't help us understand exactly why animals should suffer simply because Adam and Eve sinned. What did animals do wrong to deserve this punishment?

J. W. Rogerson, emeritus canon of Sheffield Cathedral who was head of the department of Biblical Studies at Sheffield University in England before retiring, offers a similar defense of traditional view. He claims there is a contrast between the creation that existed before the Flood and that which existed after it. Before the Flood all creatures were vegetarians, but after it the dominion mandate spoken of in Genesis 9:1–4 "introduces an element of hostility" among us, especially between animal life and human beings. Paradise is lost. Animals now fear and dread us because into our hands they have been delivered. After the Flood "the human race is given authority to eat meat, provided that the blood is drained from it."[18]

Rogerson understands full well that his understanding goes against the views of modern readers—post-Darwinian readers—that there never was a "violence-free" period of time in the evolutionary scheme of things before the supposed Flood. He candidly admits the reason for holding his particular view is because he cannot explain or justify the existence of natural evil and the sufferings of animals otherwise. By his lights it "is preferable to say that natural evil is not the will of God . . . than to try to justify natural evil or to explain it away."[19] Just look at this Biblical scholar squirm, retreat, and take an indefensible position because of the serious nature of the problem natural evil presents to his faith. It causes Rogerson to deny the geological and biological evidence for the age of the universe in order to maintain it. It requires him to either adopt a young six-thousand-year-old creation, or more than likely, the idea that there were three billion years before the arrival of human beings on earth in which all animals were vegetarians. And he adopts this view based upon a historically conditioned interpretation of an ancient, superstitious, mythological biblical text. His viewpoint seems ludicrous to modern scientifically literate readers. This is a high price to pay in order to hang on to his faith in the face of the *Darwinian Problem of Evil*. In my opinion, such a faith isn't worth hanging on to.

Apparently Rogerson has never read where Augustine cautioned fellow Christians against being ignorant of the sciences in front of non-believers who know better. Augustine wrote:

> It is a disgraceful and dangerous thing for an infidel to hear a Christian, presumably giving the meaning of Holy Scripture, talking nonsense on these topics; and we should take all means to prevent such an embarrassing situation, in which people show up vast ignorance in a Christian and laugh it to scorn.... If they find a Christian mistaken in a field which they themselves know well and hear him maintaining his foolish opinions about our books, how are they going to believe those books in matters concerning the resurrection of the dead, the hope of eternal life, and the kingdom of heaven, when they think their pages are full of falsehoods on facts which they themselves have learnt from the experience and the light of reason?[20]

But it's even worse than what Rogerson shows awareness of, for while he rejects science in order to support his Biblical interpretation of the world despite the overwhelming scientific evidence, not even the Bible supports his claims. It is *not* the case that the God of the Bible created us all as vegetarians, and so it is *not* the case that by returning to the vision of paradise represented in Isaiah that we will return to the supposed Garden of Eden's paradise.[21]

At least Paul Copan, the president of the Evangelical Philosophical Society, is trying to harmonize what these specific Biblical texts lead us to accept. At least he's trying to heed Augustine's caution about scientific ignorance. Copan is not completely consistent, for while he admits that "animal death occurred before human beings existed," he also says that not until the fall of Adam and Eve did human death enter the world. The reason why he accepts the results of evolutionary biology for animals but not for humans is inconsistent with the facts and shows deference for believing in an ancient so-called inspired text over the results of modern science. Still, based on the Biblical texts, Copan argues, "human beings and various animals were meat eaters before the Flood of Noah."[22]

There is a good amount of biblical evidence for Copan's claim. After God pronounced his sentence on Adam and Eve for their sin and as he was banishing them from the Garden he made for them "garments of skins, and clothed them" (Genesis 3:21). Where would these skins come from? What was done with the meat of the animal killed? Or did God just kill an animal for its skin, like the elephant poachers of today's African jungle do for ivory tusks? If the animal was a burnt sacrifice to God on behalf of their sin, surely Adam and Eve ate some of the meat too.

There is much more to consider. In Copan's words: "God tells human beings to 'rule over the fish of the sea' (Gen.1:28). What could this mean apart from permission to eat them? Abel kept sheep, presumably to eat (4:2–4). Noah himself distinguished between clean and unclean animals (7:2), which clearly assumes the edibility of meat prior to the Flood." Copan is surely right about this. We also read where Jabal, who existed before the Flood as a descendant of Cain, "was the father of those who dwell in tents and have cattle" (Genesis 4:20). The same problems arise. Why did Jabal raise cattle if he was a vegetarian? We see this same carnivorous view reinforced when it comes to Psalm 104:20–22, which speaks of the time when God created the world. Copan argues of this Psalm: "There is no clear biblical indication that carnivorous activity is the result of sin and could not have existed before the Fall; rather as Psalm 104 suggests, all organisms have their rightful place in the food chain."[23]

In the poetical book of Job we see God's discourse about the glory of his original creation where there is carnivorous activity (Job 38:38–41, 39:26–30). After mentioning these texts Copan exclaims, "No herbivore here!" and concludes, "Animal death and the food chain are presupposed as part of God's creation—without apology or qualification." He admits, "the paleographic/geological evidence bears out that carnivorous animals—not to mention thorns and thistles or earthquakes and hurricanes—existed before the Fall, it was only after the Fall that human beings became vulnerable to and endangered by them."[24]

This last comment by Copan needs to be examined more closely before we move on. Again, he said, "it was only after the Fall that human beings became vulnerable to and endangered by them." Christian thinkers who believe all suffering occurs after a human moral failure must deny that there was pain and suffering before such a fall. Peter van Inwagen suggests one partial defense of this traditional answer as it relates to human animals like us. As an inventor of stories, Van Inwagen tells us one he thinks justifies the literal Genesis account of the fall of Adam and Eve as the cause of all suffering in the world. He imagines a world created and guided by God over the evolutionary span of time that first produced clever primates and then *Homo sapiens*. God raised these primates to rationality and made them into human beings who were given "preternatural" or "paranormal powers." Van Inwagen writes:

> Because they lived in the harmony of perfect love, none of them did any harm to the others. Because of the preternatural powers, they were able somehow to protect themselves from wild beasts (which they were able to tame with a look), from disease (which they were able to cure with a touch) and from random, destructive natural events (like earthquakes), which they knew about in advance and were able to escape. There was thus no evil in the world. And it was God's intention that they should never become decrepit with age or die, as their primate forbearers had. But, somehow, in some way that must be mysterious to us, they were not content with this paradisiacal state. They abused the gift of free will and separated themselves from their union with God. The result was horrific... they now faced destruction by the random forces of nature, and were subject to old age and natural death... and became playthings of chance.[25]

Van Inwagen's story is supposed to offer a conception, albeit bizarre, that after Adam and Eve sinned in the Garden of Eden their "preternatural powers" were stripped from them, and they consequently began to suffer at the hands of predatory animals. Presumably animals themselves subsequently became "playthings of chance," so they began to be subject to the power of evil and fallen human beings at that point. Van Inwagen contends that given the existence of God, "the story is true for all anyone knows." He "doesn't see any reason to reject any of it," even if he admits he's not at all sure about "preternatural powers."[26]

What are we to make of such a story? Does it sound reasonable to a "neutral agnostic," as he thinks it should be? No, not at all. This is a bizarre story, an ad hoc one, that although possible, for all we know is extremely improbable and not supported by any evidence at all. If all we need are possibilities unrelated to the actual evidence to help solve the problem of suffering and sin, then any possible story will do. Why doesn't he just tell the literal creationist story where God instantaneously created the whole universe in six literal twenty-four-hour days? Why not tell a story where human beings could make themselves invisible when threatened by the environment so they couldn't experience any suffering before the Fall into sin? Why not tell a story where snakes, scorpions, spiders, and bullet ants had venom but that the venom was miraculously neutralized? The whole reason van Inwagen doesn't tell such stories is that he knows the evidence is against them. He knows such stories would be ad hoc, created out of the blue to defend a position he cannot defend any other way. So the question Van Inwagen fails to answer is why his particular story has any more going for it than any of these other stories he could have told. The question for him is why the evidence against these other stories doesn't count against his own particular story. My claim is that he cannot answer this question. The only reason he even entertains it is because he somehow thinks the Genesis story depicts a Fall, something that biblical scholars themselves dispute.

What, then, can we make of the differences between the Genesis 1:26–28 pre-Fall dominion mandate and the Genesis 9 post-Flood mandate? Given this other biblical evidence on behalf of carnivorous behavior found in the Bible itself, biblical scholars like Gordon Wenham argue that the post-Flood mandate is merely "ratifying the post-Fall practice of meat-eating rather than inaugurating it."[27] And so the fear and dread of the animal kingdom toward human beings mentioned in the post-Flood mandate "seems more likely to reflect the animosity between man and the animal world that followed the Fall (Genesis 3:15)."[28]

Michael J. Murray seems to agree that if moral wrongdoing in the form of Adam and Eve can leave "such catastrophic consequence in its wake, it must be the case that God created things so that the integrity of the natural order was, in some important sense, initially *dependent upon* the integrity of the moral order." But if this is the case, then God would know that the created order was "fragile," he argues. So unless "there is some reason why the fragility of nature is necessary, or why making it fragile in this way makes possible certain outweighing goods, the fragility of nature itself seems to be a puzzling defect in creation." He rhetorically asks, "What possible good reason could there be for creating the universe in such a way that the Fall of the first human pair could bring about a rewiring of brute nervous systems, thereby allowing for the possibility of pain and suffering?"[29] I know of none.

A second traditional Christian way to understand how the Fall caused animal suffering is to say it did so antecedently. Michael Murray sums this view up with these words: "God in his foreknowledge chose to prepare in advance a world with genuine evil and suffering in anticipation of the fact that it would be the dwelling of fallen humanity."[30] This is what Emil Brunner argued for along with Origen, Gregory of Nyssa, as well as Baptist theologian A. H. Strong, and most recently with modifications by William Dembski. Strong argued for what he called "anticipatory consequences," in that the world was not created perfect, anticipating the time when Adam would sin. When Adam sinned, God's protective hand was removed from humanity and they found themselves in the real world with natural disasters, pain, and death.[31] Accordingly, this solution attempts to explain the reality of evil "not as a consequence of moral evil but rather as among the necessary antecedent conditions for a universe which provides morally appropriate conditions for postlapsarian free creatures" (i.e., after the Fall). Dembski argues that just as God can answer prayers retroactively and just as the death of Jesus can forgive sins retroactively for Old Testament people, so also the Fall of humanity caused natural evils retroactively. Left unresolved is whether or not this is the case.[32] Since Genesis chapter 1 describes God's creative handiwork as "good," Dembski proposes a second creation prior to the Fall that is described in Genesis chapter 2.[33]

Murray rejects such an explanation as "implausible," as I do, because:

> [It] offers us no satisfying answer to the following questions: Why must the world have a natural history that precedes the existence of Adam at all? Wouldn't God secure all the relevant goods and avoid a massive array of evil simply by creating the universe in much the same way the young universe creationist believes it was created? If God were to so create it, none of the goods supposed to arise from animal pain and suffering would be lost, and a great deal of natural evil would have been eliminated.[34]

Christian philosopher Robert N. Wennberg concurs by arguing that it "still remains unclear how animals, who do not sin and do not incur guilt, can legitimately bear the penalty for human sin."[35] Philosopher C. E. M. Joad concludes as I do: "The hypothesis that the animals were corrupted [i.e., made into predators] by man does not account for animal pain during the hundreds of millions of years when the earth contained living creatures, but did not contain man."[36]

OPTION TWO

C. S. Lewis speculated on a different sort of answer to the problem of animal pain based on a "Satanic corruption of the beasts" prior to the existence of human beings. Having rejected the traditional answer, Lewis speculates "that some mighty created power had already been at work for ill on the material universe, or the solar system, or, at least, the planet Earth, before ever man came on the scene.... If there is such a power, as I myself believe, it may well have corrupted the animal creation before man appeared.... The Satanic corruption of the beasts would therefore be analogous, in one respect, to the Satanic corruption of man." According to Lewis, "living creatures were corrupted by an evil angelic being."[37] By "corrupted" Lewis means that the beasts were made to prey upon one another. Richard Swinburne, a philosopher and prolific apologist for Christianity, has likewise commented that human free will seems, "unable to account for the animal pain [that] existed before there were men," so supposing the existence of "fallen angels" who have brought on these other evils, "may indeed be indispensable if the theist is to reconcile with the existence of God the existence of... animal pain."[38]

Gregory A. Boyd, professor of theology at Bethel College, St. Paul, Minnesota, argues in some scholarly detail that C.S. Lewis was essentially correct to suggest such a thing, as does Michael Lloyd, who is supposed to publish a three-volume work on the problem of evil.[39] Boyd's theodicy comes from his warfare worldview, which is defended in his book, *Satan and the Problem of Evil*. Boyd believes we are part of a cosmic war, a war between God and the good angels against Satan and his evil cohorts. This world is a war zone. There is a cosmic rebellion taking place against God that was started even before God created the world. In fact, Boyd argues, God had to fight back the forces of evil just to create the world in the first place. When God's creatures did turn up on earth we were all caught up in this cosmic war whether or not we like it. There are casualties of war that take place because the battle is raging everywhere around us, called "collateral damage." That's just what happens in times of war. Innocents do in fact get hurt. Animals have gotten hurt ever since creation because the evil forces corrupted them into beings that preyed upon each other in defiance of God's intentions. Human beings have also sinned and stepped over into rebellion against God, according to Boyd. As such we have become failed ecological stewards and we do harm to animals and to each other too. This is because "in this war zone, there are few guarantees.... [T]here is no guaranteed security in this world."[40] In Boyd's eyes, God is "a sovereign chess master" who cannot predict with certainty what truly free-willed creatures will do. While God cannot predict certainties, he can predict possibilities when it comes to the day-to-day conflict. Because of this, God can always outflank the opposition such that the victory in the end is the one thing guaranteed. In the end, the forces of evil will be overthrown and destroyed. God will be victorious. His followers will enter into God's eternal rest.

But Boyd's satanic solution is simply implausible. Such an answer doesn't resolve anything, for several reasons—even if we grant the inspiration of the Bible and existence of evil angelic beings, which I dispute. It doesn't matter whether the pain and sufferings of animals are due to Adam and Eve, or to Satan and his hosts. It's the same problem moved back in time. A. Richard Kingston states this problem as well as anyone: "[If] God entrusted to fallible angelic beings such absolute control over creation that it was within their power to 'brutalize' the animal kingdom for all time, then he cannot be exonerated from all culpability for what allegedly happened. Must we not go further and say that such action would indicate either incompetence or the fact that the sufferings of the lower creatures are unimportant in the eyes of the Creator?"[41] Wennberg agrees that to have a genuine theodicy utilizing a satanic angelic rebellion, it must answer an important question: "Why did God allow Satan to do it?... Indeed, granting that there was an angelic fall, why did God not immediately nullify the consequences of that fall or restrain the activity of these rebellious forces so there would be no physical evil and no animal pain? It is that question that needs to be asked and then answered in order to have a genuine theodicy."[42]

Let me forcefully illustrate this question with an analogy. What would we say if a father did not stop a pack of wolves from running through the open doors of his house when he had the means to stop them, knowing full well that his children and pets inside would be mauled and even killed by them? What could possibly justify this inaction when it's considered his parental responsibility to protect his children and pets by stopping the wolves dead in their tracks, immediately? What could possibly justify a loving father to allow these wolves to attack his children and his pets? Would anything justify his initial inaction? Then let's say he picks up a shotgun and runs upstairs and downstairs killing them one by one. When the smoke clears he finds that his cat and dog are dead along with four out of six children, one of whom will be crippled for life. Is there any reason for praising the father for rescuing these two children when he could have stopped the wolves initially? In the end, I don't think there is a reasonable answer to this question, even granting the existence of Satan and his minions, unless Boyd does not believe in an omnipotent God, which actually concedes the whole argument.

I want you to imagine an actual cosmic war for a second. If we are in one, then I think a good God, as commander-in-chief with unlimited resources, would (1) provide more evidence that we are in such a war; (2) give his combat troops better communication about his war strategy; and (3) provide them with better armor, better weapons, and better medical treatment when harmed than he has done. There is simply too much carnage. Too many innocents suffer through natural disasters, predation, and from the evil choices of "the enemy" for me to consider our leader in this supposed cosmic war an all-good, all-knowing, all-powerful God. In addition, there is every reason to think the whole notion of Satan, or the devil, is reflective of an ancient superstitious and barbaric people who were looking for an answer to why undeserved suffering takes place on a massive scale.[43]

OPTION THREE

A third option is to say that animals have no souls, cannot think, and therefore feel little or no pain. René Descartes, known as the father of modern philosophy, had argued that all material bodies are *automata*, machines. The difference between human beings and the lower animals is that animals cannot reason or think because they have no souls. Only human beings have souls. Animals are like clocks with springs that cause them to move and make noise. One reason Descartes gives for believing animals cannot think is that "if they thought as we do, they would have an immortal soul like us. This is unlikely, because there is no reason to believe it of some animals without believing it of all, and many of them, such as oysters and sponges are too imperfect for this to be credible.... [It] is more probable that worms and flies and caterpillars move mechanistically than that they all have immortal souls."[44]

Descartes was understood by his followers, most notably Malebranche, to say that animals did not feel pain precisely because they couldn't think—

they were just machines. In a later letter to the marquess of Newcastle, Descartes clarified himself by saying that animals have life, since he regards life "as consisting simply in the heat of the heart." He also said he didn't deny that animals have "sensation, in so far as it depends on a bodily organ."[45] But his followers either didn't get that message or they probably thought pain is something more than a sensation. To them it requires thought and intelligence to experience pain, and Descartes denied they could think. So it seemed natural for people like Malebranche to take what Descartes argued to an extreme and claim that animals "eat without pleasure and cry without pain."[46] Even Andrew Linzey, the preeminent theologian on the status of animals, argues that from what Descartes wrote, the clear logic of it "creates the conclusion that animals are little more than machines."[47] Descartes' followers used this as an excuse to torture, kill, and experiment on live animals.[48] As a result, Peter Singer tells us, experimenters "administered beatings to dogs with perfect indifference, and made fun of those who pitied the creatures as if they felt pain. They said the animals were clocks; that the cries they emitted when struck were only the noise of a little spring that had been touched, but that the whole body was without feeling. They nailed poor animals up on boards by their four paws to vivisect them and see the circulation of the blood, which was a great subject of conversation."[49]

Voltaire responded to these so-called experiments by calling them "bizarre." In his own words: "Barbarians seize this dog . . . they nail him to a table and dissect him alive to show you the mesenteric veins. You discover in him all the same organs that you possess. Answer me mechanist, has nature arranged all the springs of feeling in this animal in order that he should not feel? Does he have nerves to be impassive? Do not assume that nature presents this impertinent contradiction."[50]

There can be little doubt any longer that animals feel pain depending on their central nervous systems. We have evidence of it in their increased heart beats, breathing rhythms, and in the activity in the pain centers in their brains when animals are subjected to pain stimuli. According to best-selling authors Temple Grandin and Catherine Johnson, "We know animals feel pain thanks to behavioral observation and to some excellent research on animals' use of painkillers." With regard to behavior, "dogs, cats, rats, and horses all limp after they've hurt their legs, and they'll avoid putting weight on the injured limb. That's called pain guarding. They limit their use of the injured body part to guard it from further injury."[51]

Andrew Linzey summaries the evidence in these words:

There is ample evidence in peer-reviewed scientific journals that mammals experience not just pain, but also suffering, to a greater or lesser degree than we do ourselves. The scientific reason is straightforward. Animals and humans show a common ancestor, display similar behavior, and have physiological similarities. Because of these triple conditions, these shared characteristics, it is perfectly logical to believe that animals experience many of the same emotions as humans.... In fact, the onus should properly be on those people who try to deny that animals have such emotions. They must explain how, in one species, nerves act in one way and how they act completely differently in another.[52]

An argument has been made that animals cannot anticipate the future or remember the past and so their pain is only momentary. For instance, it's claimed they don't worry about the future, nor do they have guilt and the fear of death.[53] This says nothing about their present pain, and we know they experience it. But even if it's the case they have no memory of the past and cannot anticipate the future, such a state of affairs may actually increase their present pain, for in Wennberg's words, "precisely because animals lack vivid links to the future (or to the past) physical pain may actually be worse, since there are no future oriented distractions to mitigate these powerful sensations... and it also denies animals the pleasure of happy memories and happy anticipations."[54] Human suffering, by contrast, writes Andrew Linzey, "can be softened by an intellectual comprehension of the circumstances" of the suffering itself. For instance, a visit to the dentist's chair can be painful, but human beings know why such suffering is needed. This is not the case with animal suffering, for they "experience the raw terror of not knowing."[55] So even if the argument can be made that animals do not suffer as much as humans, Wennberg argues: "The fact remains that animals suffer physical pain and suffer from negative emotions, and at times they suffer considerably." So "whether animals suffer more or less than humans is not quite to the point."[56] But, in fact, animals can remember, show evidence of guilt, joy, fear, and curiosity, and there is evidence they think and draw conclusions as well (see note).[57]

It's amazing to us that anyone ever thought otherwise about animals. But with the rise of evolutionary science we now know we, too, are animals (highly evolved ones, who feel pain, sometimes intense pain), and since we're related to the animal kingdom, animals must share in the pain and suffering that we experience because they are our predecessors. There's a reason why warm-blooded animals like to stay warm: being cold hurts them. Even the desire to eat for sentient creatures must motivate them to hunt and kill, otherwise—without hunger pains—they would die. Just observe a small-bodied spider that has obviously not eaten in a while, and he will attack a much larger bee or cricket with an intensity that is both amazing and ugly to behold. The literature on the complexities of this argument is growing exponentially, but I see no reason to pursue such an obviously wrongheaded kind of argument any further. As Christian philosopher Robert Wennberg said: "To seek to exonerate God by appealing to the possibility of a state of affairs that I myself cannot help but believe not to be the case, is not to argue with full integrity," therefore, "consistency at least requires that we seek a response that acknowledges the reality of animal pain."[58]

OPTION FOUR

According to this view, God doesn't care about animals. God is indifferent to their pain. During a discussion/debate I had with David Wood on the *Infidel Guy* online radio show, Wood suggested that God just may not care that much about animals. This echoes what Peter Geach has argued:

> The Creator's mind, as manifested in the living world, seems to be characterized by mere indifference to the pain that the elaborate interlocking teleologies of life involve.... Sympathy with the pains of animals whose nature we share is...a virtue in men.... But it is not a virtue that can reasonably be ascribed to the Divine Nature. God is not an animal as men are, and if he does not change his designs to avoid pain and suffering to human beings, he is not violating any natural sympathies as Dr. Moreau did. Only anthropomorphic imagination allows us to accuse God of cruelty in this regard."[59]

Peter van Inwagen rightly argues against Geach by saying it "proves too much," for a parallel argument can be made that given these same conditions God is "under no obligation to eliminate or minimize the physical suffering of human beings" either.[60] Van Inwagen reverses Geach's argument by asking why someone could not accept the following argument: "God is not an animal as men are, and if he does not change his designs to avoid pain and suffering to human beings, he is not violating any natural sympathies as Hitler did. Only anthropomorphic imaginations allow us to accuse God of cruelty in this regard."[61]

So, if Geach is correct, God's goodness is seen as something different than our goodness. I am not indifferent to the pain of the law of predation in the world. Nor am I indifferent to any pains of my dog or cat. I'll do everything I can reasonably do not to hit a small animal while driving down the road. I'm against needless and unreasonable animal experimentation, and almost all of it is needless anyway—maybe all of it. And I'm totally against trapping animals, especially just for their furs, or in hunting them for their trophy heads, or killing elephants for their ivory tusks. To say God is indifferent to these kinds of things means I have no way to assess whether or not God is good. The only standard I have for knowing whether God is good is based on my standards of goodness. If God has an entirely different standard of goodness, then why should I believe him to be good at all?

This view, that a perfectly good God is indifferent to the pain of most of his creatures, is simply repugnant to thinking people. How can a perfectly good God not care when one of his creatures is suffering? In order to answer the problem of animal suffering by saying God doesn't care that much about it, or that he's indifferent to it, means God isn't perfectly good. This answer simply denies the omnibenevolence of God, and as such, isn't an answer at all. It concedes the argument. It denies God is the kind of God demanded by Christian theology.

Most Christians have disagreed with Geach. Most Christians consider God as a being who cares for all of his creatures by virtue of the fact that he created them. While no Christian has to go as far as Saint Francis of Assisi, he characterizes the complete opposite viewpoint. He called all creatures, no matter how large or small, even crickets, by the endearing terms of "brother" and "sister," because they all had the same creator. Robert Wennberg states it this way: "To conclude that there are evils that we, but not God, recognize and abhor is to attribute to God an unacceptable moral ignorance. Or to claim that God knows that physical suffering is an evil but that he is still indifferent to it would be to attribute to God a moral fault—indifference to known evil."[62]

OPTION FIVE

One reason why it's believed God may be indifferent to the sufferings of animals is because God is much more interested in human soul making. John Hick makes this argument in these words:

> The justification of animal pain is identical with the justification of animal existence. And from the point of view of the divine purpose of soul making, animal life is linked with human life as the latter's natural origin and setting, an origin and setting that contribute to the "epistemic distance" by which man is enabled to exist as a free and responsible creature in the presence of his infinite Creator. If, then, the animal kingdom plays this part in this indirect way in the forming of man as a child of God in this "eighth day of creation," the process must be justified by its success.[63]

What we find is that Hick's God is using animals as a means to an end. They only have instrumental value and no intrinsic value. Their intense suffering doesn't matter to God so long as they have been used by him to produce human beings who can be made into his children. Is it even reasonable to believe the same ends can't be achieved without such a vast scale of animal suffering anyway? I think not.

Now it's one thing to use inanimate objects as a means to an end. I can use a hammer to help nail down a roof, for instance. The hammer feels no pain, so there's no problem using it as a means to an end. But when it comes to using sentient creatures as means to an end, disregarding their inaudible cries for help, that's another matter. If a theist can sit by and watch as a fawn is slowly burned to death in a forest fire or as a cat kills a mouse or as killer whales drown a humpback whale calf, and not question whether her God is perfectly good and caring to all of his creatures, then I'm baffled. Besides, if God is justified in abusing animals for instrumental ends, he could also be justified in abusing humans for the same reasons. After all, humans could be considered a different species than God.

In the end, Hick's God is a speciesist who falls under all of the same criticisms that human beings fall under when they treat animals with utter disregard and disrespect. Peter Singer's book *Animal Liberation*, is the Bible for this type of criticism. Singer argues that discrimination against animals simply because they belong to a different species is an injustice, in the same manner that it's an injustice to discriminate against other people based upon the color of their skin. According to Singer, the interests of all sentient beings are worthy of equal consideration and respect depending on their capacities for thought.[64]

OPTION SIX

This Christian option is that God may resurrect all sentient animals to a new life, either on a new earth, or in heaven itself, thus rewarding them for their service to God and to man. Early church fathers Irenaeus, John of the Cross, and Athanasius all believed this, as do some modern Christian thinkers like C. S. Lewis (with regard to "tamed" animals), Robert Wennberg, Jay McDaniel, John F. Haught, Christopher Southgate, Jürgen Moltmann, and Keith Ward, who claims for instance that: "Immortality for animals as well as humans, is a necessary condition of any acceptable theodicy."[65] Jurgen Moltmann claimed of an animal resurrection that: "If we were to surrender [such a] hope for as much as one single creature, for us God would not be God."[66]

The reason why Christopher Southgate believes all types of animals will go to heaven is because of (1) "specific scriptural texts," (2) "the conception that human life is richest when in the presence of other creatures," and (3) the need to "marry the evident lack of blessedness in the lives of many creatures."[67] I doubt that the first two reasons have any bearing on the existence of a heaven for animals (or humans for that matter). Nonetheless, how can three billion years of animal suffering just to fill heaven with all of those resurrected animals be morally justified? If heaven is meant to compensate or reward sentient creatures for their sufferings on earth, then this does not morally justify their sufferings. Otherwise anyone can torture any sentient creature, including another human being, and simply compensate them for their sufferings. Rewarding animals in a heaven made for them simply does not make their sufferings on earth morally justifiable.

There are also some significant problems with regard to an animal heaven. What kinds of bodies will each creature have in heaven? Will a bear or a shark or an eagle still be carnivorous? Will a mosquito or leech still need to suck blood? Since their bodies have a direct bearing on who they are, if they lack these bodies will they be the same creatures in heaven? Will they also need to live in the same kind of habitat? Will there be both cold and hot regions in heaven? Will there be wetlands and deserts?

Mountains and oceans? Will all species of animals even be in heaven, or just a select few, Lewis's "tamed animals"? Would we really want scorpions, alligators, ticks, snakes, spiders, and skunks in heaven with us? Will all parasites be there? What rational criteria can distinguish between animals that will be in heaven from those that aren't there? Or would there be separate heavens for each species? As far as I can tell, a heaven with all creatures in it would look like the actual world.

Southgate admits these types of questions are "difficult" ones. He writes that it is "very hard to imagine any form of being a predator that nevertheless does not 'hurt or destroy' on the 'holy mountain' of God (Isaiah 11:9). What could the life of a predator look like in the absence of the second law of thermodynamics, and the imperative of ingesting ordered energy to ward off the ever-present slide into decay?" According to him these kinds of questions are the ones "theologians can never resolve, any more than we can say what would be fulfillment for the parasitic organisms that so exercised Darwin, or for the bacteria and viruses that only thrive as pathogens."[68] All he can basically do is quote from John F. Haught, who said: "it is not beyond reason to trust that [God's] eternal care could also transform local *cosmic contradictions* into a wider harmony of contrasts, that is, into an unfathomable depth of beauty, and that our own destiny beyond death admits of conscious enjoyment of this beauty as well."[69] But we're on this side of heaven, and on this side we want to know how those "cosmic contradictions" can be reasonably resolved before we can believe that there is a heaven for them (or us) in the first place. Southgate and Haught cannot simply say God can do these things without offering us a reasonable explanation for how this can happen. After all, Haught is the one who called them cosmic *contradictions* in the first place.

OPTION SEVEN

This option is actually a related set of answers combining several different Christian options to the problem best argued for by Michael J. Murray. He doesn't necessarily accept all of the answers he offers in his book, *Nature Red in Tooth and Claw*, some of which are ultimately inconsistent, but he cannot rule them out either. So I'll just deal with what I consider his best combination of answers.

Murray suggests that it is intrinsically good for God to create a universe that begins from a state of chaos and leads up to order rather than instantaneously created by fiat, and that such a manner of creating is an outweighing good of the sufferings it produces. In Murray's view, the emergence of human beings like us in an environment like ours is going to require "a spectrum of precursor organisms with increasingly more complex mental capabilities." He continues, "In order to have organisms which, like us, are capable of intellectual reflection, deliberation, agency, morally significant action, etc., there must first be less-complex organisms which have only more primitive capabilities such as the ability to experience pleasure and pain, or sentience."[70]

He suggests it is good that human beings exist in a regular, law-like environment where human soul making is possible and where they have freedom to exercise it. In such an environment pain and suffering "will be inevitable for corporal, sentient beings," and as such is "required to preserve the integrity of sentient physical organisms engaged in intentional actions."[71] Additionally, he says it's quite reasonable to think human beings living in such an environment "will be essentially dependent on nonhuman animals in a variety of ways. If they are not necessary for food, they are at least a necessary part of an ecosystem in much the same way they seem to be in the actual world; i.e., for spreading pollen and seeds, for replenishing atmospheric carbon dioxide, and so on. For these and other reasons, embodied physical humans cannot live without animals," while the animals that exist are well-suited for a meaningful existence in this environment and they may experience an eternal future as well.[72]

Murray also argues that divine hiddenness is a requirement for morally significant human freedom, so he would expect that we cannot know all of God's reasons for the sufferings of this world. But he also rejects Kenneth Miller and Michael Corey's arguments for divine hiddenness when they claim that if God had created by fiat a fully formed universe six to ten thousand years ago, it would make God's existence so evident and obvious that creatures would no longer have significant moral freedom.[73] Against them both Murray argues it's hard to believe that the sufferings of animals throughout geological time are to be preferred over a scenario where God simply introduced "deceptive evidence" misleading us to conclude the universe is much older than it is without such suffering. He also argues that prior to 1859, when Darwin published the *On the Origin of Species*, vast numbers of people actually did believe the universe was created by fiat a few thousand years ago, and that this did not significantly affect their moral freedom.[74]

Murray charges that in order to dispute his claims the skeptic must give a detailed description of a world that has at least as good or a better balance of good over natural evil than the actual one contains. According to him, attempting to do this "seems hopeless." It would require an account of the world whereby any suggested alteration "could be pulled off without incurring the cost of a worse overall balance." It is this, he claims, that "cannot be done."[75]

In a way, Murray's proposal is not unlike Dinesh D'Souza's claim with regard to why there are earthquakes like the underwater one that created the 2004 Indonesian tsunami, slaughtering over a quarter of a million people and millions of animals.[76] The answer D'Souza proffered is that without these earthquakes our planet couldn't support creatures like us. D'Souza's answer assumes a natural cause-and-effect world without divine interference. However, the question is whether this answer is what we'd expect to find based upon a theistic supposition, and the answer is a resounding no, given what believers claim about an omni-God.

In the same way, Murray is asking critics to provide a detailed *natural* description of a world at least as good as or better than the existing one, without as much suffering. If I could do that, then such a world would be a different one with different natural laws producing a different ecosystem, which would produce different life forms, depending upon how radical of a deviation it is from the actual one. If Murray wants a *natural* description of a better world with the present life forms in it, this probably cannot be done precisely because he's asking for a *natural* explanation given the existing set of natural laws. This present natural world is the only one we know and the only one that could produce the life forms that presently exist in it, that is, until we get our hands on the right kinds of technologies to produce a better natural world. Richard Carrier tells us about what we have accomplished with these technologies: "No thanks to God, we got rid of his damned murderous floods, with dams, levies, and channels. What floods did that was of use, we then did with irrigation technology without all the pain and murder."[77]

Murray needs to understand that the question isn't whether I could provide a detailed natural description of a better world. The real question is whether an omniscient God could do so, and it would seem that he could. To simply respond that because God is omniscient he knows how to create a perfectly good world doesn't cut it. For it begs the question of whether God is omniscient, and I can indeed criticize his so-called creative handiwork, just like I can criticize the poor construction of a house even though I don't know enough to build one myself.

Besides, I see nothing in the world that could not be bettered by God through perpetual miracles. As David Hume wrote, the ordering of the world by natural laws "seems nowise necessary to a very perfect Being."[78] I call this the *Perpetual Miracle Objection*. I wonder if Christian theists have really thought through the implications of a God who prefers this present set of natural laws with its sufferings over constant divine, miraculous maintenance. Is their omnipotent God lazy or something? What is there that is more valuable to God about this present ecosystem that takes precedence over our sufferings? There is no moral parity here at all, just as Murray argued that there's no moral parity between the sufferings of animals through evolutionary time, and a God who introduces "deceptive evidence" to mislead us to think the universe is much older without so much intense suffering.

God could have created us much differently—easily. I've previously suggested that God could've created all creatures as vegetarians. But James A. Keller argues these types of suggestions aren't convincing "because they are inevitably incomplete":

> They are suggestions about how some features or natural laws might be changed, but they do not specify a complete set of features and natural laws, so we cannot gain a complete conception of what life would be like in a world operating in accordance with the suggested natural laws. Therefore, we cannot begin to determine whether there would be a better balance of good over evil in the new world than in this one. (For example, if all the animals in the world were vegetarians, one wonders what would keep their populations in check so as to mitigate overcrowding and mass starvation subsequent upon overgrazing.) Moreover, humans are not competent to compare the overall balance of good and evil in our world with the balance in a world with different natural laws.[79]

Contrary to Keller, God could have made fruit trees, tomatoes, carrots, grape vines, blueberry bushes, corn stalks, bananas, wheat, barley, and corn to grow as plentiful as weeds do today in areas where they are needed, or he could have changed our diets. And if for some reason this isn't enough, then God could've created us such that the process of photosynthesis would feed us off of the sun itself. Barring that, I see no reason why any creature has to eat at all, since God could perform a perpetual miracle that would provide us all with miraculously created nutrients inside our bodies throughout our lives. If he did this, no creature would ever starve to death. Since this is so, God would not even need to create any animals at all.

I see no reason why we need animals for clothes, transportation, work, or play. Clothes made from linen or cotton rather than from wool would do just fine until we invented synthetic materials. Prior to the automobile our legs would've been sufficient to get us places, or God could have created wings in addition to our arms that could be used for transportation. I see no reason why God would not have told us how to invent the combustion engine or synthetic materials anyway, if needed. And we wouldn't need oxen or horses to plow the land if we didn't need to eat.[80] God could also control any overpopulation by reducing our mating cycles in the first place (which is a much better method of doing so than natural disasters after the fact, anyway). Human beings would still have to work for a living, since we'd want a good home with the comforts of life. Cities would still need to be built and maintained. With more time on our hands we could meditate, pray, and focus on raising our families. We could do more traveling, and be better educated. We could pursue our hobbies or engage in sporting activities. And if God had done this we wouldn't know any differently.

But if there were no meat eaters of any kind, then what would happen to dead carcasses, Keller might ask. They decompose into nothing because of the help of scavenger birds, like vultures, and parasites, like maggots, (although God could have designed all bodies to dissolve naturally by innate chemical reactions once dead). I see nothing problematic with the existence of meat-eating scavengers who never kill any other creature to eat (they would be the only creatures who were not vegetarians in such a world). They only feed on carcasses that have already died.

Furthermore, if God did these kinds of perpetual miracles, then scientists would not be able to explain as many things naturally, which in turn would be a good thing for believers. The *God of the Gaps* defense would be given a boost. I've already explained in some detail why a world that couldn't be explained by natural science would help me to believe, anyway.[81] And such a world would not significantly affect morally significant human freedom, just as Murray argued that an unexplainable universe created by fiat spontaneously a few thousand years ago did not do so prior to the rise of modern science.

I see no reason at all why a perfectly good, omnipotent God would choose to create through a long evolutionary process such as we find in this world, unless we either radically alter what it means for him to be perfectly good or for him to be omnipotent, especially since he wants us to believe. The best explanation for the world of animal and human suffering is therefore evolutionarily natural selection, where nature is red in tooth and claw, precisely because this is how the fittest survive. The God hypothesis is no solution for what we see in this world.

OPTION EIGHT

The last option is the *Ignorance Defense*, which I've dealt with before (see note).[82] Christian apologist C. S. Lewis punts to that option when he wrote that the problem of animal pain "is outside the range of our knowledge. God has given us data which enable us, in some degree, to understand our own suffering: He has given us no such data about beasts. We know neither why they were made nor what they are, and everything we say about them is speculative."[83] Wennberg says when all is said and done his suggested solutions are mere "possibilities... providing faith with options that it can at least tentatively embrace as it struggles with the problem of animal suffering."[84] Echoing Wennberg, Stewart Goetz argued with regard to the issue of animal suffering:

> [It] is reasonable for the theist to be a defender and answer these questions with "I do not know," because the matter is one that lies outside our cognitive purview. One thing that is important to understand is why it is beyond our ken. The explanation for this ignorance has to do with our lack of knowledge of both a beast's nature and the purpose for which a beast exists.[85]

Granted, C. S. Lewis and others offered some reasons for thinking animal pain is not divine cruelty, but in the end they punt to ignorance. Lewis, for instance, offers two reasons in defense of his Christian view. The first reason is a deductive one unrelated to the evidence itself. He writes, "From the doctrine that God is good we may confidently deduce that the appearance of reckless divine cruelty in the animal kingdom is an illusion." However, I can easily reverse this deduction. I deduce that from the evidence of animal suffering there is no good God. Lewis's second reason is an argument by analogy. Lewis thinks he has previously offered good reasons why human pain is not divine cruelty. He claims the success of these arguments about human pain make it easier to believe animal pain is not divine cruelty either, even if he cannot specifically say why animals suffer. I, however, have argued that there is no satisfactory solution to human suffering,[86] so if my arguments succeed, as I think they do, there is no reason to think there is any good solution to animal pain either. Having mentioned these two reasons, Lewis admits: "After that, everything is guesswork."[87] And that's all he has left, guesswork, since neither he nor anyone else can specifically answer this problem. A religion that can only stand on such dubious guesswork is not a religion we have any epistemic right to accept. The intense sufferings of animals through billions of years so far, have no credible excuse and are simply incompatible with the God proposed by Christian theism.

Arguing against animal experimentation and exploitation, Andrew Linzey wrote, "Animals can never merit suffering; proper recognition of this consideration makes any infliction of suffering upon them problematic."[88] Indeed! Again, "Animals can never merit suffering." Period. It does not make a whit of difference whether human beings or God inflict this suffering upon them. There is no moral justification for it. None.

NOTES

1. Robert Wennberg lists them in *God, Humans, and Animals: An Invitation to Enlarge Our Moral Universe* (Grand Rapids, MI: Eerdmans, 2003), pp. 25–26.

2. *The Autobiography of Charles Darwin, 1809–1882* (New York; W. W. Norton, 1958), pp. 85–96.

3. *The Portable Atheist: Essential Readings for the Nonbeliever*, (Philadelphia, PA: Da Capo Press, 2007), p. xviii.

4. Ibid., pp. xix–xx.

5. *River out of Eden: A Darwinian View of Life* (New York: HarperCollins, 1996), p. 131–32.

6. Paul Waldau, "Religion and Animals," in *In Defense of Animals: The Second Wave*, ed. Peter Singer (Malden, MA: Blackwell, 2006), p. 79.

7. See the extensive documentation of this on our official Web site, "The Bible and the Treatment of Animals," to be found at http://sites.google.com/site/thechristiandelusion/Home/the-bible-and-animals, which I consider a chapter for this book in and of itself.

8. Alvin C. Plantinga, *God, Freedom, and Evil* (Grand Rapids, MI: Eerdmans, 1974), p. 28.

9. Keith M. Parsons, *God and the Burden of Proof: Plantinga, Swinburne, and the Analytic Defense of Theism* (Amherst, NY: Prometheus Books, 1989), pp. 125, 132.

10. Michael J. Murray, *Nature Red in Tooth and Claw* (Oxford: Oxford University Press, 2008), p. 37. In other words, a *defense* is appropriate only when it comes to the *logical* problem of evil. It has no effect on the *evidential* problem.

11. Ibid., p. 38.

12. Ibid., pp. 99–100.

13. Peter van Inwagen, *The Problem of Evil* (Oxford: Clarendon Press, 2006), pp. 49–55.

14. Wennberg, *God, Humans, and Animals*, pp. 310–11.

15. Another Christian solution is that God created the world as already fallen from the very start, according to liberal Christians and process theologians. I just cannot devote the space to the liberal position here. See John Hick, *Evil and the God of Love*, rev. ed. (New York: Harper & Row, 1978), where he argues that the world was created fallen. Recently James A. Keller defends process theism in *Problems of Evil and the Power of God* (Burlington, VT: Ashgate Publishing Limited, 2007). See also David Ray Griffin, *God, Power, and Evil: A Process Theodicy* (Philadelphia, PA: Westminster Press, 1976); and *Evil Revisited: Responses and Reconsiderations* (Albany: State University of New York Press, 1991). Christopher Southgate's "evolutionary theodicy" is to be found in his book, *The Groaning of Creation: God, Evolution and the Problem of Evil* (Louisville, KY: Westminster, 2008). In my opinion, a god such as this one is too small to be relevant to the needs of the created world, and as such can be safely ignored.

16. *The Bible Has the Answer* (El Cajon, CA: Master Books, 1987), pp. 116–20.

17. C. S. Lewis, *The Problem of Pain* (New York: Macmillan, 1962), p. 133.

18. J. W. Rogerson, "What Was the Meaning of Animal Sacrifice?" *Animals on the Agenda*, eds. Andrew Linzey and Dorothy Yamamoto, (Chicago: University of Illinois Press, 1998), pp. 11–12.

19. Ibid., p. 13

20. Augustine, *The Literal Meaning of Genesis*, 1.42–43, as quoted by Paul Copan in *That's Just Your Interpretation: Responding to Skeptics Who Challenge Your Faith* (Grand Rapids, MI: Baker Books, 2001) p. 152.

21. On the vision in the book of Isaiah, see Copan, *That's Just Your Interpretation*, p. 229 n. 34 and my previously mentioned post on "The Bible and the Treatment of Animals."

22. *That's Just Your Interpretation*, pp. 150–52.

23. Ibid.

24. Ibid.

25. Van Inwagen, *The Problem of Evil*, pp. 85–89.

26. Ibid., p. 92.

27. *Genesis 1–15* (Dallas, TX: Word, 1987), p. 34.

28. Ibid., p. 192.

29. Murray, *Nature Red in Tooth and Claw*, p. 83.

30. Ibid., pp. 94–96.

31. A. H. Strong, *Systematic Theology* (Old Tappan, NJ: Fleming H. Revell, 1954).

32. Of course, if Dembski believes God can answer prayers retroactively, then he should have no problem testing these prayers, as I suggested in my book *WIBA*, pp. 226–27. Pray that the Holocaust did not happen, or pray that a car accident that killed some teenagers the night before did not happen. If God can retroactively answer prayers, then as I argue this could be tested scientifically. I claim that nothing will ever change in the past and that we would remember having prayed these prayers precisely because nothing will ever change. What's his prediction?

33. William Dembski, *The End of Christianity: Finding a Good God in an Evil World* (Nashville, TN: B & H Publishing Group, 2009). In my opinion, Dembski does a good job arguing against the young-earth-creationism view of R. C. Sproul and Robert Moore, who have decided to change their minds from an old-earth creationism to the young-earth view due to the problem of animal suffering.

34. Murray, *Nature Red in Tooth and Claw*, p. 96.

35. Wennberg, *God, Humans and Animals*, p. 333.

36. C. S. Lewis (with C. E. M. Joad), "The Pains of Animals," *Animals and Christianity: A Book of Readings*, eds. Andrew Linzey and Tom Regan (New York: Crossroad, 1988), p. 59.

37. Lewis, *The Problem of Pain*, p. 135.

38. Swinburne, "The Problem of Evil," in *Contemporary Philosophy of Religion*, eds. Steven M. Cohen and David Shatz (New York: Oxford University Press, 1982), pp. 12–13. This seems to be Michael Lloyd's conclusion in "Are Animals Fallen?" in the book *Animals on the Agenda*, eds. Andrew Linzey and Dorothy Yamamoto, chapter 12.

39. See Michael Lloyd's chapter, "Are Animals Fallen?" in *Animals on the Agenda*, pp. 147–60.

40. Gregory A. Boyd, *Satan and the Problem of Evil: Constructing a Trinitarian Warfare Theodicy* (Downers Grove, IL: InterVarsity Press, 2001), pp. 238–40.

41. Kingston, in *Animals and Christianity*, p. 74.

42. Wennberg, *God, Humans, and Animals*, p. 330.

43. See chapter 21, "The Devil Made Me Do It," in my book, *Why I Became an Atheist*, pp. 383–86.

44. *Animals and Christianity*, pp. 50–51.

45. Ibid.

46. Nicolas Malebranche, *The Search after Truth*, eds. Thomas M. Lennon and Paul J. Olscamp (New York: Cambridge University Press, 1997), p. 494.

47. Andrew Linzey, *Why Animal Suffering Matters* (Oxford: Oxford University Press, 2009), p. 45.

48. On this, see Daisie Radner and Michael Radner, *Animal Consciousness* (Amherst, NY: Prometheus Books, 1996).

49. Peter Singer, *Animal Liberation*, 2nd ed. (New York: Avon Books, 1990), pp. 201–202.

50. François-Marie Arouet, *Voltaire: Philosophical Dictionary*, ed., trans. Theodore Besterman (New York: Penguin Books, 2004), p. 65.

51. *Animals in Translation: Using the Mysteries of Autism to Decode Animal Behavior* (Orlando, FL: Harvest Books, 2005), pp. 179–283.

52. Linzey, *Why Animal Suffering Matters*, p. 47.

53. On this, see George B. Wall, *Is God Really Good?* (Washington, DC: University Press of America, 1983), pp. 97–100.

54. Wennberg, *God, Humans and Animals*, p. 315.

55. Linzey, *Why Animal Suffering Matters*, p. 17.

56. Wennberg, *God, Humans and Animals*, p. 315.

57. Besides *Animals in Translation*, see also Tom Regan, *The Case for Animal Rights* (Berkeley: University of California Press, 1983), chapters 1–3; Gary Kowalski, *The Souls of Animals*, 2nd ed. (Walope, NH: Stillpoint, 1999); Donald Griffin, *Animal Minds* (Chicago: University of Chicago Press, 1992); Matthew Scully, *Dominion: The Power of Man, the Sufferings of Animals and the Call to Mercy* (New York: St. Martin's Griffin, 2002), and Robert Wennberg, "What Are Animals Like?" in *God, Humans, and Animals*, pp. 84–118. Although Michael J. Murray argues for this option, he admits that the evidence against animal pain and consciousness is "weak." He admits few will find his conclusions "compelling or even believable," in *Nature Red in Tooth and Claw*, p. 71. Right that!

58. Wennberg, *God, Humans and Animals*, p. 313.

59. *Animals and Christianity*, pp. 53–55.

60. Van Inwagen, *The Problem of Evil*, 133.

61. Ibid.

62. Wennberg, *God, Humans and Animals*, pp. 317–18.

63. John Hick, *Evil and the God of Love*, 4th ed. (London: Collins, 1975), p. 350.

64. See also Regan, *The Case for Animal Rights*.

65. Keith Ward, *Rational Theology and the Creativity of God* (New York: Pilgrim, 1982), pp. 201–202.

66. Jurgen Moltmann, *The Coming of God: Christian Eschatology*, trans. M. Kohl (Minneapolis, MN: Fortress Press, 2004), p. 132.

67. Southgate, *The Groaning of Creation*, p. 89.

68. Ibid., pp. 88–90.

69. Emphasis mine. Haught, *Deeper Than Darwin: The Prospect for Religion in the Age of Evolution* (Boulder, CO: Westview Press, 2004), p. 158.

70. Murray, *Nature Red in Tooth and Claw*, p. 184.

71. Ibid., p. 121.

72. Ibid., p. 128.

73. See Kenneth Miller, *Finding Darwin's God* (New York: HarperCollins, 1999), p. 290; and Michael A. Corey, *Evolution and the Problem of Natural Evil* (Lanham, MD: University Press of America, 2000), p. 120.

74. Murray, *Nature Red in Tooth and Claw*, pp. 175–80.

75. Ibid., pp. 147, 149 n. 24.

76. See Dinesh D'Souza, "Why We Need Earthquakes," *Christianity Today*, April 28, 2009, http://www.christianitytoday.com/ct/2009/may/12.58.html ?start=1.

77. Personal e-mail to the author, August 10, 2009.

78. David Hume, *Dialogues Concerning Natural Religion* (New York, Bobbs-Merrill, 1947), part 11, p. 206.

79. Keller, *Problems of Evil and the Power of God*, pp. 23–24.

80. Richard Carrier asks (via e-mail) that even if God created animals: "Why couldn't God give animals rational souls and speech, so we could enter into free and equal trade with them in labor and goods? Riding horses would then be no evil, nor plowing fields with oxen, if they are simply under employment, with all the same compensation, liberties, and rights as humans themselves pulling plows or rickshaws."

81. *Why I Became an Atheist*, pp. 193–94.

82. See chapter 13, "The Problem of Evil—Part 2: Objections Answered," in *Why I Became an Atheist*, pp. 243–62, where I argued on behalf of Paul Draper's and William L. Rowe's evidential arguments, and where I disputed both Stephen Wykstra's CORNEA defense and Peter van Inwagen's "massively irregular world" defense (I'll not repeat myself here). For a further criticism of the ignorance defense coming from a process theistic perspective, see Keller, "The Ignorance Defense," in *Problems of Evil and the Power of God*, pp. 73–92. With regard to Rowe's arguments, Christian philosopher William Hasker has argued that the existence of gratuitous evil is consistent with Christian theism. See his *Providence, Evil, and the Openness of God* (London: Routledge 2004), pp. 58–79; and *The Triumph of God over Evil: Theodicy for a World of Suffering* (Downers Grove, IL: IVP Academic, 2008), pp. 171–98. For a response to Hasker, see Nick Trakakis, *The God beyond Belief: In Defense of William Rowe's Evidential Argument from Evil* (Dordrecht, Netherlands: Springer, 2007), pp. 303–31. There is also an attack on Rowe's argument by Michael Almeida in "The New Evidential Argument Defeated," *Philo* 7, no. 1 (Spring/Summer 2004): 22–35, which is rebutted by Richard Carrier, "Fatal Flaws in Michael Almeida's Alleged 'Defeat' of Rowe's New Evidential Argument from Evil," *Philo* 10, no. 1 (Spring/Summer 2007): 85–90.

83. Lewis, *The Problem of Pain*, p. 129.

84. Wennberg, *God, Humans, and Animals*, p. 340.

85. Stewart Goetz, "The Argument from Evil," *The Blackwell Companion to Nat-*

ural Theology, eds. William Lane Craig and J. P. Moreland (Malden, MA: Wiley Blackwell, 2009), p. 492.

86. See chapters 12–13 in my book, *Why I Became an Atheist*, pp. 228–62.
87. Lewis, *The Problem of Pain*, p. 130.
88. Linzey, *Why Animal Suffering Matters*, p. 35.

Part 4

WHY JESUS IS NOT THE RISEN SON OF GOD

Chapter 10

JESUS: MYTH AND METHOD

Robert M. Price, PhD

I and many other scholars have argued that the Gospels are myths about Jesus, not historical records. But Christian apologists balk at the notion and deploy every argument they can against it. Since I am one of the prime targets of my friends Paul Rhodes Eddy and Greg Boyd in their landmark work of Gospel apologetics, *The Jesus Legend: A Case for the Historical Reliability of the Synoptic Jesus Tradition* (Baker Academic, 2007), I would like to respond to the book and its chief arguments and flaws. My discussion focuses on these two scholars and their work, but it will soon become clear that what I have to say applies equally to evangelical apologists in general, even those who have not taken things quite as far as Eddy and Boyd have.

* * *

What is the task of biblical criticism? It is to advance the understanding of the Bible by applying new methods to the study of the text. One hopes to learn more and new things abut the text. By contrast, what is the task of Christian apologetics? It is essentially one of retrenchment. It wants to turn the clock back on criticism and in effect to learn *less* about the Bible, to undo all that critics consider progress. The apologist makes minimal concessions to critical method, using it opportunistically to try to vindicate the

Bible as the kind of prop he needs it to be for the sake of his faith. One senses on every page that the Christian apologist wishes that the Higher Criticism of scripture had never been invented (probably by Satan) to confuse matters.

Their book takes, in the traditional style of historical apologetics, a completely deductive *a priori* approach, trying to nibble away at critical methods and conclusions with quibbling and caviling objections that are often beside the point.[1] The authors appropriate the rhetoric of postcolonial critics to make it look like only Dead White Males would hesitate to accept miracle claims. Eddy and Boyd have claimed the laurel wreath of "victim" for fundamentalism so as to dignify credulity as a method. They argue that it would be a Eurocentric, ethno-biased slur to "people's religion" the world over if we did not broaden the analogy of present-day experience (with which to judge past-event claims) to include that of various Pentecostals, third world shamans, and New Agers. The viewpoint of such a "confederacy of dunces" the authors dub a "democratized epistemology" (pp. 71–72). That is just the same sleight of hand that intelligent design creationists employ to get their quack science included in public school curricula. In fact, the approach of Eddy and Boyd is reminiscent of intelligent design propaganda at a number of revealing points, as we shall see.

Our apologists, though certainly more widely read in many relevant fields than any predecessor (certainly more than the pompous N. T. Wright), manage to have learned nothing important from their studies. For one thing, and it is perhaps the main thing, Eddy and Boyd simply cannot bring themselves to grasp the difference between methodological and metaphysical naturalism. They insist that the only reason critics refuse to acknowledge any miracle stories as probably true is that said critics are a stuck-up elite with an anachronistic commitment to a quaint creed of naturalism and/or Deism. They brand me personally as a naturalist (pp. 47, 156, despite p. 54 n. 33), though I have repeatedly rejected this label (even in public debates with Boyd). I regard it as the height of arrogant foolishness for mere mortals to pontificate on the nature and workings of a largely unknown universe. Naturalism as a philosophy has absolutely nothing to do with my historical methodology. Nor, I am convinced, does it affect, much less vitiate, the work of critics like Bultmann—or even David Hume. Boyd and Eddy manage to find various quotes from Bultmann, Robert Funk, and others in which they confess (or seem to) a personal belief in metaphysical naturalism, and here the apologists think to have found the smoking gun (46–49, etc.). But such beliefs have nothing to do with methodological naturalism (a.k.a methodological atheism, a.k.a. the surprise-free method).

Let's give it one more try. Greg? Paul? Are you listening? Troeltsch's "principle of connection" does not say we *know* or believe that all events *happen* according to unbroken, immanent cause and effect. We weren't there; we don't know. That is why we have to try to devise methods like this to tell us what most *probably* happened. All we can do is to *assume* a cause-and-effect nexus, just like the TV weatherman. We use the only reasonable guide we have. And experience tells us that whenever a scientist or historian has stopped short, shrugged, and said, "Well, *I* can't explain it! I guess it must be a miracle!" he has later regretted it. Someone else was not willing to give up, and, like a detective on a *Cold Case Files* show on TV, he or she did manage to find the neglected clue. Willard Scott does not pretend to know for a fact that a sovereign God will not reach down and stop the lightning bolt from starting a forest fire tomorrow. He does not know that the nostrils of El Shaddai or Jupiter Pluvius will not stir up a Tsunami next week. He can do no more than extrapolate from current, known trends what is *probably* going to happen. Big news: we can trace only factors that we can trace, though for all we know, there may be others.

Likewise, with Troeltsch's "principle of analogy" (pp. 48–49). There is no claim here (nor in poor, much-maligned Hume) that nothing out of the ordinary happens or ever can happen. ("What? You mean a politician told the truth last night?") There is no dogma, no certitude, that miracles do not and never can occur. We don't have a time machine; we don't know what did or didn't happen. Again, that's why we have to fashion these conceptual instruments, crude though they may be, to try to surmise what *probably* happened, which is all we can ever "know." And analogy forbids us to deem "probable" any event without reliable corroboration from some analogy with present-day experience.

I am a good historian when I get home, plop down in front of the TV, switch it on, see an image of a giant creature smashing Tokyo, and do *not* infer, "Oh! I must be watching CNN!" Is it because I know darn well that monsters do not and cannot exist? I know no such thing! Cryptozoology tells us we may yet discover lingering dinosaurs hidden away here and there (though none is likely to be this big). All I *know* is that I have seen the likes of this big boy in a number of Toho Studios flicks over the years, and that this is *probably* Gojira or Baragon, and that I am *probably* watching the Sci-Fi channel, not CNN. Analogy impels me toward the matching genre. Thus, if Buddhist devotional lore provides a close analogy to the Matthean tale of Peter walking on the water and sinking as he becomes distracted, but no experience of today provides any analogy—what am I to conclude? Should I not, especially in view of the obvious homiletical motif of both stories, conclude that Matthew's story is *probably* another legend? Why tar me with the brush of unbelieving naturalism? (Please note by the way, that in my book *The Incredible Shrinking Son of Man*,[2] I *never* invoke the mere presence of miracles in the narrative as a reason to reject a Gospel story as historically improbable.)

Nothing in Hume or Troeltsch or Bultmann, that I can see, bids us reject miracle claims without weighing the evidence. It is just that, given the limitations imposed upon us (until we invent the time machine, that is), we cannot detect "probable miracles" even if they happened! Historical inquiry cannot touch them, even if time travel would show them to have been real! I believe this was the position of Karl Barth. Barth knew that faith and historiography entailed very different epistemologies.[3] Faith claims to be able to do an end-run around the data and to obtain certainty about an ostensible miracle via some other way. But what way is that? It is, I think, nothing more than *the will to believe*. Listen to the parting words of Greg Boyd and Paul Eddy:

> Our historiographical conclusions, of course, do not yet come close to the surrendered, trusting relationship to the living Christ that lies at the heart of the Christian faith. But no amount of strictly historical reasoning or evidence can take one to *that* point. At best, historical reasoning can point in a more or less probable direction. To speak now as Christian theologians: the Holy Spirit, personal commitment, and covenant trust must carry one the rest of the way.[4]

But they have been speaking as Christian theologians—not historians—all along. In all their determination to build into the historical-critical method a "recognition" of miracles as probable, they have been trying to smuggle in a decision to believe. They imagine themselves to have maintained a strict separation between a supposedly "historical" acceptance of miracles as probable events of the past, as distinct from religious belief *about* those events. They aver that the historian, *as* historian, should accept that Jesus rose from the dead. But then they say it would take a hat-switch to the theologian's role to decide that this miracle held salvific significance. I would suggest instead that in arguing for a "resurrection" to be accepted as a "supernatural" (not just an anomalous) event, Boyd and Eddy have already smuggled in soteriology, much as in that scene in *Animal House* when the Food King cashier catches hapless freshman Pinto trying to sneak past her with his sweater and pants stuffed grotesquely with roasts, hams, and packages of ground meat.

Why can they not see that to come to a point of feeling stumped and then throwing up one's hands and exclaiming, "God did it!" has the exact same value as saying, "God only knows!"? So why not just say they don't have the explanation—rather than claiming that they do—that it defies explanation just as much as that puzzle they are invoking it to explain! To jump the gun and say "God did it!" rather than "God only knows" is to wave one's theological wand to transform agnosticism into fideism. In the last analysis, Boyd and Eddy are biblicists whose "historical" judgments are simply a matter of the will to believe. They know that would never pass for historical method, so they engage in what Freud called projection. While the fault is their own, vitiating the probabilistic method of historians via "the obedience of faith," they project the fault onto the genuine critic, urging that if he would only accept the bare possibility of the miraculous, he could start being honest with the text. But, beneath their shameful shell game, our authors are exalting faith and calling it historical judgment.

The phoniness of their enterprise is evident from the way they have to misrepresent Hume (pp. 29, 40–42, 61–63) and Bultmann (pp. 44, 49, 51, 75, etc.). Hume held the door open for precisely the "out" Boyd and Eddy ask us to entertain: Hume already allows us to accept a miracle report, provided any naturalistic explanation would sound even more far-fetched than a supernatural one.[5] In appealing to the universal facts of human experience, Hume is being neither deductive nor circular. He is merely appealing to what everyone knows: the frequent reports of the extraordinary we hear from UFO abductees, Loch Ness Monster fans, people who see ghosts or who claim psychic powers, always seem to turn out to be bunk upon examination. Ask Joe Nickell. Ask James Randi. Ask the evangelical stage magician Andre Kole, who exposed Filipino "psychic surgeons." So someone reports to you that he has seen his Uncle Mel alive again after his cremation. Are you going to believe him? Even if you believe Jesus rose from the dead, I think you will not be quick to conclude that Uncle Mel did, too. What would you say are the chances your friend is mistaken? Probably pretty high. If your friend introduced you to the living Uncle Mel, I bet you would immediately doubt whether it was really he who was cremated, as if it was all some kind of joke. Everybody would think you were pretty silly if you took to the streets proclaiming that Uncle Mel had risen from the dead.

This whole notion of granting that a miracle happened, or that the supernatural intervened, when we can find no adequate naturalistic explanation is headed in the wrong direction. Pretty soon *any* miracles the Bible says happened will fall into the same bag. Elijah called down fire from the sky to roast hundreds of Samaritan soldiers? Well, no naturalistic explanations are going to be able to account for *that*, so Boyd and Eddy will say they're entitled to believe it. Why? Because there's a compelling reason to say that it happened. And what is that reason? It's simply that the Bible says it happened! What other reason can there be if the normal pointers to historical probability are absent? We see in the long run that Boyd and Eddy just want us to believe what the Bible says, and when we don't, they flog us with the wet noodle of "naturalistic presuppositions."

Here we see a twin to Michael Behe's fraudulent "irreducible complexity" argument against evolution. He points to transitional features required as stations on the way toward a creature evolving toward something with survival value. But the transitional version does not yet possess the "envisioned" survival value. Half an eye has no utility. The creature has to make it the next step, and the next, until finally it reached greater eyesight with its survival value. What gets it there? Evolution, you see, must have proceeded according to the plan of an "intelligent designer." (Behe does not admit to being on chummy enough terms to call him by his name: God.) In the same way, Eddy and Boyd will not, they say, presume to read Christian theology into what they claim is a mere research result: yes, the supernatural must have intervened to work this miracle, but that hardly implies it is a marvelous work and a wonder wrought by Jehovah. Oh no: that would be a further step, a step of faith.

Eddy and Boyd would no doubt protest that they are not calling for belief in God, as if "the supernatural" were not merely a transparent mask like Michael Behe's "intelligent designer." But it is clear they are. Here's why. Witness their endless lambasting of Bultmann and his ilk for refusing to accept Gospel events that are parallel to the experiences of third world peoples. This is very puzzling, since Bultmann freely admits that Jesus did what he and his contemporaries regarded as miracles—both healing and exorcism.[6] Whatever you may want to make of them, Bultmann said, you have to admit they might have happened because such things, such scenes, occur today. Isn't this what Boyd and Eddy demand? You see, here is the nub of the matter: it is apparently not good enough to admit that anomalous events occurred. No, Bultmann's unforgivable sin is that he will not jump from this diving board and confess, *as a historian*, that Jesus did miracles by the power of Jehovah God.

I call Behe's "irreducible complexity" argument fraudulent because it was refuted long before he made it. George Gaylord Simpson addressed the same claim in his *The Meaning of Evolution* (1949), supplying a page full of examples of extant living creatures with every conceivable degree of light sensitivity, together with an explanation of how each tiny increment of light sensitivity has increased survival value. No mystery there. Nor is there any case of New Testament miracle stories that cannot most readily be explained, à la Occam's Razor, naturalistically (as an overblown retelling or an outright fiction). And this is most especially true of the resurrection stories. (Boyd and Eddy certainly do nothing to make a historical resurrection seem impossible to deny—just see Richard Carrier's "Why the Resurrection is Unbelievable" in the present volume). Now Barth may have been right: maybe God did raise Jesus from the dead in space-time-history, but the fact is irrecoverable by the historical method. Fine, whatever. But don't dress up the will to believe as some fancy epistemology, much less the "open historical-critical method." Nor is this gambit anything new: over thirty years ago in *The End of the Historical-Critical Method?* Gerhard Maier called the same shell game the "historical-biblical method."[7]

Boyd and Eddy pull another fast one when they attack and deride the postmodern doctrine of "incommensurability" (pp. 56–57) in order, as they imagine, to pull it out from under Van A. Harvey, who had the goods on them and their approach forty years ago in *The Historian and the Believer*.[8] Harvey says the historian cannot simply jump out of his historical skin to allow himself to embrace the beliefs possible to the ancients with their very different raft of assumptions. Here and elsewhere, Boyd and Eddy speak of biblical critics as an insular group of snobs who abdicate all responsibility for their beliefs, merely acquiescing to the suppositions of the momentary *Zeitgeist* (pp. 74–75). No one can give Harvey a fair reading and come out thinking he means this. His book, in fact, is filled with *reasons* he and his critical colleagues in the modern age have abandoned ancient credulity in favor of fine-tuned historical method. But if Harvey can be caricatured as a poster boy for passive subjectivity (as if to say, "we can't help being the mouthpieces of our age"), then Boyd and Eddy have exempted themselves from having to take his actual arguments seriously.

In doing this, our apologists pivot to wrap themselves in the postcolonial outrage against the Dead White Males of Western academia. How dare the Higher Critics exclude the beliefs and experiences of the third world and the miracle-mongering ancients! We must instead construct an affirmative action epistemology that will include their beliefs, too. What hypocrisy all this is! For Boyd and Eddy will go on to argue in a later chapter that the ancients were *not* particularly credulous, were indeed just as skeptical of claimed miracles as the moderns are! They need to argue this way just long enough to promote the idea that the early Christians must have had good reasons to believe in the resurrection, and so on, rather than just believing any old rumor someone told them (pp. 64–66). It is a way of pretending that the ancients were critical historians who would never have believed in Jesus' miracles unless they were forced to do so by the Humean caveat that when naturalistic rationalizations become too far-fetched, all that remains is belief in a miracle. So what were they? Were they critical moderns before their time, so we can accept their conclusions about miracles that we ourselves cannot witness? Or were they easy believers in demons and spirits and wonders, which Boyd and Eddy would forbid us from being skeptical about since we must embrace "democratized epistemology"? In either case they want their cake and eat it too, and as such they are not being responsible historians.

Another egregious case of Janus apologetics, facing both ways at once, is Boyd's and Eddy's argument that the resurrection of Jesus cannot have been borrowed from polytheistic mythemes (pp. 91–132). Their first step is to circumscribe a magic zone from about 165 BCE to 70 CE when there was no Jewish inclination to accept Hellenistic influence. They figure that the Hasmonean victory over the Seleucid Hellenizers put an end once and for all to the temptation to Hellenize. Hellenization began to rear its ugly head again only after the Roman victory over Jews. This strikes me as a gratuitous assumption. Indeed, the fact that there is during their magic period much evidence of Jewish anti-Hellenistic zealotry surely means the "danger" of influence continued. You don't strengthen the fortifications when there is no enemy at the door. And no evidence of Hellenization? What about the astrology of the Dead Sea Scrolls? Ah, er, it's not what it looks like! The presence of horoscopes at Qumran doesn't mean the sectarians actually used or believed in them, say the apologists. Perish the thought! It was probably because they needed them to write scholarly refutations of them! And second- to third-century synagogues with mosaics of Hercules, Dionysus, and the Zodiac? Purely decorative, that's all. Come on! Obviously you don't decorate your *house of worship* with images of gods you find abhorrent! And this was just at the time Yahweh Judaism was getting stronger and stronger, they claim! Judaism just was not a solid monolith even at this time, much less in Jesus' time.

Our authors find it necessary to misrepresent Margaret Barker, too (p. 100). She argues very powerfully (in *The Older Testament* and *The Great Angel: A Study of Israel's Second God*) that popular Judaism had not embraced the monotheism of the Exilic prophets yet, even in spite of priestly indoctrination and interdiction.[9] She ventures that Jesus as the resurrected Son of God was a direct survival of Israelite polytheism. Boyd and Eddy cannot seem to get through their learned heads that Barker is not talking about a Jewish embrace of pagan mythemes. Her point is that mythemes, which the rabbis later reinterpreted (explained away) as pagan, were always indigenously Israelite, shared with Canaanite neighbors, not borrowed from them. Thus there is no need to posit some repulsive borrowing from hated paganism to account for easy Jewish familiarity with dying and rising gods. Ezekiel knew the daughters of Jerusalem were engaged in ritual mourning of the slain god Tammuz even in the days of the Exile (8:14). Baal and Osiris were well known in Israel, too.

Boyd and Eddy indulge in overkill when it comes to the dying and rising gods, summarizing Jonathan Z. Smith's failed case for dismantling this ideal type (pp. 143–45) with not even a footnote referring to, much less rebutting, my detailed refutation of Smith in *Deconstructing Jesus* (Prometheus Books, 2000). They follow Bruce Metzger (pp. 136, 140), Edwin Yamauchi (p. 144) and other apologists in arguing, absurdly, that the *Mystery Religions* borrowed the dying and rising god mytheme from Christianity —even though early Christian apologists like Tertullian, Firmicus Maternus, and Justin Martyr admit the pagan versions were earlier (even insisting the devil fabricated the Gospel events long before they happened with Jesus)! Some dying and rising god cults we know for a fact were earlier, so this borrowing can't have gone the other way around as they pretend anyway.[10]

So there was no need to go to paganism for the resurrection doctrine/

myth. It was homegrown in earlier Israelite polytheism. One need not throw up one's hands in mock bafflement that the Christian resurrection faith could not have come from paganism, so it must have been ignited by a real resurrection! This is like saying space aliens must have built the pyramids. It's a ridiculous argument, but the apologists see *how* ridiculous it is only once they have to refute someone else's use of it against them! What about the worship of Menachem Mendel Schneerson, the Lubavitcher Rebbe, believed by most of his followers during his lifetime to be the Messiah, though he never said so? He died, and immediately his fans predicted his soon return in glory and began hailing him as God incarnate! Now where did they get such a notion, which non-Lubavitcher Jews, needless to say, do not exactly welcome? If it sprang spontaneously from messianic adoration, and overnight after the Rebbe's death, there would seem to be no miracle required to explain how Jewish disciples soon ascribed incarnate divinity to Jesus, right? Oh no! The cases are not similar at all, Boyd and Eddy tell us (pp. 150–51). The Lubavitchers must have *borrowed it from Christianity*! Yeah, that's really likely. Hasidic Jews borrowing myths from the religion they hated most! If Jesus' disciples wouldn't have stooped to borrowing theology from pagans, there is even less likelihood Hasidic Jews would have cribbed from Christianity.

We are treated to another fine display of nimble apologetical pirouetting when Boyd and Eddy discuss the question of ancient Palestinian Jewish literacy. They make a good enough case for widespread literacy (pp. 239–51). I never doubted it. Why are they interested? Because this fact enables them to speculate (or to borrow the old speculation of Edgar J. Goodspeed) that the Gospels are not dependent exclusively upon oral transmission. Matthew *might have* taken notes (p. 252). One must infer that Boyd and Eddy would feel uncomfortable with merely word-of-mouth connections between Jesus and the Gospels. No, written sources would be a more secure link, so by all means let's posit them. (Myself, I cannot help thinking of the scene in Nikos Kazantzakis's *The Last Temptation of Christ* when Jesus picks up such a sheaf of notes Matthew has been making, and he rebukes him for writing lies about him! Just as George Washington's friend and biographer admitted fabricating stories and sayings that he felt would communicate "the real Washington" better than any known facts.)

But then it's one hundred eighty degrees around to exploit recent theories of oral transmission of epics, poems, and sagas. Though we just heard how literate first-century CE Jewish culture was, now we learn that it was instead a largely oral culture, like the various African tribes, Balkan shepherd communities, and Pacific islanders on whom the whole cottage industry of orality studies, stemming from Milman Parry (*The Making of Homeric Verse*) and Albert Lord (*The Singer of Tales*), base their theories. The point of trying to subsume the Gospels under this rubric is to maximize the reliability of the underlying oral tradition. Apologists like to make a great deal of the fact that local history and lore may be transmitted faithfully for generations within such a closed framework, under the watchful supervision of both lore-masters who sing or chant the traditions and their audiences who are like children with a bedtime story, refusing to countenance any significant variations. So far this sounds like a folkloristic vindication of the old apologetics dictum that Gospel reliability is guaranteed by the "retentive mind of the oriental." Except that closer examination disappoints. The crown jewel of the "controlled local oral tradition" approach, the work of Kenneth Bailey (*Poet and Peasant*, etc.), has been thoroughly debunked by Theodore J. Weeden.[11] Boyd and Eddy admit this, but it doesn't matter to them, since they say it was a crummy example anyway (pp. 238 n. 1, 262 n. 84). They're just asking you to accept Bailey's conclusions, regardless.

Based on these studies, they insist that oral balladeers were faithful transmitters of detailed material (pp. 260–66). But then it turns out that these performers cared little for specific wording, focusing only on the general gist. Uh-oh. Then it turns out that the order of pericopes varies almost at random with the whim of the balladeer (pp. 253–54). We are starting to get very close to form criticism here, though Boyd and Eddy, who hate form criticism (for understandable reasons) do not seem to see it. We must not, they urge, impose twenty-first-century standards of accuracy onto ancient oral texts (pp. 256, 260). Yes: this is exactly the point of the form critics! The only difference is another parallel to intelligent design creationist arguments: Boyd and Eddy will allow only differences in wording within a recognizable story or saying. They will not countenance changes big enough to make one saying into a new one with a different point, to retell one story so much that it becomes another (say, stilling the storm becoming walking on the water in order to still the storm). This is exactly like the creationist willingness to admit the occurrence of "micro-evolution" within "kinds" of animals so long as one does not posit "macro-evolution" from one "kind" to another. Boyd's and Eddy's fear of "macro-evolution" in the Jesus tradition is the dread of having to admit that a saying or story no longer truly represents what Jesus actually did or said. As they urge critics to do, perhaps

Eddy and Boyd ought to be a bit more critical of the agendas underlying their scholarly methods.

They sneer at the form-critical axiom that particular forms in which the sayings or stories meet us in any way reflect the *Sitz-im-Leben* of their use (p. 295). They fear, rightly, that to admit this would be halfway to admitting the materials have been designed to serve their purpose and are thus tendentious fictions. But then they do not mind at all following Joanna Dewey and Christopher Bryan in taking certain *formal* features as implying the public performance of the Gospel of Mark for evangelistic purposes (p. 358). Isn't that inference from formal features to *Sitz-im-Leben?* Maybe it's not so perverse an approach after all.

Form critic Dennis E. Nineham long ago pointed out how the Gospel pericopes, short and sweet and streamlined as they are, just do not read like eyewitness testimony. For that we would expect the kind of "table talk" we get in, say, the Acts of John: "Once I said to Jesus . . . , and he said to me . . ." Our gospel pericopes sound like they have been rubbed smooth by the currents of constant repetition. Boyd and Eddy are happy to point to ethnographic studies that show even actual eyewitness recollections may, the first time out, be put into traditional forms for transmission, verbal time capsules, and that in this manner vivid details and distinctive features may be sacrificed from the very beginning (pp. 274–75). Similarly, they aver, the dynamics of oral tradition dictate that what is actually stated, preserved in explicit wording, presupposes an informational background outsiders are unlikely to know, with the result that even good, on-the-spot recollections may not sound like it (pp. 285–86). Well, that helps a lot! Boyd and Eddy obviously imagine they have given themselves permission to read the clipped and stereotyped mininarratives of the Gospels as eyewitness testimony despite appearances. But all they have actually shown is that, even if there *should* chance to be real eyewitness testimony in the Jesus tradition, *we can no longer recognize it as such*! Formal considerations will have obliterated any evidence of eyewitness origin.

Another case of transforming agnosticism into fideism concerns the *Mythic Hero Archetype* to which the life of Jesus in the Gospels conforms in its entirety, with no incidental, "secular," or genuine biographical detail left over. Boyd and Eddy point out the obvious: that sometimes known historical figures actually live up to the archetype (p. 149). Of course: that is why Joseph Campbell and others have made so much of it. The problem is that the more completely people's life stories conform to the mythic-literary form, the less likely it becomes that their stories are genuinely historical. At such a point they risk becoming lost behind the stained glass curtain, unless they have left a trail of historical "bread crumbs." Augustus Caesar did; Jesus did not.

It is especially ironic that Boyd's favorite example of a real-live archetypal hero is Scot William Wallace, whose exploits came to the screen in the film *Braveheart*. Boyd likes to make Wallace a real-life Jesus, implying that the Gospel Jesus could have been just as real (p. 149). It does not occur to Boyd that we actually have a great deal more historical evidence for Wallace, including actual documents of the period, thus proving my point: like Augustus Caesar, but unlike Jesus, we can independently confirm some historical facts about him from more reliable, nonmythical information. We have no such information about Jesus. All we have are the myths. And as every Wallace historian agrees, the mythical narratives about Wallace, which come closest in form and content to the Gospels, are often wildly inaccurate and invent a great deal, such that if we didn't have any independent way to check their claims, we would have no idea what to trust in them.[12] That's exactly our situation for Jesus.

Boyd and Eddy are relieved at last not to have to trouble themselves with the destructive intricacies of redaction criticism. Again, they defend the right of oral singers and tradition-transmitters to vary details in the telling as they prefer, and they do not see that this is no different from redaction criticism. They suggest that some of the differences of which Hans Conzelmann (*The Theology of St. Luke*) and Willi Marxsen (*Mark the Evangelist*) and Günther Bornkamm (with Hans Joachim Held and Gerhard Barth, *Tradition and Interpretation in Matthew*) made so much are not changes made by writers at their desks, but rather the slavish recording of whole oral performances in which the oral tridents had made *ad hoc* variations (pp. 252–57). Uh, what's the difference? Why could you not trace a redactional agenda in an oral performance (see especially p. 254)?

But Boyd and Eddy skip past that. Their main point is that oral tradents could not and would not have expected their audience to notice tiny differences in details. Lacking the opportunity of the modern TV viewer who can pause and rewind even a live TV show to catch what was said a moment ago, the listener of a live oral performance in the ancient world simply would not have been able to keep up with and catalogue the sorts of changes redaction critics think they discern when comparing Mark to Luke and Matthew, and so on. So far, this is a point well taken. But it seems to prove too much: it implies that such oral-performance variations could never have survived into written transcripts, since who could have remembered them? I don't think this has occurred to Boyd and Eddy. Their point is rather that all the tendential patterns of redaction Conzelmann and company think they have found must be *sheer illusion, completely accidental.* Slips of the balladeer's tongue. I find it difficult to credit that anyone familiar with the work of the redaction critics can believe this. But I find it quite easy to believe that apologists who do not *want* to know what the redaction critics have to tell them would take the easy way out, embracing a pious know-nothing-ism.

This is a prime example of what I mean when I charge that evangelical apologists want to know less about the Bible, not more, to turn back the clock on criticism, to reenter the Sunday School Toyland of fundamentalism. "It was long ago and it was far away, and it was so much better than it is today."

So if we do not dismiss the findings of the redaction critics as so much hallucination, we begin to realize that the "orality studies" approach is inappropriate. We begin to realize that Boyd and Eddy are just shopping for a paradigm congenial to apologetics. Here *Heilsgeschichte* has turned into *Bullgeschichte.* If the Gospels are in practice so readily understood and profitably studied as written works amenable to the methods of reading and analyzing, then I think it is safe to forget about the politically correct "noble savage" paradigm of African tribal lore-masters and Eskimo chanters. The Gospels seem to be true literary works, so let's treat them that way. That is what Burton L. Mack and Vernon K. Robinson are doing when they point out the similarity of the Gospel pronouncement stories to the Hellenistic *chreia* so common in Greco-Roman classrooms, where students demonstrated they understood the gist of a Socrates or a Diogenes by fabricating a pronouncement story appropriate to each man's reputation. I'm afraid that's bad news for apologists, for it provides a natural paradigm accounting for the Gospel materials independent of any access at all to supposed eyewitnesses.

Does that rule out any possible oral-traditional basis to the written Gospels? No. I don't mean to discount that, just to point out that the possible parallels Boyd and Eddy insist on are not the only ones, or even the best ones available. They seem so sure that oral cultures would not allow for a mass fabrication of traditional units that would serve only to legitimize this practice or that belief of some faction of the community. But it was field studies of the Trobriand Islanders that led Bronislaw Malinowski to formulate his categories of myths, including legitimization myths.

Closer to home, there is the well-known mass production of spurious tendential *hadith* falsely ascribed to the Prophet Muhammad. The early guardians of hadith felt it was their job to shepherd the growing tradition into the directions they thought best by *making up* opinions and deeds of the Prophet. We do not know if early Christian tradents engaged in such activities, but neither do we know that they behaved like Serbian shepherds or African lore-masters! Given the choice, the Islamic paradigm would seem a lot more likely, if only because it is closer to home historically and religiously (and, given the contradictory messages of the different Gospel Jesuses even *within* the canon, it seems directly confirmed in the evidence). At any rate, the wholesale hadith-forging industry is at least as attractive an option for understanding the developing Jesus tradition. It is based on a well-known oral-traditional matrix and matches perfectly the model adopted by Bultmann and the form critics. If oral tradition "really" worked as Boyd and Eddy say it must, we cannot explain the phenomena of the hadith.

Likewise, this same thing applies to the Nag Hammadi Gospels! They, too, claim to stem from eyewitnesses. They, too, offer us many sayings ascribed to Jesus. If instead we admit they are historically spurious, we admit that it was nothing for early Christians to ascribe their own best thoughts and revelations to their Lord. How typically contrived and double-tongued for our apologists to begin by quoting the old "not I but the Lord" text as the rule for all early Christians as attesting the universal early Christian tendency to segregate Christian intuitions from dominical sayings—and then to isolate the prophecies of the Risen Christ through John of Patmos and his canonical book of Revelation as some aberration unrepresentative of early Christians generally! For if the latter were even possibly typical of early Christian practice, then Bultmann would be justified in chalking up some Jesus-attributed sayings to Christian prophecy. And then Pandora's box is opened.

Boyd and Eddy gleefully point out what so many other retrenchers before them have: if the needs of the church dictated what Jesus would be made retroactively to say, why do we not find so many of the "hot" issues of early Christianity discussed by Jesus (p. 305)? Why, for instance, was he not made to mouth someone's opinion on the issue of Gentile conversion and circumcision? But he *was*: that must be the point of Mark 7:14–19, where we find a rationalist repudiation of the idea that nonkosher food renders one unclean. That must be the point of Thomas 53: "His disciples say to him, 'Is circumcision worthwhile or not?' He says to them, 'If it were, men would be born that way automatically. But the true circumcision in spirit has become completely worthwhile.'" Would not Jesus be made to address the issue at stake in the Cornelius story of Acts 10–11, missionaries eating Gentile food? But he *does* address it, in Luke 10:7, where the seventy, in contrast to the twelve (in other words, future missionaries to the Gentiles), are told to "eat and drink what they set before you." The Gentile Mission as a whole? What do you think the Great Commissions, not to mention the distance-healings of the children of Gentiles, are all about? Table fellowship with Gentiles, as in Antioch? That's the point of Jesus being shown to be eating with "sinners." Eating meat offered previously to idols? Someone must have realized that Jesus could not plausibly be pictured addressing this in Jewish Palestine, so they left this one in the form of a post-Easter prophecy (Revelation 2:20), a concern for verisimilitude not often observed. The role of women in the community? That is the point of Luke 10:38–42, where, depending on how one understands it, the issue is either women serving the Eucharist (Martha) or women embracing the stipended, celibate life as "widows" and "virgins" (Mary). Speaking in tongues? Matthew 6:7 ("when you pray, do not say '*batta*' as the heathen do") is against it; the late Mark 16:17 ("they will speak with new tongues") is for it.

By contrast, Boyd and Eddy utterly fail to meet the challenge of G. A. Wells: if Paul had our fund of Jesus sayings available in oral tradition, why does he not settle issues at once with a dominical saying, for example, on payment of taxes to Caesar, on celibacy, on fasting? And when Boyd and Eddy follow James Dunn and others in the bluff that all the parallels between epistolary maxims and Gospel sayings are unattributed allusions to the Gospels by the Epistle writers, it is just pathetic. If the point is to win obedience to the teaching of Jesus, who in his right mind would not pull rank by explicitly quoting from the words of Jesus himself?

Boyd and Eddy continue their march into yesteryear with an appeal to take with renewed seriousness Papias's authorial ascriptions of the Gospels of Matthew and Mark (pp. 290–91). He was in a good position to get the facts from the eyewitness apostles, was he not? Well, then, I ask, must we also accept what Papias says about Judas Iscariot swelling up bigger than an oxcart and pissing live worms (J. A. Cramer's *Catena in Acta SS. Apostolorum* on Acts 1:8)?[13] The sole surviving example (Irenaeus, *Against Heresies*, 5:33:3–4) of Papias's collection of Jesus traditions supposedly derived from "the Elders" sounds like a garbled quote from the Syriac Apocalypse of Baruch 29:5.

I suppose the clearest, most outrageous example of Boyd and Eddy advocating old-time fundamentalism and calling it criticism is their defense of harmonization, indeed, their attempt to elevate it to an axiom of criticism! They proudly point to a pair of reports about the hanging of two men; according to one report, they were strung up from trees, but according to another, they depended from a bridge. A contradiction, no? What do you know? News photos demonstrated that both were true! For some unknown reason, the bodies were displayed first in one circumstance, then the other! Strange but true. And so it would turn out, if we had the photos, in every case of Gospel contradictions they could be solved (pp. 421–26). Oh, would it? It seems to me that Eddy and Boyd are trying to persuade us to make the exception into the rule. Do they really think every secular, nonbiblical "apparent contradiction" can be resolved in such a way? If not, what's the point of invoking this example? We are henceforth to baptize the improbable into the probable. But as F. C. Baur said long ago, the true critic admits that anything is possible but asks "What is probable?"

Finally, let me venture to agree with Greg Boyd and Paul Eddy on one major methodological point. Although they quote me out of context on the question, my approach is to assume the burden of proof in challenging the historical accuracy of any and every bit of Gospel material I analyze. I believe it is best and only natural not to dismiss any of the Gospel sayings or stories unless there seems to be some problem, for example, an anachronism, a contradiction. And never do I count it against a story when it involves ostensible supernaturalism. I do not want to beg the question. See my Gospel analyses in *Deconstructing Jesus* and *The Incredible Shrinking Son of Man*, and you will see my approach. What Boyd and Eddy do not like are the results I have come to in this manner. Naturally they would prefer to be able to rule them out of court *a priori* by accusing me of sweeping away all the material on the basis of a naturalistic bias, which in fact I do not hold.

One may render the following verdict on the case the authors have made on rehabilitating the historical reliability of the Synoptic Gospels: Nice try, but no good.

NOTES

1. Ken Olson of Duke University has also surveyed their apologetically tendentious and questionable methods in his critical review of their book at *Review of Biblical Literature Online* (December 2008), http://www.bookreviews.org/pdf/6281_6762.pdf.

2. Robert M. Price, *The Incredible Shrinking Son of Man: How Reliable Is the Gospel Tradition?* (Amherst, NY: Prometheus Books, 2000).

3. See William F. Hordern's crystal-clear summary of Barth's view in "Faith, History and the Resurrection," [a symposium] appendix to John Warwick Montgomery, *History & Christianity* (Downers Grove, IL: InterVarsity Press, 1974), pp. 86–87.

4. Boyd and Eddy, *Jesus Legend*, p. 454.

5. David Hume, "Of Miracles," in *On Religion*, ed. Richard Wollheim (New York: Meridian Books, 1964), p. 211.

6. Rudolf Bultmann, *Jesus and the Word*, trans. Louise Pettibone Smith and Erminie Huntress Lantero, (New York: Scribner, 1958), p. 173.

7. Gerhard Maier, *The End of the Historical-Critical Method?* (St. Louis, MO: Concordia, 1977).

8. Van A. Harvey, *The Historian and the Believer: The Morality of Historical Knowledge and Christian Belief* (New York: Macmillan, 1966).

9. Margaret Barker, *The Older Testament: The Survival of Themes from the Ancient Royal Cult in Sectarian Judaism and Early Christianity* (London: SPCK, 1987) and *The Great Angel: A Study of Israel's Second God* (Louisville, KY: Westminster/John Knox Press, 1992).

10. See Tryggve N. D. Mettinger, *Riddle of Resurrection: "Dying and Rising Gods" in the Ancient Near East* (Coronet Books, 2001).

11. Theodore J. Weeden, "Theories of Tradition: A Critique of Kenneth Bailey," *Foundations and Facets Forum*, New Series 7/1 (Spring, 2004): 45–69.

12. For the documentary and historical evidence, and legendary fabrications, about Wallace see: Alan Young and Michael J. Stead, *In the Footsteps of William Wallace* (Stroud, Gloucestershire: Sutton, 2002); Andrew Fisher, *William Wallace*, 2nd ed. (Edinburgh: John Donald, 2001); and Joseph Stevenson, *Documents Illustrative of Sir William Wallace, His Life and Times* (Edinburgh: The Maitland Club, 1841).

13. Vol. 3, p. 12, reproduced in Robert M. Grant, ed., *Second-Century Christianity: A Collection of Fragments: Translation of Christian Literature* (London: SPCK, 1946), p. 67.

Chapter 11

WHY THE RESURRECTION IS UNBELIEVABLE

Richard Carrier, PhD

J ohn Loftus has more than adequately defended the *Outsider Test for Faith* (OTF) in chapter four. If he's right, and he is, it is simply unreasonable to believe anything extraordinary that hasn't passed that test. So what happens when we apply that test to the resurrection of Jesus? As the apostle Paul aptly declared, "if Christ has not been raised, then our preaching is vain, and your faith is vain" (1 Corinthians 15:14). And he was right. If the resurrection of Jesus is unbelievable, then so is Christianity. Since, as I'll show, the resurrection does not pass the OTF, neither does Christianity.

SEEING MIRACLES FROM THE OUTSIDE

Fifty years after the Persian Wars ended in 479 BC Herodotus the Halicarnassian asked numerous eyewitnesses and their children about the things that happened in those years and then wrote a book about it. Though he often shows a critical and skeptical mind, sometimes naming his sources or even questioning their reliability when he has suspicious or conflicting accounts, he nevertheless reports without a hint of doubt that the temple of Delphi magically defended itself with animated armaments, lightning bolts, and collapsing cliffs; the sacred olive tree of Athens, though burned by the Persians, grew a new shoot an arm's length in a single day; a miraculous flood-tide wiped out an entire Persian contingent after they desecrated an image of Poseidon; a horse gave birth to a rabbit; and a whole town witnessed a mass resurrection of cooked fish!

Do you believe these things happened? Well, why not? Herodotus was an educated man, a critical historian, and he consulted eyewitnesses, and he clearly saw nothing to doubt in these events.[1] So why should we? If you're smart, reasonably educated, and honest, you'll have to admit your doubts here are rather strong. And I'm sure if someone came knocking on your door, insisting these things were true, you'd defend your doubts as entirely reasonable. So think for a moment what you'd say to them. I bet you'd come up with several good rules of thumb about what kinds of stories to believe or doubt. You'll say, for example, that these sorts of things don't really happen because nothing like them happens today, certainly never when you're around. Cooked fish don't rise from the dead. Rabbits don't pop out of horses. Temples don't defend themselves with miraculous weather and floating weapons. The oceans do not selectively drown blasphemers. And tree limbs take much longer to grow than a single day. You know these things because of your own experience, as well as that of countless other people, especially after centuries of scientific research. But you also know people lie, even if for what they think is a good reason. They also exaggerate, tell tall tales, craft edifying myths and legends, and err in many ways. As a result, as we all well know, false stories are commonplace. But miracles, quite clearly, are not.

So what is more likely? That miracles like these really happen, while you and everyone else you trust, including every scientist and investigator for the last few centuries, just happens to have missed them all? Or that these are just tall tales? I think the latter. And I suspect you agree. But that's just one rule of thumb we all live by. Your doubts become stronger when you can't question the witnesses; when you don't even know who they are; when you don't have the story from them but from someone else entirely; when there is an agenda, something the storyteller is attempting to persuade you of; when the witnesses or reporters are a bit kooky or disturbingly overzealous. And so on. We all think this way, and rightly so. Any of these factors will call into question the stories we're told, and many apply here. We don't really have any of Herodotus's stories from the witnesses themselves, we don't know who exactly they are or how trustworthy or level-headed they were, we don't know what agenda they might have had, we can't question them, we don't even get to hear anyone else question them—nor do we hear from anyone who was also there and might have seen things differently. For all these reasons and more, we rightly dismiss such wonders as fun tales that simply aren't true.

IF WE DON'T BELIEVE HERODOTUS, WE CAN'T BELIEVE THE GOSPELS

I see no relevant difference between the marvels in Herodotus and the many and varied tales of the resurrection of Jesus. Even the most fundamentalist of Christians don't believe half of them. When the Gospel of Peter (yes, Peter) says a Roman centurion, a squad of his soldiers, and a gathering of Jewish elders all saw a gigantic cross hopping along behind Jesus as he exited his tomb, and then saw Jesus grow thousands of feet tall before their very eyes, there isn't a Christian alive who believes this. And yet that was among the most popular Gospels in the Christian churches of the second century, purportedly written by someone who was alive at the time. So why don't Christians believe Peter's Gospel anymore? Well, for many of the same reasons we don't believe the marvels of Herodotus. But why then believe any of the *other* Gospels, those according to Matthew, Mark, Luke, and John?

The Gospel of Matthew claims that as Jesus died:

> The veil of the temple tore in two from top to bottom, and the earth quaked, and the rocks were rent, and the tombs were opened, and many bodies of holy men who had fallen asleep were raised, and coming out of the tombs after Jesus' resurrection they entered into the holy city and appeared to many. And then the centurion and those who were watching Jesus with him, when they saw the earthquake and the rest that happened, were quite terrified, saying, "Truly this was the Son of God!" (Matthew 27:51–54)

How is this any less fantastic than the Gospel of Peter? None of the other Gospels report anything like this. Nor in fact does any other historian or writer of that place or period. Somehow all the educated men, all the scholars and rabbis of Jerusalem, failed to notice any rock-splitting earthquake, or any hoard of walking dead wandering the city, or any of the numerous empty tombs they left behind. The lone exception among all these wonders is the miraculous tearing of the temple curtain, which Matthew and Luke both borrow from Mark, but still no Jew ever seems to have noticed this, apparently not even the priests whose only job was to attend to that very curtain.[2]

Like the tall tales in Herodotus, we don't hear any of this from any of the actual witnesses. In this case we don't even know their names, even though there are supposed to have been a lot of them, including high-ranking Roman officers and temple priests. There also had to have been thousands of witnesses to so devastating an earthquake, and hundreds of witnesses to the hoard of resurrected dead. We're never told who. And we don't hear any of this from *them*. Worse, we don't even know for sure who Matthew is, or when exactly he wrote, or where, or who his sources were—except we know he copied Mark almost verbatim, and then embellished his story with fantastic details like these. But we don't know who Mark is, either, or when or where *he* wrote or who *his* sources were. Even so, he never heard of any of this stuff either. Nor do we know who Luke or John were, or when or where they wrote, or who any of their sources were. The authors of John (and yes, that's plural) claim they got their information from some anonymous disciple (John 21:24 and 19:35) who is never clearly named and nowhere mentioned in any other Gospel, yet it's generally agreed that "John" wrote last of all—well after the other three Gospels were already circulating—and that "his" entire story fundamentally con-tradicts the others in countless details. And yet *his* authors hadn't heard of any of Matthew's marvels *either*.

Just read the resurrection accounts yourself, the ones Christians are supposed to believe (Mark 16, Matthew 28, John 20–21, and Luke 24, with Acts 1:1–14), and you'll see far too many contradictions to plausibly rec-oncile, as well as patent wonders that you wouldn't believe from Herodotus, and certainly shouldn't believe coming from complete unknowns, working from unidentified sources, without any evidence of a critical analysis of any conflicting or suspect details. Matthew's account is particularly amusing:

> As it began to dawn ... Mary Magdalene and the other Mary came to see the tomb. And behold! There was a great earthquake, for the Angel of the Lord descended from Heaven, and came and rolled back the stone from

the door, and sat upon it. His appearance was as lightning, and his gown white as snow. And for fear of him the guards shook and became as dead men. And responding [to this], the Angel said to the women, "Don't be afraid, for I know you seek the crucified Jesus. He isn't here, for he has risen, as he said. Come, see the place where the Lord lay!" (Matthew 28:1–6)

Compare this to Mark's version of the same event:

Mary Magdalene, and Mary the mother of James, and Salome…came very early to the tomb as the sun was rising. And they were saying among themselves, "Who will roll away the stone from the door of the tomb for us?" and when they looked up, they saw that the stone had been rolled back, for it was very large. And when they went inside the tomb they saw a young man sitting on the right side, dressed in a white robe, and they were amazed. And he said to them, "Don't be amazed. You seek Jesus, the Nazarene, who was crucified. He is risen. He isn't here. Behold the place where they laid him!" (Mark 16:1–6)

Basically the same story. Except in Matthew the young man sitting inside the tomb has become an angel descending from heaven, causing an earthquake and paralyzing some guards that Mark has no idea were ever there. Now imagine you're a police officer who arrives at the scene of a bank robbery and finds an empty vault and two tellers. One says they went to get some money and found the vault empty and no one was there except a young man inside in a white suit—who has since mysteriously vanished, but at the time said "Don't worry! We took it for a good cause!" Already a suspicious story. But then the other employee says when they went to the vault, a robot with a jet-pack descended from the sky, paralyzed two United States marines who were guarding that vault for some reason, then single-handedly tore it open, revealing that somehow (as if by magic) it was already empty, and then this flying robot sat on top of the vault door and said "Don't worry! We took it for a good cause!" Now be honest. Would you *ever* believe the second witness? I doubt you'd have much confidence even in the first one's already very odd story, much less the second's wild tale. And yet when it comes to Jesus, we don't get to interview *any* witnesses like this. We just get to hear what some unknown guy decades later said someone *else* saw, with no idea how he even knows that, or who told him (or why we should believe *them*).

There is no good reason to treat these stories any differently than those we find in Herodotus, certainly not if these claims are to pass the OTF. Yet at least we know when and where he wrote; and something of who he was and how he got his information; and that he was trying to report the facts as best he could find them out; and that he personally had no agenda here, no need for us to believe him, and no great mission he was trying to accomplish by telling these tales. Not so for the Gospels. So when it comes to miracles, if we don't believe Herodotus, we surely can't believe the Gospels. That's why *I* don't believe Jesus rose from the dead: it simply isn't a plausible event, and is not supported by any sources I trust.

If this were any other religion, say the Heaven's Gate cult or a growing sect of Victor Hugo worshippers, then that would be the end of it. No one would need any further argument. After all, if a bunch of well-dressed men went around knocking on doors claiming Victor Hugo rose from the dead, and all they had to prove it were their own creepy convictions, some wild miracle tales written decades after the fact by unknown persons who never even say how they know anything they claim to know, and some vaguely obsessive letters written by one guy who claims he saw Hugo's heavenly ghost, you'd tell them to go away. And you'd never feel any need to inquire further. Because we all know poppycock when we hear it.

But these are weird times. We live in an age of science and reason, and yet millions of people still seriously believe the world's dead will rise again when an immortal superman flies down from outer space to destroy the earth. I'll be honest with you: people who believe things like that scare me. But I have to deal with them every day, and one thing I've learned is that they get very angry and indignant when we close the door on them, telling them to go away without having examined all their many papers and books. Then they pontificate proudly that because we didn't give their bizarre claims a fair shake, clearly we're just biased, and we deserve the worst of all eternal tortures as punishment for our lazy audacity, and thank goodness superman will kill us from outer space soon. (Did I mention scary?) To put an end to this pompous rhetoric, I've given them far more than they're due, extensively researching their claims to the very core, learning the ancient languages, studying the relevant histories and cultures and documents, and examining their best arguments. Which is all generally more than they ever do in return. Now, with all that, and a PhD in ancient history to boot, they can't say I don't know what I'm talking about.

THE EVIDENCE

Apart from just "feeling" that it's true, or being told so in a dream, or seeing ghosts or hearing voices, and other equally dubious grounds for belief today (you wouldn't believe such things from any other religion), there are really only two kinds of evidence that Jesus rose from the grave, and neither provides enough evidence to believe it. These are early Christian writings and the fact that Christianity began with a belief that Jesus rose from the dead. All other evidence simply repeats the claims of the New Testament (NT), or fabricates claims no one believes anymore (like that wild tale from the Gospel of Peter).

Of course, many beliefs have arisen in history despite being untrue, so the fact that Christianity began with a weird belief is not enough reason to believe it, any more than we should believe the angel Moroni gave Joseph Smith some magical gold tablets or that Haile Sellassie is Jesus Christ. That leaves the NT, which is recognized by biblical scholars the world over as an arbitrary hodgepodge of dubious literature of uncertain origins and reliability.[3] Curiously absent from the record are any actual eyewitness accounts of what Jesus said or did, either in life or at his resurrection, any records of events by historians or authorities or correspondents from the same time and place, any inscriptions erected or documents composed by the earliest churches, any neutral or hostile accounts from outsiders observing the orig inating events of the Christian religion, any court documents from the many early trials reported in Acts, or anything written by Jesus himself—or in fact any of his disciples, since hardly any scholar today believes Peter's Epistles are authentic (and none believe his Gospel is authentic), and no other document in the NT claims its author was a disciple—not even the Gospels, contrary to common assumption. Though the authors of the Gospel of John (and they alone) claim to have used something written by a disciple as their source, since they don't even confess to know his name, we can doubt that. In any event, we don't have that alleged source-document, any more than we have Joseph Smith's heavenly gold tablets.

Already, just from what's *missing*, we can tell the evidence is poor. But let's still look at the little that managed to survive. For Christianity to pass the OTF, we must treat all this evidence the same way we treat Herodotus or any ancient writer—all the more, since we have no reason to believe the authors of the NT documents were any more honest or critical or infallible than any other men of their time, and there's plenty of evidence to suspect they were less so. Yet that means, just as with the stories in Herodotus, since a man rising from the dead is an extraordinary claim, we can only believe it if we have extraordinary evidence. Do we?

WHY WE NEED EXTRAORDINARY EVIDENCE

Denying that extraordinary claims require extraordinary evidence is among the rhetoric now resorted to by those who genuinely expect superman to fly down from outer space and kill me. So I have to say something about this first. If I tell you I own a car, I usually won't have to present very much evidence to prove it because you've already observed mountains of evidence that people like me own cars. But if I say I own a nuclear missile, you have just as much evidence that "people like him own nuclear missiles" is *not* true. So I would need much more evidence to prove I owned one, to make up for all the evidence I *don't* have from any supporting generalization. Just think to yourself what it would take for me to convince you I owned a nuclear missile, and you'll see what I mean. In contrast, the odds of winning a lottery are very low, so you might think it would be an extraordinary claim for me to assert "I won a lottery." But lotteries are routinely won. We've observed countless lotteries being won and have tons of evidence that people win lotteries. Therefore, the general claim "people like him win lotteries" is already confirmed, and so I wouldn't need very much evidence to convince you that I won. So "I won a lottery" is not an extraordinary claim. But "I own a nuclear missile" clearly is.

Now suppose I told you "I own an interstellar spacecraft." That would be an even more extraordinary claim—because there is no generalization supporting it *at all*. Not only do you have tons of very good evidence that "people like him own interstellar spacecraft" is *not* true, you also have no evidence this has ever been true for *anyone*—unlike nuclear missiles, which you know at least exist. Therefore, the burden of evidence I would have to bear here is truly enormous. Just think of what it would take for you to believe I really did have an interstellar spacecraft, and again you'll see what I mean.

Once you realize the common sense of this, it's obvious that extraordinary claims require extraordinary evidence. To deny that's true is simply irrational.[4] But there is no more evidence supporting the generalization that "people like Jesus get resurrected from the dead" than there is for people owning starships. Therefore the claim that Jesus arose from the dead is an extraordinary claim, and thus requires extraordinary evidence —more evidence, even, than I would need to convince you I own an interstellar spacecraft.[5] For you actually have evidence confirming the generalization that "there *can be* an interstellar spacecraft." We could build one today with present technology. But we have no comparable evidence at all confirming the generalization that "there *can be* miraculous resurrections from the dead." That doesn't mean miracles must be impossible. It only means we have less evidence that miracles are possible than we have that interstellar spacecraft are possible. And that means the claim that Jesus rose from the dead *is even more extraordinary* than the claim that I own an interstellar spacecraft. Think again of the kind of evidence I would need to convince you I had such a vehicle. I should need *more evidence than that* to convince you Jesus rose from the dead.[6] Just as would be required to convince you a whole village witnessed a pot of cooked fish rise from the dead, or anything else as incredible.

THE EPISTLES

So is the evidence that extraordinary? Let's start with the letters. There are twenty-one Epistles in the NT. None are dated, so we can only guess at when they were written. Of these, thirteen claim to be written by Paul. But scholars now agree that in fact only seven of these letters are likely authentic. The remaining six are forgeries. That means someone else forged them in his name, pretending to be Paul, probably after his death. The authorship of the remaining letters is also questioned. Most scholars agree 1 and 2 Peter are forgeries, too, while the authorship (actual or intended) of the remaining letters is uncertain, since no one really knows for sure who any of these people are.[7]

But the fact that so many forgeries got into the Bible already confirms how little we can trust anything in the NT.[8] Just their presence there, indeed their very creation, proves a pervasive dishonesty among early Christians, as well as the gullibility of their peers. And neither fact warrants much confidence in the remainder of what Christians said or believed. Indeed, besides readily producing and believing many forgeries and lies (and all the personal claims made in the forged letters, such as in 2 Peter, are indeed outright lies), the earliest Christians seem to have guided themselves by very fallacious methodologies when it came to deciding who or what to believe, trusting the mere appearance of sincerity over any real inquiry or interrogation, assuming someone who seemed to perform miracles must be telling the truth, being too easily persuaded by 'secret messages' in scripture, 'communications' in dreams, and the merely intuitive 'feeling' of being instructed directly by God.[9]

In fact, Paul reveals the earliest Christians were hallucinating on a regular basis, entering ecstatic trances, prophesying, relaying the communications of spirits, and speaking in tongues—so much, in fact, that outsiders thought they were lunatics (e.g., 1 Corinthians 14). The whole book of Revelation, for example, is a veritable acid trip, and yet it got into the Bible as an authoritative document. That's how respectable even the craziest of hallucinations were. Not only were they constantly channeling spirits and speaking in tongues and having visions of angels and strange objects in the sky, they were also putting on faith-healing acts and exorcising demons by laying on hands and shouting words of power.[10] In other words, the first Christians behaved a lot more like crazy cultists than you'd ever be comfortable with. These aren't the sort of people whose testimony you would ever trust if you met them today. And if you wouldn't trust what they said now, you shouldn't trust anything they said then.

But what do the Epistles even say? As far as evidence Jesus actually rose from the dead, almost nothing. As Paul says:

> I make known to you, brethren, that the Gospel I preached is not according to [any] man. For neither did I receive it from [any] man, nor was I taught it, except through a revelation of Jesus Christ.... when it was the good pleasure of God...to reveal his Son in me, so I could preach him among the Gentiles. I did not confer with flesh and blood right away. Nor did I go to Jerusalem to see those who were apostles before me, but I went off into Arabia, and then back to Damascus. Then only after three years did I go to Jerusalem to visit Cephas...and [even then] I remained unknown by face to [any of] the churches in Judaea. (Galatians 1:11–18)

So Paul tells us he received the Gospel by revelation alone. No one taught it to him. He learned it only in a vision. What Gospel did he learn this way? He tells us:

> For I make known to you, brethren, the Gospel I preached to you, which you also accepted and in which you now stand.... For I delivered to you

first of all what I also received: that according to the scriptures 'Christ died for our sins,' and that he was buried, and that according to the scriptures 'he was raised on the third day,' and that he appeared to Cephas, then to the twelve, then he appeared to over five hundred brethren at once (of whom most remain until now, but some have fallen asleep), then he appeared to James, then to all the apostles, and last of all he appeared to me, too. (1 Corinthians 15:1–8)

Note that Paul begins both reports with the exact same phrase: "I make known to you, brethren, that this is the Gospel I preached." So Paul says the Gospel he preached was not handed down to him through any human testimony. He learned it directly from God through a revelation, and he says this is the same Gospel he taught his Christian churches. He even went on preaching it for three whole years before he spoke to any eyewitnesses about it, and in all that time he was personally unknown to anyone in the whole of Judea (so he can't have spoken with them earlier, and he clearly implies he didn't).

Paul never mentions having any other evidence for the resurrection of Jesus. He never mentions anyone finding an empty tomb, for example, or the testimony of a Doubting Thomas, or anything else. He learned it from scripture and revelation, and that's it (e.g., Romans 16:25–27). Paul was thus convinced by evidence we would never accept from a cult leader in any other religion. So his evidence does not pass the OTF. Yet Paul never mentions anyone else having any other evidence, either. All those before him, he says, only *saw* the risen Jesus just like he did, and he tells us he saw the risen Jesus only in a vision. There is no other evidence mentioned in any of the Epistles.

THE GOSPELS

Even before we look at their stories, the Gospels don't pass the OTF. We don't know the actual source of any of the information in them. We don't know who really wrote them, or when, or where. We don't know who got to read them before the second century or if anyone investigated their claims in any useful way. We can't even establish that the four Gospels are independent, since Luke and Matthew clearly copied extensively from Mark (often verbatim), and what they changed or added often doesn't agree between them or is outright contradictory. Even when they agree on some additional things Jesus said (which Mark seems not to have known), they have Jesus saying these things in completely different times and places, as if their sources really didn't know when or where Jesus said them, so they each had to make something up. John, meanwhile, contradicts the other three, more even than they contradict each other, and in the most fundamental ways. And since scholars agree his Gospel was written last, and has been meddled with by other unknown authors, and it appears to have reworked stories from Luke, we can't trust his authors had any real sources of their own either.[11]

That's what we *don't* know. What we *do* know is that the Gospels were written with an agenda, a deliberate aim to persuade, to turn people toward belief in Christ and the embrace of Christian morals. And we know they were written long after Paul's Epistles, by members of a fanatical cult who believed their dreams were communications from God, that their intuition was guided by the Holy Spirit, and that they could find information about Jesus secretly hidden in the Bible—and whose leaders regularly hallucinated, occasionally lied, and often fabricated documents. They also doctored them. We know Mark did not write verses 16:9–20, for example. Those were "snuck in" later by dishonest Christians. John's Gospel appears to have ended originally at 20:30–31. But someone seems to have tacked on a whole extra ending (John 21) that egregiously reworks a completely different story Luke had already placed long before Jesus died (Luke 5). Then this person invented a fake, yet nameless, witness for it. (Or the reverse is the case, and John 20:18–31 was interpolated before the original ending of John 21). You might even know the famous story of the adulteress saved by Jesus' famous quip, "Let he who is without sin cast the first stone" (John 7:53–8:11). That's now known to be a forgery, too; it was deceitfully inserted after the fact. There was even a copy of Acts circulating in the second century that's over 10 percent longer than the one now in the Bible, demonstrating that Christians had no qualms about adding all kinds of material to their books.[12] Which means we have no way of knowing what got added to the version we now have in the Bible, or indeed any of the other Gospels or Epistles (or what was changed or taken away, for that matter). There were actually whole basketfuls of fake books written by Christians, too, including over a dozen more Gospels, a few additional Acts, various bogus letters and correspondences, even wild fantasies about the deeds of Jesus in his childhood. With so much meddling and forgery indisputably coming from early

Christians, why should we trust the "canonical" Gospels any more than the rest? We already know they were meddled with, and we know many of the canonical *Epistles* were outright forged.[13]

Combine what we *don't* know with what we *do* know, and there is no sound basis for trusting what the Gospels tell us about anything we can't corroborate elsewhere or don't already have reason enough to believe. The existence of improbabilities, contradictions, propaganda, evident fictions, forgeries and interpolations, and legendary embellishments in them has been exhaustively discussed in the modern literature, and most scholars agree the Gospels contain a goodly amount of these things. In fact, I think it's pretty clear the earliest of them—the Gospel according to Mark, the original story later embellished by all the others—was not even written as history, but as a deliberate myth. The author of Mark never says he is writing anything else. And we can clearly see the difference. Consider just one example.

When Mark says the Roman governor Pontius Pilate had a custom of releasing a prisoner on the annual holiday, and the Jews cried for Barabbas, and to crucify Jesus in his place (Mark 15:6–15), what we surely have is myth, not fact.[14] No Roman magistrate (least of all the infamously ruthless Pilate), would let a murderous rebel go free, and no such Roman ceremony is attested as ever having existed. But the ceremony so obviously emulates the Jewish ritual of the scapegoat and atonement, *in a story that is actually about atonement*, that its status as myth is hard to deny. Barabbas means "Son of the Father" in Aramaic, yet we know Jesus was deliberately styled the "Son of the Father" himself. Hence we have two sons of the father, one is released into the wild mob bearing the sins of Israel (murder and insurrection), while the other is sacrificed so his blood may *atone* for the sins of Israel. This is an obvious imitation of the Yom Kippur ceremony of Leviticus 16, when two goats were chosen each year, and one was released into the wild bearing the sins of Israel, while the other's blood was shed to atone for the sins of Israel. Conclusion? Mark crafted a mythical narrative to convey what Hebrews 9–10 says about Jesus as the final Yom Kippur, thus telling us, with his own parable, to reject the sins of the Jews (especially violence and rebellion) and embrace instead the eternal salvation of atonement offered in Christ. Had this story appeared in any other book, we would readily identify it as myth and not historical fact. As fact, it's hopelessly implausible. As myth, it makes perfect sense.

Matthew did the same thing, radically refictionalizing the resurrection narrative, for example, to echo the story of Daniel in the lion's den, thus again communicating the "true meaning" of the Gospel without any evident interest in historical fact.[15] And Luke appears to have fabricated his Emmaus narrative (in Luke 24:13–34) to emulate the epiphany of Romulus, the mythical founder of Rome who—just like Jesus—was the Son of God incarnate, was born of a virgin, was killed by the corrupt leaders of the city, was subsequently resurrected from the dead, appeared to the living on a road to the city, and ascended to heaven to rule from on high.[16] Even John added stories never before heard (like John 2) that seem more symbolic than true. Scholars have documented countless other examples of mythmaking in the Gospels.[17]

For all these reasons, we can't trust the Gospels as historical accounts of what really happened because we wouldn't trust documents like this from any other religious tradition. Acts is similarly untrustworthy, proven by the fact that it gets completely wrong fundamental events in the church, as we know from the letters of Paul (who was an eyewitness to them).[18] That leaves us with no trustworthy evidence that Jesus ever really rose from the grave. We have nothing better than we have from Herodotus. And since we don't believe Herodotus's claims of the miraculous, we shouldn't believe the New Testament's.

HOW CHRISTIANITY BEGAN

We don't really know how Christianity began. We can't trust our sources, and we have no idea who *their* sources were or how faithful they were to them. We have no eyewitness accounts, and the only author we can definitely place near the faith's origin tells us almost nothing about how or why it began. So we can only talk about what is most likely, given everything we know about the way the world really works. If any unextraordinary series of natural events can explain all the evidence we have, and if we don't have any of the extraordinary evidence we would need to confirm an extraordinary explanation instead, then we can't believe the extraordinary, for then the ordinary is more probable. Yet many unextraordinary explanations are possible, so we have no sound reason to prefer an extraordinary one.

There are really only two facts that need explaining: why the first Christians claimed to see Jesus "risen from the dead," and what happened to the body. To take the second first, we don't really know whether the body went missing, or even that the first Christians believed it did. The

Epistles never mention a missing body. In Acts no one ever investigates his grave or says it was empty. And the Gospels freely invent stories, so their stories about a missing body could be invented, too. It's quite possible the first Christians believed Jesus rose in an entirely new body, leaving the old one in the grave.[19] For as Paul tells us, the body that dies is *not* the body that rises (1 Corinthians 15:37–38). So they wouldn't even need to believe the body had gone missing. And even if they did believe the body had gone missing, they could believe that even if the body *wasn't* missing. For any evidence to the contrary they could simply dismiss as a trick, just as the Heaven's Gate cult dismissed all evidence against their claim that an alien spaceship was photographed behind comet Hale-Bopp.[20] In fact, contrary to the Gospel tales, Jesus might actually have been buried in the ground, in which case it wouldn't even have been possible to check.[21] But even if the body did go missing, when *other* bodies go missing we never assume they rose from the dead—because we know it's far more likely they were misplaced or stolen. And for all we know, *either* could have happened to the body of Jesus.[22] Since none of these possibilities can be ruled out on the evidence we have, since all are compatible with that evidence, and none require anything as extraordinary as a corpse coming back to life, we have no sound reason to believe the latter. We might not know what happened. But we can know it wasn't that.

That leaves only one thing to explain: why the first Christians claimed to see Jesus "risen from the dead." The Gospels can't be trusted on this, and we already saw what the Epistles say: the only reason they ever give is that the scriptures told them Jesus would rise, and then they had revelations of the risen Jesus. As the Epistles reveal, these people regularly hallucinated and 'channeled spirits.' So for them the risen Jesus was just another hallucinated encounter with the divine. If we trust Paul's list of appearances (1 Corinthians 15:5–8), Jesus clearly wasn't around anymore, because Paul says he only 'appeared' on isolated occasions, to highly select people, which certainly suggests revelatory experiences, not 'Jesus the house guest' hanging around until he flew away. Paul even implies there was only one occasion when such a revelation was experienced by many believers "at the same time," but he doesn't tell us what they saw (1 Corinthians 15:6). We know masses of people hallucinating together can *believe* they saw the same thing, and such hallucinations can be stirred by ecstatic trance-inducing behaviors, especially in religious cults populated by regular hallucinators and trancers—as the Christians demonstrably were, prophesying and speaking in tongues en masse (as shown in 2 Corinthians 12 and 1 Corinthians 14:26–30). In fact, functional schizotypes are prone to congregating into cults like this and just as prone to this kind of hallucinatory behavior. Such phenomena is well-documented in people and cults generally, and requires no extraordinary explanation.[23]

Paul even tells us what inspired these hallucinations: he says the scriptures told them that Christ would rise from the dead. So, inspired by scripture, he and others hallucinated a Jesus telling them exactly that.[24] The well-studied phenomenon of cognitive dissonance reduction could have played a powerful role in setting all this in motion, if the followers of Jesus were desperate enough to rationalize his death.[25] But just their apocalyptic expectation that the world was about to soon end could have been enough. Many Jews believed the final sign of the end would be the arrival of the Messiah and the resurrection of the dead, and Christians from the very beginning believed the resurrection of Jesus was that sign, the "firstfruits" of that expected apocalyptic resurrection (1 Corinthians 15:20). Some Jews even expected the end would shortly follow the death of the Messiah (Daniel 9:25–27). Christians believed Jesus was the Messiah, and he had died. The end was nigh. Desperately needing confirmation they were right, they imagined proof: the beginning of the resurrection in Jesus.[26]

It's also possible the first Christians *claimed* to have had these visions even when they didn't. They could have done so simply to join, lead, or support a movement whose moral goals they approved and believed should be implemented and preached to society for the good of their fellow man (or his salvation from immanent doom). We know this would have been a successful strategy of social mobility. As long as you stuck by your story even unto death, you would be successful in maintaining your honor and status within the group, as well as your surviving family's. And since this would serve to inspire others to adopt your message of moral and social reform, if you sincerely believed those reforms would make the world a better place (or save many from God's wrath), and you were willing to sacrifice anything, even your life, for this greater good, then pious lies about visions and revelations would be an effective tool to accomplish these altruistic goals.[27] I've met enough 'liars for Christ' to believe this quite possible. But those same motives could also inspire genuine hallucinations confirming what the apostles most wanted to hear, especially if they were naturally prone to such altered states of consciousness, as some people are and the early Christians appear to have been.

Any combination of these possibilities would explain the claim that Jesus was raised from the dead and later seen risen. Yet everything above rests on established knowledge, nothing very extraordinary, certainly nothing as extraordinary as a miracle.[28]

Even martyrs lend no credence. Later converts were not eyewitnesses, and from eyewitnesses we have no testimony. In fact, that so-called 'eyewitnesses' were willing to die rather than recant their testimony to some extraordinary fact is neither reliably attested nor inherently improbable, and thus is not extraordinary evidence. For most of them we have no reliable record of their deaths at all, and for the rest we have no such record that any could have avoided death by recanting, or that their resolve rested on anything more tangible than hallucinations or moral defiance. Christianity had many elements typical of other martyr cults, which facts are alone sufficient to explain a willingness to die.[29] Ultimately, the fact that so many other religions have willing martyrs demonstrates that such willingness is no more likely for a true religion than a false one.

WHERE'S THE EXTRAORDINARY EVIDENCE?

None of the evidence is extraordinary enough to justify believing an extraordinary explanation. All the evidence we have is ordinary and has ordinary explanations. In fact, those ordinary explanations actually explain the evidence *better*. Consider the conversion of Paul. Though we sometimes hear that James was a skeptic until his dead brother Jesus appeared to him, in fact only the Gospels suggest James had ever doubted, and only early in his brother's ministry—there is no evidence he was not already a loyal believer by the time Jesus died. Which makes Paul unique: as far as we know, he is the only skeptic in the entire world who got to see the risen Jesus. Since Paul's turnabout is unique, we must expect the causes of his conversion to be unique.

We may never know. We don't have much to go on, and we have little to trust. But it would not be unlikely for just *one* of the hundreds opposing the church to have come to admire the moral convictions and ideals of the Christians, then to have become overwhelmed by guilt at having done them (or even God's plan) so much harm, and then to have found a way out of the resulting cognitive dissonance by hallucinating a vision of Christ, joining their movement, and, in penance, actually helping them further their social and moral reforms. Paul might even have feared the Christians' predictions of the coming divine judgment were true and thus decided he had better get on board and spread the word. The fact that his conversion elevated Paul from a relative nobody taking orders from a Jewish elite he had come to despise to a respected and powerful authority taking orders from no one might also have played a part. But the hardships involved suggest he had a genuine passion for the moral and social mission of the early Christians or even its apocalyptic convictions. And whether he fabricated his way into a mission for the greater good, or his natural tendency to hallucinate constructed the experience he needed to persuade him to find such a way out of his torment, entirely natural causes of his conversion can be imagined without proposing anything extraordinary. Though such a conjunction of causes would be uncommon, Paul's conversion *was* uncommon, thus *confirming* an ordinary explanation. Had the extraordinary been at work, Paul would not have been alone.

Only an ordinary explanation can easily explain why Jesus only appeared to die-hard believers, and then, much later, to only *one* of millions of outsiders across the entire planet. If God himself were really appearing to people, and really was on a compassionate mission to reform and save the world, there is hardly any credible reason he would appear to only one persecutor rather than to all of them. But if Paul's experience was entirely natural and not at all divine, then we should expect such an event to be rare, possibly even unique—and, lo and behold, that appears to be the case. Paul's conversion thus supports the conclusion that Christianity originated from natural phenomena, and not from any encounter with a walking corpse. A walking corpse—indeed a flying corpse (Luke 24:51 and Acts 1:9–11) or a teleporting corpse (Luke 24:31–37 and John 20:19–26)— could have visited Pilate, Herod, the Sanhedrin, the masses of Jerusalem, the Roman legions, even the emperor and senate of Rome. He could even have flown to America (as the Mormons actually believe he did), and even China, preaching in all the temples and courts of Asia. In fact, being God, he could have appeared to everyone on earth. He could visit me right now. Or you! And yet, instead, besides his already fanatical followers, just one odd fellow ever saw him.

If Jesus was a god and really wanted to save the world, he would have appeared and delivered his Gospel personally to the whole world. He would not appear only to one small group of believers and one lone outsider, in one tiny place, just one time, two thousand years ago, and then give up. But if Christianity originated as a natural movement inspired by ordinary hallucinations (real or pretended), then we would expect it to arise in only one small group, in one small place, at just one time, and especially where, as in antiquity, regular hallucinators were often respected as holy and their hallucinations believed to be divine communications. And that's exactly when and where it began. The ordinary explanation thus predicts all we see, whereas the extraordinary explanation predicts things we don't see at all.

The unreliability of the Christian documents now offered in support of the resurrection is also just what we should expect if Christianity had an entirely natural origin, whereas if God himself inspired its founding and wanted it to flourish, he would have made it impossible for forgeries and fictions to get into His Book. Instead, all Bibles that contained the true word of God could have been miraculously indestructible and unalterable by any human effort. No meddler could then change what it said, or add or take anything away, and its imperviousness to all earthly harm would confirm God's approval of what it said. If *I* were God, *I* would appear to everyone and prevent any meddling with my book, and since I can't be cleverer or more concerned for the salvation of the world than God, this must be what he would do, too.[30] So once again, an ordinary explanation predicts what we see, the extraordinary explanation doesn't.

That Christianity was just a natural product of its time and culture also predicts a great deal more. It explains why Christianity shares so many things in common with the religions of its day (from various Jewish sects to pagan mystery cults), including notions that would seem strange in any other cultural context yet were common at the time, like incarnation, resurrection, blood sacrifice, and vicarious atonement. Even the idea of a god having a son makes no sense, except then, under the Roman Empire, when many gods were believed to have sons.[31] Christianity thus looks like an ordinary product of its time, not a supernatural miracle from a universal God.[32]

CONCLUSION

That Jesus rose from the dead is an extraordinary claim, which requires extraordinary evidence. We have none. Christianity thus fails the OTF. We have no more reason to believe Jesus rose from the dead than that a pot of fish did. Christianity is also a theory, and as such, it makes predictions.

Those predictions didn't come true. Any ordinary explanation of all the same evidence also makes predictions. But those predictions *did* come true. Christianity is therefore disconfirmed.

This conclusion still follows even if God exists and miracles and the supernatural are real. But it follows even more if they aren't. And I see no reason to believe they are. I find no adequate evidence for believing any of the metaphysical agencies the resurrection of Jesus requires. The evidence strongly supports the conclusion that there are no angels, transmutations, flying or teleporting holy men, or gods of any kind, much less a god routinely engaged in producing miraculous wonders of the sort the Bible depicts throughout. Hence it's perfectly reasonable to conclude that people simply don't rise from the dead because we can plainly see no god is doing anything like that. The world just doesn't work that way, as we all well know.[33] In the absence of any adequate evidence to the contrary, Jesus rising from the dead is simply no more plausible than a mass resurrection of cooked fish or a horse birthing a rabbit. And until I'm provided with enough evidence to warrant believing otherwise, there is no reason I should.

NOTES

1. See Richard Carrier, "The Spiritual Body of Christ and the Legend of the Empty Tomb," in *The Empty Tomb: Jesus beyond the Grave*, eds. Robert Price and Jeffery Lowder (Amherst, NY: Prometheus Books, 2005), pp. 168–82. Herodotus records the cited miracles in *Histories* 8.37–38, 8.55, 8.129, 7.57, and 9.120; and discusses methods and sources in *Histories* 1.20–21, 2.29, 2.123, 4.14, 4.29, 5.86-87, 6.53–54, 8.55, 8.65, and so on. Herodotus is just an example. Ancient and medieval literature was filled with incredible stories no one believes anymore. For examples, see Richard Carrier, *Sense and Goodness without God* (Bloomington, Indiana: Author-House, 2005), pp. 211–52.

2. On the priests attending the veil: Mishnah, *Sheqalim*, *Yoma* 5:1, and *Middot* 1:1h.

3. This scholarly consensus on the NT is well surveyed in Bart Ehrman, *Jesus Interrupted* (New York: HarperOne, 2009), *The New Testament* (New York: Oxford University Press, 1997), and in *The New Interpreter's Bible: New Testament Survey* (Nashville: Abingdon Press, 2005).

4. Literally: rejecting this principle constitutes rejecting logic. Formally, Bayes' theorem entails $P(h|e.b) = [P(h|b) \times P(e|h.b)] / [[P(h|b) \times P(e|h.b)] + [P(\sim h|b) \times P(e|\sim h.b)]]$, in which extraordinary claims are defined by $P(h|b) \rightarrow$

0, and believability by $P(h \mid e.b) > 0.5$, and a strong explanation of the evidence by $P(e \mid h.b) \rightarrow 1$, which entails for an extraordinary claim to achieve believability (even when that claim is a strong explanation of the evidence), $P(e \mid {\sim}h.b) \rightarrow 0$. In other words, even in the best possible case, in order for an extraordinary explanation to be believable, the evidence (as a whole) must be extraordinarily improbable on any other explanation but the extraordinary one and in direct proportion (i.e., the more extraordinary the claim, the more extraordinarily improbable the evidence must otherwise be). On Bayes' theorem and its application to history see Richard Carrier, "Bayes' Theorem for Beginners: Formal Logic and Its Relevance to Historical Method," in *Caesar: A Journal for the Critical Study of Religion and Human Values* 3, no. 1 (2009): 26–35.

5. The idea of "more" evidence need not mean only quantity but can include quality and any other measures of evidentiary strength. Formally, "more evidence" for any explanation h, when h is already a strong explanation *and* extraordinary, is defined according to Bayes' theorem as any evidence that reduces $P(e \mid {\sim}h.b)$; that is, the less probable the evidence would be on any *other* explanation, the "more" it supports the extraordinary explanation. There are two other ways to have "more" evidence, but neither pertains here: (1) evidence that increases $P(e \mid h.b)$ is also "more" but can never make a difference in believability in the case just defined; and (2) contrafactually, if miracles like the resurrection were commonplace (as common as people winning lotteries, for example), then "resurrection" would not be an extraordinary claim, and thus would not require extraordinary evidence, so if God started behaving today like the incredible miracle worker the Bible depicts he was, that could also provide "more" evidence for the resurrection.

6. For more examples and discussion see Richard Carrier, "Why I Am Not a Christian," *The Secular Web*, 2006, http://www.infidels.org/library/modern/richard_carrier/whynotchristian.html and the epistemological analyses of Matt McCormick, *The Case against Christ: Why Believing Is No Longer Reasonable* (forthcoming), and Chris Hallquist, *UFOs, Ghosts, and a Rising God: Debunking the Resurrection of Jesus* (Reasonable Press: 2009).

7. On these facts, see references in note 3.

8. On the ubiquity and significance of forgeries in early Judaism and Christianity, see John Loftus, *Why I Became an Atheist* (Amherst, NY: Prometheus Books, 2008), pp. 167–76.

9. See Richard Carrier, *Not the Impossible Faith: Why Christianity Didn't Need a Miracle to Succeed* (Raleigh, NC: Lulu, 2009), pp. 161–218, 281–85, 329–68, 385–405; and chapter five, "Christian Rejection of the Natural Philosopher" in *The Scientist in the Early Roman Empire* (forthcoming).

10. See, for example, 1 Corinthians 12–14; 2 Corinthians 12; Hebrews 2; Galatians 1:12, 2:2; Ephesians 1:17, 3:3; 1 John 4:1; Mark 16:17–18; Acts 2:16–18; and Justin Martyr, *Dialogue with Trypho* 30. For discussion of these phenomena in

the early church, see Gordon Fee, *The First Epistle to the Corinthians* (Grand Rapids, MI: Eerdmans, 1987), pp. 590–99, 652–713. The book of Acts also claims regular hallucinations and dream communications, which were believed by the earliest Christians without hesitation: 2:1–4, 2:17–18, 7:55–57, 9:3–7, 10:9–17, 16:9–10, 22:6–11, 26:12–19, 27:21–25.

11. Again, on these facts, see references in note 3. But on what is claimed regarding the Gospel of John specifically, see Herman Waetjen, *The Gospel of the Beloved Disciple: A Work in Two Editions* (New York: T & T Clark, 2005); C. K. Barrett, *The Gospel according to St. John*, 2d ed. (Philadelphia: Westminster Press, 1978): pp. 15–26; C. H. Dodd, *Historical Tradition in the Fourth Gospel* (Cambridge: Cambridge University Press, 1963); see also, Carrier, "Spiritual Body," pp. 155–56, 191–93; Loftus, *Why I Became an Atheist*, pp. 329–32; Robert Price, *The Pre-Nicene New Testament* (Salt Lake City: Signature Books, 2006), pp. 665–718; and Andrew Gregory, "The Third Gospel? The Relationship of John and Luke Reconsidered" in *Challenging Perspectives on the Gospel of John*, ed. John Lierman (Tübingen: Mohr Siebeck, 2006), pp. 109–34 (although Gregory argues the reverse thesis, he nevertheless summarizes the scholarship arguing the authors of John knew the Gospel of Luke).

12. Carrier, *Not the Impossible Faith*, pp. 186–87.

13. On how rampant Christian forging and meddling with documents was, see Bart Ehrman, *Misquoting Jesus* (New York: HarperSanFrancisco, 2005), *Lost Christianities* (New York: Oxford University Press, 2003), *Lost Scriptures* (New York: Oxford University Press, 2003), and *Orthodox Corruption of Scripture* (New York: Oxford University Press, 1993). See also note 8.

14. Jennifer Maclean, "Barabbas, the Scapegoat Ritual, and the Development of the Passion Narrative," *Harvard Theological Review* 100, no. 3 (July 2007): pp. 309–34. That even Mark's idea of placing women at the empty tomb has a mythical basis, see Carrier, *Not the Impossible Faith*, pp. 297–321.

15. Demonstrated in Carrier, "The Plausibility of Theft," in *Empty Tomb*, pp. 360–64.

16. Arnold Ehrhardt, "Emmaus, Romulus und Apollonius," in *Mullus: Festschrift Theodor Klauser*, eds. Alfred Stuiber and Alfred Hermann (Münster, Westfalen: Aschendorff, 1964), pp. 93–99; and Carrier, "Spiritual Body," pp. 180–81, 191; and Carrier, *Not the Impossible Faith*, p. 33.

17. See, for example, Randel Helms, *Gospel Fictions* (Amherst, NY: Prometheus Books, 1988) and Thomas Brodie, *The Birthing of the New Testament* (Sheffield: Sheffield Phoenix Press, 2004).

18. Contrast the chronology and depiction of events in Galatians 1–2 with that of Acts 9, 10, and 15, or just Galatians 1:22 with Acts 7:58–8:4. On the mixed reliability of Acts in general, see Richard Pervo, *The Mystery of Acts* (Santa Rosa, CA: Polebridge, 2008), Richard Pervo, *Acts: A Commentary* (Minneapolis, MN: Fortress Press, 2009), and Carrier, *Not the Impossible Faith*, pp. 173–87.

19. See: Carrier, "Spiritual Body," with "Spiritual Body FAQ," http://www
.richardcarrier.info/SpiritualFAQ.html. Many other scholars have argued this:
Bruce Chilton, *Rabbi Paul* (New York: Doubleday, 2005), pp. 57–58; Peter Lampe,
"Paul's Concept of a Spiritual Body," in *Resurrection: Theological and Scientific Assess-
ments*, eds. Ted Peters et al. (Grand Rapids, MI: Eerdmans, 2002), pp. 103–14; Gre-
gory Riley, *Resurrection Reconsidered* (Minneapolis, MN: Fortress Press, 1995); Dale
Martin, *The Corinthian Body* (New Haven, CT: Yale University Press, 1995); Adela
Collins, "The Empty Tomb in the Gospel according to Mark," in *Hermes and
Athena*, eds. Eleonore Stump and Thomas Flint (Notre Dame, IN: University of
Notre Dame Press, 1993), pp. 107–40; C. F. Moule, "St. Paul and Dualism: The
Pauline Conception of the Resurrection," *New Testament Studies* 12 (1966): 106–23;
and James Tabor, "Leaving the Bones Behind: A Resurrected Jesus Tradition with
an Intact Tomb," in *Sources of the Jesus Tradition*, ed. R. J. Hoffmann (forthcoming).

20. For this and other examples of beliefs impervious to evidence see Carrier,
"Plausibility of Theft," pp. 355–57; and Kris Komarnitsky, *Doubting Jesus' Resurrection* (n.p.: CreateSpace, 2009), pp. 48–76, whose whole book is a must read.

21. Jesus may indeed have been buried in the ground and not in a tomb:
Komarnitsky, *Doubting*, pp. 10–47; Peter Kirby, "The Case against the Empty
Tomb," in *Empty Tomb*, pp. 233–60.

22. Evidence the body could have been misplaced: Richard Carrier, "The
Burial of Jesus in Light of Jewish Law," in *Empty Tomb*, pp. 369–92, with "Burial of
Jesus FAQ," http://www.richardcarrier.info/BurialFAQ.html; and Jeffery Jay
Lowder, "Historical Evidence and the Empty Tomb Story," in *Empty Tomb*, pp.
261–306. Evidence it could have been stolen: Carrier, "Plausibility of Theft," with
"Plausibility of Theft FAQ," http://www.richardcarrier.info/TheftFAQ.html.

23. See S. Day and E. Peters, "The Incidence of Schizotypy in New Religious
Movements," *Personality and Individual Differences* 27, no. 1 (July 1999): 55–67; C.
Claridge and G. McCreery, "A Study of Hallucination in Normal Subjects," *Per-
sonality and Individual Differences* 2, no. 5 (November 1996): 739–47.

For an excellent discussion of this fact (and references to further scholarship),
see Komarnitsky, *Doubting*, pp. 77–97, with extensive support in Carrier, "Spiritual
Body," pp. 151–54, 182–97; "Burial of Jesus," pp. 387–88; and "Isn't the Idea of
'Visions' Implausible?" in Carrier, "Spiritual Body FAQ," http://www.richard
carrier.info/SpiritualFAQ.html#visions; Keith Parsons, "Peter Kreeft and Ronald
Tacelli on the Hallucination Theory," in *Empty Tomb*, pp. 433–51; and James
Crossley, "Against the Historical Plausibility of the Empty Tomb Story and the
Bodily Resurrection of Jesus," *Journal for the Study of the Historical Jesus* 3, no. 2
(June 2005): 171–86.

The internal and comparative evidence is even more thoroughly discussed in
Michael Goulder, "The Baseless Fabric of a Vision," in *Resurrection Reconsidered*, ed.
Gavin D'Costa (Oxford: Oneworld Publications, 1996), pp. 48–61; "The Explana-

tory Power of Conversion Visions," in *Jesus' Resurrection: Fact or Figment: A Debate between William Lane Craig & Gerd Lüdemann*, eds. Paul Copan and Ronald Tacelli (Downers Grove, IL: Intervarsity Press, 2000), pp. 86–103; Gerd Lüdemann, *The Resurrection of Jesus* (Minneapolis, MN: Fortress Press, 1994), *What Really Happened to Jesus* (Louisville, KY: Westminster John Knox, 1995), and *The Resurrection of Christ* (Amherst, NY: Prometheus Books, 2004).

Modern examples are numerous: Roland Littlewood, "From Elsewhere: Prophetic Visions and Dreams among the People of the Earth," *Dreaming* 14, nos. 2–3 (June–September 2004): 94–106; Felicitas Goodman et al., *Trance, Healing, and Hallucination* (New York: Wiley, 1974); Edward Rice, *John Frum He Come: Cargo Cults & Cargo Messiahs in the South Pacific* (Garden City, NY: Doubleday, 1974); I. C. Jarvie, *The Revolution in Anthropology* (London: Routledge, 1964); Peter Worsley, *The Trumpet Shall Sound: A Study of "Cargo" Cults in Melanesia*, 2nd ed. (London: MacGibbon & Kee, 1968).

24. On how this could have happened, see comparative evidence in Komarnitsky, *Doubting*, pp. 98–129, with additional discussion in Carrier, "Spiritual Body," pp. 151–52, 158–61, and "Burial of Jesus," pp. 387–88; and a more recent find that might have been involved: Israel Knohl, "'By Three Days, Live': Messiahs, Resurrection, and Ascent to Heaven in Hazon Gabriel," *The Journal of Religion* 88, no. 2 (April 2008): 147–58.

25. Most persuasively argued in Komarnitsky, *Doubting*, pp. 48–76, supported by Carrier, "Burial of Jesus," p. 392 n. 55.

26. Jesus might even have enhanced his followers' apocalyptic belief by making it a centerpiece of his ministry. See Bart Ehrman, *Jesus: Apocalyptic Prophet of the New Millennium* (New York: Oxford University Press, 1999); and John Loftus's chapter "At Best Jesus Was a Failed Apocalyptic Prophet" in the present volume.

27. For why this would make sense within the culture of the time, see Carrier, *Not the Impossible Faith*, pp. 281–85; and Carrier, "Whence Christianity? A Meta-Theory for the Origins of Christianity," *Journal of Higher Criticism* 11, no. 1 (Spring 2005): 22–34 (though "Passover" is there conflated with "Yom Kippur"; Jesus was figured as fulfilling both). On the powerful role of public honor and shame in motivating even suicidal behavior in antiquity, see Carrier, *Not the Impossible Faith*, pp. 219–45, 259–96.

28. That no miracle was needed for Christianity to succeed is extensively argued in Carrier, *Not the Impossible Faith*.

29. See Carrier, *Not the Impossible Faith*, pp. 219–45, with: Alan Segal, "Apocalypticism and Millenarianism: The Social Backgrounds to the Martyrdoms in Daniel and Qumran," in *Life After Death: A History of the Afterlife in Western Religion* (New York: Doubleday, 2004), pp. 285–321; W. H. C. Frend, "Martyrdom and Political Oppression," in *The Early Christian World*, ed. Philip Esler (London: Rout-

ledge, 2000), 2: 815–39; Arthur Droge and James Tabor, *A Noble Death: Suicide and Martyrdom among Christians and Jews in Antiquity* (San Francisco: Harper, 1992); Robin Lane Fox, "Persecution and Martyrdom," *Pagans & Christians* (New York: Alfred A. Knopf, 1987), pp. 419–92.

30. Against the bizarre rebuttal that God wouldn't give us *any* good evidence lest he coerce us into belief, see Carrier, *Sense and Goodness without God*, pp. 285–86, and "Why I Am Not a Christian" (particularly section 1, "God Is Silent"), http://www.infidels.org/library/modern/richard_carrier/whynotchristian.html#silentgod. That the "official" visions of Jesus ended with Paul also makes more sense if Jesus never really rose from the dead: Carrier, "Spiritual Body," p. 195.

31. For yet other examples of how the evidence could have been better yet in fact supports the contrary, see Loftus, *Why I Became an Atheist*, pp. 192–96. That many key (yet weird) elements of the Jesus story were not unique but in fact typical of religions of that era, see Carrier, *Not the Impossible Faith*, pp. 17–20 and "Spiritual Body," pp. 180–82; Tryggve Mettinger, *The Riddle of Resurrection: "Dying and Rising Gods" in the Ancient Near East* (Stockholm: Almqvist & Wiksell International, 2001); Alan Dundes et al., *In Quest of the Hero* (Princeton, NJ: Princeton University Press, 1990); and Charles Talbert, *What Is a Gospel?* (Philadelphia, PA: Fortress Press, 1977).

32. Formally, on Bayes' theorem, since an extraordinary explanation entails $P(h|b) \to 0$, but the evidence (as just demonstrated) is actually more probable on ~h than h, entailing $P(e|\sim h.b) > P(e|h.b)$, it follows that $P(h|e.b)$ must necessarily be < 0.5, which means such an extraordinary explanation isn't believable *even if* $P(e|\sim h.b) \to 0$ (which still follows even if $P(h|b)$ is merely < 0.5, and miracles are certainly far less common than that).

33. See Carrier, *Sense and Goodness without God* and "Why I Am Not a Christian."

Chapter 12

AT BEST JESUS WAS A
FAILED APOCALYPTIC PROPHET

John W. Loftus

I n their chapters for this part of the book, Price and Carrier have surveyed ample reasons not to believe the extraordinary claims of the
New Testament (NT). But even if you believe the NT is reliable, Christianity still remains untenable. I'll argue that even if the NT is somewhat
reliable, then Jesus was an apocalyptic prophet in the tradition of other
Jewish apocalyptists beginning in the Old Testament (OT) and stretching
down through John the Baptist to Paul the Apostle. These apocalyptists all
predicted an impending apocalypse, or ending of the world. I'll argue that
Jesus was a *failed* apocalyptic prophet because the "Son of Man" did not
come in his generation as predicted, nor did the consummation of the ages,
also known as the *eschaton*, from which we get the word eschatology.

This presents Christians with a serious and even fatal problem for their
faith, which is largely unrelated to any skeptical doubts about the possibility of miracles. We can derive this conclusion from the relevant texts
themselves. Either Jesus was a failed prophet or the NT isn't even somewhat reliable. Either way, this falsifies Christianity. If we cannot trust the
NT, then the basis for Christian beliefs fail. But if Jesus was an apocalyptic
prophet, then surely he wouldn't get something so important so dead
wrong.[1]

Jewish/Christian apocalyptic writings are encoded revelations using cryptic signs that predict an impending apocalypse. The authors describe horrible events to fall on pagans who are not among God's chosen ones. They express a sort of verbal eschatological revenge upon their oppressors for their wicked deeds. After the apocalypse is to take place, they also predicted the establishment of God's new kingdom on a new, refashioned earth with God's people reigning over the nations.[2]

To see a history of these types of apocalyptic movements since the days of Jesus, I recommend Jonathon Kirsch's readable and illuminating book, *The History of the End of the World*.[3] From the Montanists in the early second century CE to modern writers like Hal Lindsey, author of *The Late Great Planet Earth*, and in almost every generation in between, there have been millenarian predictions of the consummation of the ages. In our day, Tim LaHaye and Jerry B. Jenkins have vividly described the supposed impending doom of the world and the coming again of Jesus in their *Left Behind* book series.

Various millenarian doomsday prophets have set dates for the apocalyptic end of the world in the great and final battle of Armageddon. They have also played what Jonathon Kirsch calls "pin the tail on the anti-Christ"[4] by naming people from the Pope to Mohammed, Napoleon, Hitler, Mussolini, Henry Kissinger, Saddam Hussein and even Barack Obama as the anti-Christ. Some of these cult movements have been violent and dangerous, like those initiated by Charles Manson, Jim Jones, David Koresh, and Marshall Applewhite.

Given the propensity of human beings to be fascinated with the end of the world, and given the many doomsday prophets throughout history, it should not surprise us if the Jesus cult movement was just another one of them. These predictions and movements are a dime a dozen, so to speak, and to this date they have all been wrong. At best, the Jesus cult fits this same profile. And its predictions failed, too.

JESUS WAS AN APOCALYPTIC PROPHET

There has been a great deal of scholarly work done to try to find the core of who Jesus was and what his central message was, if he had one at all. He is thought of as a Jewish cynic, a wise sage, a mystic, a miracle worker, a social reformer, a revolutionary liberationist, the Son of God, and even a fictional character.[5] Attempting to figure out who was the "real" Jesus is difficult because, as John P. Meier reminds us, "the vast majority" of his deeds and words are "irrevocably lost to us today."[6] Nonetheless, the dominant view among mainline Christian theologians ever since Albert Schweitzer's 1906 masterpiece, *The Quest of the Historical Jesus*, is that Jesus was an apocalyptic prophet. Some of the most important modern defenders of such a view are E. P. Sanders in *The Historical Figure of Jesus*;[7] Dale C. Allison in *Jesus of Nazareth: Millenarian Prophet*;[8] Bart D. Ehrman in *Jesus: Apocalyptic Prophet of the New Millennium*;[9] and Paula Fredriksen in *From Jesus to Christ: The Origins of the New Testament Images of Jesus*.[10]

To understand who Jesus was and what he may have said, scholars use several different criteria to distinguish between what he may have actually said from what was placed on his lips by the Gospel redactors in a post-Jesus setting when the concerns of the church took priority. Criteria such as "coherence" with other sayings, "dissimilarity" with the surrounding culture, "multiple attestation" in the various strata of Gospel development, and "embarrassment" are all used in combination to determine this. But before scholars can actually use these criteria, they need some overall understanding of the major themes in the Gospels themselves.

Dale Allison of Pittsburgh Theological Seminary contends that "our first move is not to discover which sayings...are authentic. Rather we should be looking for something akin to what Thomas Kuhn once called a 'paradigm,' an explanatory model or matrix by which to order our data." This means that the "initial task is to create a context, a primary frame of reference, for the Jesus tradition, a context that may assist us in determining both the authenticity of traditions and their interpretation." He continues: "It would seem to follow that we should initially be concerned less with refining our criteria of authenticity than with worrying about how to establish a story that can usefully arrange our mass of data into coherent patterns." Therefore, he argues, "we should not attempt to determine the authenticity of items within the Jesus tradition until we have established an interpretative framework."[11]

The best interpretative framework to understand Jesus is within the context of the Jewish apocalypticism of his day, if we're to understand him at all. We see Jewish apocalypticism everywhere, stemming from such texts as Isaiah 24–27, Daniel, Zechariah 9–14, parts of 1 Enoch, Sibylline Oracles, the Testament of Moses, 4th Ezra, 2nd Baruch and the Apocalypse of Abraham. The Dead Sea Scrolls show apocalyptic elements in them, especially the War Scroll, where there is a war between the "children of the light" and the "children of darkness," during which God intervenes in the seventh battle and the Sons of Light are given their victory.[12] Paula Fredriksen tells us that both the Essenes (who probably had a community at Qumran) and the Pharisees embraced the apocalyptic. The Essenes "saw themselves as living on the edge of time, in the very last days; and they dedicated every moment and aspect of life to preparing, after their fashion, for the coming Kingdom of God." The Pharisees "were as much touched by eschatological hopes as most other Jewish groups."[13] So, in this contextual milieu, it's not difficult at all to think Jesus believed and taught what others did in his day. In fact, this is what we would expect to find. To say otherwise would require evidence to the contrary. But the evidence from the NT is against claiming otherwise.

When we first turn to the canonical Gospels, we notice that Jesus is a baptized convert to John the Baptist and his apocalyptic message. John preached that the long-awaited hope for the restoration of Israel was coming soon: "the kingdom of God was at hand" (Matthew 3:1–2). His message was of an impending judgmental warning to unrepentant sinners to repent and "flee from the coming wrath" of God, because God's judgmental "axe is already at the root of the trees..." (Luke 3:7–9). After Jesus was baptized by John, we see him taking up John's message when he preached: "'The time has come,' he [Jesus] said. 'The kingdom of God is near. Repent and believe the good news!'" (Mark 1:15).

Jesus is often compared to Judas the Galilean (6 CE), John the Baptist (30 CE), and Theudas (45 CE), who all shared a fundamental eschatological hope for the restoration of Israel to be the light unto the nations.[14] Since this was the whole contextual milieu of that day, it would be extremely odd if we found that the NT writers, beginning with Paul, believed such a hope was to be fulfilled in their generation if Jesus didn't also think so. That Jesus carried on John the Baptist's message in his ministry can be seen in eight dominant themes appearing over and over in the NT. Allison documents them in a descending scale beginning with the ones emphasized the most: (1) the kingdom of God, (2) future reward, (3) future judgment, (4) persecution of the saints, (5) victory over evil powers, (6) a sense that something new is here or at hand, (7) the importance of John the Baptist, and (8) reference to the "Son of Man." Allison argues that these eight major themes "readily invite an eschatological interpretation. When put together, they foretell a utopia, labeled 'the kingdom (of God).'... We have here the standard pattern of Jewish messianism, which is also found in millennial movements worldwide—a time of tribulation followed by a time of unprecedented blessedness."[15] Allison admits the conclusion about Jesus and his millenarian cult "is not the verdict reached by self-evident steps from self-evident truths and clear observations," yet he argues that "the millenarian Jesus is indeed almost, if not quite, clear to demonstration."[16]

The most essential element in an eschatological prophetic community is a charismatic leader who makes a prediction of an impending doom in the immediate future. Without this prediction there would be no sense of urgency, no need to form a community, and no need to prepare for it in the present. It must be near. It must be soon. It must be an immediate concern. Allison tells us: "The expectation of supernatural renewal in the offing is one of the central energizing elements in all millenarian movements, which typically expect imminent, total, ultimate, this-worldly collective salvation."[17]

In what has become known as the "Olivet Discourse" or the "Little Apocalypse," in Mark chapter 13, we find Jesus instructing his disciples about the time when the temple would be destroyed and the "Son of Man" is to come. Making a crystal-clear reference to a prophecy in the book of Daniel (9:26–27) about "the abomination that causes desolation" (Mark 13:14) referring to the destruction of Jerusalem in 70 CE (cf. Matt 24:25, Luke 21:20), Jesus tells his disciples that the "Son of Man" will come shortly afterward:

> But in those days, following that distress, the sun will be darkened, and the moon will not give its light; the stars will fall from the sky, and the heavenly bodies will be shaken. At that time men will see the Son of Man coming in clouds with great power and glory. And he will send his angels and gather his elect from the four winds, from the ends of the earth to the ends of the heavens. Now learn this lesson from the fig tree: As soon as its twigs get tender and its leaves come out, you know that summer is near. Even so, when you see these things happening, you know that it is near, right at the door. I tell you the truth, this generation will certainly not pass away until all these things have happened. (Mark 13:24–31)

Given what we know about the apocalyptic milieu in which Jesus preached, and granting that this passage at least derives from a tradition that stems from the lips of Jesus, as I'm doing in this chapter,[18] his disciples would understand exactly what he meant. The sign of the coming "Son of Man" was the distress and tribulation surrounding the destruction of

Jerusalem in 70 CE. The lesson of the fig tree merely reinforces the point that just as they can predict when summer is coming because the fig leaves blossom, so also can they know the "Son of Man" is coming when Jerusalem is destroyed. And as such, the very generation of people living in his day will witness this apocalyptic event, which clearly echoes what we read earlier in Mark 9:1 when Jesus says to his disciples, "I tell you the truth, some who are standing here will not taste death before they see the kingdom of God come with power" (cf. Matthew 16:28, Luke 9:27).

Theologians have tried to construe the word "generation" in the "Little Apocalypse" to mean "race," as in, "this race of people will certainly not pass away until all these things have happened." But that is not the obvious, natural reading, given the whole context. Edward Adams, senior lecturer in New Testament studies at King's College, London, states it forthrightly: "It is virtually certain that 'this generation' means the generation living at the time of utterance. The time frame in this verse is thus the lifetime of Jesus' own contemporaries."[19] The translation "race" wouldn't make any sense here anyway, since one wonders with Robert Price, what would be the sense of saying: "'This race of people will not pass away before all these things transpire,' if 'these things' included the testing and salvation of this very race."[20] Besides, no Jew of that day would ever consider the possibility that his or her race of people could ever "pass away," given their assuredness of special divine promises of permanence, as we shall see.

The imminence of the *eschaton* is further reflected in Matthew's Gospel when Jesus is found saying to his disciples: "I tell you the truth, you will not finish going through the cities of Israel before the Son of Man comes" (10:23). Speaking to the Sanhedrin during his trial, Jesus reportedly said, "you will see the Son of Man sitting at the right hand of the Mighty One and coming on the clouds of heaven." (Mark 14:16; cf. Matthew 26:64). The meaning is obvious.

The rest of the NT writers interpreted Jesus in this natural way. The apostle Paul, himself an apocalyptist, was the first NT author to reassure believers that while some time has passed since the days of Jesus and though some have died, "the day of the Lord" will still take place suddenly, without warning, any day, like "a thief in the night" (1 Thessalonians 5:1–2). Paul even expected that some of the people he was writing to would still be alive to experience the coming of the Lord (1 Thessalonians 4:15), including himself. Elsewhere Paul also writes:

What I mean, brothers, is that the time is short. From now on those who have wives should live as if they had none; those who mourn, as if they did not; those who are happy, as if they were not; those who buy something, as if it were not theirs to keep; those who use the things of the world, as if not engrossed in them. For this world in its present form is passing away. (1 Corinthians 7:29; cf. 1 Corinthians 15:20, 2 Corinthians 6:2, Romans 13:11) (See note.)[21]

Later we find the author of 1 John saying he knows it's the "last hour" and even expects to be alive when "the Holy One" comes (2:18, 28). Still later we have the author of the book of Revelation repeatedly saying that the "time is near" or that Jesus will be coming "soon" (1:1; 3:11; 22:6–7, 10, 12, 20).

The imminent coming of the *eschaton* is reinforced by the radical "interim ethic" we find in the Gospels as well. Jesus tells his disciples such things as to sell all and give to the poor (Luke 12:33), which would serve the double purpose of helping the poor and preparing their own hearts for the *eschaton*. He told his disciples not to worry at all about the future (Matthew 6:34), to follow him immediately rather than take the time to bury a father (Matthew 8:22), and to forsake and even hate their parents for him (Matthew 10:37). According to Bart Ehrman, Jesus "urged his followers to abandon their homes and forsake families for the sake of the kingdom that was soon to arrive. He didn't encourage people to pursue fulfilling careers, make a good living, and work for a just society for the long haul; for him, there wasn't going to be a long haul."[22] This best explains why Jesus' ethic isn't livable, as much as Christian commentators have tried to make it appear so, because there was a "long haul" after all.[23]

RECENT OBJECTIONS

Until 1994, James Charlesworth, an internationally recognized expert in Jesus research, could claim that "One of the strongest consensuses in New Testament research is that Jesus' mission was to proclaim the dawning of God's Rule, the Kingdom of God. Research on Mark 9:1 has convinced virtually every specialist that Jesus' teaching was emphatically apocalyptic and eschatological."[24] But even as he wrote this, several scholars were already calling this picture of Jesus into question, such that there is more to Jesus than just that of an apocalyptic prophet. Jesus also advocated social reform. It's now argued that a doomsday prophet with hopes of an other-worldly existence would not be a social reformer. So David Gowler tells us in a 2007 book that: "Any portrait of the historical Jesus must come to terms with Jesus as both an apocalyptic prophet and a prophet of social and economic justice for oppressed people. Any portrait that does not integrate both these aspects generates a caricature of Jesus of Nazareth."[25]

Because Jesus was interested in social reform, Marcus Borg who is one of the leading pioneers of this recent scholarship, argued that Jesus must have rejected John's apocalyptic message sometime during his ministry, but that his disciples later adopted it again.[26] In other words, for some un-explained reason, Jesus rejected John's message in the middle of his ministry, and then for another unexplained reason his disciples later rejected Jesus' message to revert back to an apocalyptic one. Dale Allison argues that such a scenario is improbable because "it posits two discontinuities." He writes: "My reconstruction more simply posits a continuity that is in line not only with John's baptism of Jesus but with the fact that Christianity's oldest extant document explicitly attributes its apocalyptic scenario to Jesus (1 Thessalonians 4:13–5:11, see 4:15)."[27] About this, E. P. Sanders likewise argues: "It is almost impossible to explain these historical facts on the assumption that Jesus himself did not expect the imminent end or transformation of the present world order"; such "desperate" measures like these he said, merely show "the triumph of wishful thinking."[28]

In any case, the unified scholarly consensus no longer exists. So in 2008, fourteen years after telling of a unified consensus, Charlesworth offered a more nuanced view by maintaining that "leading scholars" still think the primary mission of Jesus "was to declare the coming Kingdom of God or, better, God's Rule."[29] And Charlesworth still claims "Jesus' authentic message was fundamentally eschatological," because for Jesus:

> All time, past and present, was focused on the immediate present. The attempts to understand Jesus' eschatology and discern the time of the fulfillment of God's Rule have myopically focused on the Greek New Testament text. Greek has a temporal sense of past, present, and future. Jesus perceived time in Semitic concepts: fulfilled time and unfulfilled time. Thus, Jesus imagined God's Rule as a mixture as fulfilled and unfulfilled time in the present. He could ponder a future action as fulfilled, as did the prophets when they perceived how God had completed a task that has not yet been experienced by humans.[30]

Charlesworth argues that Jesus' teaching (especially in some parables) "is often a mixture of realizing eschatology and futuristic eschatology," but it's eschatology just the same, even if Jesus didn't have "a preoccupation with the end of time."[31] Furthermore he says: "we should not expect Jesus to be a systematic theologian, or one who was not human. Surely, the historian is not the only one who can imagine a first-century prophet at times thinking that God's Rule was soon to be fully present and at other times pondering that only God knows that time."[32]

So even if there is no "thoroughgoing eschatology" found in Jesus or in the NT, as Schweitzer claimed, "leading scholars" still think eschatology is a dominant theme. And I don't see a real problem in combining Jesus' role as a social reformer with his apocalyptic message anyway. Dale Allison, probably the leading scholar in the field, shows how Jesus could be both:

> He did not proclaim the wonderful things to come and then pass by on the other side of the road. He rather turned his eschatological ideal into an ethical blueprint for compassionate ministry in the present, which means that, in addition to saying that things would get better, he set out making it so. Jesus' eschatological hope and his humanitarianism cannot be sundered because they were both products of his infatuation with divine love. God's loving devotion to the world requires that it not suffer disrepair forever, and God's love shed abroad in human hearts ... cannot wait for heaven to come to earth: it must, therefore, before the end, feed the hungry and clothe the naked.[33]

Allison further argues that:

> Consistency is the hobgoblin of non-apocalyptic minds. And if [Jesus] was a social prophet, that does not exclude his having been an apocalyptic prophet. Others have been both. The reason is obvious: as eschatological expectation and instruction cannot cover all of life, no successful apocalyptic prophet can afford to be a monomaniac. So using a criterion of consistency to delete apocalyptic elements from Jesus' speech because they contradict the sapiential elements is no more plausible than arguing that people who pray for God to heal them cannot go to the doctor, or that those who teach that Jesus will come again cannot insist that even now he lives in their hearts.[34]

In fact, since the eschatological kingdom was expected soon and since entrance into it demanded repentance, as John the Baptist and Jesus both preached, then we would expect Jesus to be a social reformer who preached and practiced social justice, just like the prophets of old (Micah 6:8). Doing so was required of someone who desired to be part of the new, coming, eschatological kingdom. Jesus is found to be saying this eschatological event could happen any day and will definitely happen in his generation. *Since Jesus is only found to be saying that his generation would see this event rather than predicting the very day it will happen (Matthew 24:36), there is still a reason to do justice on earth while waiting for it.* Case in point is that televangelists like Pat Robertson and his ilk are part of the "Christian Right" which seeks sociopolitical change, and yet they also think Jesus will come soon, probably in our generation.

JESUS WAS A *FAILED* APOCALYPTIC PROPHET

So if Jesus was an apocalyptic prophet, then he was a failed one, just like every other doomsday prophet in history—before and after him. The eminent New Testament scholar, James D. G. Dunn, admits this in what is surely to be his *magnum opus*: "Jesus had entertained hopes which were not fulfilled. There were 'final' elements in his expectation which were not realized. Putting it bluntly, Jesus was proved wrong by the course of events."[35] And yet the Jesus cult survived even after these failed predictions. But that isn't too unusual. Many cult groups survive after experiencing a failed prophecy of the end of times. Whether or not they survive depends on how they reinterpret what took place. The survival of the cult group depends on how they view the failed prophecy from hindsight. To understand this when it comes to the Jesus cult we need some historical background.

After the destruction of Jerusalem and deportation of Jewish leaders to Babylon in 586 BCE, the prophet Jeremiah spoke of seventy years for the restoration of Israel (25:11–12; 29:10) with a new covenant (chapter 31). Prophetic numbers like these were not meant to be taken literally, since the number seven symbolizes completeness while seventy is roughly the span of a man's life. Nonetheless, it was a serious problem for later Jews as the years passed and it wasn't fulfilled. The Davidic dynasty, after all, was supposed to be an eternal one (2 Samuel 7:11–16, Psalm 89:36–37), but it was never reestablished as predicted (Jeremiah 33:14–18; Isaiah. 11:1–9;

Ezekiel 34:22–24, 37:24; Micah 5:2). So in trying to make prophesy fit, the prophets Haggai (2:20–23) and Zechariah (4: 6:9–13) both claimed that in their day Zerubbabel was going to be the Messiah. Since this didn't turn out as predicted, the prophetic institution was thrown into a crisis. This crisis first started when the monarchy ceased to exist, since the monarchy both legitimized the prophetic institution and provoked it due to kingly transgressions. Jeremiah's failed prophecy was the final straw that forced the later pseudonymous author of Zechariah 13:2–5[36] and Malachi (4:4–5) to say prophecy would cease until such time as the final prophet would come (cf. 1 Maccabees 4:46; 9:27). When prophecy ceased, there was a corresponding rise of apocalyptic literature. Apocalyptic literature predicted the coming apocalypse, unlike prophetic literature, which stressed immediate judgments upon people who were unfaithful to God's covenant. Apocalyptic literature expressed in cryptic language the next thing on God's timetable, the full restoration of Israel and the Davidic dynasty in a Messiah who would reign over all the nations.

Four centuries had gone by after Jeremiah's prophecy, and no fulfillment was in sight. The first fully apocalyptic book was Daniel, in which we see Jeremiah's prophecy altered to mean something different. It was not meant to be "seventy years," but rather "seventy weeks of years" (Daniel 9:25–27). This meant the prophecy was to be fulfilled in the second century BCE, when the book of Daniel was composed.[37] Old Testament scholar Bernard Anderson explains Daniel's prophecy:

> The first seven weeks (49 years) apparently extend from king Zedikiah to Joshua the High Priest (587–538 BCE), who was in office in the days of Cyrus; the sixty-two weeks (435 years) extend from the return from the Exile to the assassination of the High Priest Onias III (538–171 BCE); and the last week covers the reign of Antiochus Epiphanes. During the first half of this week (171–168 BCE), Antiochus showed some lenience toward the Jews; but during the last half (168–164 BCE), in which the author of Daniel was living, Antiochus attempted to abolish Jewish religion and desecrated the Temple by installing an altar to Zeus of Olympus…which came to be, by a malicious pun, "the abomination of desolation."[38]

But the prophesied restoration of Israel and the apocalyptic *eschaton* did not happen in that day either. Even an evangelical like Kenton L. Sparks admits this: "It is to my mind that it is quite clear that the author of

Daniel, like the authors of countless other Jewish apocalypses, expected the kingdom of God to appear in his lifetime... these expectations clearly turned out to be incorrect.... in fact we are still waiting for it.[39]

That this was still a problem in the first two centuries CE is evidenced by the fact that apocalyptic hopes like these incited several Jewish eschatological movements. There were the Zealots and the Sicarii in the days of Jesus, who had a role to play in the *Great Jewish Revolt* against Roman rule, which led to the fall of Jerusalem in 70 CE, and the massacre at Masada in 74 CE. Then Esdras, writing in about 90 CE, was given a divine interpretation of a vision he had: "The eagle, whom thou sawest come up from the sea, is the kingdom which was seen in the vision of thy brother Daniel. But it was not expounded unto him, therefore now I declare it unto thee" (2 Esdras 12:10–12). And he does, but this won't detain us here only to note his prophecy failed as well. These apocalyptic hopes also inspired the Bar Kokhba Revolt (ca. 132–136 CE). Simon bar Kokhba, the commander of the revolt, was proclaimed the long-awaited Messiah who would restore the Jewish people to rule over the nations. Some of these movements were violent ones in the hopes of providing the faithful spark that would ignite God's wrath. Others were quietist ones like the Jesus cult. Stemming from John the Baptist, they called people to repent and be baptized in order to prepare themselves for what God himself was about to do for them. In these apocalyptic movements we find some divergences of opinion, true, but as Fredriksen argues, they all shared "the belief that the End was fast approaching and the final restoration of Israel was at hand.... The forces of good will utterly vanquish the hostile powers, demonic or human, and the Kingdom of God will finally, truly be established."[40]

In the NT, about six centuries after Jeremiah's prophecy and two centuries after the book of Daniel, it was claimed that Jesus was the predicted prophet "like unto Moses" (Acts 3:20–22, see Deuteronomy 18:18). According to the Gospel of Luke, Jesus came to announce that these things were starting to be fulfilled in his own day in what is known as his "Nazareth Manifesto" sermon (Luke 4:14–21). It was to be an eschatological *Jubilee* (cf. Leviticus 25:13; Isaiah 58:6, 61:1–11) where the captives would be set free and the land would be given back to Israel, its rightful owners. Israel would finally be restored to her glory in the coming new age.[41]

But if we grant that this original prediction stems from Jesus, it "was continually threatened by the simple passage of time," argues Fredriksen. "Successive disappointments gave rise to new interpretations as the tradition reworked what was too central to relinquish." "Reconceiving Jesus and the Kingdom, Christian tradition in various ways continually adjusted itself... as its central prophecy failed. And as part of its adjustment to this unexpected future, the tradition grew away from its own past."[42]

The apostle Paul was the first person to reinterpret the failed prophecy gradually in his own lifetime. He had expected to see an immediate apocalyptic *eschaton,* as already noted in his earlier letters. So how did Paul sustain such a belief through twenty-five years of preaching? Fredriksen makes a plausible case that he did so because he came to believe that through his ministry to the Gentiles he was helping to bring in the *eschaton.* When he completes his ministry the end will come when God will save "all Israel" by "an eschatological miracle."[43] Thus, "The interim before the Kingdom came would last as long as Paul's mission itself."[44] Only when the "full number of the Gentiles" came into God's kingdom through Paul's ministry would the End come (Romans 11:25).

Paul's view came about during the debates he had with the "circumcision party" over the fact that there were "Too many Gentiles, too few Jews, and no End in sight."[45] The circumcision party argued that only after the Kingdom came "would Gentiles as such be redeemed." So they blamed Paul for the fact that the Kingdom had not yet appeared because he was not reaching out to Israel. Paul came to see this problem differently. The reason why the End had not come and the reason why the Jews were not responsive to the Gospel was because this was all part of God's plan. God hardened the hearts of the Jews so that through Paul's ministry God would save the full number of Gentiles, and then the End would come (Romans 9–11). But Paul died and the End didn't come.

With Mark's "Little Apocalypse," as we saw earlier, Daniel's prophecy was altered to foretell the destruction of Jerusalem soon after Jesus' own time (later to be destroyed in 70 CE), which was a prelude for the *eschaton* to happen in a few years.[46] Yet this too did not happen. So by virtue of "the criterion of embarrassment," we find evidence that later NT authors altered and tried to explain away this failed prophecy of Jesus.[47] They did so in the exact same manner that the multitude of other failed millenarian prophetic groups have done. This is an essential element for surviving as a group after such a failed prophecy did not materialize, and this is what we see time and again with regard to these types of failed prophecies in the Bible. The biblical writers progressively changed their position regarding the *eschaton* and the restoration of Israel, just as Paul before them did.[48]

After Mark's Gospel there are subtle changes made with each subsequent canonical Gospel, as the prophesied *eschaton* did not happen. The Gospel of Matthew, written decades after Mark, makes subtle changes to the text. In Mark's Gospel the disciples asked a question specifically about the destruction of the temple: "Tell us, when will these things happen? And what will be the sign that they are all about to be fulfilled?" (13:4) Nothing was asked about the coming of the "Son of Man" or the end of the age because it was assumed that the destruction of the temple and Jerusalem would be the only signs needed for when the "Son of Man" would come. But in Matthew's Gospel the disciples ask not only about the destruction of the temple in Jerusalem, but now they additionally ask Jesus about the sign of "your coming" along with the end of the age (24:3). In Matthew's Gospel more than just the destruction of the temple was needed as a sign for the end of the age and the coming of the "Son of Man." The reason is because by the time Matthew's Gospel was written, the temple had already been destroyed and the *eschaton* had not yet happened.

While Mark's Gospel merely told believers to be on guard while waiting for this eschatological event (13:33), Matthew's Gospel elaborates on this warning for almost an entire chapter in three parables (24:45–25:30). Matthew agrees with Mark that this series of events will happen in that generation, of course (24:34), it's just that the goal posts have been moved. In his day there is more of a need to stress patience than before, since the faithful are becoming impatient. And according to Matthew when the "Son of Man" comes, he will reward the righteous with the kingdom and cast the unrighteous into eternal fire (25:31–46). These are events which were to follow immediately upon his coming, since that's the progression of the events depicted in Matthew.

In the even later two-part Luke–Acts we find the goal posts are moved a little further. Luke drops a few words from what we first read in Mark 9:1, where Mark's Jesus says, "I tell you the truth, some who are standing here will not taste death before they see the kingdom of God *come with power*" [emphasis added]. The last three words are missing in Luke's version (9:27). As far as Luke is concerned, the disciples were *not* promised that they would see the kingdom "come with power." Of this slight but "huge" difference, Ehrman tells us that with the deletion of these three words Luke's Jesus, "does not predict the imminent arrival of the Kingdom in *power*, but simply says that the disciples (in some sense) will see the Kingdom."[49] Luke also attempts to distance Jesus from the erroneous expectation that the kingdom appearing in power will take place immediately by blaming such a false expectation on others when introducing the parable of the ten minas: "While they were listening to this, [Jesus] went on to tell them a parable, because he was near Jerusalem and the people thought that the kingdom of God was going to appear at once" (19:11).

And the disciples do indeed see the kingdom according to Luke. They already experienced it since they were personally with the Messiah-king, Jesus: "Once, having been asked by the Pharisees when the kingdom of God would come, Jesus replied, 'The kingdom of God does not come with your careful observation, nor will people say, "Here it is," or "There it is," because the kingdom of God is within (i.e., 'among') you'" (Luke 17:20–21). So Luke first introduces a distinction between the "already here" and the "not yet." The kingdom was "already here" Luke says, even though the kingdom coming with "power" had not yet happened. This same distinction is something we see reflected in the later non-Pauline letter of Ephesians (2:6) and in Hebrews (12:22–24), although these authors believed in a future *eschaton* as well (cf. Ephesians 1:10, Hebrews 10:37–38). Of this change of perspective Bart Ehrman stresses:

> Luke continues to think that the end of the age is going to come in his own lifetime. But he does *not* seem to think that it was supposed to come in the lifetime of Jesus' companions. Why not? Evidently because he was writing after they had died, and he knew that in fact the end had not come. To deal with the "delay of the end," he made the appropriate changes in Jesus' predictions.[50]

Some scholars conclude from Luke 17:20–21 that Jesus was not an apocalyptic prophet, but this is a slender reed to hang that conclusion on (just two verses). Bart Ehrman tells us that this saying "is found only in Luke (i.e., it is not multiply attested), a Gospel, as we've seen, that went some way to tone down the apocalyptic dimensions of our earlier sources."[51] For these reasons, E. P. Sanders does not think Jesus even spoke these words, but even if so, "they cannot be used to prove that he said nothing about a future cosmic event." For as Sanders argues, "one cannot take Luke 17:20–21 as canceling out the large number of sayings about the future kingdom—including those that immediately follow in Luke." (i.e., 22–37).[52] In my opinion, the two similar verses in the Gnostic *Gospel of Thomas* (3, 113) also alter what Jesus predicted, as did Luke, since it was written early in the second century.[53]

We find the final word of Jesus on the topic from the author of Luke–Acts just before he ascended into heaven. We see the disciples asking Jesus, "Lord, are you at this time going to restore the kingdom to Israel?" (see Acts 1:6–8). Here we see that the disciples didn't think Jeremiah or Daniel's prophecies had been fulfilled yet, otherwise why would they be asking about the restoration of Israel? The author of Acts simply has Jesus responding that the disciples should not be concerned with the timing of the prophecy but instead focus on their mission with the help of the coming Holy Spirit. Two chapters later, Peter is reported to say that Jesus "must remain in heaven until the time comes for God to restore everything, as he promised long ago through his holy prophets" (Acts 3:21). So according to what the author of Acts tells us, by putting these specific words on the lips of Peter, the *eschaton* was not supposed to happen in Peter's lifetime, but rather sometime in the future. What started out as an urgent call to action based upon an immediate *eschaton* has now been altered to cover up a failed prophecy.

Such talk of an imminent *eschaton* is completely removed in John's Gospel. In Dale Allison's words, this Gospel: "focuses not on Jesus coming on the clouds of heaven in the future but on the Spirit coming to believers in the present. It emphasizes not that the dead will someday arise but rather that the living can even now enjoy eternal life. It teaches not the impending defeat of evil in a cosmic judgment but the routing of the devil at Jesus' crucifixion." It's as though the "Evangelist systematically set out to translate the literal into the figurative, sought to reinterpret, in terms of present religious experience, the apocalyptic mythology he found in the Jesus tradition."[54]

Indeed! At the end of the Gospel of John we even see an attempt to explain away the fact that the last living "disciple whom Jesus loved" had died without these predictions coming true. Since Jesus had said his disciples would see the *eschaton* in their day (cf. Mark 9:1, 13:30; Matthew 10:23) "a rumor" started that this last disciple would not die before it took place. This presented a serious problem to the church as the disciples began to die out one by one until the only one still alive was the "disciple whom Jesus loved." To dispel such a rumor we're told this: "Jesus did not say that he would not die; he only said, 'If I want him to remain alive until I return, what is that to you?'" (John 21:20–23).

E. P. Sanders sums what happened so far in these words: "Jesus originally said that the Son of Man would come in the immediate future, while his hearers were alive." After Jesus died and after they claimed he resurrected, Sanders continues:

[H]is followers preached that he would return immediately—that is, they simply interpreted "the Son of Man" as referring to Jesus himself. Then, when people started dying, they said that some would still be alive. When almost the entire first generation was dead, they maintained that one disciple would still be alive. Then he died, and it became necessary to claim that Jesus had not actually promised even this one disciple that he would live to see that great day.[55]

In the book of Revelation the author moves the goal posts a little farther. In chapter 13 we find a beast who is identified with the Roman Emperor Nero, through the cipher language of using numbers to double as letters, called gematria, so that 666 adds up to Nero Caesar (13:18). So if Revelation was written during Nero's reign, then the *eschaton* had a statute of limitations with the people alive at that time. If, however, as Bart Ehrman and others argue, parts of Revelation were written in the 60s CE, during Nero's reign (ca. 54–68 CE) before the destruction of Jerusalem, and subsequently edited at the end of Domitian's reign around 95–96 CE, then an older tradition formed the basis of the present book (see note).[56] This older tradition was reworked to show that the *eschaton* would instead take place during Domitian's reign because it didn't take place during Nero's reign as previously predicted. The connection between the two rulers was easy enough to make, since it was believed Nero would return from the dead to persecute the faithful once again,[57] and because Domitian reinstated Nero's persecutions. In any case, the author assures us that this event was to happen "soon," in his day. But it did not happen.

Later, when the pseudonymous second letter to the Thessalonians was written at the end of the first century[58] to reassure Christians that Jesus would indeed return, unlike some who thought he had already done so (2:1–2), and unlike others who quit their jobs to wait for it to happen (3:6–15), additional signs must take place first. A rebellion must take place and "the man of sin" be revealed who will "exalt himself over everything that is God" (2:3–12). And although the power of this "man of sin" (or anti-Christ) is already at work in the world, he is being held back until the "proper time" when he will be revealed and later destroyed when Jesus returns in glory.

By the time the even later second-century pseudonymous Epistle of 2 Peter was written,[59] scoffers were mocking the claim that Jesus would soon return. Christians themselves were doing the scoffing since this letter was written to admonish them. These things were an embarrassment to the church of that time. The answer given was that with the Lord, "a day is like a thousand years, and a thousand years are like a day. The Lord is not slow in keeping his promise, as some understand slowness...the day of the Lord will come like a thief" (2 Peter 3:3–10). This answer falls on deaf ears. It comes across as an excuse for why the *eschaton* didn't occur in the very generation Jesus said it would. This is just what apocalyptic movements do with the prophetic texts when their prophecies fail. They use what has been aptly described as "secondary exegesis" (à la Dale Allison) to reinterpret them, and this is exactly what we see in the NT.

CHRISTIANS HAVE FAILED TO EXPLAIN AWAY THIS FAILED PROPHECY

My working hypothesis has been that the best explanation for the different claims in the NT of the timing of the *eschaton* is because later authors kept moving the goal posts as time marched on. By contrast, we have a splintered array of eschatological theories coming from Christians who are trying to interpret and harmonize the NT with itself as if it were the inspired word of God and consistent in every respect. In light of nearly two thousand years and no return of Jesus in sight, Christian eschatological theories are in a major crisis.

One way to observe whether a theory is in crisis is to note how many versions of that theory there are. When it comes to Christian eschatology, there are Historicist, Preterist, Futurist, and Idealist versions of it. Specific millennial views include premillenialism, postmillennialism, and amillennialism. Then there is dispensational premillenialism with pre-, mid-, and post-tribulational rapture viewpoints, even though there is no room in the NT for the idea of a rapture separated from the final *eschaton*.[60] There also are partial and full preterist views. There are so many questions and disputes between Christians over this issue that the evidence seems clear: attempts to harmonize the statements in the NT are a failure. Christians misunderstand what is going on in the NT writings themselves. The authors were reinterpreting these prophecies just like every failed doomsday cult has done in order to survive as a community. Dale Allison reminds us that these "after the fact rationalizations are almost inevitable: it is easier to deceive oneself than to admit self-deception."[61] And he argues the "evidence that this happened in early Christianity is substantial."[62]

Today's Christian doomsday prophets are doing the same things we have seen ever since Jeremiah issued his prophecy of the restoration of Israel. They dodge the impact of the NT texts describing an imminent *eschaton* with a coming "Son of Man" by claiming God's clock stopped with the advent of the church and will start up again in the last days when the tribulation begins, called the *Great Parenthesis*. Or they'll claim that when God's word says "soon" it's from God's perspective rather than ours. Robert Price counters such nonsense:

> But what sort of revelation is it that is couched in terms unintelligible to those for whose sake it is vouchsafed? Given God's infinite expanse of cosmic eons, what could "soon" possibly mean if it bears no relation to our own use of the word? After all, if God is talking to human beings, he has to use human terms if he wants to be understood. And if he really meant, "I am coming thousands of years in the future," why didn't he just say so?[63]

In our day a major reinterpretation of these prophecies has been offered by the Canon of Westminster, N. T. Wright, who argues in his book, *Jesus and the Victory of God*,[64] that the prophecies of Jesus took place in his generation just as Jesus predicted. He argues that what Jesus and the early Christians predicted was not a cosmic ending of the universe in their day, but rather socio-political and spiritual change. They used the apocalyptic language of cosmic destruction but applied it metaphorically, not literally, to describe the destruction of the temple and Jerusalem, which took place in 70 CE. The coming of the "Son of Man" was not about Jesus' second coming but rather about his coming into the presence of God after his sufferings. Jesus was vindicated by virtue of his resurrection from the dead and who was later manifested on earth in the destruction of Jerusalem. He is now reigning victorious over the world. The greatest enemy isn't the Roman occupiers but Satan and his cohorts. As such, the greatest battle is not against the Romans but the liberation from sin.

Christians fall into two groups based on Wright's arguments. Partial preterists claim there will be a future *parousia* (i.e., Jesus returning in the sky), while full preterists like Wright deny it. It's ironic that Wright hopes that with his construal of these prophecies it might lessen the conflict in the world (p. xv), but in fact it has done the exact opposite. Reconstructionists have adopted it to advocate a theocracy, like Gary Demar in *Last Days Madness: Obsession of the Modern Church American.*[65] Their argument is that if Jesus now reigns over the world, then he does so in part through Christians. What follows for them is that Jesus wants a theocracy.

While there are many nuances to his case, this will suffice for my critique of Wright, since it should be enough simply to show there is abundant evidence that the NT writers believed the language of cosmic catastrophe was to be taken literally, not metaphorically. They literally expected a cosmic conflagration at the predicted *eschaton*, which did not happen in their generation, contrary to Wright, and as such, the apocalyptic predictions of the *eschaton* could not have been fulfilled in their day.

The eschatological language in the NT was thought by the early church fathers as depicting literal cosmic events, as seen in Papias (as reported in Eusebius, *Ecclesiastical History* 3:39:12), Justin Martyr (*Dialogue with Trypho* 80), Irenaeus (*Against Heresies* 5:32–36), Tertullian (*Against Marcion* 3:24), the Montanists (Epiphanius, *Panarion.* 49:1:2–3), and Lactantius (*The Divine Institutions* 7:24–26). From all of this Allison says they "all believed, because they read their Bible literally, in a rather worldly millennium involving a transformation of the natural world."[66]

Given the cosmology of the Bible that Edward Babinski shows us in chapter 5, it's clear what believers would think of the following language in Mark 13:24: "But in those days, following that distress, the sun will be darkened, and the moon will not give its light; the stars will fall from the sky, and the heavenly bodies will be shaken." To people like Wright, who claim this language is metaphorical, Allison asks:

> Why then suppose that Mark 13:24 is less prosaic than, let us say, 1 Enoch 70:6, which foretells that one day the stars "will change their course and their activities, and will not appear at the times which have been proscribed for them," or that it is less realistic than *The Epistle of Barnabas* 15:8, which says that when the Son of God abolishes the time of the lawless one, God "will change the sun and the moon and stars," or that it is less literal than Lactantius, *Divine Institutions* 7:24, where we are told that, during the millennium, the moon will shine like the sun and the sun will be seven times brighter than it is now?[67]

While Allison admits there is indeed some metaphorical language in the Bible with regard to beasts and the moon turning into blood, he concludes:

> My own judgment is that we have so many similar texts because so many people have longed for the same thing, namely, supernatural judgment and repair of a fallen world; and it would strike me as peculiar to suppose that, whereas ancient Jews and Christians looked into the future and saw metaphorical darkness, metaphorical earthquakes, and metaphorical stars, so many others who have looked into the future have seen literal darkness, literal earthquakes, and literal stars.[68]

Edward Adams extensively documents these kinds of things more than sufficiently in his book, *The Stars Will Fall from Heaven: Cosmic Catastrophe in the New Testament and Its World*, as do Jonathan T. Pennington and Sean M. McDonough, editors of *Cosmology and New Testament Theology*.[69] It's hard to believe that Jesus didn't think the stars will fall from heaven on that day (Mark 13:24), or that the early Christians didn't think Jesus would literally come on the clouds and take Christians up into the air with him (e.g., Mark 13:26–27, Acts 1:9–11, 1 Thessalonians 4:13–18), with one person snatched away right next to others who are not taken, even from their very beds as they sleep (Matthew 24:36–44, Luke 17:26–35). The fact that no one would know the exact hour when this would happen (e.g., Mark 13:32–37) entails that a singular apocalyptic event was meant, which is contrary to Wright's hypothesis. It's also highly unlikely that the writer of Hebrews did not think the heavens (sky) and earth would be shaken (12:25–29, cf. 1:10–12), or that the author of 2 Peter did not think that "the earth will be burned up" (3:5–13), or that the author of Revelation did not think heaven would literally roll up like a scroll and that every mountain and island will be removed from its place on that day (6:12–17).

Clearly the events expected by Jesus and his followers were cosmic in scope, and soon to occur. It was not only going to be the end of all of the kingdoms of men on earth but a total cosmic catastrophe in which the stars literally fall from heaven and the present earth is burned up, after which God inaugurates a literal kingdom with the "Son of Man" reigning on a new earth from a new Jerusalem, in their very day. This prophesied event did not happen.

So Christians must choose. Either the NT isn't even somewhat reliable, or Jesus was a failed apocalyptic prophet. In either case this falsifies Christianity.

NOTES

1. I thank Dr. Felipe Leon for calling my attention to this whole problem, and I thank Richard Carrier for some helpful comments on this chapter. Paul Tobin has a good discussion of this issue in his book, *The Rejection of Pascal's Wager: A Skeptics Guide to the Historical Jesus* (Authors Online Book, 2009), pp. 455–70.

2. For a helpful description of Jewish apocalyptic literature, see John J. Collins, *The Apocalyptic Imagination: An Introduction to Jewish Apocalyptic Literature*, 2nd ed. (Grand Rapids, MI: Eerdmans, 1998). See also *The Encyclopedia of Apocalypticism*, vol. 1, *The Origins of Apocalypticism in Judaism and Christianity*, ed. John J. Collins (New York: Continuum International, 2000).

3. Kirsch, *History of the End* (New York: HarperCollins, 2006). See also Bernard McGinn et al., *The Continuum History of Apocalypticism* (New York: Continuum, 2003).

4. Kirsch, *History of the End*, p. 126.

5. Probably the best three books discussing the claim that Jesus was a fictional character are Robert M. Price, *Deconstructing Jesus* (Amherst, NY: Prometheus Books, 2000), Earl Doherty, *The Jesus Puzzle* (Ottawa: The Age of Reason Publications, 2005), and Richard Carrier, *On the Historicity of Jesus Christ*, forthcoming, which I have not yet seen.

It can be very difficult to establish what may have happened in the past, so agnosticism about the historicity of Jesus is a reasonable position. On the poor evidence of historical evidence, see chapter 8 in my book, *Why I Became an Atheist.* When it comes to the historicity of the founder of the Jesus cult, the dominant theory, in Earl Doherty's words, is this: "In their fervor and distress following the crucifixion, the followers of Jesus…ran to their Bibles and began to apply all manner of scriptural passages to him, especially those looked upon as messianic by the Jewish thinking of the time. But they turned as well to contemporary Hellenistic mythology about the Logos, supplementing it with the Jewish equivalent in the figure of personified Wisdom, throwing in for good measure…myths about descending-ascending heavenly redeemers." Earl Doherty argues instead for an alternative skeptical theory:

> [T]he Christian movement was not a response to any human individual at one time and location. Christianity was born in a thousand places, out of the fertile religious and philosophical soil of the time, expressing faith in an intermediary Son who was a channel to God, providing knowledge, love and salvation. It sprang up in many innovative minds like Paul's, among independent communities and sects all over the empire, producing a variety of forms and doctrines. Some of it tapped into tradi-

tional Jewish Messiah expectation and apocalyptic sentiment, other expressions were tied to more Platonic ways of thinking. Greek mystery concepts also fed into the volatile mix.... Paul and the Jerusalem brotherhood around Peter and James were simply one strand of this broad salvation movement, although an important and ultimately very influential one. Later, in a mythmaking process of its own, the Jerusalem circle with Paul as its satellite was adopted as the originating cell of the whole Christian movement. (http://www.jesuspuzzle.humanists.net/jhcjp.htm)

The reason why a vast majority of scholars do not accept the skeptical theory is not necessarily because they are believers, although most of them are. It's because the dominant theory seems to be a simpler one. It is much simpler (and hence easier) they conclude, to conceive of an original movement with a human founder that splintered into a multiple number of groups than it is to conceive of a multitude number of similar groups arising at the same time across the known world who soon came together to identify themselves as Christians.

A recent book of five views discussing this issue is *The Historical Jesus: Five Views*, eds. James K. Beilby and Paul Rhodes Eddy (Downers Grove, IL: InterVarsity Press, 2009). Unfortunately, the apocalyptic view of Jesus did not get a chapter of its own, probably because the editors are evangelicals and they tend to ignore it.

6. In *A Marginal Jew*, vol 1, (New Haven, CT: Yale University Press, 1991), pp. 22–23.

7. (New York: Penguin Books, 1993), especially pp. 169–204.

8. (Minneapolis, MN: Fortress Press, 1998).

9. (Oxford: Oxford University Press, 1999).

10. 2nd ed. (New Haven, CT: Yale University Press, 2000). A discussion/debate on these issues can be found in *The Apocalyptic Jesus: A Debate*, ed. Robert J. Miller (Santa Rosa, CA: Polebridge Press, 2001). Probably the best resource to consult about the quest for the historical Jesus is Gerd Theissen and Annette Merz, *The Historical Jesus: A Comprehensive Guide* (Minneapolis, MN: Fortress Press, 1996).

11. Allison, *Jesus of Nazareth*, pp. 36, 45. As an aside, I think establishing such a framework is also important for dating the books the NT. With an improper framework, people will date the books incorrectly. It's at least part of the solution.

12. Such a context for the life of Jesus is shown in John Dominic Crossan, *The Historical Jesus: The Life of a Mediterranean Jewish Peasant* (New York: HarperSanFrancisco, 1991), pp. 3–226.

13. Paula Fredriksen, *From Jesus to Christ: The Origins of the New Testament Images of Jesus*, 2nd ed. (New Haven, CT: Yale University Press, 2000), pp. 88–90.

14. Mark 6:14, 8:28; Matthew 11:7–19; Acts 5:35–39. Cf. Josephus, *Antiquities of the Jews* 18:5, 20:97–98, 169–72; and *Wars of the Jews* 2:261–3, 6:284–85.

15. Allison lists nine other major themes on that same descending scale: (9)

God as Father; (10) loving/serving/forgiving others; (11) special regard for the unfortunate; (12) intention as to what matters most; (13) hostility to wealth; (14) extraordinary requests/difficult demands; (15) conflict with religious authorities; (16) disciples as students and helpers; (17) Jesus as miracle worker. According to Allison, items (9)–(11) tell us that Jesus "was a teacher of compassion"; items (12)–(15) tell us he was "a moral rigorist"; items (15)–(16) tell us he was a "well-known teacher"; and item (17) "probably explains in great measure... why people paid attention to what he had to say." Allison, *Jesus of Nazareth*, pp. 46–49 (see also pp. 61–69, 78–94).

16. Ibid., pp. 51, 96.

17. Ibid., p. 154.

18. It should be noted that Robert Price disputes that this "Little Apocalypse" actually comes from the lips of Jesus in his book, *The Paperback Apocalypse: How the Christian Church Was Left Behind* (Amherst, NY: Prometheus Books, 2007), pp. 101–107. If he's correct, then the synoptic Gospels are probably not even somewhat reliable. Nonetheless, even though Price and others can object to the authenticity of "The Little Apocalypse" because most apocalyptic literature was written anonymously, not all of it was. And unless we're willing to say the whole NT tradition is inauthentic, the original founder of the Jesus cult was not the apostle Paul. For according to him he persecuted Christians, which means the Jesus cult, in some form or other, already existed prior to his conversion (see Galatians 1:13, cf. Acts 8:1–3, 9:1–19, 23:3–16, 26:9–18).

19. Edward Adams, *The Stars Will Fall From Heaven: Cosmic Catastrophe in the New Testament and Its World* (New York: T & T Clark, 2007), p. 164.

20. *Paperback Apocalypse*, p. 160.

21. It's quite clear in Paul's' genuine letters that he expected the apocalyptic end of the world. This is just one of the reasons why the Pastoral letters are rejected by most scholars as genuinely Pauline (i.e., 1 and 2 Timothy, and Titus), for which see Paul Tobin's chapter in this book. In one Pastoral Epistle we find the author altering what Paul wrote in 1 Corinthians (7:17–31), urging instead that unmarried women should marry and bear children (1 Timothy 5:14). In another we find the author making provisions for his death without having personally experienced the coming kingdom of God, which Paul had predicted he would see (1 Thessalonians 4:15–17, cf. 2 Timothy 2:1–14). It's also argued that since the letters of Colossians (3:18–41) and Ephesians (5:21–6:9) include household rules detailing the duties of members in a household, this goes against what Paul said in 1 Corinthians 7, so they must be forgeries as well (cf. also 1 Peter 2:13–3:12). See Bart D. Ehrman, *The New Testament: A Historical Introduction to the Early Christian Writings*, 3rd ed. (Oxford: Oxford University Press, 2003), pp. 372–94.

22. Ehrman, *Jesus: Apocalyptic Prophet of the New Millennium*, p. 244. Dale Allison would find fault with Ehrman's characterization here, since Jesus was

mostly speaking to his disciples who were told to leave everything to follow him. They had no need to be instructed about a fulfilling career precisely because they had chosen to follow him. See Allison's chapter, "The Problem of Audience" in *Resurrectiong Jesus* (New York: T & T Clark, 2005), pp. 27–55. However, the fact remains that Jesus did not offer advice to anyone to pursue a fulfilling career, nor did the evolving church think it was important to incorporate any such advice into the Gospels.

23. As Paula Fredriksen argued, "No human society could long run according to the principles enunciated in the Sermon on the Mount." *From Jesus to Christ*, p. 100. On the ethic of Jesus, see Michael Martin, *The Case against Christianity* (Philadelphia, PA: Temple University Press, 1991), pp. 162–72; and Dan Barker, *Godless, How an Evangelical Preacher Became One of America's Leading Atheists* (Berkely, CA: Ulysses Press, 2008), pp. 178–202.

24. James H. Charlesworth, "Jesus Research Expands with Chaotic Creativity," in *Images of Jesus Today*, ed. James H. Charlesworth and Walter P. Weaver (Valley Forge, PA; Trinity, 1994), p. 10.

25. David B. Gowler, *What Are They Saying about the Historical Jesus?* (New York: Paulist Press, 2007), p. 142. On this, one need look no farther back than Marcus J. Borg, *Jesus: A New Vision: Spirit, Culture, and the Life of Discipleship* (New York: HarperSanFrancisco, 1987). Borg fleshes out this new vision in a subsequent book, *Meeting Jesus Again for the First Time: The Historical Jesus & the Heart of Contemporary Faith* (New York: HarperSanFrancisco, 1994). In this later book he claimed that the "pre-Easter Jesus was noneschatological" (p. 29). Borg's precise denial is found in these words: "what is being denied is the notion that Jesus expected the supernatural coming of the Kingdom of God as a world-ending event in his own generation." (p. 29).

26. In *Apocalyptic Jesus: A Debate*, pp. 31–48.

27. Ibid., p. 85.

28. *Historical Figure of Jesus*, p. 183.

29. James H. Charlesworth, *The Historical Jesus: An Essential Guide* (Nashville, Abingdon Press, 2008), p. 97.

30. Ibid., p. 104.

31. Ibid., p. 99.

32. Ibid., p. 101.

33. Dale Allison, *The Historical Christ and the Theological Jesus* (Grand Rapids, MI: Eerdmans, 2009), p. 113.

34. Quoting a preview draft of Dale Allison's forthcoming *Constructing Jesus: Memory and Imagination* (Grand Rapids, MI : Baker Academic, 2010).

35. *Jesus Remembered* (Grand Rapids, MI: Eerdmans, 2003), p. 479.

36. For arguments that a different author wrote Zechariah 9–14, see the entry written by David L. Petersen, professor of Old Testament, Iliff School of The-

ology, Denver, CO, in *The Anchor Bible Dictionary*, ed. D. N. Freedman, (New York: Doubleday, 1996): "Zechariah, Book of."

37. To see this argued even by an evangelical scholar, see Kenton L. Sparks, *God's Word in Human Words: An Evangelical Appropriation of Critical Biblical Scholarship* (Grand Rapids, MI: Baker Books, 2008), pp. 116–18. Sparks argues that when we consider the prophecies in the book of Daniel, it becomes clear that they are "amazingly accurate and precise" up until a certain point where they "fail." He wrote: "Scholars believe that this evidence makes it very easy to date Daniel's apocalypses. One merely follows the amazingly accurate prophecies until they fail. Because the predictions of the Jewish persecutions in 167 BCE are correct, and because the final destiny of Antiochus in 164 BCE is not, it follows that the visions and their interpretations can be dated sometime between 167 and 164 BCE" (p. 117).

38. *Understanding the Old Testament* (Englewood Cliffs, NJ: Prentice-Hall, 1957), pp. 525–26. See also the commentary on this passage in Andre Lacocque, *The Book of Daniel* (Atlanta, GA: John Knox Press, 1979).

39. Sparks, *God's Word in Human Words*, p. 225.

40. For instance, when God intervenes on "the Day of the Lord," He will either "lead the battle against the forces of Evil (*Zechariah*, *Assumption of Moses*), or else he will send his prophet Elijah to anoint his Messiah, who will lead the Army of God. Or perhaps he will send his Messiah himself (*2 Baruch*), or delegate the military duties to a nonhuman hero figure, the Son of Man (*2 Esdras*)," Fredriksen, *From Jesus to Christ*, p. 84.

41. Since this sermon is the key that the author of Luke uses to characterize the ministry of Jesus, it seems a bit improbable to think some kind of tradition like this does not stem from the founder of the Jesus cult himself.

42. Fredriksen, *From Jesus to Christ*, p. 135.

43. Ibid., p. 170.

44. Ibid., p. 165.

45. Ibid., p. 169. See also pp. 165–70.

46. On this see Randel McCraw Helms, *The Bible against Itself: Why the Bible Seems to Contradict Itself*, (Altadena, CA: Millennium Press, 2006), pp. 153–65.

47. E. P. Sanders tells us: "An unfulfilled prophecy is much more likely to be authentic than one that corresponds precisely to what happened, since few people would make up something that did not happen and then attribute it to Jesus," in *Historical Figure of Jesus*, p. 182.

48. To read a very helpful description of the cognitive dissonance of the early disciples and their need to resolve it concerning the unexpected death of Jesus, see Kris Komarnitsky, "The Belief That Jesus Died for Our Sins and Was Raised," in *Doubting Jesus' Resurrection: What Happened in the Black Box?* (CreateSpace, 2009), pp. 48–76. If this can happen with the death of Jesus, it can surely happen with regard to his failed prophecies of an imminent apocalypse.

49. Ehrman, *Jesus Apocalyptic Prophet of the New Millennium*, p. 130 [emphasis original].

50. Ibid.

51. Ibid., p. 177.

52. *Historical Figure of Jesus*, pp. 176–77.

53. See Richard Valantasis, *The Gospel of Thomas* (New York: Routledge, 1997), pp. 12–21. I recommend Paul Tobin's discussion of this in *The Rejection of Pascal's Wager*, pp. 464–67.

54. *Historical Christ and the Theological Jesus*, p. 100.

55. *Historical Figure of Jesus*, p. 180.

56. In *The New Testament: Historical Introduction to the Early Christian Writings*, 3rd ed. (Oxford: Oxford University Press, 2003), pp. 469–70 Erhman writes: "most investigators think that parts of the book were written during the 60s of the Common Era, soon after the persecution of the Christians under Nero." And yet there are important clues suggesting the book wasn't completed until around 95 CE during the rule of Domitian. The earliest external evidence is provided by Irenaeus in *Against Heresies* 5.30.3, who said Revelation was seen at the end of the reign of Domitian, so this implies a date of 95–96 CE. The most important internal clue is that the code word *Babylon*, which is used to signify Rome, "came to be used by Jews to designate Rome as the chief political enemy of God only after the destruction of Jerusalem in 70 CE (e.g., 4 Ezra 3, 2 Baruch 10)," claims Ehrman. Adela Yarbro Collins argues the solution that best explains all of the internal evidence is that "an older tradition" was "incorporated and reinterpreted by the author of Revelation." For a more detailed discussion, see Collins, "Revelation, Book of," in *The Anchor Bible Dictionary*, vol. 5, ed. D. N. Freedman (New York: Doubleday 1996), pp. 700–708; and her book *Crisis and Catharsis: The Power of the Apocalypse* (Philadelphia, PA: Westminster Press. 1984), pp. 54–83.

57. Says Ehrman in *New Testament*, p. 472: "Historians have long known of a group of ancient Jewish books called the Sybilline Oracles, which predict that one of the most hated of the Roman emperors, Caesar Nero, will return from the dead to wreak havoc on the earth—making him comparable to the one who recovers from a death-inflicting wound" (see Rev. 13:3). Thus the eighth beast "who was and is not" spoken of in Revelation 17:11 "alludes to the return of Nero as eschatological adversary," argues Collins in "Revelation, Book of," in *The Anchor Bible Dictionary*, vol. 5, p. 701.

58. On this see Ehrman, *New Testament*, pp. 376–78.

59. On the Dating of 2 Peter, see Ehrman, *New Testament*, pp. 456–58.

60. See Price, *Paperback Apocalypse*, pp. 123–43.

61. *Jesus of Nazareth*, p. 94

62. Ibid., p. 64.

63. *The Paperback Apocalypse*, pp. 159–60. This, of course, is part of the *Problem of Miscommunication*, which I wrote about in chapter 7 of this book.

64. (Minneapolis, MN: Fortress Press, 1996).

65. 4th ed. (Atlanta: GA: Vision Books, 1999).

66. *Jesus of Nazareth*, p. 157.

67. Ibid., p. 161.

68. In *Jesus and the Restoration of Israel: A Critical Assessment of N.T. Wright's "Jesus and the Victory of God,"* ed. Carey C. Newman (Downers Grove, IL: InterVarsity Press, 1999), pp. 138–39.

69. (New York: Continuum International, 2008).

ADDENDUM

For a list of the many predictions made by NT authors that the "Son of Man" and/or "the Lord" were "coming soon," see Dr. James D. Tabor, *New Testament Texts on the Imminence of the End*, http://www.religiousstudies .uncc.edu/JDTABOR/apocalyptic.html and Edward T. Babinski, *The Lowdown on God's Showdown* (2001), http:/secweb.infidels.org/?kiosk=articles &id=86.

Part 5

WHY SOCIETY DOES NOT DEPEND ON CHRISTIAN FAITH

Chapter 13

CHRISTIANITY DOES NOT PROVIDE THE BASIS FOR MORALITY

David Eller, PhD

Imagine someone said to you that English provided the only basis for grammar. After you overcame your shock, you would respond that English is certainly not the only language with a grammar. You would add that grammar is not limited to language: understood broadly as rules for combination and transformation, many phenomena have a grammar, from sports to baking. Nor is grammar the sole or essential component of language: language also includes sound systems, vocabularies, genres, and styles of speech. And you would remind the speaker that grammar does not depend on *human* language at all: some nonhuman species, including chimps and parrots, can produce grammatical—that is, orderly and rule-conforming —short sentences. Ultimately, you would want to explain that English does not "provide a basis" for grammar at all but rather represents one particular instance of grammar. English grammar is definitely not the only grammar in the world and even more definitely not the "real" grammar.

The person who utters a statement like "English provides the only basis for grammar" either understands very little about English (and language in general) or grammar, or the person is expressing his or her partisanship about language (i.e., pro-English)—or, more likely, the speaker is doing both. Thus, the person who utters a statement like "Christianity provides the only basis for morality" either understands very little about

Christianity (or religion in general) or morality, or the person is expressing his or her partisanship about religion (i.e., pro-Christianity)—or, more likely, the speaker is doing both. But, as a savvy responder, you would answer that Christianity is certainly not the only religion with morality. You would add that morality is not limited to religion: understood broadly as standards for behavior, many phenomena have a morality, from philosophy to business. Nor is morality the sole or essential component of religion: religion also includes myths, rituals, roles, and institutions of behavior. And you would remind the speaker that morality does not depend on *human* religion at all: some nonhuman species demonstrate moral—that is, orderly and standard-conforming—behavior. Ultimately, you would want to explain that Christianity does not "provide a basis" for morality at all but rather represents one particular instance of morality. Christian morality is definitely not the only morality in the world and even more definitely not the "real" morality.

In this chapter, then, we will first explore what religion and morality actually are. We will show that other religions have their own moralities and that morality does not depend on Christianity. Further, we will show that nonreligion can also provide "a basis" for morality, that morality does not depend on religion. We will even show that nonhumans can have a sort of, or a precursor to, morality—that morality does not depend on humanness. Finally, we will clarify how religion is related to morality and why it often appears that morality depends on religion but *that this is part of the ideology of religion, not the nature of morality.*

WHAT IS RELIGION? WHAT IS MORALITY?

Not surprisingly, much of the confusion and (what passes for) debate about religion and morality boils down to a misunderstanding of both. There have been many attempts to define each term, most not so much wrong as highly biased. Accurately understanding religion and morality separately will help to make the relationship between them more comprehensible and will automatically dispense with the notion that morality depends on or is "provided by" any particular religion—or any religion at all.

Perhaps it is easiest to approach the problem of what religion or morality is by establishing what it is not. Let us start with religion. Many people, Christian or under the influence of Christianity, define religion as "belief in God" or, only slightly more generally, "belief in one god." This is, of course, not a definition of religion in any way but rather a description of their particular religion. It is reminiscent of the opinion of Parson Thwackum in Henry Fielding's novel *The History of Tom Jones*, who said, "When I mention religion I mean the Christian religion; and not only the Christian religion, but the Protestant religion; and not only the Protestant religion, but the Church of England." It is utterly inadequate and more than a bit egocentric.

Other, more serious, attempts have been made to define religion, in psychology, sociology, anthropology, and biology. Some emphasize individual experience (especially the "transcendent feeling" or the "oceanic feeling," etc.); others stress ritual or myth or belief or institutions or, inevitably, morality. In reality, all of these are *aspects* of religion, but none of them is the essence or *sine qua non* of religion: there are religions without god(s), without (much) ritual, without (much) myth, without (many) institutions, and—depending on who you talk to—without morality. Rather, all of these are potential elements or building blocks of religions, in what many contemporary theorists have suggested as a "modular" approach to religion. In other words, according to thinkers like Pascal Boyer[1] and Scott Atran,[2] religion is not a "thing" at all but a composite of basic elements which, most critically, are not fundamentally "religious" in and of themselves. That is, there are religious rituals and there are nonreligious rituals; there are religious stories and there are nonreligious stories; there are religious institutions and there are nonreligious institutions; and, most importantly for our present purpose, there are religious moralities and there are nonreligious moralities. All of these are *human* phenomena, not specifically or exclusively *religious* phenomena.

If there is, nevertheless, one quality that religions seem to share, it is what has been called "agency." Agency essentially means "intelligence" or "will" or, perhaps most profoundly, "intention." Agents are the kinds of beings who have intelligence or will or intention, who are not mere objects of natural forces but who make some *choices* on the basis of their own *nature* and *interests*. Agents are, in short, "persons," and human beings are the agents or persons with which we are most familiar. As Graham Harvey puts it:

> Persons are those with whom other persons interact with varying degrees of reciprocity. Persons may be spoken *with*. Objects, by contrast, are usually spoken *about*. Persons are volitional, relational, cultural and social

beings. They demonstrate intentionality and agency with varying degrees of autonomy and freedom. That some persons look like objects [or do not have visible appearance at all] is of little more value to an understanding of [religion] than the notion that some acts, characteristics, qualia, and so on may appear human-like to some observers. Neither material form nor spiritual or mental faculties are definitive.[3]

What is important is that humans are inveterate agent-detectors, looking for will or intention or purpose or goal-oriented behavior in each other and in the world around them. And we tend to find it, whether or not it is there. Thus, the characteristic feature of religion is the claim that there are nonhuman and superhuman agents in the world, lacking some of the "qualia" of humans (like bodies or mortality) but possessing the most important one—mind or personality or intention. This "religious perspective," if you will, humanizes the world or, more critically, *socializes* the world, because these nonhuman religious agents (like a god) not only *can* be spoken with but also *must* be spoken with. They are understood by members of the religion to be a real and inescapable part of their social world. This leads us to a definition of religion offered by Robin Horton almost fifty years ago:

> [I]n every situation commonly labeled religious we are dealing with action directed toward objects which are believed to respond in terms of certain categories—in our own culture those of purpose, intelligence, and emotion—which are also the distinctive categories for the description of human action. The application of these categories leads us to say that such objects are "personified." The relationship between human beings and religious objects can be further defined as governed by certain ideas of patterning and obligation such as characterize relationships among human beings. In short, religion can be looked upon as an extension of the field of people's social relationships beyond the confines of purely human society. And for completeness' sake, we should perhaps add the rider that this extension must be one in which human beings involved see themselves in a dependent position vis-à-vis their nonhuman alters.[4]

If religion is the expansion of society to include nonhuman and superhuman agents, then what is morality? Much ink has been spilled on this question too, most of it also biased, egocentric, and inadequate. Let us, as before, start with what morality is not. First and foremost, morality is not any particular rule or principle or set of rules or principles. That is, morality as such is not chastity or marital fidelity or honesty or nonkilling; these are all specific (although perhaps widely held) moral claims or issues but not "morality" in and of itself—any more than theism is "religion" in and of itself.

Further, and more surprisingly, morality is not essentially about "goodness," if only because "goodness" is completely relative. In other words, while people of a certain moral temper might consider prohibiting same-sex marriage to be "good," no doubt most same-sex couples consider it "not good." Likewise, if some remote tribe believed it was "good" to sacrifice humans or to throw virgins in volcanoes to appease the volcano god, this behavior was "not good" for the victims. "Good" must always and necessarily be "good for someone" or "good for some purpose." It also goes without saying that morality is not what is "pleasurable" or "makes you happy," since occasionally the things that might give you pleasure—like sex or taking someone's property—are not deemed moral.

Finally, and most surprisingly, morality is not essentially about "prosocial" behavior. This is a common misconception, but of course it depends on one's particular view of what society ought to be. Morality tends to be equated, first of all, with only the "positive" or "beneficial" values and behaviors, like altruism or generosity and love. But indisputably, any morality, including Judeo-Christian morality, accepts that there is a time to kill and a time to heal, a time to love and a time to hate, a time for war and a time for peace. When called upon (often by religion), killing and hating and warring are delightfully moral, even the highest and noblest thing we can do, a virtual commandment. More, "prosocial" is another relative term: killing witches may be "good for society" but is not good for witches, who are part of society. Banning gay marriage or preventing abortion may be good for one person's notion of society and not good for another person's. Worse yet, hardly anyone ever acts for the "good of society" but rather for some more local and personal good: most of us would act more altruistically toward our family or friends than toward strangers or enemies. We would kill to defend ourselves and our property, and the law sometimes recognizes this as a praiseworthy action (note the "make my day" laws that allow killing an intruder in your home). Finally, many things that preoccupy the Christian moral sensibility have little or nothing to do with prosociality, like nakedness or premarital sex; other cultures have adopted the exact opposite stance on these issues and have been happy and successful. At the same time, other cultures have their own moral preoccupations, like covering a woman's face and figure in some Muslim countries, which do not constitute "moral" concerns in Christian countries in the first place.

If morality is not any of these things fundamentally, then what is it? Michael Shermer's stab at the question in his *The Science of Good and Evil* makes a decent first approximation: morality, he says, refers to "right and wrong thoughts and behaviors in the context of the rules of a social group."[5] What this terse statement reminds us is that (1) morality always refers back to a set of rules and (2) each social group may have its own set of such rules. Therefore, as in the case of religion, we should look for the essence of morality in some larger and deeper area than the details of any particular moral system.

The answer can be sought in our new understanding of religion. Why are humans such obsessive agency detectors? Because we, as an inherently social species, are necessarily interested in the actions and intentions of other members of our group (which may include, we now realize, non-human agents as well). Therefore, we need to evaluate each other's behavior—to be able to determine the meaning of that behavior, the intention of that behavior, and the predictability of that behavior. Indeed, the very existence of society depends on, one might even say *is*, a shared set of standards for the interpretation, evaluation, and prediction of behavior.

In a word, humans—hopelessly social creatures that we are—do and must engage in the *appraisal* of each other's actions. Morality is one form of such appraisal. Morality is a kind of talk about behavior, a discourse or language about which behaviors we commend and which behaviors we condemn. As Kai Nielsen has said it better than just about anyone:

> Moral language is the language we use in verbalizing a choice or a decision; it is the language we use in appraising human conduct and in giving advice about courses of action; and finally, it is the language we use in committing ourselves to a principle of action. Moral language is a *practical* kind of discourse that is concerned to answer the questions: "What should be done?" or "What attitude should be taken toward what has been done, is being done, or will be done?"[6]

In short, as a social process of behavioral appraisal, "morality functions to *guide* conduct and *alter* behavior or attitudes."[7] Of course, it does not do so infallibly or in isolation.

We say that morality does not guide and alter behavior infallibly because the existence of moral rules and of other people's moral outrage does not guarantee consistently and exclusively "good" behavior. Despite the presence of moral injunctions against killing and stealing, for instance, some folks persist in killing and stealing. Even worse, despite the fact that morality supposedly serves as a "conversation stopper," a bedrock basis for behavior and behavioral appraisal, the presence of moral injunctions has not ended and does not appear about to end the moral conversation. Instead, humans can and do argue about what the standards of appraisal are, what they mean, and when and how to apply them. Does "Thou shalt not kill" mean *all* killing, or merely "murder" (i.e., illicit killing)? Does it mean that you should avoid all killing, or only try to minimize killing (say, in war)? Does it mean killing anything at all, or only killing humans? (So much for carnivorism—or eating of any kind!)

So humans constantly appraise each other's behavior and intentions (partly to determine *future* behavior), and they do so in relation to some group standard of behavior—some collective sense of what is "approved" or "disapproved" behavior. These standards unarguably differ across religions and cultures (although some big items do frequently appear). But morality is ultimately nothing more than a special case of the more general human predilection to appraise behavior and to erect systems and standards of appraisal. Even more, morality is not the only form that such appraisal systems/standards and such appraisal language can take. "Morality" is one entry in the universe of appraisal-talk, of which there are many other entries. What I mean is that "moral" and "immoral" are two labels that can be attached to behaviors depending on their conformity to group standards. But there are other labels, too, available to members to praise or denounce (and hopefully *affect and control*) behavior: legal/illegal, sane/insane, mature/immature, normal/abnormal, polite/impolite, ethical/unethical, professional/unprofessional, and so on. None of these other pairs of terms quite overlaps with moral/immoral.

As Nielsen also explains, "Not all practical discourse is moral discourse. Not all conduct is moral conduct and not all advice or appraisal of conduct is moral advice or moral appraisal. Nor are all attitudes or dispositions to action moral attitudes or moral dispositions to action."[8] That is, not every behavioral issue is a "moral" issue, and not every standard of behavior is a "moral" standard. As we mentioned, most Westerners do not regard the display of a woman's face or arms to be a moral concern at all, and some tribes like the Warlpiri or the Yanomamo did not regard public nakedness to be a moral concern. The Jains consider eating vegetables or killing insects to be a moral problem, while the average Westerner does not. Nietzsche once asserted that there are no moral facts; in truth, there are no universal moral questions.

Finally, just as religion can and should be decomposed into more fundamental building blocks that are not "religious" in themselves, morality can and should be decomposed into more fundamental building blocks that are not "moral" in themselves. Shermer calls these "premoral sentiments" and includes among them:

> [A]ttachment and bonding, cooperation and mutual aid, sympathy and empathy, direct and indirect reciprocity, altruism and reciprocal altruism, conflict resolution and peacemaking, deception and deception detection, community concern and caring about what others think about you, and awareness of and response to the social rules of the group.[9]

Haidt and Graham condense the rudiments of morality down to five "psychological preparations for detecting and reacting emotionally to issues related to harm/care, fairness/reciprocity, ingroup/loyalty, authority/respect, and purity/sanctity."[10] Most of these, it can be noticed, have little to do with religion and could easily stand without religion.

MORALITY WITHOUT CHRISTIANITY

So Christianity has its own behavioral interest and its own appraisal language—or perhaps we should say interests and appraisals, since not all Christians seem to agree on the details of "Christian morality." It cannot even be claimed that Christianity is the only basis for a *single* morality, let alone for *all* morality. For example, some Christians think that dancing is bad, while others do not; some think that coffee or alcohol are bad, while others do not.

Different religions have their particular behavioral rules and appraisal terms. Judaism was heralded as a religion of justice long before Christianity was invented; the word "justice" occurs dozens of times in the Torah/Old Testament, and the book of Job is centered on it (see Alan Dershowitz's *The Genesis of Justice* for a discussion of the evolution of justice in the Torah's first book[11]). Here, as in many of the cases to follow, "morality" might not quite be the right word to describe the specific concerns, but the concerns are recognizable as manifestations of an appraisal discourse. For instance, the Big Ten of moral rules were written centuries before the Gospels, with their admonitions against killing and stealing and lying and bearing false witness. But as anyone with minimal familiarity with the Judeo-Christian scriptures knows, not all of the "ten commandments" are "moral" in the conventional sense of the term. There is nothing "moral" (in the sense of "prosocial" or "altruistic") in having no other gods before some god, or in avoiding graven images ("or any likeness of any thing that is in heaven above, or that is in the earth beneath, or that is in the water under the earth," as Exodus 20:4 orders and which the average Western Christian utterly ignores), nor in keeping the Sabbath, nor in not coveting your neighbor's possessions (which is the engine of Western capitalism).

What most Christians seem to conveniently forget is that the so-called "ten commandments" are neither the only rules nor the main rules in Judaism. Why, after the first tablets were broken, the Hebrew god gave Moses a new set *with different commandments* in Exodus 34, such as to keep the feast of unleavened bread, to offer the firstborn to their god (presumably by sacrifice, since they are also instructed not to offer the blood of sacrifice along with leaven), to observe the feast of weeks, and to assemble the men-children three times a year. Most modern Christians, if they have even heard of these rules, do not obey them and do not regard them as "moral" worries.

Judaism also has a concern for "sin," but a cursory examination shows that "sin" is not the same thing as the modern Christian concept of "immorality." Sin in ancient Judaism was more akin to uncleanness or impurity: the dietary laws do not say it is "immoral" to eat pork or shellfish but that those substances are an "abomination," and a woman is unclean after birth, not immoral. And Judaism's behavioral rules are hardly exhausted with the ten (or twenty) orders but are famously said to run to 613 *mitzvot* or commandments. Among these mandates are that every man should write a copy of the Torah for himself,[12] wear the *tefillin* or phylactery on the head and arm,[13] not reap his entire field,[14] and exempt a bridegroom from public labor or military service for one year;[15] that a widow whose husband had no children should not marry anyone other than her dead husband's brother;[16] that one not kiss or hug or wink at or skip with a relative lest one commits incest;[17] that one not borrow money at interest;[18] and one of my personal favorites, that one release any servant that one "buys" after six years.[19]

Islam is another well-known religion with a clear set of "moral" principles. According to the first lines in the Qur'an, Allah (simply the Arabic for "god") is beneficent and merciful, a judge, and one who keeps humans on the right path. More specifically, Islam provides the standard for determining what behaviors are good or bad. An action is *fard* if it is obligatory; performing the action is meritorious, and not performing it is punishable. An action is *halal* if it is allowed or permitted, but not required; performing the action is neither good nor bad, moral nor immoral. An action is *makruh* if it is disapproved, though not forbidden. Finally, an action is *haram* if it is forbidden or prohibited or unlawful; performing the action has negative religious consequences.

Among the foods that are *halal* are milk, honey, fish, fruits, vegetables, and meat—as long as it is sacrificed according to Muslim ritual (throat slit and drained of blood, never strangled or bludgeoned to death). A foodstuff is *haram* if it contains or comes into contact with blood, pigs, dogs, reptiles, alcohol, animals with protruding canine teeth, or animals won by betting or gambling. But ingestion is hardly the only area of moral concern. A man should not wear gold ornaments or silk clothes, although a woman may; women should not wear tight or transparent clothing, and in more than a few societies, should be veiled from head to toe to show their modesty and preserve their honor. No one should alter their physical features in pursuit of beauty, and all excess is disapproved. Gold and silver utensils are *haram*, as are pure silk sheets and bedspreads. Keeping dogs inside the house as pets is forbidden, too, as are songs that praise wine and encourage drinking, all forms of gambling and lottery, and movies that depict or incite sex, greed, crime, deviance, or false belief.

Just to show how very "moral" Islam is, in May 2009 Saudi Arabia actually held a "Miss Beautiful Morals" pageant. The contestants were all heavily veiled, as is proper, since the women were not being judged on their physical beauty (and would definitely not be seen in bathing suits by strange men). Rather, as pageant founder Khadra al-Mubarak asserted, "The idea of the pageant is to measure the contestants' commitment to Islamic morals.... The winner won't necessarily be pretty. We care about the beauty of the soul and the morals."[20] And the categories in which the women were judged included "discovering your inner strength," "the making of leaders," and "Mom, paradise is at your feet." Now *there* is a commitment to morality the likes of which Western Christianity has not achieved.

Outside the Western/Abrahamic religions, Hinduism is premised on the concept of *dharma*, the transcendent order of the universe and the duty that it imposes on humans. Failure to act in accordance with the *dharma* generates *karma*, which functions like a kind of moral weight or dirt or rust on the *atman* or soul. The entire caste system, the division of society into different and unequal social and occupational groups, is a moral imperative, resting on the spiritual purity or impurity of individuals; and many moral regulations go along with it, including who may or may not marry or even eat with someone else. One's specific moral demands depend on one's caste status: if one is *pariah*, one's moral duty is to perform dirty jobs; and if one is *kshatriya*, one's moral duty is to lead, to fight, to kill, and to die. The *Bhagavad Gita*, the beloved sacred tale of the warrior Arjuna, affirms that neither killing nor dying is a moral problem for the *kshatriya* warrior, since it is by definition meritorious, even mandatory, that a soldier slay and be slain and, even more fundamentally, the soul cannot be injured by death anyhow.

Buddhism has an elaborate and demanding set of behavioral strictures; one could argue with justification that Buddhism is more morality than religion. The very beginning of the Buddha's teaching is the "Eightfold Path," the discipline to observe right view, right intention, right speech, right action, right livelihood, right effort, right mindfulness, and right concentration. These "rights" go beyond the Judeo-Christian requirement to eschew lies and false witness: to observe right speech, the Buddhist must abstain from lies and deceit as well as slander and malicious words as well as harsh or hurtful words as well as idle chatter. But the Eightfold Path is only the most general of moral rules. The Buddhist should obey the ten precepts, to avoid harming any living thing, taking anything not freely given, misbehaving sexually, speaking falsely, ingesting alcohol or drugs, eating untimely meals, dancing/singing/miming, using garlands or perfumes or other adornments, sitting in high seats, and accepting gold or silver. Actually, the list of Buddhist ethical regulations is much more extensive.

Jainism may have the most stringent morality of all. A religion related to Hinduism and Buddhism, Jainism condemns all injuring of all living beings, even insects and microbes—the concept of *ahimsa* or no-harm. This is why some Jains can be seen wearing masks and drinking through a strainer lest they swallow an insect, or sweeping the path ahead of them

with a small broom lest they trample one. A Jain must minimally be a vegetarian, but that is only the beginning: they should eat only plants that are
already dead, so as to avoid injuring the plant. They cannot be farmers
because farming harms living things; they should not be blacksmiths
because the hammering hurts the anvil and the bench. They must also, like
Buddhists, avoid attachment to life, whether this be food, clothing, family
members, or their own body. Jains who commit themselves to a more rigorous religious life also renounce travel, owning weapons, eating during
night time, and contact with their spouse; they pledge to meditate frequently during the day, live a monk's life as fully as possible, and ultimately
become a complete ascetic by dwelling naked in the forest and dying
proudly of self-starvation.

These are only some of the major "world religions." Every ancient and
tribal religion included its own moral standards, some similar to Christianity, some foreign to Christianity, some absurd to Christianity. And the
feeling was mutual.

MORALITY WITHOUT RELIGION

While religions have a lot—and a lot of different—moral compunctions,
morality is not limited to religion. If we understand morality properly, as
one expression of the human concern to organize one's (and others')
behavior according to standards of appraisal, then there are at least four
other potential bases for moral determination and moral evaluation:
nature, reason, philosophy, and culture.

There are many people who assert that morality is "natural" or "real"
or "objective," and therefore independent of religion; in fact, they use
(supposedly) natural/real/objective standards to judge, and often to
reject, religious "morality." I am not, for reasons not manageable in this
chapter but hopefully obvious in this chapter, one of these people; morality is too diverse and contradictory to be natural or real or objective, and
the total lack of agreement on moral answers—or even moral questions—
contradicts the notion of a single "real" morality (as it does the notion of
a single "real" language). Nevertheless, for those who use nature or reality
as their standard of moral judgment, theirs is no more inadequate and no
more ridiculous than some religious standard.[21]

Related to the idea of real morality is the idea of rational morality, that is, that one can determine the morality of one's and others' actions by reason and analysis. By starting from the relevant facts, one applies logic and critical thinking, possibly weighs the alternatives, and chooses the "moral" course of action. To be sure, this begs the question of which are the relevant facts and of how to weigh the alternatives. For instance, I asked a moral rationalist to explain the morality of abortion to me, and he answered that a fetus does not have a complete and functioning brain, that only beings with complete and functioning brains are persons, and therefore that it was morally acceptable to terminate a fetus. The problem with this manner of "reasoning" is that it stipulates the key terms of the debate (is a complete and functioning brain the definition of "personhood," and is lack of personhood a justification for killing?) and ignores issues of interest and of value conflicts. Even so, this approach is not inferior to, and is often superior to, religious brands of morality.

Philosophers since Socrates have struggled with the problem of "the good." They have made little headway and will make no more so long as they insist on finding *the* good way to act or live, but the exercise shows that one *can* philosophize about ethics and morality without reference to religion. In fact, in his dialogue entitled *Euthyphro*, Plato stalled on whether an action is good because some god(s) ordain(s) it or whether the god(s) ordain(s) it because it is good. The dilemma is crucial because if an action is good with or without god(s), then we do not need god(s) to tell us what is good; we can philosophize it out for ourselves. And if an action is good only because some god(s) say(s) that it is, then the action is not good in itself; its goodness is purely arbitrary and contingent on the whim of the god(s).

Since Plato's time, philosophers have offered a number of analyses of morality or ethics. One popular approach to morality is personal interest or egoism: people do, or should do, what is best for themselves; interestingly, early (and some modern) theorists of capitalism see informed egoism as the principle on which markets in particular and societies in general do and should operate. (Others regard egoism as the very antithesis of morality.) Utilitarianism argues that the best and most ethical course of action is the one that promises to produce the most pleasure and the least pain, presumably for the most people (or else it is just egoism again): humans thus become moral calculators, adding up pleasures, subtracting pains, and arriving at the most congenial sums. The fact that moral choices often cost pleasure and cause pain complicates this calculation, and of course how one compares relative pleasures and pains (say, mine against yours) is a problem.

Immanuel Kant argued that morality flows from the perception of *duty*, that some actions are required of us simply because they are required of us. Moral actions are "imperatives," he said, and "categorical" imperatives at that. A hypothetical imperative is the sort of requirement that relates means to ends: if you want to drive a nail into a board, it is a hypothetical imperative to use a hammer. A categorical imperative is not a means to an end. In fact, Kant insists that we should not treat other people as means at all; rather, we should think about the maxim underlying our action—for example, the maxim underlying my aversion to stealing is "you should not steal"—as if it were a universal rule. The maxims of moral action are universal or universalizable rules.

Aristotle, on the other hand, appraised behavior in terms of *virtue*, which is part of the character of persons. Living and acting virtuously was, as they say, its own reward—the cause and the effect of moral choices. A person who lived in the condition of *eudaimonia* (well-being, happiness, flourishing) behaved in ways to express and perpetuate this healthy state; of course, the person had to be educated and trained to be virtuous in the first place. Among the virtues were the eight "moral virtues" of prudence, justice, fortitude, courage, liberality, magnificence, magnanimity, and temperance. Further, a virtue was always the middle way between two vices (in the case of courage, the vices would be cowardice and foolhardiness).

Other philosophical grounds for morality have been proposed, including justice and fairness and human rights. All of these really amount to little more than synonyms for morality and to formalizations of a *particular* form or view of morals or ethics. But Aristotle's observation about the training of virtue raises the point about the cultural basis of morality. Culture, of which religion is inevitably a part, is a source of behavioral expectations and behavioral appraisal far beyond the part contributed by religion. Any culture provides all kinds of norms for human comportment, from what clothes to wear to how to eat at the dinner table to how to treat other people. Some of these norms are influenced by or derived from a culture's religion, and some have no relation to the religion at all. Indeed, "moral" reactions often take the form more of cultural disdain than supernatural disapproval—it is more a matter of "what we do or don't do around here" than "what the supernatural beings want."

MORALITY WITHOUT HUMANITY

Humans—especially but not exclusively religious humans—have a tendency to imagine that morality is some unique human gift, sublime, ethereal, even "spiritual" or "supernatural." This is one reason why many (like C. S. Lewis) have been inclined to attribute "the moral sense," the very possibility of having morality or being a moral species along with the details of any specific moral system, to some source outside of humanity. Morality seems to them *unprecedented* in the natural world, transcendent and inexplicable.

This attitude is a combination of hubris, ignorance of the world around us, and more than a small dose of Christian exclusivism—the suggestion that humans are unlike anything else in existence. But humans are not unlike anything else in existence; we are natural beings too, a species that developed historically and continuously from nonhuman precursors. And just as we can find traces (clear and strong traces) of our physical characteristics in other species, so we can find traces of our psychological and even moral characteristics in them as well.

The question that is generally not asked in the discussion of morality, but that should be asked, is not "what is the basis of morality?" and certainly not "what is the true morality?" and not, as some well-intentioned thinkers have done, "why be moral?" Asking "why be moral?" is no more sensible than asking "why be linguistic?" or "why be bipedal?" Rather, the correct question is *why are humans a moral species?* That is, what is it about us that makes us the kind of beings who are capable of "morality," who have "moral" interests and invent "moral" systems?

A great deal of literature has accumulated over the last couple of decades to address this question, although Darwin predicted it more than 130 years ago. In his *The Descent of Man*, first published in 1871, he mused that morality was not really such a mystery at all but rather that "any animal whatever, endowed with well-marked social instincts, the parental and filial affections being here included, would inevitably acquire a moral sense or conscience."[22] If this is so, then we should expect to find rudiments, evolutionary traces, or "building blocks" of "morality" in the nonhuman natural world. And of course we do.

The details of the research into the evolution of morality are too vast and too varied to explore in depth here. All we need to establish is that some ancestral precursors to morality can be found in nonhuman species. Since Darwin, an accelerating line of investigation has developed, as early as Edward Westermarck's 1908 *The Origin and Development of the Moral Ideas* and reaching critical mass with E. O. Wilson's 1975 *Sociobiology: The New Synthesis*. Since then, the effort has yielded conceptual and empirical studies like Peter Singer's 1981 *The Expanding Circle*, Robert Wright's 1994 *The Moral Animal: The New Science of Evolutionary Psychology*, Marc Hauser's 2000 *Wild Minds: What Animals Really Think*, and his 2006 *Moral Minds: How Nature Designed Our Universal Sense of Right and Wrong*, Michael Shermer's aforementioned *The Science of Good and Evil*, Richard Joyce's 2006 *The Evolution of Morality*, and the many works of primatologist Frans de Waal, including *Primates and Philosophers: How Morality Evolved*.

The core of this research is that "morality" is not utterly unique to humans but has its historical/evolutionary antecedents and its biological bases. "Morality" does not appear suddenly out of nowhere in humans but emerges gradually with the emergence of certain kinds of beings living certain kinds of lives. This is not to assert that animals have full-blown "morality" any more than they have full-blown language. It is to assert that, just as some prehuman beings have "linguistic" capacities, some prehuman beings also have "moral" capacities.

The key to the evolutionary theory of morality is that *social* beings tend reasonably to develop interests in the behavior of others and capacities to determine and to influence that behavior. This might start most obviously with offspring: parents of many species show concern for their offspring, disadvantage themselves for their offspring (for instance, by spending time feeding them), and put their own lives at risk for their offspring (the notorious problem of "altruism"). Some species exhibit these same behaviors toward adult members of the "family," or toward adult members of the larger social group, or ultimately, in humans, to all members of the species and perhaps to other species as well. In this regard, human "morality" is an extension of more "short-range" helping behaviors.

With such costly but prosocial behaviors, we have taken a long step toward "morality." Or, as Shermer puts it, the capacity and tendency to have "moral sentiments" or moral concerns evolved out of the "premoral" feelings and tendencies of prehuman species. Frans de Waal and other animal watchers have accordingly gathered an enormous amount of data on prehuman "morality," including sharing, indications of "fairness," gratitude, self-sacrifice, sympathy and comforting, and many more. O'Connell has been able to catalogue hundreds of reported cases of "empathy" and "moral" behavior in chimps,[23] and it has been observed in an extraordinary variety of species, from birds to elephants to primates.

As de Waal reminds us, social living depends on social "regularity," which he characterizes as a "set of expectations about the way in which oneself (or others) should be treated and how resources should be divided."[24] Individuals without some sense of what to expect from others—and of what others expect of him or her—would not be properly "social." And this social regularity entails some method for handling exceptions and deviations: "Whenever reality deviates from these expectations to one's (or the other's) disadvantage, a negative reaction ensues, most commonly protest by subordinate individuals and punishment by dominant individuals."[25]

Thus, a certain amount of regularity and predictability in behavior is a requisite for social coexistence and for the eventual formation of "morality." However, it is only one component. As in the case of religion, "morality" is not a single, monolithic thing or skill but a composite phenomenon of multiple skills and interests. To reach premoral behavior, and ultimately human morality, a variety of other pieces must be in place. One of the essential pieces is a certain degree of "intersubjectivity," the ability to understand (and therefore hopefully predict) the thoughts and feelings of others. Beyond the mere awareness of others' thoughts and feelings is the capacity to *share* them in some way, what de Waal calls "emotional contagion." As beings approach "moral" status, they develop the capacity to *experience* the experiences of others. Fortunately, some of the most fascinating recent work has identified a basis for this phenomenon in so-called mirror neurons in the brain. Mirror neurons, as the name suggests, imitate or mimic the activity of other parts of the brain—or of other brains. Experiments have shown that "neurons in the same area of the brain were activated whether the animals were performing a particular movement... or simply observing another monkey—or a researcher—perform the same action."[26] This provides a literal biological foundation for empathy: individuals with mirror neurons, including humans and other primates, can actually feel what others feel.

Other premoral habits and skills include the ability to inhibit one's own actions and to remember, which is crucial for preserving and learning from previous interactions with the same individuals. A third is the ability to detect and respond to "cheaters" or those who violate expectations. A fourth is "symbolic" thought, ultimately in the form of language and even quite abstract thought about "rules" and "principles." Few, if any, nonhuman animals meet all of these qualifications, but then neither do very young human children—proving that "morality" is a developmental achievement. However, many or most of these talents exist in nonhuman species, and by the time these talents all appear together in one species, namely humans, we have a patently unmysterious and unsupernatural "moral" sensibility. The fact that nonhumans do not have human morality, de Waal reminds us, is no reason to discount the natural, prehuman roots of "morality":

> To neglect the common ground of primates, and to deny the evolutionary roots of human morality, would be like arriving at the top of a tower to declare that the rest of the building is irrelevant, that the precious concept of "tower" ought to be reserved for its summit.
>
> Are animals moral? Let us simply conclude that they occupy several floors of the tower of morality. Rejection of even this modest proposal can only result in an impoverished view of the structure as a whole.[27]

CONCLUSION: WHAT'S RELIGION GOT TO DO WITH IT?

We have proved that Christianity is not the only basis for morality, since religion of any kind is not required for morality nor is humanity even required. Let the silly and biased claim never be uttered again.

But what is the relationship between Christianity and morality? There certainly appears to be a connection. The relationship is the same one as between any religion and its local morality system. It consists of two parts: first, the religion as a source of specific *moral claims* and second, the religion as *a legitimation of those moral claims.*

We have seen that all religions contain behavioral instructions or norms of some sort or another; however, the details of these instructions vary wildly. Each religion advances its particular *version* of morality and backs it up with its own promises and threats (hell, reincarnation, bad *karma*, or whatever). To be sure, there are some commonalities across these religion-inspired moral systems, but *what is specifically religious in moralities is not universal or important, and what is universal and important in moralities is not specifically religious.* Humans, like all social beings, have codes and consequences for behavior; religions add to that natural and nonreligious base a layer of diverse, trivial, irrational, and divisive—and as often as not, *immoral*, viewed from outside the religion—bits and pieces. Frankly, human morality would be better off without the religious additions.

More critical, but regularly overlooked, is the legitimation effect of religion on morality (and on many other aspects of human life, like marriage or political institutions). The problem comes down to this: why *this* moral claim or moral system as opposed to some other? Why is *this* way of marrying or eating or dressing or living "moral" instead of *that* way? In a word, on what *authority* is this moral claim/system based? There are various possibilities: a moral (or social) system might be based on tradition or popular opinion or majority vote or some theory (like Marxism) or, in the end, force. None of these is a very adequate base, though, because (1) we could disagree and (2) we could be wrong.

What religion does for morality and for society in general *is move the authority, the responsibility, for rules and institutions out of human hands*. Each religion adds some idiosyncratic elements to the nonreligious human tendency to create and enforce behavioral norms and appraisals and then *attributes the whole system to a nonhuman and superhuman source*. Individually and collectively, our relationship to (putatively) religion-given morality is thus not creation or criticism but *obligation*: "the moral" is that which we as members of the group must do and which is the most praiseworthy to do and the most reprehensible not to do. This also solves the problem of the diversity of moral codes and commands: the moralities of different religions and societies have little in common except the fact that those behaviors are the most obligatory in their group. Other rules exist, but their seriousness is not as great: violating a lesser obligation might be impolite or childish or abnormal, but violating a big obligation is immoral. But what is a big and "moral" obligation in one religion/society may be a small one in another—or not a moral obligation or issue at all.

In the end, the return of morality back to earth, to the natural world and the human world, puts morality in the hands of the humans who create and sustain it in the first place. It does not "solve" the moral problems of humanity—since there is still no agreement on what the solution or what the very problems are—but it empowers us to be the ones to decide. It is humans and only humans who must struggle and negotiate and compete to arrange "moral" affairs, but then we were always alone on this mission, and religion—as history plainly and painfully shows—was never much help anyhow.

NOTES

1. Pascal Boyer, *Religion Explained: The Evolutionary Origins of Religious Thought* (New York: Basic Books, 2001).

2. Scott Atran, *In Gods We Trust: The Evolutionary Landscape of Religion* (Oxford: Oxford University Press, 2002).

3. Graham Harvey, *Animism: Respecting the Living World* (New York: Columbia University Press, 2006), p. xvii.

4. Robin Horton, "A Definition of Religion, and Its Uses," *Journal of the Royal Anthropological Institute of Great Britain and Ireland* 90 (1960): 211.

5. Michael Shermer, *The Science of Good and Evil: Why People Cheat, Gossip, Care, Share, and Follow the Golden Rule* (New York: Times Books, 2004), p. 7.

6. Kai Nielsen, *Why Be Moral?* (Amherst, NY: Prometheus Books, 1989), p. 39.

7. Ibid.

8. Ibid., p. 40.

9. Shermer, *Science of Good and Evil*, p. 31.

10. Jonathan Haidt and Jesse Graham, "When Morality Opposes Justice: Conservatives Have Moral Intuitions that Liberals May Not Recognize," *Social Justice Research* 20 (March 2007): 98.

11. Alan Dershowitz, *The Genesis of Justice: Ten Stories of Biblical Injustice that Led to the Ten Commandments and Modern Law* (New York: Warner Books, 2000).

12. Dueteronomy 31:19. The analysis for these commandments (notes 12 through 19) comes from "A List of the 613 Mitzvot" published on "Judaism 101," http://www.jewfaq.org/613.htm. The published list, in turn, is explicitly derived from the writings of Rabbi Moshe ben Maimon, also known as Maimonides, whom the list compiler regards as the most widely accepted of the mitzvah commentators. Readers may find that the original passages in scripture do not always appear to support these interpretations, which only goes to show how subjective such "moral" regulations are.

13. Deuteronomy 6:8.

14. Leviticus 19:9; Leviticus 23:22.

15. Deuteronomy 24:5.

16. Ibid.

17. Leviticus 18:6.

18. Deuteronomy 23:20.

19. Exodus 21:2.

20. CBS News, "Saudi's 'Miss Beautiful Morals' Pageant," http://www.cbsnews.com/stories/2009/05/07/world/main4998112.shtml?source=RSSattr=World_4998112.

21. [Editor's note: Although Dr. Eller still finds them unconvincing, for two

defenses of this kind of secular moral realism, see Richard Carrier, *Sense and Goodness without God* (Bloomington, Indiana: AuthorHouse, 2005), pp. 291–348, and Gary Drescher, *Good and Real* (Cambridge: MIT Press, 2006).] Sam Harris also defends this in his forthcoming book, *The Moral Landscape: How Science Can Determine Human Values* (New York: Free Press, 2010).

22. Charles Darwin, *The Descent of Man and Selection in Relation to Sex*, 2nd ed. (London: John Murray: 1882 [1871]), p. 98.

23. S. M. O'Connell, "Empathy in Chimpanzees: Evidence for Theory of Mind?" *Primates* 36 (1995).

24. Frans de Waal, *Primates and Philosophers: How Morality Evolved* (Princeton: Princeton University Press, 2006), p. 44.

25. Ibid., p. 44–45.

26. Thomas S. May, "Terms of Empathy: Your Pain in My Pain—If You Play a Fair Game," *Brain Work* 16 (May–June 2006): 3.

27. De Waal, *Primates and Philosophers*, p. 181.

Chapter 14

ATHEISM WAS NOT THE CAUSE OF THE HOLOCAUST

Hector Avalos, PhD

In his remonstrance against the New Atheist's claims that religion has led to massive human slaughters, Dinesh D'Souza, the conservative commentator, assures us that "Nazism... was a secular, anti-religious philosophy that, strangely enough, had a lot in common with Communism."[1] Thus, D'Souza is able to charge atheism in Nazi Germany with some 10 million deaths, including that of 6 million Jews. Actually, for D'Souza, the atheist regimes of Joseph Stalin and Mao Zedong take the top two spots in the list of atheist violence. Altogether, D'Souza affirms that these big three atheist regimes have killed about 100 million people.[2]

D'Souza is typical of many Christian apologists whose best response to the genocides committed by self-described Christians is that atheists have killed even more. In fact, D'Souza calculates that "deaths caused by Christian rulers over a five-hundred year period amount to only 1 percent of the deaths caused by Stalin, Hitler, and Mao in the space of a few decades."[3] Witches and Jews are some of the groups that D'Souza grudgingly concedes may have been killed due to Christian violence.

I have already discussed at length the fallacies of viewing Stalinist violence just in terms of atheism.[4] Most of Stalinist violence resulted from forced collectivization, and recently published documents show the complicity of church authorities in the Stalinist agenda.[5] D'Souza does not provide a single document or statement by Stalin that shows that he was collectivizing or killing for atheist reasons.

Moreover, communism, in the sense of a system of collectivized property, is a biblical notion found already in Acts 4:32–27. That Christian communist system also results in the killing of a married couple (Acts 5:1–11) that reneged on their promise to surrender their property. Thus, the principle of killing those who did not conform to collectivization of property is already a biblical one. The defense that it was simply lying about turning over property that was the motive for the deaths of Ananias and Sapphira overlooks the brute fact that the value of life was put below handing over all their property. For instead of just being expelled, they were killed. Stalin or Mao probably would have done the same thing. Since communism is advocated by some biblical authors, then Maoist and Stalinist deaths cannot simply be attributed to atheism, as enforcing collectivization can be deadly in both atheist or Christian forms.

In addition, D'Souza does not have the competence to evaluate claims of Maoist violence because it requires extensive training in Chinese language and documents to check the accuracy of the information provided in English sources. Since I also do not have the expertise in Chinese to evaluate Maoist violence, I will not address Maoism here. What I do know is that D'Souza does not provide a single quote from Mao or even a translated Chinese document for his assertions that Mao killed because of atheism.

In any case, this chapter will analyze in greater depth the argument that the deaths caused by Hitler should be attributed to some form of Darwinist atheism, something especially argued by Richard Weikart in his book, *From Darwin to Hitler* (2004).[6] Weikart's book is one of the sources for D'Souza's pronouncements. In fact, I shall argue that:

- Hitler's holocaust, rather than the result of some form of Darwinist atheism, is actually the most tragic consequence of a long history of Christian anti-Judaism and racism.
- Nazism follows principles of killing people for their ethnicity or religion enunciated in the Bible.

In addition, I will show that many of D'Souza's claims rely on poor research techniques and a superficial knowledge of Christian anti-Judaism.

ETHICAL PRINCIPLES AND NUMBERS

According to the United Nations Convention against Genocide (also called the first Geneva Convention), genocide describes "acts committed with the intent to destroy, in whole or in part, a national, ethnic, racial or religious group."[7] There is no ethical distinction between killing a religious group or an ethnic group. There is no ethical distinction between killing a racial or a national group. All are equally banned by the United Nations standards. This is important because D'Souza often tries to mitigate religious violence by claiming, usually without documentation, that some acts attributed to religious violence are really cases of ethnic/racial violence.

Moreover, D'Souza often leaves unexplained what it is about warring ethnic groups that makes them so opprobrious to each other. D'Souza fails to see that ethnicity can be created and/or exacerbated by religious differences. For instance, according to biblical accounts, the creation of the Hebrew ethnic group is traced to the calling of Abraham to form his own separate lineage (Genesis 12:1–7), even though he was not different "ethnically" at that point from the rest of his kinship group.[8] Abraham's lineage was further differentiated by adhering to monotheism and adding some religiously mandated practices (e.g., endogamy, circumcision) that set them apart from their neighbors (see Genesis 17:12, 24:3–4).

A similar phenomenon occurred between Christians and Jews. The initial conflict was between Jews who accepted Jesus as the Messiah and Jews who did not (see John 5:18, Acts 17:2–5, Galatians 2:11–16). Such Jews really did not differ "ethnically" from each other. While it is clear that some persons in the New Testament (NT) regarded themselves as Jewish and Christian, eventually "Jews" became those who retained the traditional religion of their ancestors, and did not accept Jesus as the Christ. The Catholic Church then reinforced the separate religious identity of Jews through marriage laws, professional restrictions, spatial separation in ghettos, and distinctive garb, which made Jews even more different and even more identifiable targets.[9] Yet it was a perceived Jewish antagonism to Christ that was often the stated initial reason for such actions. Thus, when Pope Paul IV issued his bull, *Cum nimis* (1555), which established a ghetto for Jews, his introductory rationale was that the Jews' "own guilt has consigned them to perpetual servitude."[10] Thus, one cannot divorce ethnicity and religion as easily as D'Souza attempts to do.

D'Souza also focuses on numbers more than on the ethical principle that it is wrong to kill groups of human beings based on their race, ethnicity, nationality, or religion. But if, as D'Souza seems to think, genocide is always evil, then the numbers don't matter as much as does the principle. If D'Souza does not think genocide is always evil, then he is no less a moral relativist than atheists, and now we would have only his arbitrary reasons for justifying it.

So, let's suppose that two genocidal groups, X and Y, were following the same principle of killing all members of some group that they had targeted for ethnic or religious reasons. We will label the victims of Group X as Target 1 and the victims of Group Y as Target 2. However, let's further suppose that Target 1 was an ethnic tribe that only had a thousand people, while Target 2 was a religious group composed of a million people. In tabular form:

Victimizer:	Group X	Group Y
Size of Victimized Group:	1,000	1,000,000

Now, would the reprehensibility of the principle of genocide change if Group X only killed one thousand while Group Y killed one million? Of course not, because we can reasonably suppose that if Target 1 had been composed of a million members, then Group X might have killed a million.

So an ethical sleight-of-hand is being deployed by D'Souza in his numbers game insofar as he supposes that Christianity is somehow morally superior because it simply had lesser numbers of people available for killing in some target groups. Consider that even by D'Souza's admission, Christian witch-hunts killed some 100,000 persons in Europe.[11] But if the principle of killing witches did not change, then we might have had 10 million witches killed if witch-hunters had managed to find and kill that many.

The fact that we had only 100,000 victims of witch-hunts just means that the target group was smaller, but not that the goal of total extermination was different. Thus, we must judge genocide's morality not just by the absolute numbers of people killed but also by the proportion of the target group slated to be killed. Since the presumed extermination goal for Hitler or for Christian witch-hunters is both 100 percent, the moral reprehensibility of Hitler and the witch-hunters are morally equal. Their acts of genocide also would be equally banned by the United Nations standard.

Therefore, the only thing D'Souza accomplishes is to show that Christianity is not morally superior in its principles of genocide. Christians can and have sought to kill entire groups of people. It is simply a historical accident that there were different sets of numbers for atheist versus Christian regimes, even if we allow D'Souza's erroneous assumption that Hitler represented an atheist regime. Otherwise, D'Souza's argument is akin to claiming that Hitler should be given credit for killing only 6 million Jews because that is all he managed to round up.

NAZISM AND CHRISTIAN ANTI-JUDAISM

Contrary to D'Souza's contention that Nazism is an anti-religious philosophy, Nazism is part of a long history of Christian anti-Judaism. Nazism does not represent a radical departure from traditional Christian attitudes toward Jews. This much is admitted by the Catholic historian, José M. Sánchez: "There is little question that the Holocaust had its origin in the centuries-long hostility felt by Christians against Jews."[12]

The fact that Nazism is simply an updated form of Christian anti-Judaism is evidenced by how closely the Nazi plan for Jews resembles that of the father of Protestant Christianity, Martin Luther (1483–1546). In order to understand this link, we present an actual extract of Luther's seven-point plan, issued in 1543 in his tract, *On the Jews and Their Lies*:

> First, to set fire to their synagogues or schools and to bury and cover with dirt whatever will not burn, so that no man will ever again see a stone or cinder of them.
>
> This is to be done *in honor of our Lord and of Christendom*, so that God might see that we are Christians, and do not condone or knowingly tolerate such public lying, cursing, blaspheming of his Son and of his Christians....
>
> Second, I advise that their houses also be razed and destroyed....
>
> Third, I advise that all their prayer books and Talmudic writings, in which such idolatry, lies, cursing, and blasphemy are taught, be taken from them.
>
> Fourth, I advise that their rabbis be forbidden to teach henceforth *on pain of loss of life* and limb....
>
> Fifth, I advise that safe-conduct on the highways be abolished completely for the Jews.
>
> Sixth, I advise that usury be prohibited to them, and that all cash and treasures of silver and gold be taken from them and put aside for safekeeping....

> Seventh, I recommend putting a flail, an ax, a hoe, a spade, a distaff, or a spindle into the hands of young strong Jews and Jewesses and letting them earn their bread in the sweat of their brow, as was imposed on the children of Adam (Gen. 3 [:19]).[13]

Every single point in Luther's plan was implemented by Nazi policy. For example, during Kristallnacht, the horrific anti-Jewish rampage of 1938, Jewish synagogues, businesses, and homes were burned or ransacked, just as Luther's first and second points direct. Moreover, whether by coincidence or not, Kristallnacht spanned Luther's birthday on November 10. Jewish literature was burned by the Nazis just as is stated in Luther's third point. Rabbis were certainly forbidden to teach, as directed by Luther's fourth point. The arrests and shipment of Jews to concentration camps certainly would be consistent with Luther's fifth point. Jewish property, including works of art, was confiscated by the Nazis, thus paralleling Luther's sixth point. Luther's seventh point had a correspondence in Nazi labor camps, with their infamous *Arbeit macht frei* ("work liberates") slogan.

The plans are so similar that even Martin H. Bertram, a Lutheran Luther scholar and the translator of Luther's anti-Jewish tract, states: "It is impossible to publish Luther's treatise today, however, without noting how similar his proposals were to the actions of the Nationalist Socialist regime in Germany in the 1930s and 1940s."[14] And when one looks at how Hitler viewed Luther, all we need to do is consult *Mein Kampf*: "Beside Frederick the Great stands Martin Luther as well as Richard Wagner."[15]

Catholic Christians have an even longer history of anti-Judaism. Canon Sixteen of the Council of Elvira (ca. 306), for instance, prohibited marriage between Christians and Jews.[16] Thus the Nazi Nuremberg laws, which prohibited marriages between Germans and Jews, are simply an extension of a Christian tradition, not a radical departure as D'Souza would have us believe. While anti-Judaism reaches back to the NT, it is in the Middle Ages that we begin to witness some of the most brutal and systematic Christian attacks on Jews.[17] In part, the codification of Catholic canon law was responsible for a more uniform policy toward the Jews.[18] And despite signs of tolerance shown in canon law at times, the reality is that Jews were expelled from England in 1290 and from France in 1306. Of course, by 1492, Spain also expelled the Jews.

In any event, the First Crusade, which aimed to capture the Holy Land from Muslims, generated a new wave of systematic anti-Jewish violence.

The First Crusade was proclaimed in 1095, and the first contingents began to make their way eastward in 1096. These contingents, composed mostly of laypersons, were held responsible for most anti-Jewish violence. Hordes of "crusaders" stormed into towns such as Cologne, Mainz, and Worms, and left some three thousand Jews dead.[19] Many of the Jews caught in those pogroms refused to convert to Christianity. According to one Jewish chronicle, the following rationale for martyrdom was uttered:

> After all things, there is no questioning the ways of the Holy One, blessed be He...Who has given us His Torah and has commanded us to allow ourselves to be killed and slain in witness to the Oneness of His Holy Name. Happy are we if we fulfill His will and happy is he who is slain or slaughtered and who dies attesting to the Oneness of His Name.[20]

These Jews, victimized by Christians, certainly saw hatred against them as rooted in religion. D'Souza's defense that at least Medieval Jews could have converted to Christianity, as opposed to the case in Nazi Germany, fails by the United Nations standard.[21] One cannot kill any group based on their ethnicity or religion, and so the opportunity to convert does not make a difference.

So does D'Souza think that if the number of Jews available for killing in those Medieval German cities would have been greater, then fewer Jews would have been killed? On the one hand, church authorities did denounce these pogroms. On the other hand, the laity may have acted the way they did because of words such as those of Pope Innocent III, who on October 9, 1208, issued the following announcement concerning heretics and Jews to Philip II Augustus, the king of France:

> In order that the Holy Church of God, arrayed like a fearful battlefront, may proceed against its cruelest enemies, to exterminate [*ad exterminandum*] the followers of wicked heresy, which like a serpent or an ulcer, has infected the entire province, we have caused garrisons of Christian soldiers to be called together...[22]

Notice that, even if not always carried out literally, the idea of exterminating groups of people (heretics, Jews) is already there, as is the use of medicalized genocidal language ("ulcer...infected") also common to Nazism.[23]

The fact that Hitler saw what he was doing as a continuation of Catholic policy is confirmed by a conversation he had on April 26 1933, with Hermann Wilhelm Berning, bishop of Osnabrück, Germany. According to a report recorded in *Documents on German Foreign Policy.*

> [Hitler] then brought up the Jewish question. In justification of his hostility to the Jews he referred to the Catholic Church, which had likewise always regarded the Jews as undesirables and which on account of the moral dangers involved had forbidden Christians to work for Jews. For these very reasons the Church had banished the Jews to the ghetto. He saw the Jews as nothing but pernicious enemies of the state and Church and therefore he wanted to drive the Jews out more and more, especially from academic life and public professions.[24]

As the famed Holocaust historian, Guenter Lewy, summarized this meeting, "Hitler was merely doing what the Church had done for 1,500 years."[25] Indeed, Hitler simply had much better logistics and technology to do what some Medieval Christians wanted to do to the Jews. There were also many more Jews living in Germany by Hitler's time. Thus, D'Souza should be counting the increases in target populations, not just general populations, to judge the proportionality of atheist and religious violence.

How Religious Was Nazi Anti-Judaism?

D'Souza contends that Nazism was an "antireligious philosophy," but he offers meager indisputable evidence for his claim. If we wish to know motives, a reasonable procedure is to seek the reasons people give for what they do. If we follow this procedure, then the following statement by Hitler in *Mein Kampf* is most relevant:

> Hence today I believe that I am acting in accordance with the will of the Almighty Creator; by defending myself against the Jew, I am fighting for the work of the Lord.[26]

But D'Souza dismisses Hitler's statement as evidence that Hitler meant what he said.[27] Instead, D'Souza suggests that a better source for Hitler's thoughts on religion is Allan Bullock, author of a book titled *Hitler and Stalin: Parallel Lives* (1993). As D'Souza phrases it: "From an early age, historian Allan Bullock writes, 'Hitler had no time at all for Catholic teaching, regarding it as a religion fit only for slaves and detesting its ethics.'"[28] This is clearly a deflective tactic since D'Souza does not explain why Bullock knows what Hitler thinks better than Hitler himself. It is usually poor history when one substitutes a secondary source (i.e., Bullock) for a primary source (i.e., Hitler). Moreover, even if Hitler detested Catholic teachings, D'Souza confuses atheism with anti-Catholicism. And the above quotation was not the only time Hitler invoked God, religion, or Christianity to explain his policies in *Mein Kampf*. Hitler also stated: "For God's will gave men their form, their essence and their abilities. Anyone who destroys His work is declaring war on the Lord's creation, the divine will."[29] In the meeting with Berning, Hitler insisted that "neither a personal life could be built without Christianity nor a state."[30]

Yet another attempt to avoid the obvious implications of Hitler's statements is D'Souza's appeal to the propagandistic aspect of Hitler's *Mein Kampf*. D'Souza claims that "Hitler himself says in *Mein Kampf* that his public statements should be understood as propaganda that bears no relation to the truth but are designed to sway the masses."[31] D'Souza does not cite a direct quote from Hitler for this claim and only refers us to pages 177–85 of *Mein Kampf*, which again reflects poor scholarship. D'Souza does not seem to realize that his gross generalization about *Mein Kampf*'s bearing "no relation to the truth" creates a case of self-referential incoherence. If Hitler's propaganda always hides the truth, then it follows that the very statement about how he was using propaganda must be false. And does Hitler not really believe that Jews are evil because what he says in *Mein Kampf* has no relation to the truth? Rather, a better historical procedure is to presume that an author meant what he said about what he believed unless proven otherwise. Nothing Hitler said disproves that he believed he was doing God's will.

Moreover, D'Souza leaves unexplained why Hitler could have thought that his anti-Jewish rhetoric would sway the masses unless the masses were receptive to an anti-Jewish message. This is important because the masses of which D'Souza speaks identified themselves largely as Christians. For example, a Nazi report indicates that by 1938, 51.4 percent of SS members were identified as Protestant, 22.7 percent were Catholic, and 25.7 percent were "God-believers" (*Gottgläubigen*).[32] Since anti-Judaism was not associated with Darwin's own writings, then it is a history of Christian anti-Judaism that would be much more effective in convincing the Christian masses.

POSITIVE CHRISTIANITY

Another aspect of Nazism that D'Souza dismisses without much investigation is the Nazi idea of Positive Christianity. The term dates from as early as Point 24 of the Nazi Party Program of 1920, which says:

> The Party as such reflects the viewpoint of a positive Christianity without being bound confessionally to any specific denomination. It battles the Jewish materialistic spirit.[33]

Again, anti-Judaism was one of its main tenets, and that simply follows a long history of Christian anti-Judaism. It is not a radical departure from historically orthodox Christianity in that sense.

If one reads *The Myth of the Twentieth Century*, a treatise on Nazism by Alfred Rosenberg, who is credited with authorship of that Party Program of 1920, one will understand that he saw Positive Christianity as a restoration of the original and purer teachings of Christ.[34] Indeed, Rosenberg tells us that Christ's life is what should be meaningful for Germans.[35] Rosenberg repudiated the idea of Christ's sacrifice as a Jewish corruption, and saw Jesus as a great figure whose true work, the love of one's race, has been distorted by organized Christendom into a universal love, instead of a love restricted to one's racial group (especially as he interpreted Leviticus 19:18 and 25:17).

That is why Rosenberg called it "positive Christianity" (*positive Christentum*), which he explicitly contrasted to the "corrupt" form represented by the "etrusco-asiatic clergy" (*etrusco-asiatische . . . Priesterherrschaft*), which encompassed Roman Catholicism.[36] Thus, for Positive Christianity, the mere word "Christianity" often meant the Judaized and clerically organized form seen in Roman Catholicism, which was not equivalent to what Jesus had in mind. Being opposed to "Christianity," therefore, did not mean opposing the religion of Christ or opposing religion.

In fact, *Der Mythus* is replete with biblical quotations. Some of Rosenberg's interpretations of the Bible were ones upon which even Jewish scholars could agree. For example, he notes that Leviticus 25:17, which states "thou shalt not take advantage of thine neighbor," refers to fellow Hebrews, and not to everyone else.[37] But this interpretation of "thine neighbor" is consistent with the interpretation of Harry M. Orlinsky, the great Jewish biblical scholar.[38] Rosenberg also thought that the Gospel of John best preserved some of the teachings of Jesus. He commented thus: "The Gospel of John, which still bears an aristocratic spirit throughout, strove against the collective bastardization, orientalization and Judaization of Christianity."[39] It is in the Gospel of John (8:44) where Jesus himself says that the Jews are liars fathered by the devil. That verse later shows up on Nazi road signs, whereas no quotes from Darwin were ever on Nazi road signs.[40] That verse has echoes in the title of Luther's tract (*On the Jews and their Lies*), as well as the longer original title of *Mein Kampf* (*[My] 4 and 1/2 Years of Struggle against Lies...*).

Yes, Rosenberg syncretized Christian concepts found in the NT with Germanic myths, and myths of his own creation or adaptation. But how does Rosenberg's biblical exegesis and syncretism differ from what other self-described Christians have been doing throughout history? Indeed, many scholars argue precisely that Christianity was the result of combining Jewish with Hellenistic ideas. In understanding themselves as restorers of early Christianity, Positive Christians are no less Christian than the first Lutherans or Anabaptists. Indeed, Positive Christianity had great forebears among early Christians who rejected Judaism. This includes Marcion (second century), the Gnostic Christian who repudiated the Old Testament (OT) entirely, and promoted a canon consisting only of an expurgated Gospel of Luke and some of Paul's Epistles. Marcionism repeats itself in Christian history, especially among some Anabaptist groups and Christian theologians (e.g., Friedrich Schleiermacher).[41]

In short, if we use the same logic used by many Christian theologians who radically reinterpret the Hebrew Bible for Christian practice, we could also argue that Positive Christianity does not represent so much an anti-Christian movement, as it does a reinterpretation of Christianity, a phenomenon which is a standard part of Christian history. That is why we have some 25,000 Christian groups today, some of which believe radically opposite things. To say that Marcionites, Lutherans, or Positive Christians are not really Christians is to make a theological judgment more than a historical judgment.

What's So Negative about Positive Christianity?

Not only does D'Souza exhibit a woeful misunderstanding of Positive Christianity, but the main objections he launches against it are extremely superficial. For D'Souza, Positive Christianity cannot count as Christianity because it "was obviously a radical departure from traditional Christian understanding, and was condemned as such by Pope Pius XI at the time."[42] The latter case alone shows D'Souza's theological prejudices because he assumes that whatever Pope Pius condemns must represent a false Christianity. And of course, the claim that an Aryan Christ is a radical departure from traditional Christian understanding comes as news to anyone who has ever studied the long history of Christian art, where Christ is routinely painted as a white European. According to Epiphanius Monachus (eighth or ninth century), a Greek monk from Constantinople, Jesus "stood six feet tall, his hair was long, goulden-colored, and not very thick...."[43] So, how is a Nazi Aryan Christ such a radical departure?[44]

D'Souza also neglects to tell his readers that before Pope Pius XI distanced himself from Nazism in his famous 1937 encyclical (*Mit Brennender Sorge* / "With Burning Sorrow"), that same Pope had signed, "at the time," a Concordat with the Nazis in 1933, which even Hitler credited with helping to further his "struggle against international Jewry ("*der Kampf gegen das internationale Judentum*").[45] And note how D'Souza does not question whether Pope Pius XI has political rather than lofty humanitarian motives for his reproof of the Nazis in 1937. D'Souza does not question whether Pius XI meant what he said, as he does when Hitler says he is following God's will.

Yet when one reads that 1937 encyclical, Pope Pius XI admits compromising with Nazi Germany:

> When, in 1933, We consented, Venerable Brethren, to open negotiations for a concordat, which the Reich Government proposed on the basis of a scheme of several years' standing... We were prompted by the desire, as it behooved Us, to secure for Germany the freedom of the Church's beneficent mission and the salvation of the souls in her care, as well as by the sincere wish to render the German people a service essential for its peaceful development and prosperity. Hence, despite many and grave misgivings, We then decided not to withhold Our consent for We wished

to spare the Faithful of Germany, as far as it was humanly possible, the trials and difficulties they would have had to face, given the circumstances, had the negotiations fallen through.[46]

Why does that not qualify as a political move since it is meant to protect the interests of a distinct group (Catholics)? Why can't we say that Vatican hierarchy did not mean what it said in 1937 either? And were none of the Pope's advisers familiar with *Mein Kampf*, which had been published nearly a decade before 1933?

In fact, Diego von Bergen, the Reich's ambassador to the Holy See, reported that while the Pope was saying one thing, Eugenio Pacelli, the Cardinal Secretary to the Vatican and the man who would become Pope Pius XII, promised that "normal and friendly relations...would be restored as soon as possible" between the Vatican and the Nazis after that encyclical.[47] Indeed, by 1939, Archbishop Cesare Orsenigo, the nuncio to Berlin, was busy opening a gala reception for Hitler's fiftieth birthday in Berlin.[48] So much for the Catholic hierarchy repudiating the Nazi regime.

Otherwise, it all depends on whether one views the mission of the Catholic Church as worthy of such a compromise, and that is a theological judgment. If Hitler believed that God wanted him to kill Jews, there is no way to verify that that mission was any less from God than when Pope Innocent III wanted to exterminate Jews or other heretics in the Middle Ages. Otherwise, D'Souza would have to explain why Pope Innocent III was right to say God wanted him to exterminate Jews or heretics in the Middle Ages, but God would not have wanted the same thing for Hitler in the twentieth century.

HOW ANTI-RELIGIOUS WAS HITLER?

Misunderstanding the difference between Positive Christianity and the rest of Christianity is what has led D'Souza and others to transform any of Hitler's supposed anti-Christian views into antireligious views. There is a logical problem, of course, with the claim that being anti-Christian or being anti-Catholic means being antireligious. Religion is much broader than Christianity or Catholicism.

More importantly, for part of his evidence, D'Souza appeals to Hitler's *Table Talk*, which supposedly records the Fuehrer's more private thoughts.

However, the reliability of this source for determining Hitler's views is most questionable. Four major versions of *Table Talk* exist, here named after the main editors or translators and the years of publication: (1) Henry Picker (German, 1951, 1963, 1976); (2) François Genoud (French translation only, 1952); (3) H. R. Trevor-Roper (English, 1953, 1973, 2000); and (4) Werner Jochmann (German, 1980). These records are usually organized internally by the date in which Hitler held a conversation.

The problems with *Table Talk* have been studied carefully by Richard Carrier.[49] From my perspective, as an academic historian, there are at least three problems with using this source: (1) There are no extant manuscripts from Hitler's own hand of this source. We have no audio tapes to verify the transcripts. What we have are reputed copies which often have been filtered through Martin Bormann, Hitler's adjutant. The fact that versions agree sufficiently to propose a common source does not necessarily prove that this common source was Hitler himself. (2) The versions are sometimes discrepant. Some passages are missing from the edition of Trevor-Roper relative to the edition of Picker. So it is difficult to tell what comes from Hitler and what comes from the editors. (3) Trevor-Roper authenticated the Hitler Diaries, despite the fact that they later proved to be forgeries.[50] Genoud is also a questionable character who may have been involved in forgery. And as Carrier has shown, both the Genoud and Trevor-Roper editions often egregiously mistranslate the original German.

In addition, a main intermediate in all known versions of *Table Talk* is Hitler's personal secretary, Martin Bormann, who was known for his anti-Christian views.[51] So sometimes we may be reading Bormann's thoughts rather than Hitler's.[52]

We also know, from other sources, that Hitler disagreed with Bormann and also disagreed with his own supposed views expressed in *Table Talk*. For example, Albert Speer, who was Hitler's personal architect, said:

> Even after 1942 Hitler went on maintaining that he regarded the church as indispensable in political life. He would be happy he said in one of those teatime talks at Obersalzberg, if someday a prominent churchman turned up who was suited to lead one of the churches—or if possible both the Catholic and Protestant churches reunited.[53]

Speer also reports cases where Hitler contravened anti-Christian actions by his underlings.[54]

So, if we use only the most reliable sources, D'Souza definitely has not proven his case. D'Souza does not cite a single instance in *Mein Kampf*, a source indisputably ascribed to Hitler, where the latter says his motives are atheistic. Yet we can find a number of places in *Mein Kampf* where Hitler, no less than Martin Luther, claims to be following the will of God.

But even if we were to regard *Table Talk* as a reliable source, Hitler's antireligionism is not as clear as D'Souza claims because D'Souza conflates anti-Christianity with atheism. Of the quotes D'Souza provides, the one that would best makes his case is: "through the peasantry we shall be able to destroy Christianity."[55] But D'Souza does not provide a page number to Hitler's *Table Talk*, and his corresponding footnote just refers to "Hitler's *Table Talk* (New York: Enigma Books, 2000)," which is an edition associated with Hugh Trevor-Roper.[56] This is, at best, very sloppy documentation, and it raises the question of whether D'Souza is even reading *Table Talk* firsthand.

Moreover, D'Souza does not reveal the full sentence, which is actually found in *Hitler Speaks*, a historically discredited book authored by Hermann Rauschning: "But it is through the peasantry that we shall be really able to destroy Christianity because there is in them a true religion rooted in nature and blood."[57] Thus, in this fuller version, Hitler's alleged goal is a better religion ("true religion"), not no religion.

If D'Souza had read the various versions of *Table Talk* carefully, he would also find a lot that contradicts his claim that Hitler was antireligious. For example, in a conversation reported for October 14, 1941 (Trevor-Roper edition), Hitler remarks:

> An educated man retains the sense of the mysteries of nature and bows before the unknowable. An uneducated man, on the other hand, runs the risk of going over to atheism (which is a return to the state of the animal)....[58]

Hitler adds:

> One may ask whether the disappearance of Christianity would entail the disappearance of belief in God. That's not to be desired. The notion of divinity gives most men the opportunity to concretise the feeling they have of supernatural realities. Why should we destroy this wonderful power they have of incarnating the feeling for the divine that is within them?[59]

Thus, even here Hitler makes a difference between not believing in Christianity and not believing in God. In fact, in the original German of the *Table Talk*, Hitler expresses his expectation of eternal life in heaven and his actual disdain for those who mock the providence of God, declaring instead that he thinks he may have been chosen by God, and that it is our belief in a Creator that separates us from the animals.[60]

And it is in *Table Talk* that Hitler clearly distinguishes the original teachings of Christ from the corrupt form that became known as "Christianity." He said (on October 21, 1941) that:

> Originally, Christianity was merely an incarnation of Bolshevism the destroyer. Nevertheless, the Galilean, who later was called the Christ, intended something quite different. He must be regarded as a popular leader who took up His position against Jewry.[61]

In any case, Hitler's actions against any churches are not necessarily more anti-Christian or antireligious than Protestant destruction of Catholic churches, or Catholic destruction of Protestant shrines. For instance, King Henry VIII (1491–1547), who initiated the English Reformation, did not see himself as anti-Christian or antireligious when he demolished Catholic monasteries. Christian kings often killed clerics and persecuted churches that disagreed with them.[62] What we are seeing in Nazism is a sectarian war or an intrareligious war, which should not be confused with antireligionism.[63]

HOW DARWINIST WAS NAZISM?

Despite all the evidence that Nazism is a continuation of Christian anti-Judaism, D'Souza assures us that Darwinism is really behind Nazism. For his evidence, D'Souza refers us to the work of Richard Weikart, as follows:

> If Nazism represented the culmination of anything, it was that of the nineteenth-century and early twentieth-century ideology of social Darwinism. As historian Richard Weikart documents, both Hitler and Himmler were admirers of Darwin and often spoke of their role as enacting a "law of nature" that guaranteed "the elimination of the unfit." Weikart...concludes that while Darwinism is not a "sufficient" intellectual explanation for Nazism, it is a "necessary" one. Without Darwinism there might not have been Nazism.[64]

As in the previous cases, D'Souza does not seem to have the expertise to evaluate the claims of Weikart. I have already offered a number of lengthy critiques of Weikart, but here I will summarize some of the problems with using Weikart's book.[65]

First, the very notion that Darwinism was "necessary" for Nazism is disproven by Luther's 1543 plan for the Jews. By 1543 one could achieve a program that even Luther scholars admit resembles Nazism, and there was no Darwin then. Weikart forgets Luther altogether, and he hardly mentions a long history of Christian anti-Judaism which certainly would be more important than Darwinism. Most Germans were not as familiar with Darwin's books as they were with the Bible or with anti-Jewish traditions of German figures, such as Luther.

D'Souza never provides any direct quotation to show that Hitler was an admirer of Darwin. In fact, D'Souza seems to be unaware of Weikart's exact views on Hitler's references to Darwin. Weikart has been quoted as saying:

> It's true that Hitler hardly ever mentioned Darwin by name (the only direct mention of Darwin I have been able to find is an account by a colleague Wagener).[66]

Yet even "hardly ever" is deceptive because Weikart admits that the only direct reference to Darwin by Hitler does not come from Hitler at all. Hitler, however, mentions Luther, and praises him in *Mein Kampf*. That alone tells us that, for Hitler, Luther was important enough to mention a few times, but Darwin never was.

Moreover, D'Souza and Weikart also ignore evidence that Darwinism was specifically banned in Nazi Germany, at least in 1935. Evidence derives from this directive in a list of banned books in Nazi Germany compiled by an exhibit of the University of Arizona library: "Writings of a philosophical and social nature whose content deals with the false scientific enlightenment of primitive Darwinism and Monism (Häckel)."[67]

WEIKART'S DARWINISM

A principal problem with Weikart's thesis is that he begins with this very restrictive definition of "Darwinism":

> When I use the term Darwinism in this study, I mean the theory of evo-
> lution through natural selection as advanced by Darwin in *The Origin of
> Species*.[68]

It is puzzling why Weikart restricted his definition of Darwinism just to
what is found in *On the Origin of Species* (1859), especially as that book says
really nothing about human evolution or racial struggle. Consequently,
Weikart has to keep redefining "Darwinism" to include other works of
Darwin and whatever perversions of Darwinism he can find. This flaw is
all the more important because he has criticized other recognized historians for not adhering to their definitions. Thus, in a review of a book by
Annette Wittkau-Horgby, Weikart remarks, "Wittkau-Horgby thus does
not adhere to the definition of materialism she starts with...."[69] To avoid
constantly moving the definitional goal post for Darwinism, Weikart could
have defined Darwinism more broadly, and said "... as advanced by Darwin
in his works." Since, for Weikart, misinterpretations of Darwin still count
as "Darwinism," then he actually should say: "... as advanced by Darwin in
his books and in various interpretations of his work, whether those interpretations are right or wrong."

Weikart's willingness to count misrepresentations of Darwin as Darwinism, however, is not consistently applied to other writings that the
Nazis misrepresented. For example, in his review of Richard Steigmann-
Gall's *The Holy Reich*, Weikart remarks: "Many German pantheists used
religious— even Christian—terminology, but they often redefined it."[70] So,
when Nazi writers use pantheistic terminology, then they are pantheists,
but when they use Christian terminology, then they are not really Christians, but pantheists. Redefining Christian terms absolves one from being
Christian, but redefining Darwin will still brand one a Darwinist. This logical inconsistency is tendentious and serves to deflect responsibility from
Christianity.

All this is important because none of Darwin's works, and especially
not *On the Origin of Species*, is concerned with anti-Judaism. Anti-Judaism is
an essential component of Nazism, and one that is shared, not with
Darwin's books, but with early Christianity (e.g., John 8:44, Revelation
2:9–10). Again, even if Darwin had an anti-Jewish agenda, most Germans
would not be as familiar with Darwin's books as they were with the Bible.

RACIALIZATION OF JEWS

D'Souza claims that at least Medieval Jews could have converted to Christianity while Nazi Darwinist eugenics had racialized Jews to the point where the latter could not change their identity. As I have argued, this really does not make a difference in condemning genocide based on religion or ethnicity. But the idea that Jews were a racial category, not just a religious category, already had a long history in Christianity before Darwin.

Consider Hitler's idea of "purity of blood" (*Reinhaltung des Blutes*).[71] This notion did not begin with Darwin, nor was it even discussed as such by Darwin in *On the Origin of Species*. Instead, Hitler's specific terminology corresponds quite closely to Catholic Spanish terminology (*limpieza de sangre*/"cleanliness or purity of blood") applied against Jews in Spain. In particular, Juan Martinez Siliceo, the archbishop of Toledo, proposed legislation in 1547 based very specifically on this *limpieza de sangre*.[72] Statutes enacted in Toledo in 1449 also focused on blood purity as a means to discriminate against Jews who had converted but were not Spaniards by "blood."

As even Jewish scholars have noted, many biblical figures can be interpreted as advocating forms of eugenics before the term was even invented. Rabbi Max Reichler, one of the authors of *Jewish Eugenics and Other Essays* tells us:

> To be sure eugenics as a science could hardly have existed among ancient Jews; but many eugenic rules were certainly incorporated in the large collection of Biblical and Rabbinical laws. Indeed there are clear indications of a conscious effort to utilize all influences that might improve the inborn qualities of the Jewish races and to guard against any practice that might vitiate the purity of the race or "impair the racial qualities of future generations" either physically, mentally, or morally.... The very founder of the Jewish race, the patriarch Abraham, recognized the importance of certain inherited qualities, and insisted that the wife of his "only beloved son" should not come from "the daughters of the Canaanites," but from the seed of a superior stock.[73]

D'Souza provides really nothing comparable, other than a secondary reference to Weikart, that would show that Darwin's *On the Origin of Species* had any notions of blood purity or eugenics even close to this. As it is, D'Souza seems to be confusing *natural selection*, the main concept behind *On the Origin of Species*, with *artificial selection* which was an essential part of Nazism.

If we look at Hitler's own racialist rationales, we find that he appeals to the Bible, not to *On the Origin of Species*, for support. One example is this statement from *Mein Kampf* concerning race mixing:

> ...it is one of those concerning which it is said with such terrible justice that the sins of the fathers are avenged *down to the tenth generation*.... Blood sin and desecration of the race are the original sin in this world....[74]

But whence comes Hitler's notion that blood desecration is a sin down to the tenth generation? It is not from any of Darwin's works. Rather, it is from Deuteronomy 23:2–3 (RSV):

> No bastard shall enter the assembly of the LORD; even to the tenth generation none of his descendants shall enter the assembly of the LORD. No Ammonite or Moabite shall enter the assembly of the LORD; even to the tenth generation none belonging to them shall enter the assembly of the LORD for ever.

Hitler adds that "To bring about such a development is, then, nothing else but to sin against the will of the eternal creator."[75]

And where do we find the notion that race mixing is a sin? It is not from *On the Origin of Species*. But it is in Ezra 9:1–2 and 12:

> The people of Israel, the priests, and the Levites have not separated themselves from the peoples of the lands with their abominations...For they have taken some of their daughters as wives for themselves and for their sons. Thus *the holy seed has mixed itself* with the peoples of the lands, and in this faithlessness the officials and leaders have led the way... Therefore give not your daughters to their sons, neither take their daughters for your sons, and never seek their peace or prosperity, *that you may be strong*, and eat the good of the land, and leave it for an inheritance to your children for ever. [emphasis mine]

Notice that the purpose of endogamy is "*so that you may be strong*," which exemplifies a classic eugenic concept of improving some desired trait through proper breeding. Thus, *Mein Kampf* indicates that it is the Bible, not *On the Origin of Species*, that seems to be the more direct influence for Hitler.

RACIAL STRUGGLE PART OF CHRISTIANITY

Weikart tags as particularly Darwinian the notion of history as a racial struggle. Weikart has repeatedly used the following quote from *The Descent of Man* to support this contention:

> At some future period, not very distant as measured by centuries, the civilised races of man will almost certainly exterminate and replace throughout the world the savage races.[76]

But this quote is out of context. The proper context is a lament for this extinction—not an endorsement of it. This lament is even clearer if one reads further, where Darwin observes that, in fact, "savages did not formerly waste away" until modern civilizations (not modern races) encroached upon them, since in classical times "there is no lament in any writer of that period over the perishing barbarians."[77] Hence Darwin believed superior culture and technology, not inferior blood, was exterminating "the savage races."

And history as a racial struggle is very much part of Christian history. Already in 1853, and a few years before Darwin's *On the Origin of Species* was even published, George Fitzhugh, the American proslavery advocate, had a racial struggle framed in a survival-of-the-fittest matrix when he said:

> Members of Congress of the Young American party, boast that the Anglo-Saxon race is manifestly destined to beat out all other races, as the wire-grass destroys and takes the place of other grasses.[78]

And contrary to Weikart's claim that the spiritual orientation of Judeo-Christianity resisted such racialist ideas, Robert Knox, the famous Scottish racialist writer, says:

> Now, whether the earth be overpopulated or not, one thing is certain—the strong will always grasp at the property and lands of the weak. I have been assured that this conduct is not at all incompatible with the highest moral and even Christian feeling.[79]

Indeed, John Campbell, a proslavery Christian writer, saw racial struggle as an essential part of the history of mankind, and he quotes Knox for part of his 1851 essay, "Negro-Mania":

The antagonism of races is working itself out in every instance where two races are put in collision by the quicker or slower extinction of the inferior and feebler race.... Knox has shown us everywhere the white blood treading down and exterminating the darker races. "The Saxon (he remarks) will not mingle with any dark race, nor will he allow him to hold an acre of land in the country occupied by him... There is no denying the fact that the Saxon—call him by what name you will—has a perfect horror for his darker brethren."[80]

In general, Weikart seems blissfully unaware of an abundance of Pre-Nazi Christian racialist literature that would show that Nazism is not a departure from Christian history whatsoever.

CONCLUSION

D'Souza fails spectacularly in his efforts to paint Nazism as an "anti-religious philosophy" responsible for ten million deaths. First, D'Souza provides almost no documentation for his claims, and what he does provide comes mostly from secondary sources. He is apparently unable to read primary German sources in the original language. He also confuses any efforts against organized Christianity with antireligionism. But even in *Table Talk*, a questionable source used by D'Souza, Hitler makes clear that being against Christianity is not the same as being against belief in God.

D'Souza's numbers game simply hides the fact that both theistic and nontheistic morality can result in genocide. Any differences in the number of deaths is more an accident of history than a difference in a principle that can justify the killing of groups based on ethnicity, race, nationality, or religion. By the United Nations standards, Christian acts of genocide have failed just as much as those of Maoists or Stalinists because they were all equally devoted to the extermination of 100 percent of their respective target groups.

But the most significant problem with D'Souza's argument is his convenient amnesia about a long history of Christian anti-Judaism before Hitler and Darwin were even born. The calling for the extermination of heretics and Jews in France by Pope Innocent III in the Middle Ages did not need Darwinism. And Luther's murderous seven-point plan, which is nearly identical to that of Nazism, proves beyond a doubt that Darwinism certainly was not "necessary" to achieve a Nazi vision (see chart below). Nazism, indeed, was very much at home in a long tradition of Christian anti-Judaism.

A COMPARISON OF HITLER'S ANTI-JEWISH POLICIES AND POLICIES ADVOCATED IN ANY OF THE WORKS OF MARTIN LUTHER AND CHARLES DARWIN

Hitler's Policies	Luther	Darwin
Burning Jewish Synagogues	Yes	No
Destroying Jewish Homes	Yes	No
Destroying Sacred Jewish Books	Yes	No
Forbidding Rabbis to Teach	Yes	No
Abolishing Safe Conduct	Yes	No
Confiscating Jewish Property	Yes	No
Forcing Jews into Labor	Yes	No
Citing God as Part of the Reason for Anti-Judaism	Yes	No

NOTES

1. Dinesh D'Souza, *What's So Great about Christianity* (Washington, DC: Regnery, 2007), p. 215.

2. D'Souza, *What's So Great*, p. 215. D'Souza is particularly responding to the arguments of Sam Harris, *The End of Faith: Religion, Terror, and the Future of Reason* (New York: W. W. Norton, 2005); Daniel Dennett, *Breaking the Spell: Religion as a Natural Phenomenon* (New York: Viking, 2006); and Richard Dawkins, *The God Delusion* (Boston: Houghton Mifflin, 2006).

3. D'Souza, *What's So Great*, p. 214.

4. Hector Avalos, *Fighting Words: The Origins of Religious Violence* (Amherst, NY: Prometheus Books, 2005), pp. 325–34.

5. See especially, Tatiana A. Chumachenko, *Church and State in Soviet Russia: Russian Orthodoxy from World War II to the Krushchev Years*, trans. Edward E. Roslof (Armonk, NY: M. E. Sharpe, 2002).

6. Richard Weikart, *From Darwin to Hitler: Evolutionary Ethics, Eugenics, and Racism in Germany* (New York: PalgraveMacmillan, 2004).

7. A Summary of the United Nations Agreements on Human Rights at: http://www.hrweb.org/legal/undocs.html#CAG.

8. For recent discussions on theories of ethnicity, see Richard H. Thompson, *Theories of Ethnicity: A Critical Appraisal* (New York: Greenwood Press, 1989). For ancient Israel, see Kenton Sparks, *Ethnicity and Identity in Ancient Israel: Prolegomena to the Study of Ethnic Sentiments and Their Expression in the Hebrew Bible* (Winona Lake: IN: Eisenbrauns, 1998).

9. See further, Solomon Grayzel, *The Church and the Jews in the XIIIth Century* (New York: Hermon Press, 1966); Kenneth R. Stow, *Catholic Thought and Papal Jewry Policy, 1555–1593* (New York: Jewish Theological Seminary of America, 1977).

10. Stow, *Catholic Thought*, p. 295; Latin (p. 291): *quos propia culpa perpetua servituta submisit.*

11. D'Souza, *What's So Great*, p. 208.

12. José M. Sánchez, *Pius XII and the Holocaust: Understanding the Controversy* (Washington, DC: Catholic University of America Press, 2002), p. 70.

13. Martin Luther, "On the Jews and Their Lies," trans. Martin H. Bertram in *Luther's Works: The Christian in Society IV*, ed. Franklin Sherman (Philadelphia, PA: Fortress Press, 1971), pp. 268–72.

14. Martin Luther, "On the Jews," p. 268 n. 173. See also William Montgomery McGovern, *From Luther to Hitler: The History of Fascist-Nazi Political Philosophy* (Cambridge, MA: Houghton Mifflin, 1941)

15. Adolf Hitler, *Mein Kampf,* trans. Ralph Manheim (Boston: Houghton Mifflin, 1971), p. 213; German (p. 232): *Neben Friedrich der Grossen stehen hier Martin Luther sowohl als wie Richard Wagner.* Our German text is from Adolf Hitler, *Mein Kampf* (München. Müller, 1938). Henceforth, we refer to this source as "German (page number)."

16. On the Council of Elvira, see Louis H. Feldman, *Jew and Gentile in the Ancient World: Attitudes and Interactions from Alexander to Justinian* (Princeton: Princeton University Press, 1993), pp. 373, 380, 398.

17. For a Catholic scholar's view of this period, especially in light of Vatican II, see Edward A. Synan, *The Pope and the Jews in the Middle Ages* (New York: Macmillan, 1965).

18. John Y. B. Hood, *Aquinas and the Jews* (Philadelphia: University of Pennsylvania Press, 1995), p. 25.

19. See Robert Chazan, *In the Year 1096: The First Crusade and the Jews* (Philadelphia, PA: Jewish Publication Society, 1996), p. 129.

20. Shlomo Eidelberg, *The Jews and the Crusaders: The Hebrew Chronicles of the First and Second Crusades* (Madison: University of Wisconsin Press, 1977), p. 31.

21. D'Souza, *What's So Great*, p. 218.

22. Grayzel, *The Church and the Jews*, p. 133; Latin text on p. 132. Innocent (Grayzel, *The Church and the Jews*, pp. 92–93) paradoxically also subscribed to the Augustinian idea of keeping some Jews alive as a sign of unbelief, and so he also

believed that one should "not destroy the Jews completely" (Latin: *ne deleveris omnino Judeos*). On this latter idea, see Jeremy Cohen, *Living Letters of the Law: Ideas of the Jew in Medieval Christianity* (Berkeley: University of California Press, 1999).

23. For this aspect of Nazism, see Götz Aly, Peter Chroust, and Christian Pross, *Cleansing the Fatherland: Nazi Medicine and Racial Hygiene*, trans. Belinda Cooper (Baltimore, MD: Johns Hopkins University Press, 1994).

24. Paul R. Sweet, ed., *Documents on German Foreign Policy, 1918–1945, from the Archives of the German Foreign Ministry* (Washington, DC: United States Printing Office, 1949), series C, vol. 1, p. 347.

25. Guenter Lewy, *The Catholic Church and Nazi Germany* (New York: De Capo Press, 2000), p. 51.

26. Hitler, *Mein Kampf*, p. 65 / German (p. 70): *So glaube ich heute im Sinne des allmächtigen Schöpfers zu handeln: Indem ich mich des Juden erwehre, kämpfe ich für das Werk des herrn.*

27. D'Souza, *What's So Great*, p. 217.

28. Ibid.

29. Hitler, *Mein Kampf*, p. 562 / German (p. 630): *Denn Gottes Wille gab den Menschen einst ihre Gestalt, ihr Wesen und ihre Fähigkeiten. Wer sein Wert zerstört sagt damit der Schöpfung des herrn, dem göttlichen Wollen, den kampf an.*

30. Sweet, *Documents on German Foreign Policy*, series C, vol. 1, p. 347.

31. D'Souza, *What's So Great*, p. 217.

32. Richard Steigmann-Gall, *The Holy Reich: Nazi Conceptions of Christianity, 1919–1945* (Cambridge: Cambridge University Press, 2003), p. 221. For a study of the anti-Jewish receptivity of the German masses, see Daniel Goldhagen, *Hitler's Willing Executioners: Ordinary Germans and the Holocaust* (New York: Little, Brown, 1996).

33. Alfred Rosenberg, *Das Parteiprogramm: Wesen, Grundsätze und Ziele der NSDAP* (Münich: Zentralverlag der NSDAP, 1922 [25th edition, 1943]), p. 13: *Die Partei als solche vertritt den Standpunkt eines positiven Christentums, ohne sich konfessionell an ein bestimmtes Bekenntnis zu binden. Sie bekämpft den jüdisch-materialistischen Geist…* [my English translation].

34. Alfred Rosenberg, *Der Mythus des 20, Jahrhunderts: Eine Wertung der seelisch-geistigen Gestaltentkämpfe unserer Zeit*, (München: Hoheneichen Verlag, 1938). Steigmann-Gall (*The Holy Reich*, pp. 92–93) contends that Rosenberg's book was not highly regarded within the Nazi Party. However, Albert Speer (*Inside the Third Reich*, trans. Richard and Clara Winston [New York: Macmillan, 1970], p. 115), Hitler's personal architect, says that "the public regarded the book as the standard text for party ideology."

35. Rosenberg, *Der Mythus*, p. 74.

36. Ibid., p. 78: *Das positive Christentum gegenüber dem negativum der auf der etrusco-asiatische Vorstellung zuruckgehende Priesterherrschaft und des Hexenwahns.*

37. Alfred Rosenberg, *Race and Race History and Other Essays*, ed. Robert Pois and trans. Jonathon Cape (New York: Harper & Row, 1970), p. 180.

38. See Harry M. Orlinsky, "Nationalism-Universalism and Internationalism in Ancient Israel," in *Translating and Understanding the Old Testament: Essays in Honor of Herbert Gordon May*, eds. Harry Thomas Frank and William L. Reed (Nashville, TN: Abingdon, 1970), pp. 206–36, especially pp. 210–11.

39. Rosenberg, *Der Mythus*, p. 75. My translation of the German: *Gegen diese gesamte Verbastardierung, Verointalisierung und Verjudung des Christentums wehrte sich bereits das durchaus noch aristokratischen Geist atmende Johannesevangelium*. Robert Pois's edition (*Race and Race History and Other Essays*, p. 70) translated *Johannesevangelium* as "evangelical teachings of St. John," which obscures Rosenberg's more specific reference to the book we call the Gospel of John.

40. For illustrations of Nazi road signs with this verse, see Robert P. Ericksen and Susannah Heschel, *Betrayal: German Churches and the Holocaust* (Minneapolis, MN: Fortress Press, 1999), fig. 6.

41. For a history of the canon and Marcionism among Anabaptists, see my article "The Letter Killeth: A Plea for Decanonizing Violent Biblical Texts," *Journal of Religion, Conflict, and Peace* 1, no. 1 (Fall 2007): http://www.plowshares project.org/journal/php/article.php?issu_list_id=8&article_list_id=22.

42. D'Souza, *What's So Great*, p. 217.

43. Frederic W. Farrar, *The Life of Christ as Represented in Art* (London: Adam and Charles Black, 1901), p. 84.

44. See further, Susannah Heschel, *An Aryan Jesus. Christian Theologians and the Bible in Nazi Germany* (Princeton: Princeton University Press, 2008).

45. My quote is from the minutes of a meeting of the Nazi government on July 14, 1933. My source is Walther Hofer, ed., *Der Nationalsozialismus: Dokumente 1933–1945* (Frankfurt: Fischer Taschenbuch Verlag, 1976), p. 130.

46. *Mit Brennender Sorge*, at http://www.newadvent.org/library/docs_pi11mb .htm.

47. Telegram from Diego von Bergen to Eugenio Pacelli as preserved in Raymond James Sontag et al., eds., *Documents on German Foreign Policy, 1918–1945, from the Archives of the German Foreign Ministry* (Washington, DC: United States Printing Office, 1949), series D, vol. 1, p. 991.

48. See Richard Phayer, *The Catholic Church and the Holocaust, 1930–1965* (Bloomington: Indiana University Press, 2000), p. 45.

49. See Richard Carrier, "Hitler's *Table Talk*: Troubling Finds," *German Studies Review* 26, no. 3 (2003): 561–76.

50. For a history of the Hitler Diaries, see Charles Hamilton, *The Hitler Diaries: Fakes That Fooled the World* (Louisville: University Press of Kentucky, 1991) and Robert Harris, *Selling Hitler* (New York: Pantheon Books, 1986).

51. Steigmann-Gall, *The Holy Reich*, pp. 243–60.

52. Carrier, "Hitler's *Table Talk*," p. 573.

53. Speer, *Inside the Third Reich*, p. 113.

54. Ibid., p. 114.

55. D'Souza, *What's So Great*, p. 218.

56. Ibid., p. 327 n. 12.

57. Hermann Rauschning, ed., *Hitler Speaks: A Series of Conversations with Adolf Hitler on His Real Aims* (London: Thornton Butterworth, 1939; Reprint: Whitefish, MT: Kessinger, 2007), p. 63. On the unreliability of this source, see Steigmann-Gall, *The Holy Reich*, pp. 28–29.

58. H. R. Trevor-Roper, ed., *Hitler's Table Talk, 1941–1944: His Private Conversations* (London: Phoenix Press, 2000), p. 59.

59. Trevor-Roper, ed., *Hitler's Table Talk*, p. 61.

60. Carrier, "Hitler's *Table Talk*," pp. 566–72 (all four statements appear in the entry dated the afternoon of 27 February 1942, in the original German).

61. Trevor-Roper, ed., *Hitler's Table Talk*, p. 76. Hitler routinely equated "Bolshevism" and "Judaism." He also believed Jesus was an Aryan whose true message was corrupted by the Jewish Paul (Carrier, "Hitler's *Table Talk*," p. 572).

62. See further, Peter A. Dykema and Heiko Oberman, eds., *Anticlericalism in Late Medieval and Early Modern Europe* (Leiden: Brill, 1993), which also discusses various conflicts between Protestants and Catholics.

63. Diego von Bergen, the German ambassador to the Vatican, specifically reported that the Pope feared that "a 'third' faith is being organized and encouraged" in addition to Catholicism and Evangelical faiths (*Documents on German Foreign Policy*, series D, vol. 1, p. 988). This shows that the Vatican saw Nazi religion as a competing faith, and not as "atheism," a term it sometimes applied to competing faiths, as well.

64. D'Souza, *What's So Great*, p. 219; Richard Weikart, *From Darwin to Hitler: Evolutionary Ethics, Eugenics, and Racism in Germany* (New York: Palgrave, 2004).

65. For my critiques of Weikart, see "Avalos contra Weikart: Part I: General Problems with Dr. Weikart's Methods," at http://debunkingchristianity.blogspot .com /2008/05/avalos-contra-weikart-part-i-general.html; and "Avalos Contra Weikart: Part II: Weikart's Seven Darwinian Aspects of Nazism," at http:// debunkingchristianity.blogspot.com/2008/06/avalos-contra-weikart-part-ii-weikarts.html. See also Sander Gliboff, *H. G. Bromm, Ernst Haeckel, and the Origins of German Darwinism: A Study in Translation and Transformation* (Cambridge, MA: MIT Press, 2008).

66. Denise O'Leary, "Post-Details: Expelling the Outrage: Hitler and Darwinism," at http://www.arn.org/blogs/index.php/2/2008/04/15/ expell_ing_the _outrage_hitler_and_darwin (accessed July 3, 2009).

67. "Guidelines from *Die Bücherei*," 2:6, 1935, p. 279, at http://www.library .arizona.edu/exhibits/burnedbooks/documents.htm.

68. Weikart, *From Darwin to Hitler*, p. 9.

69. Richard Weikart, "Review of Annette Wittkau-Horgby, *Materialismus: Enstehung und Wirkung in den Wissenschaften des 19. Jahrhunderts* (Göttingen: Vandehoek und Ruprecht, 1998)," *German Studies Review* 24, no. 3 (October 2001): 610.

70. Richard Weikart, "Review of Richard Steigmann-Gall's *The Holy Reich: Nazi Conceptions of Christianity*," *German Studies Review* 27, no. 1 (February 2004): 175.

71. See *Mein Kampf*, p. 312: "keeping his blood pure" / German (p. 342): *Reinhaltung seines Blutes*.

72. See further, Linda Martz, "Pure Blood Statutes in Sixteenth-Century Toledo: Implementation as Opposed to Adoption," *Sefarad* 61, no. 1 (1994): 91–94; Albert Sicroff, *Los estatutos de limpieza de sangre: Controversias entre los siglos xv y xvii* (Madrid: Taurus, 1985); Henry Kamen, *The Spanish Inquisition: A Historical Revision* (London: Weidenfeld and Nicolson, 1997), especially pp. 242–54; Henry Kamen, *Philip of Spain* (New Haven, CT: Yale University Press, 1997), pp. 33–34.

73. Max Reichler, *Jewish Eugenics and Other Essays* (New York: Bloch, 1916), pp. 7–8.

74. Hitler, *Mein Kampf*, p. 249.

75. Ibid., p. 286.

76. Weikart, *From Darwin to Hitler*, p. 186.

77. Charles Darwin, *The Descent of Man and Selection in Relation to Sex*, 2nd ed. (New York: D. Appleton, 1909 [1874]), p. 187 (in context: pp. 185–96). See also Patrick Brantlinger, *Dark Vanishings: Discourse on the Extinction of Primitive Races 1800–1930* (Ithaca, NY: Cornell University Press, 2003).

78. George Fitzhugh, "Sociology for the South or the Failure of Free Society," in *Antebellum Writings of George Fitzhugh and Hinton Rowan Helper on Slavery*, ed. Harvey Wish (New York: Capricorn Books, 1960 [reprint of 1854 edition]), p. 61.

79. Robert Knox, *The Races of Men* (Philadelphia, PA: Lea & Blanchard, 1850), pp. 38–39.

80. John Campbell, "Negro Mania," in *E. N. Elliott, Cotton Is King and Pro-Slavery Arguments: Comprising the Writings of Hammond, Harper, Christy, Stringfellow, Hodge, Bledsoe, and Cartwright, on This Important Subject* (Augusta, GA: Pritchard, Abbott and Loomis, 1860), p. 520.

Chapter 15

CHRISTIANITY WAS NOT RESPONSIBLE FOR MODERN SCIENCE

Richard Carrier, PhD

As a new generation of historians, sociologists, and philosophers of science has proven, biblical religion was not the enemy of science but rather the intellectual matrix that made it possible in the first place. Without the key insights that Christianity found celebrated in the Bible and spread throughout Europe, science would never have happened.... The evidence is incontrovertible: It was the rational theology of both the Catholic Middle Ages and the Protestant Reformation—inspired by the explicit and implicit truths revealed in the Jewish Bible—that led to the discoveries of modern science.[1]

Belief in the rationality of God not only led to the inductive method but also led to the conclusion that the universe is governed rationally by discoverable laws. This assumption is vitally important to scientific research because in a pagan or polytheistic world, which saw its gods often engaged in jealous, irrational behavior in a world that was nonrational, any systematic investigation of such a world would seem futile. Only in Christian thought, which posits "the existence of a single God, the Creator and Governor of the universe, [one that] functions in an orderly and normally predictable manner," is it possible for science to exist and operate.[2]

T hese two quotes succinctly describe a new delusion creeping around the halls of conservative academia: the belief that Christianity not only caused modern science, but was *necessary* for modern science even to exist. As the story now goes, not only has Christianity never been at odds with science and never impeded it in any way, but it was actually the *savior* of science, the only worldview that could ever make science possible. And that's why the Scientific Revolution only ever sparked in one place: a thoroughly Christian society.

This is not only false in every conceivable detail but so egregiously false that anyone with even the slightest academic competence and responsibility should have known it was false. Which means its advocates, all of whom claim to be scholars, must either be embarrassingly incompetent, perversely dishonest, or wildly deluded. That so many scholars would be so incompetent seems improbable. That they are all lying, even more so. Of course, we've all seen the conservative political tactic of repeating a lie so often, in so many places, with such confidence, and from so many sources, that everyone begins to believe it. This may be one such lie. Or these scholars may really be this mind-bogglingly incompetent. But I'm inclined to doubt it. Delusion seems a more likely explanation for how so many can repeat a claim so demonstrably false without ever being corrected by their peers.

An obvious objection to this delusional claim is that it violates one of the most basic principles of causality: when the cause is in place, its effect is seen. Christianity fully dominated the whole of the Western world from the fifth to the fifteenth century, and yet in all those thousand years there was no Scientific Revolution. A cause that fails to have its predicted effect despite being continually in action for a thousand years is usually considered *refuted*, not confirmed. Excuses will be made, claims of impediments, but no Scientific Revolution occurred in the Eastern half of the Christian world either, which had none of the West's excuses. The East was not overrun by barbarians and remained prosperous and developed for five centuries. Such excuses are usually denied anyway—the new trend is to insist even the Western Middle Ages were shot through with an unrivaled spirit of innovation and economic and intellectual vigor. But even if you reject that and accept the West was held back, why did the Scientific Revolution still never happen in the Byzantine Empire, despite being just as Christian, and in every respect more successful? Those caught by this question usually solve it by denigrating the Byzantines as somehow the "wrong kind" of Christians.[3] But once you start down that road, the notion that *Christianity* is the solution goes out the window. Now you need a *special kind* of Christianity, which is evidently not an inevitable outcome of the original Christian Gospel. Either way, the fact remains, whether East or West, once Christians dominated the culture, no Scientific Revolution ensued. It took over a thousand more years.

So, right from the start, something is amiss. Maybe you can work your way around that conundrum. But some claims associated with this new delusion are just too obviously false. Dinesh D'Souza declares with unquestioning confidence that of all ancient religions "only" Christianity "was from the beginning based on reason" and consequently "there are no theologians" in the history of any other religion.[4] Yet surely even an attentive high-school student knows the pagan Greeks *invented* reason, in the very sense he means, developing the formal sciences of logic, philosophy, mathematics, and rhetoric. And any attentive reader of the Bible knows Christianity was from the beginning based on scripture, inspiration, and revelation, not "reason."[5] To see what a religion *actually* based on reason looks like, just look at the formal theologies of the Greco-Roman philosophers. Yes, the pagans invented theology, too.[6]

But facts aren't the only thing getting in the way of the idea that science needed Christianity. Paucity of logic is another.

COMMON FALLACIES

Most arguments for this conclusion rest on a number of common fallacies. That no effort is made to detect or avoid them is another sign of delusion.

The whole notion begins with a simple correlation fallacy: just because modern science only arose in a Western Christian culture, it does not follow that a Western Christian culture caused it (or even more absurdly, that such a culture was the only one that could). This is as fallacious as assuming that because the inventors of formal geometry were polytheists, therefore polytheism caused the invention of formal geometry, or even more absurdly, that *only* polytheists could invent it. Neither is plausible. It's simply an accident of history when formal geometry was invented, at which time the dominant religion just happened to be polytheism. In most respects the same is true of Christianity and the Scientific Revolution.

Never taken into account, for example, is that in the early second millennium any motive, to be respectable in such a strict and paranoid cultural matrix, had to be framed in terms agreeable to Christianity—indeed as *fulfilling* Christianity, if at all possible. For anything that even had a whiff of being unchristian was condemned and its advocates punished—socially to be sure, sometimes physically. This was not a time when you could enjoy the liberty of being a heretic or an atheist, much less a pagan or infidel, without facing repercussions that could put an end to your career, your freedom, or even your life. Such an atmosphere compelled everyone to find inventive ways to sell *any* new ideas as perfectly Christian, even biblical, regardless of their actual motives or inspiration. Hence finding in that period Christian or biblical arguments for embracing new ideas does not confirm Christianity or the Bible was the *cause* of those ideas, rather than just the marketing strategy required to sell them at the time.

Another fallacy is the conflation of necessary, sufficient, and contributing causes. A good case can be made that scientific thinking was actually a byproduct of early *pagan* theology.[7] But even if so, no one would conclude from this that paganism was *required*. I could point to many aspects of pagan religion that contributed to the rise of science (its increasing commitment to religious and intellectual freedom, its reliance on evidence and reason over scriptural and institutional authority, its devotional interest in nature and the stars), but it doesn't follow that *only* paganism can have these attributes. It's not even certain they're all required. Greco-Roman paganism could have been a sufficient or just a contributing cause of ancient science, but it was hardly a necessary one; and it may have provided values that helped science develop, which science could still have developed without, or that other worldviews could have encouraged just as well. So, too, Christianity.

Finally, all too frequently advocates of this new delusion repeatedly confuse reason (as the use of logic to achieve consistency) with *scientific reasoning* (testing the predictions of your claims against the evidence, using a method that aggressively searches and controls for empirical errors and fallacies, and collecting and documenting actual facts about the world by observing and confirming them). Or they confuse "science$_1$" as scientific methods, research, and progress, with "science$_2$" as the transmission and use of past science in professional practice (as by doctors, astronomers, and engineers) with no significant effort to improve it (beyond armchair revision or the refining of measurements). Very often evidence of one will be touted as evidence of the other. But that's a fallacy of equivocation. Science$_2$ can persist without science$_1$ and in fact clearly did in medieval Christianity, just as reason could be praised and pursued while scientific reasoning is hardly to be seen, as was also clearly the case through much of the Middle Ages.

HISTORICAL FANTASIES

Perhaps a well-constructed argument could avoid those fallacies. But then you'd have to get the facts straight. And no one does. The notion that science needed Christianity had many progenitors, but its fully delusional form appears to originate with a devout Catholic physicist, Father Stanley Jaki.[8] It has since filtered into the conservative Christian mindset, and is often represented as the new consensus in the history of science (even though it isn't).[9] Rodney Stark is probably its best representative. He summarizes Jaki's arguments more succinctly and intelligibly than Jaki himself, and unlike most, Stark at least attempts to cite his sources. So I'll examine his version of the argument.[10] Stark has been criticized already.[11] But not yet by an expert in ancient science and Christianity.

HISTORICAL FANTASY NUMBER 1: "NO REAL SCIENCE IN ANTIQUITY"

Rodney Stark is an excellent sociologist but a lousy historian. He has no formal training in history as a profession, or in ancient history in particular. Actually, none of the advocates of this theory do. But we needn't cite a lack of credentials. Stark's incompetence is decisively exposed in a single sentence: "Greek learning stagnated of its own inner logic. After Plato and Aristotle, very little happened beyond some extensions of geometry."[12] That Princeton University would publish a book with that sentence in it is one of the most appalling things I've ever encountered in my career (and it might be no accident that Stark had to publish his next book with Random House).

The truth is that the Greeks and Romans achieved tremendous and continual advances in science and mathematics after Aristotle. Aristotle's generation marked only the *beginning* of the history of ancient science— almost every amazing thing they discovered came after him. And they discovered a lot.[13] So in a single sentence Stark has erased the entire history of ancient science. Yet his entire argument rests on that sentence. Had he done what any scholar is obligated to do, and actually checked the current histories of ancient science, he would know this key premise, and hence the entire argument founded on it, is rubbish. Already by Aristotle's time, in the mid–forth century BCE, there were many important scientists, from Hippocrates and Eudoxus to Callistratus, Archytas, and Aristoxenus, none of whom Stark shows any awareness of. But after that, up to the end of the second century CE, I can ascertain the names of over a hundred published scientists, almost all of whose work was not preserved by medieval Christians.[14] Stark shows no awareness of any of them, either—not even the ones whose work *was* preserved.

Here's just a sample....

Aristotle performed numerous dissection and vivisection experiments in animal anatomy and physiology and composed the most scientific range of zoological works then known. Immediately afterward, his successor Theophrastus extended this work to botany and plant physiology, and also produced the first known scientific works in pyrology, mineralogy, and other fields. His successor, Strato of Lampsacus, extended their experimental method to machines and physics, by which time many of Aristotle's physical theories had been altered or abandoned. In the third century BCE a research institute was established in Alexandria, Egypt, where Ctesibius and Philo completed the first known scientific works in experimental pneumatics (the study of the behavior of air and water); Eratosthenes invented the science of cartography and was one of the first scientists in history to measure the diameter of the earth (he overshot by only 15 percent) and analyze the effect of the moon on the tides; and Herophilus became the first scientist to dissect human cadavers. In fact, Herophilus and his pupil Erasistratus originated neurophysiology, establishing with detailed experiments that the mind is a function of the brain and that specific mental functions were controlled in specific areas of the brain, and they distinguished motor from sensory nerves and mapped them throughout the body. Altogether, their study of the human body and its bones, muscles, and organs, was so thorough that we still use much of their anatomical terminology.

In Sicily, their colleague Archimedes was busy advancing the sciences of mechanics and hydrostatics, and discovering, describing, or explaining the first mathematical laws of physics. Shortly before that, Aristarchus began measuring the distances of the moon, sun, and planets (with values that were increasingly refined in subsequent centuries), and proposed the first heliocentric theory. In Rhodes a century later, Hipparchus discovered and measured celestial precession (the rotation of the zodiac over a period of 25,800 years), observed the first supernova, established the first detailed scientific star charts, made numerous advances in planetary theory, and developed the first scientific system for predicting lunar and solar eclipses. Seleucus of Babylon discovered the effect of the *sun* on the tides, not just the moon, developing the first mathematical lunisolar tide theory. Then, during the early Roman Empire, science reached its pinnacle of achievement, producing works not exceeded until the Scientific Revolution: from Dioscorides in botany, mineralogy, and pharmacology; Hero in mechanics, pneumatics, and theatrical robotics; Ptolemy in astronomy, cartography, optics, and harmonics; and Galen in anatomy, physiology, and medicine. Just to name a few. There were many more whose work is now lost, advancing fields as diverse as apiology and oceanography, to volcanology and hydrostatics.

None were shackled to any "unrevisable framework" by Aristotle[15] but freely revised and debated *all* his physical assumptions. Heliocentrists debated static and dynamic geocentrists; theories of inertia, pressure, and universal gravitation competed with Aristotelian theories of natural places; visual ray theories competed with particle theories of light, and so on.[16] By the Roman period, Aristotle's conclusion that comets were an atmospheric phenomenon was losing ground to the correct view that they were planetary bodies on wide eccentric orbits; Hipparchus had developed an increasingly correct theory of projectile motion and refuted Aristotle's belief that the heavens never change; Herophilus had refuted the Aristotelian theory that the soul resided in the heart, with precise experiments proving all thought and sensation occurred in the brain—a conclusion Galen then reinforced with a detailed study of the vocal system, demonstrating that the brain controlled human speech; Hero had experimentally refuted Aristotle's claim that a vacuum was impossible, and proven that wind was air in motion, that heated air expands and rises, and that cold air contracts and falls; and Ptolemy had abandoned Aristotle's assumption that planetary orbits had to be concentrically circular and their velocities constant. Even Aristotle's theory of a fundamental division between the sublunar and celestial realms was widely challenged and often rejected by subsequent physicists, along with almost every other doubtful aspect of his original physics.

Major advances in logic also occurred after Aristotle,[17] as well as in mathematics and physical concepts, such that almost everything credited as first proposed by medieval intellectuals, had in fact already been conceived in antiquity. For example, what we now call Ockham's Razor was already a standard methodological assumption.[18] Even Stark's dismissive "some extensions of geometry" happened to include advanced conics, plane and spherical trigonometry, and the rudiments of calculus. They even went beyond geometry, developing combinatorics and an early form of multivariable algebra. Yet medieval Christians showed such disinterest in these mathematical achievements that some were barely preserved at all, while others were literally erased from books so they could be replaced with hymns to God.[19] In fact, under Christian tenure almost all the scientific achievements of the ancients were forgotten in the West and ignored in the East, or survived only in simplistic caricatures. The few books that got copied enough to survive were rarely or barely copied at all, often not understood, and never substantially improved upon for nearly a thousand years.

As a result, for many centuries Christians didn't even know scientists after Aristotle had significantly expanded the experimental method and began confirming mathematical laws of physics, which were predictively successful, technologically useful, and thoroughly mechanical. The first correct mathematical laws likely predate Archimedes, but his treatises on statics and hydrostatics are the earliest surviving record of them. By then scientists knew that levers obey the law $D_1W_1 = D_2W_2$ (expressed geometrically) and that objects don't float because (as Aristotle supposed) it's just their nature to, they float because their density is less than the surrounding water, so the heavier water pushes up the floating object, by an amount exactly entailed by the mathematical difference in their densities, and that even sinking objects become lighter, by an amount exactly equal to the weight of the water the body displaces—which, incidentally, refuted Aristotle's notion that an object's lightness was immutably innate. By Roman times, the correct laws of reflection were also known, as well as their correct theoretical explanation (Hero proved they followed from a principle of least action), and the laws of refraction were being explored and approximated with detailed experiments. Ptolemy experimentally measured the difference in indexes of refraction for materials like glass, water, and air, discovered that the refraction angle increases with the incidence angle in a progressive relationship, and attempted to ascertain a mathematical law of refraction. Precise measurement even played a role in physiology, allowing Galen to prove the correct theory of kidney function (and explain the entire renal system) with a series of controlled experiments.[20]

Hutchinson defines modern science as an "emphasis on direct observation and experiment, precise measurement, and the formulation of laws of nature," and we've just seen the ancient pagans had all those things.[21] Stark defines modern science as "a *method* utilized in *organized* efforts to formulate *explanations of nature*, always subject to modifications and corrections through *systematic observations*" such that "it is possible to deduce from [the resulting explanations] some definite predictions and prohibitions about what will be observed."[22] That, too, accurately describes ancient science. Ancient scientists continually developed and improved their methods—right up to the end: Galen, Hero and Ptolemy all had a great deal to say about method and its improvement. Their efforts were also organized. Ptolemy's *Almagest* shows astronomers shared observations and created records for future colleagues, Galen's books repeatedly show doctors working together on anatomical research and scientists in all fields conferring with each other for information and debate, and there were many formal scientific associations, including the Museum of Alexandria. And they all aimed at producing explanations of nature, often correcting their theories with systematic observations and controlled experiments, and deducing from their theories exact predictions of what will or won't happen. Ptolemy's planetary theory could predict the position of Mars to within a straw's width twenty years in advance, and his law of refraction was almost as precise. Galen's theory of the renal and vocal systems correctly predicted the effects of specific injuries and disease as well as the normal behavior of the organs themselves. Hero could predict the precise mechanical advantages of many machines and the general behavior of air, water, and steam in the presence or absence of pressure or heat. Menelaus could predict the specific densities of different fluids and solids and their behavior in different suspending mediums. And on and on. All were empirical, all linked theory to practice, and all tested at least some of their theories against observed data. Yet Stark still maintains, with complete confidence, that "in the end all they achieved were nonempirical, even antiempirical, speculative philosophies, atheoretical collections of facts, and isolated crafts and technologies—never... real science."[23] As should now be perfectly clear, not a single bit of that sentence is even remotely true.

HISTORICAL FANTASY NUMBER 2: "PAGANS HAD A MENTAL BLOCK"

Already Stark's first fact is so embarrassingly false it's a wonder he stays employed. But it gets worse: he confidently declares reasons *why* his first fact is true, even though his first fact isn't true, thus refuting his second—since if those causes obtained, they clearly didn't have the effect predicted. So, too, any other "causes" other advocates allege for this nonexistent stagnation in ancient science.

All these "explanations" amount to claiming that pagans were suffering from various mental blocks, which only Christianity could free them from. Stark picks three popular examples:

> First, their conceptions of the Gods were inadequate to permit them to imagine a conscious Creator [so they couldn't imagine physical laws]. Second, they conceived of the universe not only as eternal and uncreated, but as locked into endless cycles of progress and decay [so they couldn't imagine scientific progress]. Third, prompted by their religious conceptions, they transformed inanimate objects into living creatures capable of aims, emotions, and desires—thus short-circuiting the search for physical theories.[24]

Even if these claims were true, Stark's theory is already refuted, for as we just saw, science flourished despite them, and it's Stark's contention that these three facts would surely have prevented that. Since they didn't, Christianity can claim no advantage in having abandoned them. Yet as Stark represents them, these claims aren't even true, nor do they make any logical sense as barriers to science to begin with. In fact, I contend they are so false or illogical, yet declared with such confidence, that Stark can only be dishonest, delusional, or incompetent. For even the most rudimentary fact checking and analysis would have exploded every one.

Pagan Theology

Pagan theology supposedly got in the way, but Stark makes little sense of this. He claims certain aspects of Platonic theology impeded science.[25] But since all ancient scientists were philosophical eclectics with strong sympathies for Stoic and Epicurean physics, and for Aristotelianism, which from its very foundation was anti-Platonist, it wasn't even possible for Platonism to impede the course of ancient science, even if it did harbor any antiscientific tendencies.[26]

More generally, pagan theology supposedly prevented a conception of an intelligible universe governed by natural laws. Hence, according to Stanley Jaki, only Christianity could produce science, for:

> The scientific quest found fertile soil only when this faith in a personal, rational Creator had truly permeated a whole culture, beginning with the centuries of the High Middle Ages... [providing] confidence in the rationality of the universe, trust in progress, and appreciation of the quantitative method, all indispensable ingredients of the scientific quest.[27]

Of course, as we just saw, the "scientific quest" had already found fertile soil in pagan antiquity. But everything else here is false, too. Ancient scientists already had confidence in the rationality of the universe (as we'll soon see), already trusted in progress (as we'll see next), and already appreciated the quantitative method (as we just saw). So Jaki's claim that only Christianity could inspire these things is clearly false.

Like other recent advocates of this new delusion, Stark emphasizes the "rationality of the universe" angle: unless you believe in a rational Creator, who made everything from nothing, you won't have any reason to believe the universe is rational or obeys discoverable laws of physics. But not only is this false, it's not even logical. D'Souza insists "the presumption" that "the universe is rational [is] quite impossible to prove" and therefore requires theological justification.[28] But that the universe is rational is *observed*. So it doesn't have to be proved. Such a belief requires no faith or theology because it rests entirely on evidence. Pagans responded to this *observation* in either of two ways: exactly the same way later Christians did, or exactly the same way modern atheists do. Neither marked any impediment to science.

Those who *didn't* believe in intelligent design had to explain where all this observed consistency and order then came from, which compelled them to scientific inquiry, precisely to discover the real causes. Hence ancient doubters and pantheists, like Strato, Erasistratus, Epicurus, or Asclepiades sought explanations in the inevitable interaction of natural laws and forces. They didn't use our "law" metaphor but others instead, like "physical necessity" and the "inherent nature" of things, but these amounted to the same thing: objects floated on water, for example, because of the inevitable interaction of innate forces in a discernible pattern. No God needed. No belief in Creation required. All is just the outcome of natural causes. Hence even atheism could be no impediment to science. To the contrary, it all but *entails* it, since there is no other way for atheists to explain what they see.

And most likely, if you weren't an atheist, you were a creationist. Most intellectual polytheists believed in a Creator who had intelligently ordered the cosmos, that this order could be discovered by the human mind, and that such discovery honored God. Scientists like Galen and Ptolemy were thus motivated to pursue scientific inquiry by their religious piety, exactly as Stark claims Christians were, and for exactly the same reasons. In Galen's scientific tour de force *On the Uses of the Parts*, a multivolume survey of human anatomy that remains one of the most empirically persuasive defenses of intelligent design ever written, he declares his pagan motives for conducting all the meticulous and exhaustive hands-on research the book documents: "I am composing this sacred discourse as a true hymn of praise to our Creator. And I consider that I am really showing Him reverence not when I offer Him" countless expensive sacrifices "but when I myself first learn to know His wisdom, power, and goodness and then make them known to others."[29] Most philosophers agreed. Seneca argued scientific inquiry was a pious enterprise superior to the sacred mysteries of pagan religion, and Cicero argued God actually designed us to pursue scientific knowledge.[30] We can find many more examples of pagans declaring theological motives for scientific inquiry.[31] So when D'Souza claims a religious "impulse" to pursue science "came originally from Christianity," we can plainly see that's false.[32] Pagan theology provided just as ample a motivation, as did atheism or pantheism.

Cyclical Theory of Time

Stark's claim that anyone who believes the world is locked in "endless cycles of progress and decay" can't conceive of "progress" is illogical: if they believe in cycles of *progress* and decay, they obviously believe in progress. You almost have to be delusional to miss such an obvious contradiction. Nevertheless, Stark irrationally insists the Greeks "rejected the idea of progress in favor of a never-ending cycle of being."[33] Not only is this illogical, it's false.

Belief in scientific progress is so well evidenced in ancient literature, it's a wonder anyone ever claimed the contrary.[34] How can Stark claim the opposite? By not checking the scholarship on the subject, or even his own evidence. To support his claim all Stark provides are various irrelevant quotations that fail to demonstrate any connection at all between ancient theories of time and a belief in progress. In fact, the ancient idea of eternal cycles could be *based* on a belief in progress: it was assumed the universe was eternal (lacking any evidence to the contrary), but it was observed that society had not reached a perfect state of advancement in all the arts and sciences, but it would have if it had been advancing for all infinite time; therefore, periodic catastrophes must destroy civilizations and all record of their achievements, forcing men to start over from scratch. Aristotle believed some scarce oral lore might survive each catastrophe, but all written record and advanced knowledge must have been lost, otherwise we would still have it.[35] Believing this in no way entails believing there is any end to progress, other than the destruction of your entire civilization—or, of course, the whole world, whose end the Christians believed was so imminent we should sooner ask why *they* would believe in progress, as to them it should seem futile.[36] The pagans at least expected many thousands of years, even tens of thousands, in which to continue their advance.

Hence it's notable that the only text Stark quotes that actually seems relevant, in fact says the *exact opposite* of what he claims. In this he may have been duped by Jaki (what excuse Jaki could have escapes me), but I think Stark's failure to check the original is a mark of either incompetence or delusion.[37] When Aristotle says everything "had been invented several times over in the course of ages, or rather times without number," Stark not only claims he is referring to technology, but that Aristotle meant "the levels of technology of his time were at the maximum attainable, precluding further progress," and (I suppose we're meant to infer) as in technology, so in science.[38] But here is the actual quotation *in context*:

> It seems it is not a new or recent discovery among political philosophers that the state ought to be divided by class and ... have public meals.... So we must suppose these and other things were discovered many times, over a long period, or rather countless times. For it seems the necessities of life teach men what's useful in and of itself, while it is reasonable to expect an increasing refinement and improvement of those things established at the start.... Therefore, one must rely on what has already been adequately discovered, but also attempt to seek out what remains to be discovered.[39]

Observe: Aristotle is specifically referring only to political organization, not technology, nor any scientific knowledge of any sort. In fact, he is only referring to two political inventions in particular: the development of a class system and of public meals, both of which he traces to long past civilizations in Crete, Italy, and Egypt. He only concludes these (and certain "other things") must have been invented everywhere because he sees them everywhere, as far back as recorded history. And he still doesn't say no progress could be made in them. Rather, when he says such things have been invented many times, all Aristotle means is that necessity is the mother of invention, and therefore wherever a certain necessity arises, we can expect to find men inventing what is necessary to deal with it. Aristotle immediately adds that there are still many things left to be discovered and *we should look for them*—exactly the opposite of what Stark claims.

Similarly, when Aristotle says "it is reasonable to suppose that each art and philosophy has been developed as much as possible and then lost again, many times over," he does not mean progress has ended in his own day, nor even that it would end anytime soon, but that in each cycle the arts progress as far as they can before some world catastrophe casts us back into another Dark Age, and we have to start over.[40] Since no such catastrophe was at hand in Aristotle's day, there is no indication he imagined his society had reached the end of its progress—to the contrary, as we see in the *Politics*, he clearly believed there was much more to be had, and even declares it our obligation to pursue it. Aristotle expresses his faith in the future advance of human knowledge in many other contexts as well.[41] There is simply no evidence, from Aristotle or any other pagan after him, of a belief in eternal cycles impacting anyone's confidence in the value and possibility of scientific progress. To the contrary, we have ample evidence that many pagans, especially scientists, not only believed in such progress, but labored for it.

Pagan Animism

We're also told pagan animism impeded science. As Stark puts it, "if mineral objects are animate, one heads in the wrong direction in attempting to explain natural phenomena—the causes of the motion of objects, for example, will be ascribed to motives, not to natural forces."[42] This is simply false. Neither Aristotle nor any scientist after him ever sought to explain much of anything in this way, except when they should have (as in the study of human and animal behavior) and when Christians did (as in the search for God's purpose and design in nature).

Again we catch Stark not reading his own sources, and instead trusting Jaki (who has no such excuse). They both imply Aristotle (and every pagan after him) believed objects fall to the ground "because of their innate love for the centre of the world."[43] But in his book *On the Heavens* Aristotle specifically argues *against* this explanation. He instead says planets or falling objects must move because of fixed innate tendencies—in our words, because they obey natural laws.[44] A strong indicator of deception, incompetence, or delusion is when you claim your sources say exactly the opposite of what they actually say, and then base your entire grand theory on that remarkable error. Yet had Stark checked the explanations of motion, or any other behavior of inanimate objects, in Aristotle or any pagan philosopher after him, he would have found the exact opposite of what he claims.

Even D'Souza knows enough to admit it was the *pagans*, beginning with the Presocratics, who originated the idea of "a universe that operates through discoverable rules of cause and effect" and thereby "replaced the idea of an 'enchanted universe' with that of a 'disenchanted' cosmos accessible to unassisted human reason."[45] D'Souza then claims "their influence was short-lived," but that's false. Far from being short-lived, it became the standard view among Greco-Roman philosophers, driving scientific progress for five centuries. All ancient scientists sought to explain everything as a conjunction of natural causes, developing mathematical laws, mechanical explanations, and theories of fixed natural properties and forces. Not one sought to explain anything in terms of the arbitrary desires of physical objects. Even the notion that the gods actively govern the world, thus rendering it capricious and unpredictable, was abandoned in favor of a consistent rational order that could be studied, understood, modeled, and predicted.

Though many among the illiterate masses retained the old animistic view, this was ridiculed by pagan intellectuals. The *Aetna*, for example, an epic Roman poem about volcanology, argues such ignorant animism must be rejected in favor of mechanical explanation, and then proceeds to describe mechanical explanations of volcanic phenomena.[46] Medical scientists from Erasistratus to Galen sought to explain all human physiology in terms of machinery or physical principles.[47] Astronomers from Posidonius to Ptolemy could certainly imagine modeling the solar system as a machine.[48] The behavior of air, water, the weather, everything was similarly explained.[49] Even when "reductively" mechanical explanations were rejected, they were not replaced with animism, but physical theories of innate natural powers—which could often be correct, such as Galen's theory of kidney filtration, which held that the kidney is no mere sieve but contains smartly engineered forces of attraction that naturally select toxins to extrude from the blood, a conclusion he proved by experiment.[50] And far from attributing planetary motion to unpredictable desires, Ptolemy attributed it to innate natural powers that obeyed mathematical laws—developing, for example, an "equal angles in equal times" law that entailed planets varied their speeds in a manner that clearly inspired Kepler's second law of equal *areas* in equal times.[51] Though Ptolemy did suspect the force that propels the planets *might* be "planetary souls," these were as fixed and predictable as Kepler's "planetary souls," being as mindless as magnets or any other physical force.[52]

Hence Stark's contention that after Aristotle ancient scientists were explaining the whole universe in terms of animistic motives is pure fantasy. That never happened. Nor is there any basis for believing it did. And a belief that's not only based on no evidence, but refuted by all the available evidence there is, certainly looks like a delusion.

The Head-Hand Divide

Though Stark doesn't rely on it, another common premise is that pagans didn't have science because there was a sharp divide between educated thinkers and those who worked with their hands—due (we're told) to some sort of aristocratic disdain for getting dirty. Since the ancients very clearly *did* have science, we already know this theory is false. But not only is the causal connection demonstrably absent, so is the alleged cause.

The evidence is abundantly clear that all ancient scientists were not only superbly educated theorists, but also master craftsmen engaging in their own hands-on experiments and even building their own instruments. All the works of Ptolemy and Hero are filled with discussion of the machines and instruments they had built, and how to build them, many of which had to be manufactured with fine precision. All the works of Galen are filled with discussion of his personal dissections and surgeries and vivisections, as well as his repeated insistence on the importance of doctors developing and maintaining their manual skills, and conducting dissections and vivisections themselves instead of relying on others, and even making their own drugs. The Renaissance anatomist Vesalius famously railed against a split between the surgeons as hands-on workers and doctors as the "books and theory" guys, but in antiquity no such split existed, as Galen amply attests and insists upon.[53] Hero similarly maintained that physicists and engineers needed both extensive book learning *and* hands-on skill, especially in metalwork, construction, carpentry, and painting.[54] So if any split ever did occur, it can only have been on Christianity's watch.

One of the most decisive proofs of this is the archaeological recovery of the world's earliest known astronomical computer, a machine built by Greek scientists shortly before 100 CE that sank in a ship off the island of Antikythera a few decades later. Using meticulous and superbly crafted epicyclic gearing, the machine calculates the day and year in several calendars, the positions of all the planets in the zodiac, as well as the sun and moon, and the phases of the moon, and predicts lunar and solar eclipses, all up to two centuries in advance, reported on a system of dials and displays.[55] This computer is superbly crafted, yet employs advanced astronomical and mathematical theory, conclusively demonstrating that pagans imagined no conflict between theory and learning, and craftsmanship and hard work. To the contrary, they had fully united them. Christians just weren't interested in preserving this knowledge.

CONCLUSION

In the colloquial sense, a delusion is any belief that is not merely false, but easily shown to be false on even a cursory check of the facts, yet held with a conviction out of all proportion to the evidence. On that count, this new idea that Christianity was not only responsible but necessary for the rise of modern science is certainly delusional. A delusion becomes pathological when this belief is held with absolute conviction even in the face of compelling evidence to the contrary. And on that count, I think people unmoved by the evidence in this chapter are not just delusional, but off their rocker.

None of the premises on which this delusion is based are true. They all misrepresent the facts or the texts, often quite egregiously. Nor are the arguments employing these premises even logically sound. But more disturbingly, this whole fantasy ignores what are, in fact, the values necessary for scientific progress: embracing curiosity as a moral virtue, elevating empiricism to the status of supreme authority in all disputes of fact, and valuing the pursuit of progress. Many ancient pagans held to all three values, so strongly and persistently that they made continual advances in scientific findings and methods. Christianity, by contrast, for a long time never esteemed these values, and in many cases even denounced them. There was nothing in the Bible or the original Christian mindset that had any tendency to favor them. Only with considerable ingenuity, and against considerable resistance, did some Christians eventually figure out a way to reintegrate these pagan values into a thoroughly Christianized culture, and then only after many centuries of nearly complete disinterest.[56]

Nevertheless, like all good delusions, this one is built on kernels of truth.

Pagans did set the stage for the end of ancient science—just not for any of the reasons Christians now claim. By failing to develop a stable and effective constitutional government, the Roman Empire was doomed to collapse under the weight of constant civil war and disastrous economic policy; and in the third century BCE that's exactly what it did. Pagan society responded to this collapse by retreating from the scientific values of its past and fleeing to increasingly mystical and fantastical ways of viewing the world and its wonders. Christianity was already one such worldview, and thus became increasingly popular at just that time.[57] But as one could predict, when Christianity came to power *it did not* restore those scientific values, but instead sealed the fate of science by putting an end to all significant scientific progress for almost a thousand years. It did not do this by oppressing or persecuting science, but simply by not promoting its progress and by promoting instead a deep and enduring suspicion against the very values necessary to produce it.

Likewise, modern science *did* develop in a Christian milieu, in the hands of scientists who *were* indeed Christians, and Christianity *can* be made compatible with science and scientific values. Christianity only had to adapt to embrace those old pagan values that once drove scientific progress. And it *was* Christians who adapted it, craftily inventing Christian arguments in favor of the change because only arguments in accord with Christian theology and the Bible would have succeeded in persuading their peers. But this was a development *in spite* of Christianity's original values and ideals, returning the world back to where pagans, not Christians, had left it a thousand years before at the dawn of the third century. Only then did the Christian world take up that old pagan science and its core values once again. And only then did further progress ensue.

Had Christianity not interrupted the intellectual advance of mankind and put the progress of science on hold for a thousand years, the Scientific Revolution might have occurred a thousand years ago, and our science and technology today would be a thousand years more advanced. This is a painful truth that some Christians simply don't want to hear or accept. Hence they flee into the delusion that it isn't true, that Christianity was instead so wonderful it not only *caused* modern science, but was *essential* to it. But, as the facts prove, that simply isn't true.

NOTES

1. From Robert Hutchinson, "The Biblical Origins of Modern Science," in *The Politically Incorrect Guide to the Bible* (Washington, DC: Regnery, 2007), p. 139.

2. From Alvin Schmidt, "Science: Its Christian Connections" in *Under the Influence: How Christianity Transformed Civilization* (Grand Rapids, MI: Zondervan, 2001), p. 221.

3. I kid you not: Lynn White Jr., "What Accelerated Technological Progress in the Western Middle Ages?" in *Scientific Change*, ed. A. C. Crombie (New York: Basic Books, 1963): pp. 272–91; Edward Grant, *Science and Religion, 400 B.C. to A.D. 1550* (Westport, CT: Greenwood Press, 2004), pp. 225–30. Grant also claims constant war impeded Byzantine science, but Western Christians and ancient Greeks were also constantly at war, and in a prosperous nation (like Byzantium) war can actually *advance* science rather than impede it: Tracey Rihll, *The Catapult: A History* (Yardley, PA: Westholme, 2007).

4. From Dinesh D'Souza, "Christianity and Reason: The Theological Roots of Science," *What's So Great about Christianity?* (Washington, DC: Regnery, 2007), pp. 84–85.

5. On the original epistemology of Christianity: Richard Carrier, *Not the Impossible Faith: Why Christianity Didn't Need a Miracle to Succeed* (Raleigh, NC: Lulu, 2009), pp. 329–68, 385–406.

6. Theology as a rational science in antiquity: Aristotle, *Metaphysics* 6.1 (1026a); Sextus Empiricus, *Against the Professors* 9.12–194 (= *Against the Physicists* 1.12–194 = *Against the Dogmatists* 3.12–194); and John Dillon, *Alcinous: The Handbook of Platonism* (Oxford: Clarendon, 1993): pp. 57–60, 86–89.

7. Persuasively argued in David Sedley, *Creationism and Its Critics in Antiquity* (Berkeley: University of California Press, 2007).

8. Most notably in Stanley Jaki, *Science and Creation* (New York: Science History, 1974), *The Road of Science and the Ways to God* (Chicago: University of Chicago Press, 1978) and *The Savior of Science* (Grand Rapids, MI: Eerdmans, 2000).

9. Prominent examples: Nancy Pearcey and Charles Thaxton, "The New History of Science" in *The Soul of Science* (Wheaton, IL: Crossway Books, 1994), pp. 15–56; Thomas Woods, "The Church and Science," *How the Catholic Church Built Western Civilization* (Washington, DC: Regnery, 2005), pp. 67–114; Schmidt, *Under the Influence*, pp. 218–47; D'Souza, *What's So Great*, pp. 83–99; Hutchinson, *Politically Incorrect*, pp. 138–56; and Stark (see following note).

10. In Rodney Stark, "God's Handiwork: The Religious Origins of Science" in *For the Glory of God* (Princeton, NJ: Princeton University Press, 2003), pp. 121–99; and "Blessings of Rational Theology" in *The Victory of Reason* (New York: Random House, 2005), pp. 3–32.

11. Andrew Bernstein, "The Tragedy of Theology: How Religion Caused and Extended the Dark Ages: A Critique of Rodney Stark's 'The Victory of Reason,'" *Objective Standard* 1, no. 4 (Winter 2006–2007): 11–37; Joseph Lucas and Donald Yerxa, eds., "The Victory of Reason: A Forum," *Historically Speaking* 7, no. 4 (March/April 2006): 2–18.

12. Stark, *Victory of Reason*, p. 20.

13. The evidence for all of this (and following) will be summarized in Richard Carrier, *The Scientist in the Early Roman Empire* (forthcoming), but is already collectively demonstrated in: Lucio Russo, *The Forgotten Revolution*, 2nd ed. (New York: Springer, 2003); Tracey Rihll, *Greek Science* (New York. Oxford University Press, 1999); G. E. R. Lloyd, *Greek Science after Aristotle* (New York: W. W. Norton, 1973); Paul Keyser and Georgia Irby-Massie, eds., *The Biographical Encyclopedia of Ancient Natural Scientists* (New York: Routledge, 2009); and the entire Routledge *Sciences of Antiquity* series.

For the Roman period specifically: Andrew Barker, *Scientific Method in Ptolemy's Harmonics* (New York: Cambridge University Press, 2000); A. M. Smith, *Ptolemy and the Foundations of Ancient Mathematical Optics* (Philadelphia, PA: American Philosophical Society, 1999); J. L. Berggren, *Ptolemy's Geography* (Princeton, NJ: Princeton University Press, 2000); G. J. Toomer, *Ptolemy's Almagest* (New York: Springer-Verlag, 1984); Karin Tybjerg, "Hero of Alexandria's Mechanical Treatises," in *Physik/Mechanik*, ed. Astrid Schürmann (Stuttgart: Franz Steiner, 2005), pp. 204–26; Bennet Woodcroft, ed., *The Pneumatics of Hero of Alexandria* (London: Taylor, Walton and Maberly, 1851); A. G. Drachmann, *The Mechanical Technology of Greek and Roman Antiquity* (Madison: University of Wisconsin Press, 1963); Rudolph Siegel, *Galen on Psychology, Psychopathology, and Function and Diseases of the Nervous System: An Analysis of His Doctrines, Observations and Experiments* (New York: Karger, 1973), *Galen on Sense Perception: His Doctrines, Observations and Experiments on Vision, Hearing, Smell, Taste, Touch and Pain, and Their Historical Sources* (New York: Karger, 1970), *Galen's System of Physiology and Medicine: An Analysis of His Doctrines and Observations on Bloodflow, Respiration, Tumors and Internal Diseases* (New York: Karger, 1968).

14. For a short list of known scientists: Richard Carrier, "Attitudes Toward the Natural Philosopher in the Early Roman Empire (100 BC to 313 AD)," PhD diss., Columbia University, 2008, pp. 562–73 (pre-Aristotle: pp. 558–61). For a thorough list, see Keyser and Irby-Massie, *Biographical Encyclopedia*. The most excruciating losses are all the scientific treatises on motion and gravity after Aristotle: Strato's *On Motion*, Hipparchus's *On Objects Carried Down by Their Weight*, and Ptolemy's *On Balances*, just to name those we know about.

15. As claimed in Jaki, *Road of Science*, p. 22.

16. As revealed in Plutarch's *On the Face That Appears in the Orb of the Moon* (= *Moralia* 920b–945d; reproduced in vol. 406 of the Loeb Classical Library, *Plutarch's Moralia*, vol. 12).

17. See Russo, *Forgotten Revolution*, pp. 218–24 and John Kieffer, *Galen's Institutio Logica* (Baltimore: Johns Hopkins Press, 1964).

18. Described in Ptolemy, *Planetary Hypotheses* 2.6 and *Almagest* 13.2.

19. For example: Reviel Netz and William Noel, *The Archimedes Codex* (Philadelphia, PA: Da Capo Press, 2007).

20. Archimedes, *On the Equilibrium of Planes* and *On Floating Bodies*; Hero, *On Mirrors*; Ptolemy, *Optics*; Galen, *On the Natural Faculties*.

21. Hutchinson, *Politically Incorrect*, p. 140.

22. Stark, *Victory of Reason*, p. 12.

23. Stark, *For the Glory*, p. 152.

24. Ibid.

25. Stark, *Victory of Reason*, pp. 18–19, and *For the Glory*, pp. 152–53.

26. See John Dillon and A. A. Long, eds., *The Question of "Eclecticism"* (Berkeley: University of California Press, 1988); H. B. Gottschalk, "Aristotelian Philosophy in the Roman World," *Aufstieg und Niedergang der römischen Welt* 2.36.2 (1987): 1079–1174 [cf. pp. 1164–71]; R. J. Hankinson, "Galen's Philosophical Eclecticism," *Aufstieg und Niedergang der römischen Welt* 2.36.5 (1992): 3505–22; Pamela Huby and Gordon Neal, eds., *The Criterion of Truth* (Liverpool: Liverpool University Press, 1989); and Tybjerg, "Hero," pp. 214–15. Explicit examples include: Galen, *On the Affections & Errors of the Soul* 1.8 and 2.6–7; Seneca, *Moral Epistles* 33; Celsus, *On Medicine* pr. 45–47.

27. Jaki, *Science and Creation*, p. viii.

28. D'Souza, *What's So Great*, p. 92.

29. Galen, *On the Uses of the Parts* 3.10 (also 17.1).

30. Seneca, *Natural Questions* 7.2 and Cicero, *On the Boundaries of Good and Evil* 5.18.(48)–5.21.(60).

31. See Carrier, "Attitudes," pp. 353–74, 396–98 (which will be reproduced in Carrier, *Scientist*).

32. D'Souza, *What's So Great*, p. 99.

33. Stark, *Victory of Reason*, pp. 18, 19.

34. Extensively proven in: Ludwig Edelstein, *The Idea of Progress in Classical Antiquity* (Baltimore, MD: Johns Hopkins Press, 1967) and Antoinette Novara, *Les idées romaines sur le progrès d'après les écrivains de la République,* 2 vols. (Paris: Les Belles Lettres, 1982). I add considerably to Edelstein and Novara's evidence in Carrier, "Attitudes," pp. 249–342 (which will be reproduced in Carrier, *Scientist*). Ancient scientists were especially optimistic: Edelstein, *Idea of Progress,* pp. 142–48; Tybjerg, "Hero," p. 211; Serafina Cuomo, *Ancient Mathematics* (London: Routledge, 2001), pp. 183–85; Ingrid Rowland and Thomas Howe, *Vitruvius* (Cambridge: Cambridge University Press, 1999), pp. 16–17; R. J. Hankinson, "Galen's Concept of Scientific Progress," *Aufstieg und Niedergang der römischen Welt* 2.37.2 (1994): 1776–89 and *Galen: On the Therapeutic Method* (Oxford: Clarendon Press, 1991), p. 86; and Mary Beagon, *Roman Nature* (Oxford: Clarendon Press, 1992), pp. 56–63, 183–90.

35. This is the thought behind Aristotle's remarks in *On the Heavens* 1.3 (270b) and *Meteorology* 1.3 (339b).

36. Many expected everything to be destroyed in a matter of years: Hebrews 1:10–2:5, 10:36–37; 1 Corinthians 1:28, 6:13, 7:29–31; 1 Thessalonians 4:15; 2 Peter 3:5–13; 1 John 2:15–18; and of course Mark 13 and Matthew 24; and so on ever since (see Bernard McGinn et al., *The Continuum History of Apocalypticism* [New York: Continuum, 2003] and Jonathan Kirsch, *A History of the End of the World* [San Francisco: Harper, 2006]).

37. Stark is simply aping Jaki, *Road of Science,* p. 24, or *Science and Creation,* pp. 113–14. Jaki had a tendency to falsely report what his sources say; for example, contrary to Jaki's assertions in *Savior,* p. 93, neither Plutarch nor Ptolemy advanced any religious objection to heliocentrism—in neither of the passages he cites do they approve of any such thing.

38. Stark, *Victory of Reason,* p. 19. Ancient technology actually advanced immensely after Aristotle: John Oleson, ed., *The Oxford Handbook of Engineering and Technology in the Classical World* (Oxford: Oxford University Press, 2008); Örjan Wikander, ed., *Handbook of Ancient Water Technology* (Leiden: Brill, 2000); Kevin Greene, "Technological Innovation and Economic Progress in the Ancient World," *Economic History Review* 53, no. 1 (February 2000): 29–59; M. J. T. Lewis, *Millstone and Hammer: The Origins of Water Power* (Hull: University of Hull, 1997); and Rihll, *Catapult.*

39. Aristotle, *Politics* 7.10 (1329b).

40. Aristotle, *Metaphysics* 12.8 (1074b).

41. See Edelstein, *Idea of Progress,* pp. 19–29 for several examples, including: Aristotle, *Sophistical Refutations* 3.34 (183b–184b), *Politics* 2.8 (1268b–1269a), *Nicomachean Ethics* 1.7 (1098a), *Metaphysics* 13.1 (1076a), *On the Heavens* 2.5 (287b–288a), and *On the Generation of Animals* 3.10 (760b).

42. Stark, *For the Glory,* p. 154.

43. Stark, *Victory of Reason*, p. 20, quoting Jaki, *Science and Creation*, p. 105.

44. Aristotle, *On the Heavens* 1.8 (276a–278a), 2.1 (283b–284a), 3.2 (300a–302a), and the whole of book 4 (307b–313b), and *Physics* 8.1 (250b–252b). Aristotle, *Metaphysics* 12.7 (1072b3) does say it's God's love and desire that sustains all natural tendencies in their unchanging arrangement (hence sustaining the laws of physics), but that's what Christians believe, too.

45. D'Souza, *What's So Great*, p. 93.

46. See P. B. Paisley and D. R. Oldroyd, "Science in the Silver Age," *Centaurus* 23, no. 1 (1979): 1–20 [cf. pp. 2–6]; F. R. D. Goodyear, "The '*Aetna*,'" *Aufstieg und Niedergang der römischen Welt* 2.32.1 (1984): 344–63 [cf. pp. 346–47].

47. Russo, *Forgotten Revolution*, pp. 146–51; Vivian Nutton, *Ancient Medicine* (London: Routledge, 2004), pp. 134–36; Sylvia Berryman, "Galen and the Mechanical Philosophy," *Apeiron: A Journal for Ancient Philosophy and Science* 35, no. 3 (September 2002): 235–53; Heinrich von Staden, "Body and Machine," *Alexandria and Alexandrianism* (Malibu, CA: J. Paul Getty Museum, 1996), pp. 85–106. Examples: Galen, *On the Natural Faculties* 3.15 and *On the Uses of the Parts* 1.2–4, 1.19, 7.14, 14.5.

48. For example: Cicero, *On the Nature of the Gods* 2.88.(34–35); Vitruvius, *On Architecture* 9.1.2, 10.1.4; and Lucretius, *On the Nature of Things* 5.96; for Ptolemy: Liba Taub, *Ptolemy's Universe* (Chicago: Open Court, 1993).

49. See Liba Taub, *Ancient Meteorology* (London: Routledge, 2003), pp. 141–61; and for examples: Hero's *Pneumatics* and *Mechanics* and Archimedes' *On Floating Bodies*.

50. See Galen, *On the Natural Faculties*.

51. Ptolemy, *Planetary Hypotheses* 2.6 and *Almagest* 9.5.

52. See Andrea Murschel, "The Structure and Function of Ptolemy's Physical Hypotheses of Planetary Motion," *Journal for the History of Astronomy* 26 (1995): 33–61; on Kepler's "soul" theory: Eric Aiton, "How Kepler Discovered the Elliptical Orbit," *The Mathematical Gazette* 59, no. 410 (December 1975): 255–57 [pp. 250–260]; on Ptolemy's whole program of finding natural laws: Alexander Jones, "Ptolemy's Mathematical Models and Their Meaning," in *Mathematics and the Historian's Craft*, eds. Glen van Brummelen and Michael Kinyon (New York: Springer, 2005), pp. 23–42.

53. See the preface to Vesalius, *On the Fabric of the Human Body* (1543). Agricola similarly had to devote the entire first chapter of his book *On Mining Operations* (1556) to defending himself against peers who rejected his study as base.

54. In a lost work quoted in Pappus, *Mathematical Collection* 8.1. For more evidence of scientists as craftsmen and the absence of any head-hand divide, see Carrier, "Attitudes," pp. 425–79 (which will be reproduced in Carrier, *Scientist*).

55. For a complete account, see Jo Marchant, *Decoding the Heavens* (Cambridge, MA: Da Capo Press, 2009).

56. On early Christian hostility to curiosity, dethronement of empiricism, and disinterest in scientific progress (and eventual warming to these ideas over a thousand years later), see Neil Kenny, *The Uses of Curiosity in Early Modern France and Germany* (New York: Oxford University Press, 2004) and *Curiosity in Early Modern Europe* (Wiesbaden: Harrassowitz, 1998); Peter Harrison, *The Bible, Protestantism, and the Rise of Natural Science* (Cambridge: Cambridge University Press, 1998) and "Curiosity: Forbidden Knowledge, and the Reformation of Natural Philosophy in Early Modern England," *Isis* 92, no. 2 (June 2001): 265–90; Lorraine Daston, *Wonders and the Order of Nature, 1150–1750* (New York: Zone Books, 1998); William Eamon, *Science and the Secrets of Nature* (Princeton: Princeton University Press, 1996); Lloyd, *Greek Science*, pp. 167–71; and Marshall Clagett, *Greek Science in Antiquity* (Salem, NH: Ayer, 1955), pp. 118–82. More evidence will be summarized in Carrier, *Scientist.*

57. For a summary of scholarship on this third-century collapse (and the fact that Christianity was not remarkably successful before then), see Carrier, *Not the Impossible Faith*, pp. 407–47 (esp. pp. 435–40 and p. 447 n. 32), which is reinforced by Ramsay MacMullen, *Christianizing the Roman Empire: AD 100–400* (New Haven, CT: Yale University Press, 1984) and *Christianity and Paganism in the Fourth to Eighth Centuries* (New Haven, CT: Yale University Press, 1997); and Robin Lane Fox, *Pagans and Christians* (New York: Knopf, 1987).

CONTRIBUTORS

Hector Avalos, PhD, is professor of religious studies at Iowa State University and author of *Fighting Words: The Origins of Religious Violence* and *The End of Biblical Studies.*

Edward T. Babinski is the editor of *Leaving the Fold: Testimonies of Former Fundamentalists*, and his writings are available at the Secular Web, Talk Origins, Debunking Christianity, and www.edwardtbabinski.us/.

Richard Carrier, PhD, is a philosopher and historian of antiquity (see www.richardcarrier.info), the author of *Sense and Goodness without God: A Defense of Metaphysical Naturalism* and *Not the Impossible Faith: Why Christianity Didn't Need a Miracle to Succeed*, and the author of three chapters of *The Empty Tomb: Jesus beyond the Grave*, ed. Robert M. Price and Jeffery Jay Lowder.

David Eller, PhD, is assistant professor of anthropology at the Community College of Denver and is the author of *Natural Atheism, Atheism Advanced: Further Thoughts of a Freethinker*, and a college textbook, *Introducing Anthropology of Religion.*

John W. Loftus, MA, MDiv, ThM, is the author of *Why I Became an Atheist: A Former Preacher Rejects Christianity* and founder of the Debunking Christianity blog, found at www.debunkingchristianity.blogspot.com.

Jason Long, PhD, is the author of *Biblical Nonsense: A Review of the Bible for Doubting Christians* and *The Religious Condition: Answering and Explaining Christian Reasoning.*

Robert M. Price, PhD, is a fellow of the Jesus Seminar, coeditor of *The Empty Tomb: Jesus Beyond the Grave,* and the author of several books, including *Deconstructing Jesus*; *The Incredible Shrinking Son of Man: How Reliable Is the Gospel Tradition?*; *The Paperback Apocalypse: How the Christian Church Was Left Behind*; and *Inerrant the Wind: The Evangelical Crisis of Biblical Authority.*

Valerie Tarico, PhD in Counseling Psychology, is the author of *The Dark Side: How Evangelical Teachings Corrupt Love and Truth.*

Paul Tobin is the author of *The Rejection of Pascal's Wager: A Skeptic's Guide to the Bible and the Historical Jesus.*